The Influence of Culture on
Human Resource Management
Processes and Practices

SERIES IN APPLIED PSYCHOLOGY
Edwin A. Fleishman, George Mason University
Jeanette N. Cleveland, Pennsylvania State University
Series Editors

Gregory Bedny and David Meister
The Russian Theory of Activity: Current Applications to Design and Learning

Winston Bennett, David Woehr, and Charles Lance
Performance Measurement: Current Perspectives and Future Challenges

Michael T. Brannick, Eduardo Salas, and Carolyn Prince
Team Performance Assessment and Measurement: Theory, Research, and Applications

Jeanette N. Cleveland, Margaret Stockdale, and Kevin R. Murphy
Women and Men in Organizations: Sex and Gender Issues at Work

Aaron Cohen
Multiple Commitments in the Workplace: An Integrative Approach

Russell Cropanzano
Justice in the Workplace: Approaching Fairness in Human Resource Management, Volume 1

Russell Cropanzano
Justice in the Workplace: From Theory to Practice, Volume 2

David V. Day, Stephen Zaccaro, Stanley M. Halpin
Leader Development for Transforming Organizations: Growing Leaders for Tomorrow's Teams and Organizations.

James E. Driskell and Eduardo Salas
Stress and Human Performance

Sidney A. Fine and Steven F. Cronshaw
Functional Job Analysis: A Foundation for Human Resources Management

Sidney A. Fine and Maury Getkate
Benchmark Tasks for Job Analysis: A Guide for Functional Job Analysis (FJA) Scales

J. Kevin Ford, Steve W. J. Kozlowski, Kurt Kraiger, Eduardo Salas, and Mark S. Teachout
Improving Training Effectiveness in Work Organizations

Jerald Greenberg
Organizational Behavior: The State of the Science, Second Edition

Uwe E. Kleinbeck, Hans-Henning Quast, Henk Thierry, and Hartmut Häcker
Work Motivation

Laura L. Koppes
Historical Perspectives in Industrial and Organizational Psychology

Ellen Kossek and Susan Lambert
Work and Life Integration: Organizational, Cultural and Individual
Perspectives.

Martin I. Kurke and Ellen M. Scrivner
Police Psychology into the 21st Century

Joel Lefkowitz
Ethics and Values in Industrial and Organizational Psychology

Manuel London
Job Feedback: Giving, Seeking, and Using Feedback for Performance Improve-
ment, Second Edition

Manuel London
How People Evaluate Others in Organizations

Manuel London
Leadership Development: Paths to Self-Insight and Professional Growth

Robert F. Morrison and Jerome Adams
Contemporary Career Development Issues

Michael D. Mumford, Garnett Stokes, and William A. Owens
Patterns of Life History: The Ecology of Human Individuality

Michael D. Mumford
Pathways to Outstanding Leadership: A Comparative Analysis of Charismatic,
Ideological and Pragmatic Leaders

Kevin R. Murphy
Validity Generalization: A Critical Review

Kevin R. Murphy and Frank E. Saal
Psychology in Organizations: Integrating Science and Practice

Kevin Murphy
A Critique of Emotional Intelligence: What are the Problems and How Can They
Be Fixed?

Susan E. Murphy and Ronald E. Riggio
The Future of Leadership Development

Margaret A. Neal and Leslie Brett Hammer
Working Couples Caring for Children and Aging Parents: Effects on Work and
Well-Being

Steven A.Y. Poelmans
Work and Family: An International Research Perspective

Robert E. Ployhart, Benjamin Schneider, and Neal Schmitt
Staffing Organizations: Contemporary Practice and Theory, Third Edition

Erich P. Prien, Jeffery S. Schippmann and Kristin O. Prien
Individual Assessment: As Practiced in Industry and Consulting

Ned Rosen
Teamwork and the Bottom Line: Groups Make a Difference

Heinz Schuler, James L. Farr, and Mike Smith
Personnel Selection and Assessment: Individual and Organizational Perspectives

Kenneth S. Shultz and Gary A. Adams
Aging and Work in the 21st Century

John W. Senders and Neville P. Moray
Human Error: Cause, Prediction, and Reduction

Frank J. Smith
Organizational Surveys: The Diagnosis and Betterment of Organizations Through Their Members

Dianna Stone and Eugene F. Stone-Romero
The Influence of Culture on Human Resource Management Processes and Practices

Kecia M. Thomas
Diversity Resistance in Organizations

George C. Thornton III and Rose Mueller-Hanson
Developing Organizational Simulations: A Guide for Practitioners and Students

George C. Thornton III and Deborah Rupp
Assessment Centers in Human Resource Management: Strategies for Prediction, Diagnosis, and Development

Yoav Vardi and Ely Weitz
Misbehavior in Organizations: Theory, Research and Management

Patricia Voydanoff
Work, Family and Community

The Influence of Culture on Human Resource Management Processes and Practices

Edited by

Dianna L. Stone • Eugene F. Stone-Romero

Psychology Press
Taylor & Francis Group

New York   London

Lawrence Erlbaum Associates
Taylor & Francis Group

New York   London

Lawrence Erlbaum Associates
Taylor & Francis Group
270 Madison Avenue
New York, NY 10016

Lawrence Erlbaum Associates
Taylor & Francis Group
2 Park Square
Milton Park, Abingdon
Oxon OX14 4RN

© 2008 by Taylor & Francis Group, LLC
Lawrence Erlbaum Associates is an imprint of Taylor & Francis Group, an Informa business

Printed in the United States of America on acid-free paper
10 9 8 7 6 5 4 3 2 1

International Standard Book Number-13: 978-0-8058-4599-0 (Softcover) 978-0-8058-4598-3 (Hardcover)

Library of Congress Cataloging-in-Publication Data

The influence of culture on human resource management processes and practices /
[edited by] Dianna Stone and Eugene F. Stone-Romero.
p. cm.
Includes bibliographical references and index.
ISBN 978-0-8058-4599-0 (alk. paper) -- ISBN 978-0-8058-4598-3 (alk. paper)
1. Diversity in the workplace--United States. 2. Personnel management--United
States. 3. Multiculturalism--United States. 4. Cultural awareness--United States. I.
Stone, Dianna L., 1947- II. Stone-Romero, Eugene F.

HF5549.5.M5I46 2008
658.30089--dc22   2007020930

**Visit the Taylor & Francis Web site at
http://www.taylorandfrancis.com**

**and the LEA and Routledge Web site at
http://www.routledge.com**

To Gene, Mavis, Joey, Patricia, Sharon, JoAnna, J., S., Q., B., S., S., and D.

DLS

To my parents, Frank J. Stone and Josephine Romero, whose love and sacrifices allowed me to have what they never had, and to my wife, Dianna.

EFS-R

Contents

Preface   *xi*

Series Foreword   *xvii*
Jeanette N. Cleveland and Edwin A. Fleishman

1   *Culture*   *1*
    Harry C. Triandis and S. Arzu Wasti

2   *A Model of the Influence of Cultural Values on Job*
    Application Intentions and Behaviors   *25*
    Dianna L. Stone, Linda Isenhour, and Kimberly M. Lukaszewski

3   *The Clash Between "Best Practices" for Selection and*
    National Culture   *53*
    Robert L. Dipboye and Stefanie K. Johnson

4   *Culture and Human Resource Management*
    Practices: Personnel Selection Based on
    Personality Measures   *85*
    Eugene F. Stone-Romero and Carol A. Thornson

5   *Designing and Delivering Training for Multicultural*
    Interactions in Organizations   *115*
    Eduardo Salas, Katherine A. Wilson, and Rebecca Lyons

6   *Culture Diversity and Performance Appraisal*
    Systems   *135*
    Gerald R. Ferris and Darren C. Treadway

7   *Culture, Feedback, and Motivation*   *157*
    Robert D. Pritchard and Satoris S. Youngcourt

8   *Compensation and Reward Systems in a
    Multicultural Context*   *181*
    Aparna Joshi and Joseph J. Martocchio

9   *Cultural Variations in Employee Assistance
    Programs in an Era of Globalization*   *207*
    Rabi S. Bhagat, Pamela K. Steverson, and James C. Segovis

10 *Work and Family Concerns and Practices:
    A Cross-National and -Cultural Comparison
    of Ireland and the United States*   *235*
    Jeanette Cleveland, Alma McCarthy, and Jodi L. Himelright

11 *A Sensemaking Approach to Understanding
    Multicultural Teams: An Initial Framework*   *269*
    C. Shawn Burke, Heather A. Priest, Christin L. Upshaw,
    Eduardo Salas and Linda Pierce

12 *Culture and Human Resource Management:
    Prospects for the Future*   *307*
    Eugene F. Stone-Romero and Dianna L. Stone

    Author Index   *313*

    Subject Index   *331*

Preface

Organizations in the United States are becoming more diverse in terms of a number of dimensions, the most important of which are the cultural norms, values, and ideologies of their members. One reason for the increase in diversity is that the population of the United States is becoming more racially diverse. More specifically, recent census data revealed that there are now over 84 million members of the four primary minority groups (i.e., African Americans, Hispanic Americans, Asian Americans, and Native Americans). In addition, the growth rates of these groups are expected to accelerate in the 21st century (U.S. Bureau of Census, 2000). Interestingly, between 1950 and 1998, the number of individuals with non-European backgrounds tripled in size due to such factors as (a) waves of immigrants from Asia, Latin America, and the Middle East, (b) relatively high birth rates among members of various minority groups, and (c) the relatively low average age of individuals in such groups (U.S. Bureau of Census, 2000). As a result of these and other trends, many organizations in the United States employ large numbers of minority group members. For instance, an article in *Fortune* (2001) reported that minority group members make up large percentages of the workforce at such firms as Advantica (49.9%), Levi Strauss (58%), Dole Foods (55.6%), Union Bank of California (54%), Avis Rent-a-Car (48%), and Walt Disney World Resorts (90%). Because members of various minority groups often have cultural values and norms that differ from those of members of the majority group, increases in racial diversity are frequently accompanied by increases in cultural diversity.

The cultural diversity of U.S. organizations also has increased as a result of the internationalization of the world economy. Recent estimates indicate that there are over 100,000 firms with international operations, and they have annual revenues in excess of $300 billion. Not surprisingly, the growth in the number of firms with international operations has been accompanied by an increase in the cultural diversity of their employees.

The increase in cultural diversity of U.S. firms may lead to substantial benefits, including increased creativity, improved decision making, and broader markets for products (Adler, 1997; Cox, 1993). However, more cultural diversity also may pose important challenges for these firms, whether or not they have multinational operations. For instance, as cultural diversity increases, firms may need to develop new strategies for managing and motivating their employees (Cox, 1993). One important reason for this is that, typically, human resource management (HRM) processes and practices in the United States have been based on values, norms, and ideologies (e.g., rugged individualism, short-term profit maximization, legalism, equity-based individual rewards) that are more common among individuals of northern and western European descent (e.g., white Anglo-Saxons) than members of various minority groups (e.g., blacks, Native Americans, Asians).

In view of the aforementioned facts, we believe that it is vital that the related fields of HRM, industrial and organizational psychology, organizational behavior, and organization theory develop a better understanding of the issues that arise in culturally diverse organizations. There are several reasons for this. First, cultural diversity has largely been ignored in the previously noted disciplines (Erez, 1994; Erez & Earley, 1993; Triandis, Dunnette, & Hough, 1994). As a result, Triandis (1994) and others (e.g., Earley & Erez, 1997; Erez, 1994; Erez & Earley, 1993) have argued that many organizational theories are underdeveloped and often fail to consider the critical role that cultural factors play in the design of organizations and the management of employee behavior. Second, although a substantial body of diversity research has focused on such variables as age, sex, race, and disability, relatively little research has considered the impact of cultural diversity on organizational processes and practices. Third, several diversity researchers have argued that because the HRM-related processes and practices (e.g., recruitment, selection, training, performance appraisal) of many U.S. firms are based primarily on values, norms, and ideologies that have northern and western European roots, they may not be as effective in organizations that are culturally heterogeneous as they are in organizations that are culturally homogeneous (Cox, 1993).

In view of the foregoing, an increasingly large number of U.S. organizations are faced with the challenge of developing HRM processes and practices that will prove functional with job applicants and incumbents who come from diverse cultural backgrounds. However, there is a paucity of theory and research to guide the development of the needed processes and practices. In view of this, the primary purpose of this book is to discuss the influence of cultural diversity on several HRM processes and practices. Other than the first chapter, which deals with the general topic of culture, the general focus of the book is on processes and practices that occur at three general phases: the pre-hire phase (e.g., recruiting), the selection phase (e.g., selection), and the post-hire phase (e.g., performance appraisal, compensation).

In Chapter 1, Harry C. Triandis and S. Arzu Wasti consider the general issue of culture from the perspective of individuals' values (e.g., individualism, collectivism). Then, they illustrate how culture influences a number of organizational processes and practices, including selection, job design, conflict resolution, and leadership. In addition, they describe the effects of culture on individuals' behavioral intentions and behaviors. The chapter concludes with a call for research that will lead to a better understanding of the role that culture plays in influencing organizations and their members.

Chapter 2, by Dianna L. Stone, Linda Isenhour, and Kimberly M. Lukaszewski, deals with the influence of culture on the propensities of individuals to apply for and accept jobs. It offers a model of the recruitment process that is based on the well-tested and supported Theory of Planned Behavior. Their model explicitly considers the influence of culture on the three antecedents of job application intentions (i.e., attitudes, subjective norms, and perceived behavioral control). They also offer a number of testable hypotheses that are based on the model. Finally, they provide a number of recommendations for practice.

In Chapter 3, Robert Dipboye and Stephanie K. Johnson deal with the relation between national culture and optimal selection practices. Among the issues considered by them are the way that culture influences various attributes of selection systems (e.g., job specification), differences between selection systems based on rational/analytic versus social/intuitive models, and individuals' reactions to selection systems. To illustrate the influence of culture, they compare selection systems found in China, Mexico, and the United States.

Chapter 4, by Eugene F. Stone-Romero and Carol A. Thornson, considers the dysfunctional consequences of selecting individuals for jobs on the basis of their standing on personality measures. This is an important issue for two reasons. One is that most personality measures are incapable of differentiating between traits and environmentally induced states. The other is that there are well-documented differences in personality across members of various cultures (e.g., national) and subcultures (e.g., race-based). These differences may lead to the stigmatization of applicants in various minority out-groups (e.g., racial minorities, women, war veterans) in the selection process. As a result, relative to members of organizational in-groups, members of such out-groups may suffer lower odds of being offered jobs.

The next six chapters deal with HRM issues that are applicable to organizational members. In Chapter 5, Eduardo Salas, Katherine A. Wilson, and Rebecca Lyons offer views on the design and delivery of training programs concerned with improving interactions among individuals in multicultural teams. In addition, they present a number of practice-based strategies for improving interactions among individuals in multicultural organizations (e.g., simulations, role play exercises). Finally, they describe strategies for maintaining workers' multicultural knowledge, skills, and abilities.

Chapter 6, by Gerald R. Ferris and Darren C. Treadway, deals with the influence of culture on performance appraisal systems and processes. The authors view performance appraisal systems as mechanisms for both ensuring accountability in organizations and influencing the behavior of employees. They describe how culture influences several appraisal-related variables, including the criteria used in appraisal, the reactions of targets to appraisals, the attributions that stem from observations of behavior, and the way in which ratees respond to appraisals. In addition, they offer a number of recommendations for research on the influence of culture on performance appraisal systems and processes.

In Chapter 7, Robert D. Pritchard and Sartoris S. Youngcourt consider the role of culture in worker motivation and responses to feedback about performance. They specify how culture influences cognitions about relations between (a) actions and results, (b) results and evaluations, (c) evaluations and outcomes, and (d) outcomes and satisfaction. In addition, they indicate how culture influences feedback seeking, feedback giving, and feedback reactions. Finally, they summarize the results of cross-cultural research on productivity measurement.

Chapter 8, by Aparna Joshi and Joseph J. Martocchio, focuses on relations between cultural variables and the nature of compensation and reward systems. More specifically, their chapter considers cross-cultural differences in individuals' affective and cognitive reactions to compensation and reward systems. Using theory and research associated with Affective Events Theory and the person–organization fit perspective, they develop a number of propositions about such reactions. Finally, they offer a number of suggestions for research on relations between cultural variables and reactions to compensation and reward systems.

Chapter 9, by Rabi S. Bhagat, Pamela K. Steverson, and James C. Segovis, is concerned with cultural variations in employee assistance programs (EAPs). The chapter begins with a history of EAPs in the United States. Next, the authors consider stress and coping in cross-cultural contexts, focusing on two dimensions of culture (i.e., individualism vs. collectivism, and vertical vs. horizontal). They also comment on the effectiveness of EAPs in the current era of globalization. Finally, they offer recommendations for cross-cultural research on EAPs.

In Chapter 10, Jeanette Cleveland, Alma McCarthy, and Jodi L. Himelright focus on cultural dimensions that influence work–family preferences. The chapter begins with a consideration of political and social influences on work and the family. Then, they describe three types of welfare state regimes. Regime type is important because it influences attitudes toward the relative importance of work and family within a nation. The description of regimes is followed by a review of values that may influence work–family issues and a detailed comparison of the United States and Ireland in terms of several factors that relate to work–family issues.

Chapter 11, by C. Shawn Burke, Heather A. Priest, Christin L. Upshaw, Eduardo Salas, and Linda Pierce, details a sensemaking approach to understanding multicultural teams. The chapter begins with a description of such teams. It then presents a model of the sensemaking process that posits that several antecedents influence team sensemaking, which, in turn, causes adaptive team coordination and team performance. The chapter concludes with a consideration of the practical implications of the model and suggestions for future research.

The final chapter of the book highlights the primary themes presented in the previous chapters and offers a summary of needed research on cultural diversity and HRM practices. It also considers methodological issues (e.g., research design, measurement, sampling) needed to extend and conduct research on the topic. As a result it serves as a point of departure for extending theory, research, and practice on the role of cultural diversity in the design and development of human resources practices in multicultural organizations.

The book should prove to be of value to several audiences. One is academicians and researchers in the related fields of industrial and organizational psychology, organizational behavior, human resource management, cross-cultural psychology, and applied social psychology. A second is HRM practitioners and researchers in industry. A third is graduate students in the above-noted fields.

Although the authors of chapters in this book are from the United States, the issues considered by them also should be of interest and value to academicians, practitioners, and graduate students in numerous other countries. The principal reason for this is that organizations in other nations often have employees who are culturally diverse. This is especially true of multinational organizations. We believe that cross-cultural issues are as important in such organizations as they are in U.S. organizations.

Overall, we hope that the views offered by the authors of the chapters in this book serve to motivate both (a) the further development of models concerned with the influence of culture on HRM processes and practices, and (b) the design and conduct of empirical research on the same topic. An improved understanding of the role that culture plays in such processes and practices should contribute to both the efficiency and effectiveness of organizations and the performance and well-being of their members.

Eugene F. Stone-Romero and Dianna L. Stone

REFERENCES

Adler, N. J. (1997). *International dimension of organizational behavior.* Cincinnati, OH: South Western College Publishing.

Cox, T. H. (1993). *Cultural diversity in organizations: Theory, research, and practice.* San Francisco: Berrett-Koehler.

Earley, P. C., & Erez, M. (1997). *New perspectives on international industrial/organizational psychology.* San Francisco, CA: New Lexington Press.

Erez, M. (1994). Toward a model of cross-cultural industrial and organizational psychology. In H. C. Triandis, M. D. Dunnette, & L. M. Hough (Eds.), *Handbook of industrial and organizational psychology* (2nd ed., pp. 559–607). Palo Alto, CA: Consulting Psychologists Press.

Erez, M., & Earley, P. C. (1993). *Culture, self-identity, and work.* New York: Oxford University Press.

Fortune (2001). Best companies for minorities. Retrieved September 15, 2001 from http://www.fortune.com/index.

Triandis, H. C. (1994). *Culture and social behavior.* New York: McGraw-Hill.

Triandis, H. C., Dunnette, M., & Hough, L. C. (1994). *Handbook of industrial and organizational psychology,*Vol. 4, Palo Alto, CA: Consulting Psychologists Press.

U.S. Bureau of the Census (2000). *Population reports.* Retrieved March 18, 2007 from http://www.census.gov/servlit/dataset/main.

U.S. Bureau of the Census. (2001). *Profiles of general demographic characteristics.* Retrieved September 29, 2001, from http://www.census.gov/prod/cen2000/dpl2kh00.pdf.

U.S. Bureau of the Census (2000). *Population reports.* Retrieved March 18, 2007 from http://www.census.gov/servlit/dataset/main.

U.S. Bureau of the Census. (2001). *Profiles of general demographic characteristics.* Retrieved September 29, 2001, from http://www.census.gov/prod/cen2000/dpl2kh00.pdf.

Series Foreword

Series Editors

JEANETTE N. CLEVELAND
The Pennsylvania State University

EDWIN A. FLEISHMAN
George Mason University

There is a compelling need for innovative approaches to the solution of many pressing problems involving human relationship in today's society. Such approaches are more likely to be successful when they are based on sound research and applications. This Series in Applied Psychology offers publications that emphasize state-of-the-art research and its applications to important issues of human behavior in a variety of social settings. The objective is to bridge academic and applied interests.

We welcome the book *The Influence of Culture on Human Resource Management Processes and Practices*, edited by Dianna L. Stone and Eugene F. Stone-Romero, into this series. Increasingly, all aspects of organizational functioning reflect permeable national boundaries. Yet much of our personal and interpersonal interactions are guided by cultural values, expectations, and attitudes. Some values transcend cultural boundaries and are mutually reinforcing. Other cultural values create interactions with high potential for conflict, misunderstanding, poor performance, and ultimately, individual and organizational ineffectiveness or failure.

It is time to disentangle our discussions of diversity and culture. To what extent do these constructs overlap? Are they distinct? As this book indicates, there is much diversity within a given culture as well as across national cultures. Much of our knowledge of human resource management (HRM) practices in organizations is based upon research conducted in single cultures or about diversity within a given country (e.g., United States, United Kingdom, or China). There is a need for more discussion and research about the influence of multiple cultures on HRM practices.

Stone and Stone-Romero bring together an impressive set of experts on culture and diversity to address specific HRM processes or practices. The distinguished Dr. Harry Triandis and S. Arzu Wasti introduce the book with a discussion of the dimensions of cultures and provide an overview of cultural links with specific HRM practices, such as selection, job design, interpersonal relationships at work, conflict resolution, training, group processes, and leadership. This chapter provides a solid foundation and point of reference for each the chapters that follow. These chapters address the links between culture and a specific HRM process or practice.

In Chapters 2, 3, and 4, more general value differences across cultures associated with individual and organizational selection are addressed. This discussion is followed by Chapters 5 through 11, in which specific HRM practices are discussed in relation to either organizational culture or using a cultural lens, individual reactions to an organizational practice. The practices include training, performance appraisal, feedback and motivation, compensation and reward systems, and team functions. In addition, the book includes chapters on both employee assistance programs and work–family concerns and practices within a global, cultural context.

The book is appropriate for undergraduate and graduate students in industrial and organizational psychology, human resource management, sociology of work, and cultural diversity within organizations. It can provide a central resource in classes on organizational psychology, strategic human resource management, and global issues in human resource management. Professionals and practitioners who increasingly interact with organizational issues at the global level will find this book essential to their work.

1

Culture

HARRY C. TRIANDIS AND S. ARZU WASTI

University of Illinois at Urbana-Champaign and
Sabanci University, Istanbul, Turkey

Culture is to society what memory is to individuals (C. Kluckhohn, 1954). It consists of what "has worked" in the experience of a group of people so it was worth transmitting to peers and descendants. Another definition of culture was provided by anthropologist Redfield (1954): "Culture is shared understandings made manifest in act and artifact" (p. 1). In short, it is shared behavior and shared human-made aspects of the society. Thus, it includes "practices" (the way things are done here) and "values" (the way things should be done). These older definitions of culture focus on what is outside the person (e.g., do people drive to the right or left). The more recent definitions also stress what is inside the person (e.g., is the self independent or interdependent of in-groups). Almost every aspect of psychological functioning is influenced, to some extent, by culture. Thus, it is best to view culture and psychology as making each other up (Cole, 1996; Shweder, 1990).

We can distinguish material and subjective culture. The tools, dwellings, foods, clothing, pots, machines, roads, bridges, and many other entities that are typically found in a culture are examples of *material* culture. *Subjective* culture includes shared ideas, theories, political, religious, scientific, economic, and social standards for judging events in the environment (Triandis, 1972). The language (e.g., the way experience is categorized and organized), beliefs, associations (e.g., what ideas are linked to other ideas), attitudes, norms, role definitions, religion, and values of the culture are some of the elements of a cultural group's subjective culture. Ideas about how to make an item of material culture constitute subjective culture as well (e.g., mathematical equations needed to construct a bridge), so the two kinds of culture are interrelated.

Subjective culture also includes shared memories, ideas about correct and incorrect behavior, the way members of culture view themselves (auto-stereotypes) and other cultural groups (hetero-stereotypes), and the way members of the culture value entities in their environment. Categorizations, associations among the categories, beliefs, expectations (e.g., what behavior will lead to what rewards), norms, role definitions, values, and broad value orientations (e.g., whether humans are intrinsically "good" or "bad"; F. Kluckhohn & Strodtbeck, 1961) are other elements of subjective culture.

Members of different cultures have characteristic lifestyles that correspond to subjective events and shared habits for paying attention to specific aspects of their environment (e.g., cues about hierarchy or hostility), and they weigh these aspects differently (e.g., in hierarchical cultures people weigh cues about hierarchy much more than cues about kindness). Such shared perceptual habits and weightings are parts of subjective culture, too. Beliefs about whether or not one can trust other people, about supernatural beings, about work and about being healthy, and about what happens after death are further aspects of subjective culture. For example, trust in individualist cultures depends on whether or not the other person behaves appropriately and as expected; in collectivist cultures it depends on whether the other person takes into account not only his or her own interests but also the interests of in-group members.

Cultures emerge because ecologies (climate, geographic features, ways of making a living) are different from place to place. For instance, if the environment has fish, people will go fishing, buy and sell fish, cook fish, eat fish, develop a rich lexicon about fish, and so on. They will also have ideas about how, where, when, and with whom to fish. They will value fish, and they may link their religious ideas with fish. They will have theories about how fish developed, ideas about how valuable fish is at different times and places, norms about how, when, and with whom to eat fish, and so on. Fish will be an important element of the economy of the culture, will be on the educational curriculum, and will figure in politics (e.g., one party might advocate restrictions on fishing, whereas another might oppose restrictions). The gods will help or spoil fishing, social life will require exchanges of fish, and so on.

In the following section, several cultural dimensions will be presented. Particular emphasis will be given to collectivism and individualism, as these cultural syndromes have benefited from rich theoretical description and empirical research (e.g., Markus & Kitayama, 1991; Triandis, 1995). Next, the implications of these cultural dimensions on several organizational phenomena, such as human resource practices, group dynamics, and leadership, will be reviewed by reference to the recent empirical research in the field. The chapter will conclude with a discussion of culture as an indirect but inevitable determinant of individual behavior.

DIMENSIONS OF CULTURAL VARIATION

Cultures differ in myriad ways and a variety of frameworks for examining cultures have been developed over the years. In the following sections, cultural dimensions that have found to be particularly important are presented.

Simple–Complex Cultures

Hunters and gatherers, but also rural cultures, are simpler than industrial societies, information societies, and urban cultures. Between these two extremes are myriad positions, such as slash-and-burn agricultural, agricultural, or industrial cultures.

Tight–Loose Cultures

Some cultures have many rules and norms about behavior and impose these norms tightly. The Taliban in Afghanistan is an example of a tight culture. It had rules about not listening to music, viewing television, flying kites, or committing myriad other "sins." Anyone who deviated from these norms was severely punished, even by execution. Other cultures are loose, with few rules or norms. Rural Thailand is such a culture. In loose cultures, when people do not do what is expected of them, others do not punish them severely and may even just smile. There are many kinds of smiles, some suggesting criticism, but nevertheless the punishment for deviation from norms is mild.

Collectivism

Collectivism is a cultural pattern found in cultures that tend to be simple, be traditional, and have many rules and norms that are imposed tightly (Triandis, 1988, 1994, 1995). One study of 186 traditional cultures found the Mbuti pygmies of the Congo were the most collectivist (Triandis, 2000). High levels of collectivism are found in rural, homogeneous, isolated cultures with much traditional shared ideology and distinct customs, where there is much discipline and punishment for not doing what the in-group expects. Self-sacrifice for the sake of the in-group is frequent.

This cultural pattern is especially likely when the population density is high, among older members of a culture, among the lower social classes (Kohn, 1969), among those who are religious (Triandis & Singelis, 1998), among those who have experienced much common fate (e.g., were attacked by an out-group), and when individual social mobility is not possible but group social mobility is (e.g., one can get more money by joining a union; Triandis & Trafimow, 2001). Collectivism can be found represented in different domains, such as politics, religion, aesthetics, education, social life, economics, or philosophy. For example, Mao's China was high in collectivism in all those domains. As China has evolved, it first allowed individual expression in the aesthetic fields, then in economics, and in social life. In the future it may allow free expression in the other domains as well.

The self, in such cultures, is perceived as very close to intimate friends and very far from enemies. It is defined by concrete entities (e.g., kinship links) and may change from situation to situation (allies one day may become enemies another day). Collectivists give priority to the goals of their in-groups over their personal goals, they see behavior as a function of both attitudes (what I like to do) and norms (what I should do), and they stay in their groups even when they are not satisfied (e.g., low divorce rates; stay in jobs they dislike). They feel more pride in the achievements of their in-group than in their personal achievements, but they feel guiltier about their transgressions than about those of their in-group. They are easily embarrassed and feel shame for actions inconsistent with in-group norms. Empathy is one of their important attributes. They are more self-critical than individualists.

People in such cultures define themselves by their relationships with groups. However, their self-definition depends on the situation. In such cultures individuals define themselves more often by using social attributes (e.g., I am a member of this group; I am a cousin) than personal attributes (e.g., I am an extrovert, I like classical music). For collectivists, context is all-important, and people are not concerned with contradictions. Thus, a member of this type of culture might say that he is "a meat-eating vegetarian." When asked to elaborate, he might say he is a vegetarian, but when others eat meat, he eats meat.

Indeed, an important attribute of collectivists is that they emphasize the context of events or stimuli (e.g., the history of an issue). Relationships with in-group members are very different from relationships with out-group members. Collectivists are suspicious of outsiders and distrust even in-group members who they feel may envy them. They perceive their in-groups as more homogeneous than their out-groups. They tend to take much time in social relationships. In fact, even if they have an urgent appointment, they will stop to talk with in-group members and do not mind being late for the appointment.

People in such cultures see the world from the outside in (Cohen, Hoshino-Browne, & Leung, 2007). Thus, they see most entities the way members of their in-group see them; that is, they use the standards of in-group members, especially the standards of their parents, to judge most entities. In a hierarchy of motives, the highest motive is service to the in-group. Ethnocentrism (people's belief that their own culture is the standard and other cultures are good only to the extent that they are like their own culture) tends to be high. They socialize their children by emphasizing obedience, reliability, cleanliness, order, and self-sacrifice within the in-group (Kohn, 1969). Their emotions tend to be engaged (close, friendly, respectful), other-focused, and somewhat self-critical (Kitayama, Markus, Matsumoto, & Noransakkunkit, 1997). Approval by others is an especially strong predictor of satisfaction in those cultures. East Asian collectivists do not display emotions in the presence of others. These attributes of collectivism may also occur in other collectivist cultures, such as those of Africa and South America, but there are no data as yet to confirm that they do occur in all collectivist cultures.

Collectivists feel a strong link to in-groups (family, tribe, village, race, religion, country, athletic team, social class). They feel sad and may cry when others are sick, absent, or die. They share their successes and failures with their in-groups. An important goal of collectivists is to fulfill their duties and obligations toward their in-groups. Collectivists see personal traits as malleable, whereas they see the social environment as fixed. Thus, they see people ready to fit into different groups. Social behavior in such cultures tends to include few but long-term and very strong links with others. People have relatively few skills for entering new groups. They tend to do what other people do much more often than people in other cultures (Bond & Smith, 1996). They are likely to help others out of duty rather than because they like them. In recreation they join relatively large stable groups (more than three persons) and rarely enjoy themselves when alone.

People in collectivist cultures expect in-group members to be supportive and helpful and are rarely directly critical. Others are supposed to behave so that they will be perceived as being "nice" (*simpatico* in Spanish, *sympatique* in French; Triandis, Marin, Lisansky, & Betancourt, 1984). On the other hand, out-group members are expected to be hostile and untrustworthy, so one is justified to behave harshly toward them. Because in such cultures maintaining good social relationships is very important, people try to save both their own face and that of the person with whom they are interacting. They often speak indirectly and may not disclose their beliefs until they know the beliefs of the other person. They use more concrete than abstract language; for example, they tend to use more action verbs than adjectives (e.g., they may say, "He did not say a word to me all evening," instead of "He is hostile.")

Collectivists do not have strong opinions, and they are likely to change their views when others have different opinions. They tend to see even physical causality as due to external forces (e.g., gravity) instead of internal forces (e.g., weight). Motivation increases following failure in these cultures, because failure is not as ego threatening (it is shared with the in-group) as it is in individualist cultures, and individuals tend to accept criticism because it leads to self-improvement.

East Asian collectivists think circularly (if something is good it will become bad, and later it will become good again) and holistically (everything is related to everything else). They use dialectical thinking (both the pro and the con aspects of an issue may have some validity depending on the context), value moderation, and tolerate contradictions, as each view may be correct in some contexts (Nisbett, 2003). They do not make the fundamental attribution error (observers see the behavior of others as due to internal factors, when the others report that their behavior is due to external factors) as frequently as do people in individualistic cultures. They are more comfortable with concrete than abstract concepts. They classify objects by focusing on relationships (e.g., cows are classified together with grass rather than with pigs). They are high in field dependence. They value what is old and common more than what is new and uncommon. They avoid confrontations and prefer methods of conflict resolution that do not destroy relationships (e.g., mediation). They see achieving a good relationship as the best outcome in conflict situations (Leung, 1997).

Morality in such cultures does not necessarily take the form found in individualist cultures (Kohlberg, 1981) but focuses instead on what is good for the in-group (Triandis, 1994). Unethical behavior that helps the in-group (e.g., lying, corruption) is more acceptable in collectivist than in individualist cultures (Triandis et al., 2001). They are more likely to punish than to reward others. When discussing others (e.g., their children), they are more likely to talk about their transgressions than about their achievements. When distributing resources within the in-group, they prefer the equality norm to the equity norm. When deciding how to divide rewards, bonuses, or provide recognition, they place more emphasis on good interpersonal relationships (e.g., that a person is "nice") than on performance. When collectivists break a norm, they tend to apologize rather than justify their actions.

Brewer and Chen (2007) make a distinction between two kinds of collectivism: relational and group. In relational collectivism, the individual has close ties with others. In group collectivism, the individual forgets who he or she is and replaces the self with the group. In short, the former kind of collectivism is personalized, whereas the latter is depersonalized. They show that when this distinction is made, many anomalous findings fall in place. For example, East Asians are relational collectivists, but Americans are both individualists and group collectivists. Thus, in all cultures there are three social orientations: individual, relational, and collective levels of the self. What differs among people across cultures is the salience and priority of these three different selves. Brewer and Chen recommend that researchers consider the *relative* endorsement of individualistic versus collectivist worldviews across different content domains.

Individualism

Individualism is a cultural pattern found in cultures that tend to be complex, modern, and tolerant of deviations from cultural norms (Triandis, 1988, 1994, 1995). In a study of 186 traditional cultures, the most individualist culture was the Ibo of Nigeria (Triandis, 2000).

Western cultures are also high in this cultural pattern. This cultural pattern is found by examining data across cultures, and in such data this cultural pattern is the opposite of collectivism. Of course, between the two extremes of collectivism and individualism, there are myriad positions and most cultures will fall somewhere in-between. Most of the findings discussed in this section have been obtained in studies carried out in the United States. It is uncertain, at this time, if the findings will generalize to all individualist cultures.

Individualism as a cultural pattern is especially likely among affluent individuals, both across culture and within culture. It is also very likely to occur among the more educated, widely traveled members of a culture; among those who have been exposed to highly heterogeneous, diverse cultures; among those raised in small families; in situations where there is fast social change; and in an American, "wild west" style open frontier. Exposure to Hollywood-made media increases individualism, because in such media the emphasis is on pleasure and fun, and rarely on doing one's duty (Triandis & Trafimow, 2001).

People in such cultures tend to think of themselves as autonomous, independent of their group (family, tribe, religion, nationality, athletic team, social class). The self is perceived as reflecting personal attributes and attitudes and is very different from both friends and enemies. They give priority to their personal goals rather than to the goals of their in-groups, and they see behavior primarily as a function of attitudes (what I like to do) and secondarily as a function of norms (what I should do). People in such cultures feel more distant from their family, especially from their parents, than is typical in collectivist cultures. Social behavior consists of many relatively superficial, short-term links with others, but individualists have good skills for entering new groups. In recreation they join different small groups or very large groups (e.g., cocktail parties) and can even have fun alone (Triandis, 1988). They tend to leave groups they do not get along with (e.g., high divorce rates, job turnover). The religions of individualists tend to be independent of groups, and if they decide to change religion they do so alone, without expecting members of their in-group to join them. When they experience psychological problems, individualists tend to seek professional help.

Individualists see the world from the inside out (Cohen et al., 2007). Thus, they see most entities according to their personal standards rather than according to the standards of other people. For example, they are motivated to achieve according to their personal standards and are satisfied if they meet these standards. Collectivists, on the other hand, tend to consider the standards of others (e.g., their parents) and are only satisfied if they meet those standards. Individualists emphasize achievement and often have difficulty accepting that others are better than they are. They see their successes as due to their own attributes and their failures as due to the difficulty of the task or the actions of others. In other words, they make the fundamental attribution error (see above) more than do collectivists. In individualist cultures motivation tends to increase after success but not after failure. In such cultures people define themselves by individual attributes (e.g., I am kind), more than by a social category (e.g., I am Muslim), and they value self-reliance. They socialize their children by emphasizing creativity, exploration, and adventure.

People from individualist cultures tend to be direct, candid, and generally themselves, not paying too much attention to the feelings of others. Their emotions tend to be disengaged (superior, proud, top of the world), self-focused, and positive (Kitayama et al., 1997). They are high in their subjective well-being (Diener, Diener, & Diener, 1995). The highest motive in individualist cultures, in a hierarchy of motives, is self-realization, whereas in collectivist cultures the highest motive is service to the in-group. Emotions, such as love, are especially important in some decisions (such as marriage) in these cultures. They favor euthanasia, because it is an individual who is in pain, so that the individual should have the right to end the pain, and the collective has no right to interfere. Choices are highly motivating in such cultures. Members like to have many choices. Privacy is also very important. Loneliness is an important clinical category in such cultures. Related to individualism is narcissism or self-absorption, which has increased between 1958 and 1998 in the United States (Triandis, 2005).

Individualists try to be consistent in their behavior; if they are reminded of previous behaviors, they are likely to try to behave in the same way. When a task at hand is simple, the more members there are in a team the more each member is likely to reduce individual effort (social loafing). When they distribute resources, individualists use the equity norm more frequently than the equality norm, no matter who needs the resources. This does not happen as much in collectivist cultures (Earley, 1989). In conflict situations they see achieving justice rather than maintaining good relationships as the better outcome (Leung, 1997). They like to confront and debate. When individualists break a norm, they tend to justify their actions rather than to apologize.

In communications, this cultural pattern is characterized by emphasis on the signal rather than the context. Individualists use abstract language such as adjectives more than do people in collectivist cultures, who tend to use more concrete language such as action verbs. Thus, they may say, "He is stubborn" rather than "He did not change his position no matter what other people told him." They see the social environment as constantly changing and persons as stable entities. Western individualists are likely to use linear thinking (e.g., if something is good, it is likely to become even better). They use analytic thinking and logic. They categorize according to common attributes rather than according to function (e.g., cows and pigs go together because they are animals; cows and grass do not go together). Contradiction and inconsistency make them uncomfortable (Nisbett, 2003).

Vertical–Horizontal Cultures

Vertical cultures are hierarchical. Status is all-important in determining social behavior. High status people expect to be obeyed without argument, and low status people obey without asking questions. Horizontal cultures emphasize equality. Every person has the right to what others have. Decisions are taken by consensus.

Time-Related Dimensions of Culture

A number of dimensions are concerned with the way people use time. In *polychronic time use* people carry on several conversations simultaneously, whereas in *monochronic time use* they carry on only one conversation at the time. In *social time* people emphasize relationships and do not pay much attention to the task. A task may take a very long time, as people do not look at their watches. Cultures also differ on the extent that people use a short or long time perspective (Triandis, 1984) and in the extent to which they plan.

Expression of Emotions

There are also cultural differences in the way people express emotions. In some cultures they suppress negative emotions. In many cultures, such as in many collectivist cultures, harmony is very important, and people will be polite even when they disagree with others, and they will not express negative emotions. In other cultures people feel free to express their emotions. Other major cultural differences involve gestures and the permissible distances between the bodies of people. For example, South Americans use small, and Japanese use large, distances when they speak in their own languages, but when they speak in English they are more or less alike (Sussman & Rosenfeld, 1982).

Other Dimensions of Culture

There are further dimensions of cultural variation. For instance, cultures with the *being* orientation emphasize the experience and the moment, whereas cultures with the *doing* orientation give importance to action and achievement. The *being-in-becoming* orientation emphasizes the way people change (F. Kluckhohn & Strodtbeck, 1961). In some cultures the emphasis is on the process (what is being done), whereas in others it is on the outcome (what was actually done). Other dimensions of culture focus on interpersonal relations. In some cultures (e.g., Africa) people believe that they have many enemies, and not believing that one has enemies is considered totally naive. In other cultures trust is widely used (Adams, 2005).

When these dimensions are combined, they result in unique cultural patterns that need to be examined separately. Thus, the combination of collectivism (C), individualism (I), horizontal (H), and vertical (V) dimensions results in cultures that emphasize particular attributes, such as conformity and obeying (VC), togetherness and cooperation (HC), uniqueness and doing one's own thing (HI), and competition and being the best (VI; Triandis, 1995). Triandis (1996) has argued that all these dimensions of cultural variation constitute the parameters of a general theory about the way culture influences people. The theory specifies that particular phenomena that have a characteristic form in cultures that are high on one of these dimensions have a different form in cultures that are low on that dimension.

A large study by Inglehart and Baker (2000) examined data from several countries and found two dimensions distinguishing countries. One dimension contrasted traditional authority with secular–rational authority. The traditional side emphasized the importance of God. The secular side emphasized permissive attitudes toward sexual and other issues. This contrast, among cultures, is positively related to individualism (more secular) and negatively to power distance (hierarchical cultures give more importance to God). The other dimension contrasted survival (emphasis on money, hard work) with well-being (leisure, friends, concern for the environment). The Northern European countries were high on both the secular and the well-being dimensions. The African and Muslim countries were on the traditional and the survival sides of the two dimensions. The other countries were in between these two sets of countries. Affluence is related to both individualism and subjective well-being and is negatively related to power distance. In other words, hierarchical societies are less affluent than relatively egalitarian societies.

Level of Analysis

The dimensions mentioned in the previous section were identified by computing data across several cultures (e.g., Hofstede, 1980, 2001). However, the examination of similar measurements within a culture gives different patterns. For example, across cultures, collectivism is the opposite of individualism. Within culture the two constructs are often orthogonal. Thus, a new name is needed to distinguish the intracultural from the intercultural level of analysis. Corresponding to collectivism is *allocentrism* (Triandis, 1995) or "psychological collectivism" (Jackson, Colquitt, Wesson, & Zapata-Phelan, 2006). Corresponding to individualism is *idiocentrism* (Triandis, 1995).

There are allocentrics and idiocentrics in most cultures; however, there are more allocentrics in collectivist and more idiocentrics in individualist cultures. The "fit" between culture and personality is important for adjustment (Ward, Bochner, & Furnham, 2001). The best adjusted are the allocentrics in collectivist cultures and the idiocentrics in individualist cultures. The allocentrics in individualist cultures try to join groups, such as associations, unions, clubs, political movements, religious institutions, or even armies, but remain dissatisfied by the lack of intimacy in social relations. The idiocentrics in collectivist cultures feel oppressed by the normative demands and try to move to another culture. If they succeed in moving to an individualist culture, they are quite successful.

INFLUENCE OF CULTURE ON ORGANIZATIONS

Organizations can differ in the same ways as cultures. Some have a tight culture (many rules and punishment for not doing what the rules specify) and others loose cultures. Some are collectivist and others individualist (Robert & Wasti, 2002). The other dimensions of cultural variation may also be present in organizations. Of course, numerous positions exist between the two poles of each of these dimensions.

In general, national culture influences organizational culture (Erez & Earley, 1993). However, numerous additional factors reflecting the macroeconomic environment, competition, the history of the organization, and the legal–political environment will also have an influence. A major factor is the decisions of the management to have an organization that will reflect universal norms or local norms. Again, many positions are possible between the two extremes of these poles.

Employee Selection

Universalistic human resource practices (e.g., selection on the basis of test scores) will be rare in collectivist cultures, whereas particularistic practices (e.g., selection on the basis of recommendations by in-group members) will be more common. Triandis and Vassiliou (1972) predicted, from subjective culture data, that Greeks and Americans would differ in the way they make employee decisions. Specifically, they predicted that in reaching employee decisions, traditional Greeks would give more weight to the recommendations of friends and relatives than would Americans and that Americans would give more weight to the recommendations of neighbors and unknown persons than would Greeks. When files of prospective employees were presented to Americans working in Greece and to Athenian employers, the predictions were supported.

Lawler and Bae (1998) examined the "males only," "females only," "no gender language," and "equal opportunity" advertisements placed in newspapers by Thai subsidiaries of Western and Japanese multinationals; the latter were assumed to be collectivist (Yamaguchi, 1994). The level of collectivism of the parent company of the multinational was associated with a high probability of using a "males only" advertisement, whereas individualism was related to the probability of using a "no gender language" advertisement. Also, countries high in individualism had laws that prohibited discrimination in employment, but that was not common in countries high in collectivism. Ozawa, Crosby, and Crosby (1996) found that their Japanese sample was more collectivist and also endorsed affirmative action to a greater degree than did their American sample. It would appear that American individualism results in people feeling some discomfort with categorical social arrangements.

In individualist cultures employers may not have as much choice in personnel decisions because in those cultures, many people seek to become self-employed and are more likely to avoid staying in large companies (Gerganov, Dilova, Petkova, & Paspalanova, 1996).

Job Design

Jobs will be designed for individuals in individualist cultures, but in collectivist cultures some job assignments will be made to groups. Erez (1997) suggests that enriching individual jobs will be the goals of managers in horizontal individualist cultures, and placing individual jobs in a hierarchy of authority and responsibility will be the goals of vertical individualist managers. Horizontal collectivist managers will emphasize autonomous work groups, self-managed teams, and quality circles, whereas vertical collectivist cultures will emphasize team work controlled by top management teams but will also use quality circles. House, Wright, and Aditya (1997) reviewed some literature suggesting that role stress is higher in vertical collectivist than in other kinds of cultures.

In a study of the human resources practices across four subsidiaries of a multinational organization, Robert, Probst, Martocchio, Drasgow, and Lawler (2000) hypothesized that empowerment would be a more successful practice in horizontal rather than vertical cultures. Their results indicated that empowerment was positively related to supervisor satisfaction in the United States but unrelated to supervisor satisfaction (and even negatively related to job satisfaction) in India. Contrary to expectation, empowerment was positively associated with supervisor satisfaction for Polish and Mexican employees, whose work environments were also considered to be relatively vertical. Robert et al. concluded that although certain vertical cultures may have a preference for hierarchy, others may tolerate it but in fact prefer a less autocratic approach. Indeed, the degree of verticality may have to be considered. India is unusually vertical because of its long tradition with the caste system.

Supervisor–Subordinate Relations and Employee Evaluation

Collectivists often control the expression of unpleasant emotions in the presence of other people, so as not to disturb the relationship. For example, Stephan, Stephan, and de Vargas (1996) found strong support for the proposition that people in collectivist cultures feel less comfortable expressing negative emotions than do people in individualist cultures. The data came from Costa Rica and the United States. People in Latino cultures, and possibly in all collectivist cultures, expect others to be "nice" (*simpatico*) during their interactions and become upset when the other person is insufficiently supportive (Triandis et al., 1984). Thus, supervisors in collectivist cultures may have to express their criticism indirectly. Nevertheless, several studies suggest that vertical collectivists accept a critical supervisor more than do individualists. For example, compared to Americans, Chinese participants regarded criticism from superiors to be more acceptable and were less negative about the critical supervisor. However, they were also more likely to perceive their status to be damaged, were less likely to accept the criticism's content, and became more demoralized after the criticism, especially when the criticism came from a high status superior (Leung, Su, & Morris, 2001).

Moskowitz, Suh, and Desaulniers (1994) found that idiocentrics were more dominant and less agreeable than allocentrics when interacting with a supervisee, but their behavior pattern was reversed when interacting with a boss. Idiocentrics have a better opinion of themselves than do most people (Heine, Lehman, Markus, & Kitayama, 1999). That is because of the self-enhancement bias of this orientation. Allocentrics often have a modesty bias, so they sometimes see themselves as less competent than other people do. The result is that in employee evaluation situations, idiocentrics often are disappointed and feel that their supervisor is biased against them and unfair.

If the evaluation results in the employee being laid off, the impact of this action is likely to be smaller in collectivist cultures where the employee can expect help from the in-group than in individualist cultures where the employee cannot expect much support from the in-group. Similarly, the effects of unemployment are more severe in the individualistic North of Italy than in the collectivist South of Italy (Martella & Maass, 2000). In that study unemployment lowered life satisfaction, self-esteem, and happiness, but the effect was stronger in the North than in the South.

Conflict Resolution

Collectivists behave very differently toward in-group and out-group members (Triandis, 1972). When in conflict with in-group members, collectivists are more tolerant, but when a threshold of conflict is reached they become extremely aggressive, even toward in-group members. When dealing with out-group members, they are very competitive and aggressive and see the conflict as "natural." Compromise is rejected. When negotiating with out-groups, collectivists often state what is non-negotiable, whereas individualists look for common ground and for areas of potential agreement. Individualists are more likely to put themselves in their opponents' shoes, whereas collectivists do this only if they are negotiating with in-group members.

The size of the in-group is an important variable. In many job relationships in East Asia, people see members of the organization as in-group and behave toward them positively. However, if the employees are strongly kin collectivists, unless they are working for family firms, they may actually engage in counterproductive organizational behaviors that are to the advantage of their in-groups (such as using the company's equipment for activities that benefit their in-group). For example, Farh, Earley, and Lin (1997) showed that protecting company resources emerged (e.g., not conducting personal business on company time) as an emic dimension of citizenship behavior in the kin collectivist Taiwanese context.

Trubinsky, Ting-Toomey, and Lin (1991) compared Taiwan and U.S. respondents and found that in conflict situations, the former were more likely than the latter to use obliging, avoiding, integrating, and compromising styles of conflict resolution, as opposed to a confrontational style. Similarly, Ohbuchi and Takahashi (1994) studied 94 Japanese and 98 American students and asked them to report on recent conflicts they had experienced. They collected 476 episodes, which they submitted to a content analysis. They found that the Japanese were much more likely than the Americans to avoid conflicts. The Japanese were motivated to preserve relationships. The findings were interpreted as being consistent with theoretical notions about collectivism (Triandis, 1989) and interdependence (Markus & Kitayama, 1991).

Leung (1997) proposed that collectivist conflict management is characterized by "animosity reduction" or "disintegration avoidance," avoidance of actions that strain the relationship and lead to its weakening and dissolution. Disintegration avoidance is especially strong when dealing with in-group members. Animosity reduction is found in intense conflicts, such as with out-groups. Leung argues that when animosity reduction is found, collectivist cultures will use problem solving and compromising conflict resolution techniques. When disintegration avoidance is found, collectivists will either yield or avoid the conflict.

Similarly, Triandis, Bontempo, Villareal, Asai, and Lucca (1988) found that Japanese participants indicated that they avoided conflict in more situations than did American participants. Gabrielidis, Stephan, Ybarra, Dos Santos-Pearson, and Villareal (1997) found that collectivists (Mexicans) displayed more concern for others (used accommodation and collaboration) than did individualists (Americans). Pearson and Stephan (1998) reported that Brazilians were more collectivist than Americans and expressed more concern for the outcomes of others than did Americans, whereas Americans focused on their own outcomes. Brazilians, as expected from theory, made more of a distinction between in-group and out-group in their negotiations than did Americans. Workers in collectivist cultures deal with conflict with their managers by joining unions, but they do not confront their managers as much as do workers in individualist cultures (see Earley & Gibson, 1998, for a review). Those with a collectivist orientation are more likely to join a trade union than those with an individualist orientation (Kelly & Kelly, 1994). Smith, Dugan, Peterson, and Leung (1998) found that individualists deal with conflict by relying on their own experience and training, whereas collectivists deal with conflict by relying on formal rules and procedures.

Training

Because collectivists are more attached and loyal to their organization, they often receive more training than individualists, who are likely to change jobs and work for a competitor organization. Also, horizontals are more likely to receive training than verticals, because the latter are expected to be supervised closely, whereas the former are supposed to be on their own, so they need to know better how to perform their tasks without help. Robert et al. (2000) predicted that training would be valued more by individualists, who would view this practice as an opportunity for advancement in terms of job knowledge and, by extension, position in the organization. However, their results showed that continuous training was positively related to job satisfaction across the Indian, Polish, Mexican, and American subsidiaries. Robert et al. suggested that collectivists from countries with less advantageous economic conditions may consider training investments valuable, as they provide an instrumental means for greater in-group support by increasing job opportunities. Earley (1994) further found that collectivists benefited from group-focused training and individualists from individual-focused training more than their colleagues with a contrasting cultural orientation.

Cross-cultural training.

A major concern is how to train expatriates to work in another culture. When collectivists and individualists come into contact, those who are bicultural (have lived a long time in another culture) are high in both individualism and collectivism, whereas Western samples tend to be high only on individualism and Eastern samples tend to be high only on collectivism (Yamada & Singelis, 1999). Thus, the bicultural individuals will require less training. Bicultural competence also can reduce depression, if the person is high in allocentrism. Lay et al. (1998) found that high bicultural competence reduced depression among allocentrics, whereas low bicultural competence increased depression among allocentrics. This makes sense, because allocentrics want to relate to others, and if they are not competent in relating to the members of the culture they are visiting, they are likely to become depressed.

Much training is required when there is a large cultural distance between the culture of the trainees and the culture of the place they are assigned to (Phalet & Hagendoorn, 1996). One way to measure culture distance, based on Hofstede's (1980) data, was presented by Zeitling (1996). He used cluster analysis and various graphic procedures. Japan is quite distant from most cultures, so one can expect that job assignment to Japan will be among the more difficult for managers from any culture. By contrast, assignments within the Scandinavian countries should be relatively easy. Americans should find it easy to work in the United Kingdom, Australia, or New Zealand. On the other hand, they are likely to find an assignment to Portugal, the former Yugoslavia, Thailand, or Taiwan to be a considerable challenge. The greater the cultural distance there is, the greater the culture shock from visiting another culture is likely to be (Ward et al., 2001). Also, when there is a large discrepancy between the personality of the visitor and the hosts, adjustment is more difficult and depression is more likely (Ward et al., 2001). Phalet and Hagendoorn (1996) reported that Turkish workers in Belgium were helped by their collectivism to adjust and be effective. Social inequality, they found, reinforced collectivism, and cultural distance lowered the achievement of these migrants.

When individualists move to a collectivist culture, they experience certain kinds of difficulties that can be overcome if they are properly trained. Triandis, Brislin, and Hui (1988) advised them to pay attention to the group membership of the people they interact with more than is necessary in their own culture. Individualists should expect more differences in the behavior of collectivists when they interact with in-group versus out-group members than is found in their own culture. They should also expect more emphasis in saving the other person's face, even if that means telling a lie. Conversely, collectivists moving to an individualist culture should pay less attention to group memberships and more attention to the idiosyncrasies of the individuals with whom they are interacting. They should avoid lying and should feel free to express themselves without worrying too much about saving the other person's face.

Training materials called *culture assimilators* (Fiedler, Mitchell, & Triandis, 1971) are helpful in increasing the comfort of the traveler. Bhawuk (1998) showed that a culture assimilator that uses individualism–collectivism theory to explain why particular behaviors are more appropriate than other behaviors in another culture is more effective than assimilators that do not use this theory.

Employee Retention

Although the North American research has typically conceptualized costs associated with leaving an organization as material or economic (such as losing pension benefits), evidence from collectivist contexts underlines the relevance of normative costs of quitting. Such costs emerge out of a concern to meet in-group expectations regarding appropriate behavior—a concern that becomes especially salient when employment opportunities are procured through these networks—as well as a necessity to maintain a reputation for loyalty, which is a crucial asset in these relationship-oriented societies. Wasti (2002) showed that allocentrics, whose continuance commitment was associated with higher levels of normative costs compared with idiocentrics, were less likely to contemplate quitting and engage in withdrawal behaviors such as tardiness.

Affective commitment, which developed from positive work experiences and organizational collectivism, was related to positive outcomes (such as lower levels of turnover intentions), withdrawal behaviors, and higher levels of citizenship behaviors and subjective well-being for both allocentrics and idiocentrics.

INFLUENCE OF CULTURE ON GROUPS AND LEADERS

Groups and Work Teams

Kirkman and Shapiro (2001) developed a model of cultural values and team effectiveness in the context of self-managing working teams. Rather than tying cultural values directly to team outcomes, they proposed two mediating variables: resistance to teams and resistance to self-management. Specifically, they argued that collectivism would be negatively related to resistance to teams, power distance and determinism (fatalism) would be positively related, but a "doing" orientation (which reflects being goal-oriented) would be negatively related to resistance to self-management. Their study, which involved samples from Finland, the United States, the Philippines, and Belgium (where values were directly measured at the individual level and country was controlled for), supported the proposed relations between collectivism and "doing" orientation.

In a more recent study, allocentrism (called *psychological collectivism* by Jackson et al., 2006) was conceived as consisting of Preference for work in groups, Reliance on members of the group, Concern for the health of members of the group, acceptance of group Norms, and giving priority to the Goals of the group. The five factors (P, R, C, N, and G) were measured with three items per factor. The 15 items had good reliability. The higher the score of the 15 items, the greater was the group's task performance and citizenship behaviors, and the lower was the frequency of counterproductive behaviors and withdrawal from the group.

Leadership

Good leaders among collectivists are warm, supportive, and also production oriented (Misumi, 1985). However, the specific behaviors that are considered "warm" are not the same in every culture (Smith & Peterson, 1994). For example, criticizing an employee in Japan requires much greater concern for "saving face" than it does in the West. A warm supervisor does not criticize directly but rather conveys the critical information though a trusted close friend of the employee to be criticized.

Being nurturing first and then demanding high production is the right way to lead in India (Sinha, 1980, 1996). Paternalism is accepted by 80% of the Japanese, 51% of representative American samples, and by around 65% in samples from middle-European countries (Hayashi,

1992). The congruence between leadership style and culture is critical for good performance by the leader's subordinates. Erez (1986) manipulated leadership style across three Israeli organizational cultures. Collectivism was highest in a kibbutz, and in that setting, participative management was most effective. In the public sector, delegation was most effective, whereas in the private sector, which was most individualist, directive leadership was most effective.

The ideal leader in horizontal cultures would be a resourceful democrat; the ideal leader in vertical cultures would be the benevolent autocrat. Promotions from within will be more common in horizontal cultures, and leadership appointments from the outside or from a high status group will be more common in vertical cultures. In horizontal cultures leadership may rotate, and leaders may treat subordinates as equals. In vertical cultures leadership reflects the cultural hierarchy (e.g., upper class or caste results in leadership even when the individual does not merit the position). Leaders in individualist cultures tend to focus on the behavior of individuals, whereas in collectivist cultures they tend to focus on the behavior of groups. The distance between leader and followers is small in the horizontal and larger in the vertical cultures. Erez (1997) suggests that decision making will be individual, and leaders will delegate authority in horizontal individualist cultures, whereas decisions will be centralized and top-down in vertical individualist cultures. In horizontal collectivist cultures there will be much group participation, whereas in vertical collectivist cultures decisions will be top-down and centralized.

House et al. (1997) reviewed literature that indicates that in horizontal individualist cultures, managers and employees pay much attention to their own experience, whereas in vertical collectivist cultures, they pay attention to formal rules. House et al. (1997) further suggest that authoritarian leadership is more acceptable in vertical collectivist cultures than in other kinds of cultures. Collectivism has been found associated with a high value on group maintenance, paternalism, in-group loyalty and harmony, treatment of in-group members with dignity, face saving among in-group members, and nonconfrontational and peaceful methods of conflict resolution. Individualists, in many studies reviewed by House et al. (1997), prefer individual to group-based compensation practices and exhibit a tendency to take risks.

A major cross-cultural study of 62 societies, which involved 170 investigators and obtained responses from 17,300 managers (GLOBE; House, Hanges, Javidan, Dorfman, & Gupta, 2004) examined some dimensions of cultural variation in addition to the ones discussed previously. They also measured societal health (e.g., "Quality of life is high in this country"), human health (e.g., infant survival per 1,000), life expectancy, general satisfaction (e.g., "Taking all things together, would you say that you are Very happy ... Not at all happy"), psychological health (e.g., "During the past few weeks, did you ever feel depressed or very unhappy?") and included several United Nations statistics, such as the Human Development Index. The data show that social health, life expectancy, and general satisfaction are high in societies that are high in individualism, low in power distance, and where people behave in a "tight" way but value "looseness." Our interpretation of the last findings is that when people behave tightly there is more predictability of social behavior, which makes life easier, but valuing looseness suggests that people are displeased with too much tightness and wish to have more tolerance for deviation from norms. Other findings show that health is high when people are "connected" with others and future oriented. These findings are consistent with the literature on the correlates of subjective well-being.

The GLOBE study examined practices (what people do) and values (what people should do) across different kinds of industry (financial services, food processing, telecommunications), organizations (several in each industry), and in the 62 societies. It distinguished institutional from in-group collectivism. The former reflects institutions that encourage collective rewards, collective distribution of rewards, and collective action. The latter involves pride and loyalty to the organization or the family. The former is a desirable cultural pattern, but the latter is not.

In addition, the study examined the cultural dimensions of Future Orientation, Gender Equality, Assertiveness, Humane Orientation, Performance Orientation, Power Concentration, and Uncertainty Avoidance. The researchers also used six culturally implied theories of leadership: Charismatic/Value-Based, Team Oriented, Participative, Autonomous, Humane, and Self-Protective. They found that in most cultures, the Charismatic form of leadership was considered desirable. The other leadership patterns were culturally contingent, but the Self-Protective (self-centered, status conscious, conflict inducer) leadership was generally undesirable. The Middle East is interesting, because the Self-Protective kind of leadership was seen to be less of a problem than it is in other cultures.

INFLUENCE OF CULTURE ON INDIVIDUALS

Behavior is a function of habits plus behavioral intentions (Triandis, 1980), multiplied by facilitating conditions. Some behaviors occur without thought, automatically. Other behaviors occur because of the person's self-instructions to do something. Behavioral intentions are a function of norms (important others think I should do this), self-definitions (I am the sort of person who does this), and the perceived probabilities that good or bad outcomes will follow the behavior. The more positive the outcomes are, the more likely the behavior is; however, if the probability of a good outcome is low, this factor may not play an important role in determining the behavior.

Facilitating conditions reflect the situation. If the person feels able to do the behavior (self-efficacy) and the situation permits the behavior to occur, then the behavior has a high probability of occurring. However, there are situations where no matter what the habits or behavioral intentions are, the behavior will not occur because facilitating conditions are zero (e.g., the person feels unable to do it, the situation does not allow doing it).

Culture has links with all those entities. The customs of the culture shape the habits of individuals. The norms of the culture, the self-definitions found in the culture (Triandis, 1989), and the structure of rewards and punishments in the culture will shape the perceived probabilities. Furthermore, in some cultures people have high self-efficacy and a good opinion of themselves, and in others they do not. Cultures weigh the variables differently. In individualistic cultures affect is given a large weight; in collectivist cultures norms are given a large weight. Perceived control (Ajzen, 1991), that is, the extent the individual feels able to do the behavior, is also important. This construct is linked to self-efficacy ("I can do it"; Bandura, 1991). Collectivist cultures often have lower self-efficacy about behaviors that are new, whereas individualist cultures often seek new behaviors. In short, culture is associated with behavior indirectly, by influencing the weight of variables that predict behavior rather than by influencing the behavior directly.

CONCLUSIONS

The challenges of the global business environment are necessitating an increasingly strategic role for the human resources function. Although our understanding of cultural influences on organizational processes and employee behavior has increased tremendously over the past decades, much of the management research remains ethnocentric. In fact, Wasti and Robert's (2004) review of the top human resource journals indicates that, across the past decade, only 6.4% of the academic human resources management (HRM) articles and 3.2% of the practitioner HRM articles dealt with cultural or international issues. Given the evidence outlined in this chapter, it is clear that future research questions and designs, as well as managerial policies and practices, should always incorporate culture as a fundamental determinant of behavior in organizational contexts.

REFERENCES

Adams, G. (2005). The cultural grounding of personal relationships: Enemy-ship in North America and West African worlds. *Journal of Personality and Social Psychology, 88,* 948–968.

Ajzen, I. (1991). The theory of planned behavior. *Organizational Behavior and Human Decision Processes, 50,* 179–211.

Bandura, A. (1991). Social cognitive theory of self-regulation. *Organizational Behavior and Human Decision Processes, 50,* 248–287.

Bhawuk, D. P. S. (1998). The role of culture theory in cross-cultural training. A multimethod study of culture specific, culture general, and culture theory-based assimilators. *Journal of Cross-Cultural Psychology, 29,* 630–655.

Bond, R., & Smith, P. B. (1996). Culture and conformity: A meta-analysis of studies using Asch's (1952b, 1956) line judgment task. *Psychological Bulletin, 119,* 111–137.

Brewer, M. B., & Chen, Y.-R. (2007). Where (who) are collectives in collectivism? Toward conceptual clarification of individualism and collectivism. *Psychological Review, 114,* 133–151.

Cohen, D., Hoshino-Browne, E., & Leung, A. K.-Y. (2007). Culture and the structure of personal experience: Inside and outside phenomenologies of the self and social world. In M. Zanna (Ed.), *Advances in experimental social psychology* (Vol. 39, pp. 1–67). San Diego, CA: Academic Press.

Cole, M. (1996). *Cultural psychology: A once and future discipline.* Cambridge, MA: Harvard University Press.

Diener, E., Diener, M., & Diener, C. (1995). Factors predicting the subjective well-being of nations. *Journal of Personality and Social Psychology, 69,* 851–864.

Earley, P. C. (1989). Social loafing and collectivism: A comparison of the United States and the People's Republic of China. *Administrative Science Quarterly, 34,* 565–581.

Earley, P. C. (1994). Self or group? Cultural effects of training on self-efficacy and performance. *Administrative Science Quarterly, 39,* 89–117.

Earley, P. C., & Gibson, C. B. (1998). Taking stock in our progress on individualism and collectivism: 100 years of solidarity and community. *Journal of Management, 24,* 265–304.

Erez, M. (1986). The congruence of goal-setting strategies with sociocultural values and its effects on performance. *Journal of Management, 12,* 585–592.

Erez, M. (1997). A culture based model of work motivation. In P. C. Earley & M. Erez (Eds.), *New perspectives on international industrial and organizational psychology* (pp. 193–242). San Francisco: Lexington Press.

Erez, M., & Earley, P. C. (1993). *Culture, self-identity, and work.* New York: Oxford University Press.

Farh, J.-L., Earley, P. C., & Lin, S.-C. (1997). Impetus for action: A cultural analysis of justice and organizational citizenship behavior in Chinese society. *Administrative Science Quarterly, 42,* 421–444.

Fiedler, F. E., Mitchell, T., & Triandis, H. C. (1971). The culture assimilator: An approach to cross-cultural training. *Journal of Applied Psychology, 55,* 95–102.

Gebrielidis, C., Stephan, W., Ybarra, O., Dos Santos-Pearson, V., & Villareal, L. (1997). Preferred styles of conflict resolution. *Journal of Cross-Cultural Psychology, 28,* 661–677.

Gerganov, E. N., Dilova, M. L., Petkova, K. G., & Paspalanova, E. P. (1996). Culture-specific approach to the study of individualism/collectivism. *European Journal of Social Psychology, 26,* 277–297.

Hayashi, C. (1992). Quantitative social research: Belief systems, the way of thinking, and sentiments of five nations. *Behaviormetrika, 19,* 127–170.

Heine, S. H., Lehman, D. R., Markus, H. R., & Kitayama, S. (1999). Is there a universal need for positive self-regard? *Psychological Review, 106,* 766–794.

Hofstede, G. (1980, second edition in 2001). *Culture's consequences.* Beverly Hill, CA: Sage.

House, R. J., Wright, N. S., & Aditya, R. N. (1997). Cross-cultural research on organizational leadership: A critical analysis and a proposed theory. In P. C. Earley & M. Erez (Eds.), *New perspectives on international industrial and organizational psychology* (pp. 535–625). San Francisco: Lexington Press.

Inglehart, R., & Baker, W. E. (2000). Modernization, cultural change, and the persistence of traditional values. *American Sociological Review, 65,* 19–51.

Jackson, C. L., Colquitt, J. A., Wesson, M. J., & Zapata-Phelan, C. P. (2006). Psychological collectivism: A measurement validation and linkage to group member performance. *Journal of Applied Psychology, 91,* 884–899.

Kelly, C., & Kelly, J. C. (1994). Who gets involved in collective action? Social psychological determinants of individual participation in trade unions. *Human Relations, 47,* 63–88.

Kirkman, B. L., & Shapiro, D. (2001). The impact of team members' cultural values on productivity, cooperation and empowerment in self-managing work teams. *Journal of Cross-Cultural Psychology, 32,* 597–617.

Kitayama, S., Markus, H. R., Matsumoto, H., & Norasakkunkit, V. (1997). Individual and collective processes in the construction of the self: Self-enhancement in the United States and self-criticism in Japan. *Journal of Personality and Social Psychology, 72,* 1245–1267.

Kluckhohn, F., & Strodtbeck, F. (1961). *Variations in value orientation.* Evanston, IL: Row, Peterson.

Kluckhohn, C. (1954). Culture and behavior. In G. Lindzey (Ed.), *Handbook of social psychology* (Vol. 2, pp. 921–976). Cambridge, MA: Addison-Wesley.

Kohlberg, L. (1981). *Essays on moral development.* New York: Harper & Row.

Kohn, M. K. (1969). *Class and conformity.* Homewood, IL: Dorsey Press.

Lawler, J. J., & Bae, J. (1998). Overt employment discrimination by multinational firms: Cultural and economic influences in a developing country. *Industrial Relations, 37,* 126–151.

Lay, C., Fairlie, P., Jackson, S., Ricci, T., Eisenberg, J., Sato, T., et al. (1998). Domain-specific allocentrism-idiocentrism: A measure of family connectedness. *Journal of Cross-Cultural Psychology, 29,* 434–460.

Leung, K. (1997). Negotiation and reward allocations across cultures. In P. C. Earley & M. Erez (Eds.), *New perspectives on international industrial and organizational psychology* (pp. 640–675). San Francisco: Lexington Press.

Leung, K., Su, S., & Morris, M. W. (2001). When is criticism not constructive? The role of fairness perceptions and dispositional attributes in employee acceptance of critical supervisory feedback. *Human Relations, 54,* 1155–1187.

Markus, H. R., & Kitayama, S. (1991). Culture and self: Implications for cognition, emotion and motivation. *Psychological Review, 98,* 224–253.

Martella, D., & Maass, A. (2000). Unemployment and life satisfaction: The moderating role of time structure and collectivism. *Journal of Applied Social Psychology, 30,* 1095–1108.

Misumi, J. (1985). *The behavioral science of leadership: An interdisciplinary Japanese research program.* Ann Arbor: University of Michigan Press.

Moskowitz, D. S., Suh, E. J., & Desaulniers, J. (1994). Situational influences on gender differences in agency and communion. *Journal of Personality and Social Psychology, 66,* 753–761.

Nisbett, R. E. (2003). *The geography of thought: How Asians and Westerns think differently and why.* New York: Free Press.

Ohbuchi, K.-I., & Takahashi, Y. (1994). Cultural styles of conflict management in Japanese and Americans: Passivity, covertness, and effectiveness of strategies. *Journal of Applied Social Psychology, 24,* 1345–1366.

Ozawa, K., Crosby, M., & Crosby, F. (1996). Individualism and resistance to affirmative action: A comparison of Japanese and American samples. *Journal of Applied Social Psychology, 26,* 1138–1152.

Pearson, V. M. S., & Stephan, W. G. (1998). Preferences for styles of negotiation: A comparison of Brazil and the U.S. *International Journal of Intercultural Relations, 22,* 67–83.

Phalet, K., & Hagendoorn, L. (1996). Personal adjustment to acculturative transitions: The Turkish experience. *International Journal of Psychology, 31,* 131–144.

Redfield, I., Introduction to Malinowski, B. (1954). *Magic, science, and religion.* New York: Anchor Books.

Robert, C., Probst, T. M., Martocchio, J. J., Drasgow, F., & Lawler, J. J. (2000). Empowerment and continuous improvement in the United States, Mexico, Poland, and India: Predicting fit on the basis of dimensions of power distance and individualism. *Journal of Applied Psychology, 85,* 643–658.

Robert, C., & Wasti, S. A. (2002). Organizational individualism and collectivism: Theoretical development and an empirical test of a model. *Journal of Management, 28,* 544–566.

Shweder, R. A. (1990). Cultural psychology—what is it? In J. W. Stigler, R. Shweder, & G. Herdt (Eds.), *Cultural psychology* (pp. 1–46). Cambridge, England: Cambridge University Press.

Sinha, J. B. P. (1980). *The nurturant task leader.* New Delhi: Concept.

Sinha, J. B. P. (1996). *The cultural context of leadership and power.* New Delhi: Sage.

Smith, P. B., & Peterson, M. F. (1994, July). *Leadership and event management: A cross-cultural survey based on managers from 25 countries.* Paper presented at the International Congress of Applied Psychology, Madrid, Spain.

Smith, P. B., Dugan, S., Peterson, M. F., & Leung, K. (1998). Individualism-collectivism and the handling of disagreement: A 23 country study. *International Journal of Intercultural Relations, 22,* 351–367.

Stephan, W. G., Stephan, C. W., & de Vargas, M. C. (1996). Emotional expression in Costa Rica and United States. *Journal of Cross-Cultural Psychology, 27,* 147–160.

Sussman, N. M. & Rosenfeld, H. M. (1982). Influence of culture, language, and sex on conversational distance. *Journal of Personality and Social Psychology, 42,* 66–74.

Triandis, H. C. (1972). *The analysis of subjective culture.* New York: Wiley.

Triandis, H. C. (1980). Values, attitudes, and interpersonal behavior. In H. E. Howe & M. M. Page (Eds.), *Nebraska Symposium on Motivation, 1979* (pp. 195–260). Lincoln: University of Nebraska Press.

Triandis, H. C. (1984). Toward a psychological theory of economic growth. *International Journal of Psychology, 19,* 79–95.

Triandis, H. C. (1988). Collectivism v. individualism: A reconceptualization of a basic concept in cross-cultural social psychology. In G. K. Verma & C. Bagley (Eds.), *Cross-cultural studies of personality, attitudes and cognition* (pp. 60–95). London: Macmillan.

Triandis, H.C. (1989). The self and social behavior in differing cultural contexts. *Psychological Review, 96,* 506–520.

Triandis, H. C. (1994). *Culture and social behavior.* New York: McGraw-Hill.
Triandis, H. C. (1995). *Individualism and collectivism.* Boulder, CO: Westview Press.
Triandis, H. C. (1996). The psychological measurement of cultural syndromes. *American Psychologist, 51,* 407–415.
Triandis, H. C. (2000). Collectivism and individualism. In Alan E. Kazdin (Ed.) *Encyclopedia of Psychology.* Vol. 2, 176–179. New York: Oxford University Press.
Triandis, H. C. (2005). Issues in individualism and collectivism research. In Sorrentino, R. M., Cohen, D., Olson, J. M., & Zanna, M. P. *Cultural and social behavior.* The Ontarion Symposium Vol. 10 (pp. 207–226) Mahwah, N.J.: Lawrence Erlbaum Associates.
Triandis, H. C., Bontempo, R. W., Villareal, M. J., Asai, M., & Lucca, N. (1988). Individualism and collectivism: Cross-cultural perspectives on self-in-group relationships. *Journal of Personality and Social Psychology, 54,* 323–338.
Triandis, H. C., Brislin, R., & Hui, C. H. (1988). Cross-cultural training across the individualism-collectivism divide. *International Journal of Intercultural Relations, 12,* 269–289.
Triandis, H. C., Carnevale, P., Gelfand, M., Robert, C., Wasti, S. A., Probst, T., et al. (2001). Culture, personality and deception: A multilevel approach. *International Journal of Cross-cultural Management, 1,* 73–90.
Triandis, H. C., Marin, G., Lisansky, J., & Betancourt, H. (1984). Simpatia as a cultural script of Hispanics. *Journal of Personality and Social Psychology, 47,* 1363–1375.
Triandis, H. C., & Singelis, T. M. (1998). Training to recognize individual differences in collectivism and individualism within culture. *International Journal of Intercultural Relations, 22,* 35–47.
Triandis, H. C., & Trafimow, D. (2001). Cross-national prevalence of collectivism. In C. Sedikides & M. B. Brewer (Eds.), *Individual self, relational self, collective self* (pp. 259–276). Philadelphia: Psychology Press.
Triandis, H. C., & Vassiliou, V. A. (1972). Interpersonal influence and employee selection in two cultures. *Journal of Applied Psychology, 56,* 140–145.
Trubinsky, P., Ting-Toomey, S., & Lin, S. L. (1991). The influence of individualism-collectivism and self-monitoring on conflict styles. *International Journal of Intercultural Relations, 15,* 65–84.
Ward, C., Bochner, S., & Furnham, A. (2001). *Psychology of culture shock.* Hove, England: Routledge.
Wasti, S. A. (2002). Affective and continuance commitment to the organization. Test of an integrated model in the Turkish context. *International Journal of Intercultural Relations, 25,* 525–550.
Wasti, S. A., & Robert, C. (2004). Out of touch? An evaluation of the correspondence between academic and practitioner concerns in IHRM. In J. Cheng & M. Hitt (Eds.), *Advances in international management* (Vol. 15, pp. 207–239). Amsterdam: Elsevier.
Yamada, A., & Singelis, T. (1999). Biculturalism and self-construal. *International Journal of Intercultural Relations, 23,* 697–709.
Yamaguchi, S. (1994). A perspective from the self: Collectivism among the Japanese. In U. Kim, H. C. Triandis, C. Kağitçibasi, S.-C. Choi, & G. Yoon (Eds.), *Individualism and collectivism: Theory, method, and applications* (pp. 175–188). Newbury Park, CA: Sage.
Zeitling, L. R. (1996). How much woe when we go: A quantitative method for predicting culture shock. *International Journal of Stress Management, 3,* 85–98.

2

A Model of the Influence of Cultural Values on Job Application Intentions and Behaviors

DIANNA L. STONE, LINDA ISENHOUR,
AND KIMBERLY M. LUKASZEWSKI

University of Texas at San Antonio, Eastern Michigan University,
and State University of New York at New Paltz

INTRODUCTION

Organizations have long been concerned with attracting highly talented employees. One reason for this is that organizational performance is often influenced by the knowledge, skill, and ability levels of their members. Another reason is that there is a growing shortage of highly talented employees in the labor force, and organizations are increasingly competing to attract these individuals. As a result, considerable theory and research in human resource (HR) management has focused on the recruitment process (Breaugh & Starke, 2000; Rynes, 1991; Vroom, 1966). Although researchers have developed a number of recruitment models, relatively little research has considered the influence that individual differences in cultural values may have on the job application process (Bretz, Ash, & Dreher, 1989; Stone, Johnson, Stone-Romero, & Hartman, 2006). This is surprising given the growing internationalization and diversity of the workforce. For instance, some reports indicate that there are over 62,000 multinational corporations operating throughout the world (United Nations Conference on Trade and Development, 2004). In addition, recent estimates (U.S. Census Bureau, 2000) indicate that over 33% of the U.S. population is now made up of minority group members (e.g., African Americans, Hispanic Americans, Asian Americans, Native Americans). Furthermore, the growth rates of these groups are expected to increase in the 21st century because of the high birth rates among these group members and the rise in immigration rates from non-European countries. Given the increasing globalization and diversity of the workforce, organizations are now concerned with developing human resources practices that can be used to attract and retain members of diverse cultural groups.

IMPORTANCE OF CROSS-CULTURAL DIFFERENCES

Given the increasing cultural diversity in the workforce, we believe it is vital to develop a better understanding of the factors that influence the attraction and retention of individuals from multicultural backgrounds. Furthermore, although some research has focused on international human resources management issues (Schuler, Dowling, & De Cieri, 1993), relatively little research has focused on the influence of cultural values on human resources policies and practices (Bentancourt & Lopez, 1993; Schuler et al., 1993; Triandis, 1994). In addition, scant attention has been paid to the impact of cross-cultural differences in values among members of subcultures within the United States (e.g., Hispanic Americans, Asian Americans, African Americans, and Native Americans). Moreover, researchers have argued that many of the models and theories in the field of industrial and organizational psychology and the related field of human resources management are underdeveloped because they fail to consider the critical role that culture plays in behavior in organizations (Erez, 1994; Erez & Earley, 1993; Triandis, 1994; Triandis, Dunnette, & Hough, 1994). Much of the existing theory and research in human resource management has focused on identifying strategies that can be used to attract and retain individuals in organizations (e.g., Huselid, 1995).

However, diversity researchers (Cox, 1993) have argued that many of our existing human resources practices (e.g., recruitment, selection, training, compensation) are based in Western European values and may not be effective with individuals from other cultural backgrounds (e.g., Hispanic Americans, Asian Americans). In particular, a number of theorists contend that the original Anglo settlers in the United States framed the nation's cultural values, and immigrants have been compelled to assimilate to these dominant cultural values (Huntington, 2004; Trice & Beyer, 1993). Similarly, the cultures and practices of work organizations have typically mirrored the dominant ideologies in the United States (Trice & Beyer, 1993). As a result, they emphasize competitive achievement, individualism, self-reliance, science and rationality, efficiency and practicality, and freedom and equality (Trice & Beyer, 1993). Not surprisingly, these values also framed many of the human resources practices in organizations. As a consequence, organizations are now faced with the challenge of developing new human resources practices that will be effective in attracting, motivating, and retaining members of the new multicultural workforce.

PURPOSES OF PRESENT CHAPTER

Given these arguments, the primary purposes of this chapter are to (a) review one of the existing models of the recruitment process, (b) present a modified model that explicitly describes the influence of cultural values on individuals' job application intentions and behaviors, (c) offer hypotheses to guide future research on the topic, and (d) consider the implications of the model for HR practices in multicultural organizations. It merits noting that we use examples of Hispanic American and Anglo American cultural values in the chapter to illustrate how differences in cultural values may affect job application intentions and behaviors. The primary reason for this is that Hispanic Americans are the fastest growing subculture in the United States, and many organizations are now composed of large percentages of employees from this subculture (U.S. Census Bureau, 2000).

CURRENT MODEL OF THE RECRUITMENT PROCESS

Although there are a number of models of the recruitment process (Breaugh & Starke, 2000; Rynes, 1991; Vroom, 1966), most of these models are based in expectancy-based theories of motivation. In particular, extant recruitment models suggest that a number of factors (e.g., recruiters, recruitment sources, administrative practices) influence individuals' motivation to apply for jobs and actual job choice. Given the overlap in these models, we consider only one representative model of the recruitment process in this chapter (Rynes, 1991). Although cultural differences are implicit in the Rynes model and other models of recruitment (e.g., Vroom, 1966), we believe these models should be expanded to explicitly consider the influence that cultural values have on the motivation to apply for jobs. Furthermore, in developing her initial model, Rynes (1991) argued that her model was designed as a point of departure for theory development on the recruitment process. Thus, in the following section we describe Rynes' (1991) initial model of recruitment and offer a modified model that explicitly considers the influence of cultural values on the job application process.

The Rynes (1991) model of the recruitment process suggests that a number of factors, including recruiters, recruitment sources, and administrative practices, affect applicants' motivation to apply for jobs and job choice. Consistent with expectancy theory, the model contends that recruitment practices influence applicants' instrumentalities, expectancies, and valences (Vroom, 1966). These latter variables are considered process variables in the model. In addition, the model posits that these three process variables influence a number of pre- and post-hire outcome variables. The pre-hire outcome variables include job and organizational attractiveness, choice intentions, recruiter attractiveness, and job pursuit. The post-hire variables include satisfaction, commitment, performance, turnover and/or retention levels. Inherent in Rynes' model is the assumption that there may be individual differences in job choice preferences and attraction to organizations. Furthermore, previous research has examined individual differences in attraction to organization (e.g., Bretz & Judge (1994)), responses to recruiters (Rynes, 1991), and responses to recruitment sources (Rynes, 1991). However, as noted previously, individual differences in cultural values are not explicitly discussed in the Rynes model. Thus, we present a model that explicates the ways in which applicants' cultural values might influence the job application process.

A MODEL OF THE INFLUENCE OF CULTURAL VALUES ON JOB APPLICATION INTENTIONS AND BEHAVIORS

Overview of the Model

The modified model of the recruitment process is based in Ajzen's (1985) Theory of Planned Behavior. This model builds on an earlier Theory of Reasoned Action, developed by Fishbein and Ajzen (1975), and suggests that the immediate antecedent of job application behaviors is a person's intentions to apply for jobs. Furthermore, the intentions to apply for jobs are a function of three major factors: individuals' (a) attitudes toward jobs, (b) subjective norms or beliefs about what referent others think about jobs, and (c) perceived control over the application process. A graphic depiction of our model is presented in Figure 2.1, after which each of the relationships in the model is discussed.

Relation between attitudes and job application intentions.

Consistent with the Theory of Planned Behavior (Ajzen, 1985), our model posits that there is a positive relation between the attitudes that individuals have about jobs and their intentions to apply for jobs. For the sake of simplicity we use examples of attitudes toward jobs in our

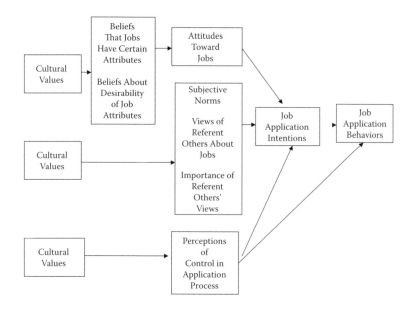

Figure 2.1 A model of the influence of cultural values on job application intentions and behaviors.

description of the model. However, we believe that applicants develop attitudes toward a number of other job application factors, including attitudes toward organizations, work groups, recruiters, recruitment sources, and administrative practices. These factors are not identified explicitly in Figure 2.1 because of space limitations.

Relation between attitudes and beliefs.

Our model also suggests that attitudes toward jobs are a function of two major factors: (a) beliefs that jobs have certain attributes (e.g., high pay levels, job challenge, friendly coworkers), and (b) beliefs about the degree to which these attributes are viewed as desirable or undesirable (see Figure 2.1). For example, the model argues that individuals develop beliefs about the degree to which a job offers opportunities for advancement or promotion before they evaluate the desirability of these advancement opportunities. In support of these arguments, considerable research has shown that the desirability of job attributes influences individuals' attraction to organizations and job choice decisions (e.g., Barber, Daly, Giannantonio, & Phillips, 1994; Feldman & Arnold, 1978; Jurgensen, 1947; Lacy, Bokemeier, & Shepard, 1983; Schwab, Rynes, & Aldag, 1987; Turban, Eyring, & Campion, 1993). Furthermore, much of this research has attempted to identify the set of job attributes that all job applicants find desirable. However, studies have shown that there may be individual differences (e.g., age, gender, personality, values) in preferences for certain job attributes (Bretz & Judge, 1994; Feldman & Arnold, 1978; Tom, 1971).

Influence of cultural values on beliefs.

Consistent with the arguments noted previously, our model hypothesizes that individual differences in cultural values will influence beliefs about the degree to which jobs have certain attributes. In addition, the model suggests that cultural values will affect the desirability of varying job-related attributes. For example, applicants who stress collectivistic values may be more likely to find jobs involving teamwork desirable than those who emphasize individualistic values. The primary reason for this is that those with collectivistic values use the group as the unit of analysis in social relationships and favor interdependence, in-group harmony, personalized relationships, and duty to one's group (Markus & Kitayama, 1991a, 1991b; Triandis, 1994). However, those who stress individualistic values believe that individuals are independent entities who are separate from the group and who have distinctive rights (Spence, 1985). As a result, individualists should find jobs that provide opportunities for achievement, autonomy, and competition more desirable than collectivists (Triandis, 1994).

In support of these arguments, previous research has shown that individuals' values and personality are related to attraction to organizations and job choice preferences (Bretz et al., 1989; Cable & Judge, 1996; Judge & Bretz, 1992; Tom, 1971). For example, results of research by Bretz et al. (1989) revealed that applicants with high needs for achievement were more likely to choose jobs in individually oriented organizations than those with low needs for achievement. In addition, a number of studies have found that the degree of congruence between individuals' values and organizational values was related to attraction to organization (Cable & Judge, 1996; Judge & Bretz, 1992; Tom, 1971). Furthermore, research by Stone, Johnson, Stone-Romero, and Hartman (2006) revealed that collectivism, power distance, and familism cultural values were related to job choice preferences.

Other research has shown that individual differences in personality are related to job choice and attraction to organizations (Bretz et al., 1989; Bretz & Judge, 1994; Turban & Keon, 1993). For instance, results of research have revealed that self-esteem and need for achievement interact with organizational factors to predict attraction to organizations (Turban & Keon, 1993). Similarly, a study by Bretz and Judge (1994) found that locus of control was related to job choice. More specifically, those with an internal locus of control preferred jobs in organizations that allowed for contest norms (i.e., upward mobility as a result of a fair contest) more than did those with an external locus of control. Researchers (e.g., Stone-Romero, 2005; Triandis, 1994) contend that individuals' values and personality are related. For instance, Triandis (1994) maintains that the ecology of a group's habitat influences cultural values and related socialization practices, which, in turn, influence individuals' personality and behavior. For instance, Triandis (1994) argues that

> In some cases, features of the culture itself require particular socialization practices. In the Andaman Islands (Gupta, 1976; Sen, 1962), located between India and Malaysia, women in one of the local tribes customarily carry their babies on their backs at all times, including while working in the field. However, this tribe does not have diapers for their babies. Of course, mothers are highly motivated to toilet-train their babies. Not surprisingly, this culture has the world's record on early toilet training—they train their babies completely by age six months! This is one case where Freud's (1909/1976) theory about socialization and personality was supported. Freud thought that an emphasis on cleanliness during early childhood will make people obsessively and compulsively neat. Such people would want "everything in its own place" and things to be done "just so." That is exactly what was observed in the tribe just described. They are very clean and compulsive. (However, they also suffer from many cases of "autointoxication"—something that happens when a person does not expel bodily fluids and excrements are needed.) In any case, in this example, we see how a particular norm (carrying the baby on the mother's back) results in a socialization pattern (severe toilet training), which results in a personality pattern (compulsiveness), which results in certain behaviors (being superclean, superneat). (p. 25)

Given these arguments, the existing research on the relations among values, personality, and organizational preferences provides indirect support for our argument that cultural values will be related to the desirability of job attributes.

Relation between subjective norms and intentions to apply for jobs.

Apart from attitudes toward jobs, our model also predicts that subjective norms, or the person's beliefs about what referent others think about jobs, influence their intentions to apply for jobs. For instance, referent others might include family members, friends, recruiters, coworkers, or supervisors. According to our model, subjective norms about jobs are based on two basic beliefs: normative beliefs and the motivation to comply with referent others' beliefs. *Normative beliefs* are the individuals' beliefs about what referent others think about the job and its related attributes. For example, individuals may have more positive attitudes toward jobs when their parents believe the jobs have high status than when they do not. In addition, our model suggests that the motivation to comply with referent others' beliefs is a function of the degree to which the person believes that the views of others are important. For instance, the more individuals believe their parents' opinions are important, the more likely they are to be influenced by their parents' views about jobs.

Likewise, our model suggests that recruiters may serve as referent others in some situations. As a result, recruiters may have more influence on applicants' job application intentions when they are viewed as important to individuals than when they are not. For instance, recruiters may have more influence on individuals when they have high status in organizations or when their backgrounds are similar to those of the job applicants. Not surprisingly, some research on recruitment provides support for these arguments (Rynes, 1991). However, research on the effectiveness of recruiters' influence attempts has typically explained a small amount of variance in job choice decisions (Rynes, 1991).

Relation between cultural values and subjective norms.

As is evident in Figure 2.1, our model also indicates that cultural values may influence the degree to which individuals are influenced by subjective norms or the opinions of referent others. For example, those individuals who are high in familism values should be more influenced by members of their families than those who are low in familism (Muniz, 2007). Similarly, individual differences in cultural values may affect the degree to which recruiters can influence individuals' job application intentions and behaviors. For instance, people who stress collectivistic or relationship-oriented values may be more influenced by recruiters' opinions than those who emphasize individualistic values. The primary reason for this is that personal relationships with recruiters may be more important to collectivists than individualists. Although these arguments seem plausible, to our knowledge no research has directly assessed these predictions.

Relation between perceived control in the application process and intentions to apply for jobs.

Apart from the impact of attitudes and subjective norms on job application intentions, our model also suggests that individuals' perceptions of control in the job application process should affect their intentions to apply for jobs. These perceptions of control are similar to Bandura's (1986) notion of self-efficacy beliefs, and they refer to a person's beliefs that he or she has the knowledge, skills, and abilities needed to apply for jobs. Furthermore, perceptions of control are thought to have a direct effect on job application behaviors and indirect effect on job application through intentions to apply for jobs. The indirect effect is based on the assumption that perceived control in the application process affects the motivation to apply for jobs. The primary reason for this is that when people believe they lack the resources needed to apply for jobs, their application intentions will be low even if they have positive attitudes toward jobs (Madden, Ellen, & Ajzen, 1992). For example, although individuals may want to apply for a job, they may believe they lack the computer skills needed to use the organization's online application systems. As a result, these individuals will have lower job application intentions than those who perceive they have the ability to use the web-based recruiting systems.

Furthermore, the model suggests that perceived control may directly affect actual job application behaviors. However, the degree to which perceived control influences actual applications is determined by the person's actual control in the situation and by other situational factors. For instance, although people are highly motivated to apply for jobs, they may perceive they do not have the requisite skills and abilities needed to perform the job. As a result, they would be unlikely to actually apply for jobs. Similarly, individuals may not apply for jobs because situational factors prevent them from accepting jobs. For instance, some individuals may lack transportation or have young children; each of these circumstances would affect their attendance rates. As a result, they may not actually apply for jobs. Although we are not aware of research on the relation between perceptions of control and actual job applications, Rynes' (1991) model of recruitment suggests that expectancies of job offers influence job choice decisions.

Relation between cultural values and perceived control in the application process.

As noted in Figure 2.1, our model also hypothesizes that cultural values may have an impact on individuals' perceived control in the application process. For example, individuals from some subcultures in a society may perceive they have less control in the job application process than others. For instance, individuals from collective subcultures may perceive that they need to form relationships with others in order to gain access to jobs. As a result, they are likely to believe they have less control in the job application process when they are required to use impersonal recruitment sources (e.g., online recruiting systems) than those with individualistic values (Stone, Lukaszewski, & Isenhour, 2005).

Similarly, individuals from some subcultures may perceive they have less control in the job application process because they do not have the values or skills needed to meet job requirements. For example, those from collectivistic subcultures may perceive their values are incongruent with the individualistic or competitive values espoused by many U.S. organizations. Likewise, individuals who value familism may be less likely to believe they fit in U.S. organizations that place emphasis on the separation of work and family than those organizations that stress work–family balance. As a consequence, individual differences in cultural values may influence perceptions of control in the application process and intentions to apply. In addition, individuals should have lower intentions of applying for jobs when they do not perceive they will be selected for jobs than when they believe they will receive a job offer. As a consequence, organizations that emphasize monocultural value systems may be less likely to attract and retain members of diverse cultures than those that emphasize multicultural values (Cox, 1993). Furthermore, these organizations may be faced with a shortage of talented employees as the workforce becomes more culturally diverse (Stone-Romero, 2005).

Interestingly, considerable theory and research on person–organization fit has shown that when individuals perceive there is a lack of fit between their values and organizational values, they are less likely to be attracted to organizations (e.g., Cable & Judge, 1996; Chatman, 1989; Kristof-Brown, 2000; Judge & Bretz, 1992). However, some recent research has argued that the perceived lack of fit between individuals' values and organizational values may serve as a barrier to diversity in organizations (Stone-Romero, 2005).

In summary, our model of the job application process suggests that beliefs about job attributes and the desirability of these attributes influence individuals' attitudes toward jobs. In addition, these attitudes, coupled with subjective norms and perceptions of control, are thought to affect individuals' intentions to apply for jobs. In turn, these intentions influence individuals' actual job application behaviors. Furthermore, our model contends that individuals' cultural values influence their beliefs, attitudes, subjective norms, perceptions of control, and intentions to apply for jobs. Thus, we believe that our modified model of the job application process has a greater capacity to explain individuals' job application behaviors than previous models. This should be especially true when job applicants come from multicultural backgrounds (e.g., Hispanic Americans, Asian Americans, African Americans). Given the predictions in the model, we offer examples of the influence of cultural values on job application intentions and behaviors in the sections that follow.

EXAMPLES OF THE INFLUENCE OF CULTURAL VALUES ON JOB APPLICATION INTENTIONS AND BEHAVIORS

In this section, we offer examples of the value of explicitly considering the cultural background of individuals in the job application process. In particular, we consider the cultural values of Hispanic Americans and Anglo Americans (hereinafter labeled Hispanics and Anglos, respectively). Although there are certainly differences among the subcultures of Hispanics who came to the United States from Latin American countries (e.g., Mexican Americans, Puerto Ricans, Cuban Americans, Colombian Americans, Argentinian Americans), research shows there are also some common threads among people who have been socialized in the Hispanic subculture (Hofstede, 1980; McGoldrick, Giordano, & Pierce, 1996). Thus, for the purpose of this chapter, the term *Hispanic* refers to those individuals who reside in the United States and who were born or trace their backgrounds to families of the Spanish-speaking Latin American nations (Marin & Marin, 1991). Unlike many other groups that have come to the United States, Hispanics have retained much of their culture and have only partially assimilated to the dominant Anglo culture.

Researchers have argued that Hispanics often share a basic set of beliefs and values, including an emphasis on collectivism, familism, a willingness to conform to the demands of people in authority, a flexible attitude toward time, and a motivation to avoid conflict in interpersonal relationships (Hofstede, 1980; McGoldrick et al., 1996). As a result of these cultural values, Hispanics are likely to have different beliefs about the desirability of job attributes and are likely to place more emphasis on the views of referent others than are Anglos. Similarly, Hispanics may have different perceptions of control in the job application process and, therefore, have different job application intentions than Anglos. In view of these cultural value differences, we consider how Hispanic cultural values might influence linkages in our modified model of the application process. More specifically, we discuss the degree to which cultural values might affect beliefs, subjective norms, perceived control, and intentions to apply for jobs.

Collectivism

Previous research on Hispanic cultures indicates that, on average, Hispanics are much more collectivistic than are Anglos (Hofstede, 1980; Marin & Triandis, 1985). Collectivists typically use the group as the unit of analysis in social relationships, and the goals of the group take precedence over individual goals (Hofstede, 1980). Most individuals who are collectivistic also favor interdependence over independence and emphasize security, obedience, duty, in-group harmony, and personalized relationships (Markus & Kitayama, 1991a and 1991b; Triandis, 1994). In contrast, those with individualistic cultural values typically favor independence, achievement, self-reliance, competitiveness, freedom, autonomy, and fairness (Markus & Kitayama, 1991a and 1991b, Perloff, 1987; Spence, 1985; Triandis, 1994).

Although there may be differences in individualism and collectivism among cultures, we caution that research also shows that there is variation among individuals within specific cultures (Triandis, 1994). For instance, within a given culture, individuals from upper socioeconomic levels are more likely to be individualistic than those from lower socioeconomic classes. Similarly, women are often more collectivistic than men (Triandis, 1994).

As noted previously, we maintain that differences in individualism and collectivism will influence (a) beliefs about the desirability of job attributes, (b) attitudes toward jobs, (c) subjective norms and the importance of referent others, (d) perceptions of control in the job application process, and (e) intentions to apply for jobs. Each of these relations is discussed in the following paragraphs.

Collectivism and beliefs about the desirability of job attributes.

Our model suggests that individual differences in collectivism and individualism will affect beliefs about the desirability of job attributes. For instance, given the definition of collectivism noted earlier, it can be argued that individuals who emphasize collectivism will be more likely to prefer jobs that offer them opportunities to work as part of a team, form relationships with others (e.g., coworkers, supervisors), and gain job security. Similarly, they may prefer positions in organizations that stress cooperation and helping others rather than individual competitive achievement. Indirect support for these arguments is provided by several studies (i.e., Blancero & Blancero, 2001; Triandis, Marin, Hui, Lisansky, & Ottati, 1984; Stone et al., 2006). For example, results of research by Stone et al. (2006) found that individuals who valued collectivism were more likely to prefer working in a diverse organization than those who emphasized individualism. Similarly, in research by Blancero and Blancero (2001), Hispanic business professionals reported that forming relationships with coworkers was critical to their job satisfaction. In addition, research by Triandis and his colleagues (1984) revealed that Hispanics often prefer interpersonal relationships with in-groups that are nurturing, caring, and respectful, whereas Anglos prefer more subordinated relationships.

Although there has been some research on the relation between collectivism and the desirability of job attributes, we believe that additional research is needed to examine this relationship. Thus, we offer the following hypothesis to guide future research.

H1: Individuals who value collectivism will believe that jobs that offer opportunities for (a) teamwork, (b) relationships with others, and (c) job security are more desirable than those who value individualism.

Collectivism and beliefs about the desirability of recruitment sources.

Our model also suggests that there should be a relation between collectivism and beliefs about the desirability of various recruitment sources. The primary reason for this is that those who value collectivism are more relationship oriented than are those who value individualism. As a result, individuals who value collectivism should find personal recruitment sources (e.g., employee referrals, networking) more desirable than impersonal sources (e.g., newspaper ads, e-recruiting). In support of these arguments some analysts have noted that Hispanics are less likely to use e-recruiting than are Anglos (McManus & Ferguson, 2003; Stone et al., 2005). Although research has examined the degree to which Hispanics use online recruiting, to our knowledge no research has examined the relation between collectivism and beliefs about the desirability of various recruitment sources. Therefore, we offer the following hypothesis to guide research.

H2: Individuals who value collectivism will believe that recruitment sources that provide opportunities to form personal relationships with others (e.g., employee referrals, networking events, job fairs) are more desirable than sources that do not allow them to form relationships with others (e.g., newspaper ads, e-recruiting).

Collectivism and subjective norms.

It can also be argued that, compared with people who value individualism, those who value collectivism will be more influenced by subjective norms. Stated somewhat differently, the views of referent others will have more influence on the job application intentions of collectivists than on the job application intentions of individualists. The primary reason for this is that collectivists are more likely than individualists to believe that the views of referent others are important. To our knowledge, only one study has provided support for this argument. Muniz (2007) found that individual differences in collectivism were related to the influence that referent others had about choice of organizations. However, to our knowledge no studies have examined the relation between collectivism and job application intentions. Therefore, we offer the following hypothesis to guide future research.

H3: The views of referent others will have more influence on the job application intentions of collectivists than those of individualists.

We also believe that recruiters should have more influence on the job application intentions of collectivists, compared with individualists. One reason for this is that collectivists are more likely than individualists to value personal relationships with recruiters. Furthermore, recruiters that form relationships with applicants may signal that the organization they represent offers opportunities to form relationships with others. Thus, those with collectivistic values may find these types of organizations as more attractive than those that do not offer the same opportunities. In support of these arguments, research has shown that recruiters' warmth and interpersonal skills influence applicants' willingness to accept jobs (Rynes, 1991). In addition, some research has shown that ethnic minorities (e.g., blacks) prefer recruiters who are similar in terms of ethnic background (Wyse, 1972, cited in Rynes, 1991). However, recruiters' ethnicity had no impact on white applicants' job acceptance intentions. Despite these results, we know of no research on the relation between individuals' cultural values and reactions to recruiters. Therefore, we offer the following hypothesis to guide future research.

H4: The relation between recruiters' influence attempts and job application intentions will be moderated by individual differences in collectivism such that collectivists' job application intentions will be more influenced by recruiters' influence attempts than will individualists' job application intentions.

Collectivism and perceived control in the job application process.

Our model also indicates that individual differences in collectivism should be related to perceptions of control in the job application process. In particular, we believe that those who value collectivism may perceive they have less control in the job application process than those who value individualism. One reason for this is that collectivists may be less likely than individualists to perceive they fit in traditional U.S. organizations that emphasize individualism and competitive achievement (Stone-Romero, Stone, & Salas, 2003). As a result, collectivists may perceive they are less likely to be selected for jobs in traditional organizations. Thus, they should have lower intentions of applying for jobs in traditional U.S. organizations than would individualists. Indirect support for these arguments is provided by research (Bretz & Judge, 1994; Turban & Keon, 1993) that revealed that values and personality interacted with organizational factors to determine attraction to organizations. In spite of these results, we know of no research that has directly examined the relation between collectivism and perceived control in the application process. Therefore, we offer the following hypothesis to guide research on the topic.

H5: The relation between individual differences in collectivistic values and perceived control in the application process will be moderated by the values of the organization.

Familism

Another cultural value that may influence job application intentions and behaviors is familism. *Familism* is defined as a value that involves strong identification and attachment to the family, and a willingness to make sacrifices to be with one's family (Marin & Marin, 1991). For example, research shows that Hispanics often place a greater emphasis on familism than Anglos do (McGoldrick et al., 1996). Furthermore, results of research by Triandis, Marin, Betancourt, Lisansky, and Change (cited in Kossek & Lobel, 1996) has shown that Hispanics are more willing than non-Hispanics to make financial sacrifices to attend family celebrations for extended family members (e.g., birthday parties for nieces, nephews). In contrast, many individuals in the Anglo culture emphasize that work should be the priority in one's life, and people should be willing to sacrifice their family life in the interests of work and achievement (Lobel & Kossek, 1996). Given these differences, it can be expected that familism cultural values should influence a number of elements in the modified model of the application process, including (a) beliefs about the desirability of job attributes, (b) subjective norms, (c) perceived control, and (d) intentions to apply for jobs.

Familism and beliefs about job attributes and desirability of job attributes.

Given the definition of familism noted in the previous paragraph, we maintain that individuals who have high levels of familism values should be more likely to find the following job-related attributes as desirable: work–family balance, personal time off to spend with family, and flexible time schedules. Support for these arguments is provided by the research of Stone et al. (2006). Results of this research found that individuals who placed a great deal of emphasis on familism were more likely to prefer jobs that offered personal time off from work than were those individuals who did not emphasize familism. Although some research has examined the relation between familism and the beliefs about the desirability of job attributes, additional research is needed on the topic; therefore, we propose the following hypothesis to guide future research.

H6: Individuals who have high levels of familism values should find jobs that offer (a) work–family balance, and (b) flexible hours as more desirable than would those individuals who have low levels of familism values.

Familism and subjective norms.

As noted previously, our model also suggests that cultural values should affect the extent to which subjective norms influence attitudes toward jobs and job application intentions. Thus, we believe that familism values should influence the extent to which individuals (a) believe their families' views about jobs are important, and (b) are motivated to comply with their families' views about jobs. For instance, a person who emphasizes familism values may be less likely to apply for a new job in another location if their families do not approve of relocation than if their family members do approve of relocation. To our knowledge, no research has directly examined the relation between familism values and the degree to which individuals are influenced by their families' views of jobs. Therefore, we offer the following hypothesis to guide future research.

H7: Individuals who have high levels of familism values are more likely to be influenced by their families' views of jobs than are those who have low levels of familism values.

Power Distance

According to Hofstede (1980), cultures vary in terms of power distance cultural values. Power distance is a value that reflects the degree to which the less powerful members of a social system expect that power will be distributed in an unequal manner in the social system and accept power differentials among individuals. The construct of power distance has also been defined as a measure of interpersonal power or influence that exists between two individuals (Stone-Romero & Stone, 1998). Cultures often vary in the degree to which they support the notion that some people have more power because of inherited (e.g., status) or acquired characteristics (e.g., education; Marin & Marin, 1991). Furthermore, societies differ in the degree to which they support deference and respect toward certain powerful groups or individuals (e.g., those who are rich or well educated) or members of professions (e.g., physicians, judges). Previous research has shown that Hispanics often value conformity and have higher levels of power distance than do Anglos (Hofstede, 1980; Marin & Marin, 1991). In contrast, research has shown that Anglos typically place more emphasis on power equality or egalitarianism than Hispanics (Trice & Beyer, 1993). Other research has shown that personal respect in interpersonal relations is very important to Hispanics, who believe that their personal power should be acknowledged in relationships (Marin & Marin, 1991).

In view of these values, it can be expected that individual differences in power distance should influence a number of elements in our modified model, including (a) beliefs about the desirability of job attributes, (b) beliefs about the desirability of recruitment sources, (c) compliance with subjective norms, and (d) perceived control in the job application process. Each of these relations is discussed in the following paragraphs.

Power distance and beliefs about the desirability of job attributes.

Our model predicts that individuals who subscribe to high power distance values will be more likely to prefer jobs in companies that offer opportunities to gain power and respect than those that do not. For instance, individuals with high levels of power distance should prefer jobs in well-known companies with good reputations. The primary reason for this is that individuals with high power distance values may perceive that the status of the organization will confer status to them and enable them to gain personal power and respect. In support of this argument, results of research by Stone et al. (2006) found that power distance was positively related to preference for jobs in companies with well-known reputations.

Our model also predicts that individual differences in power distance should be related to preferences for jobs that offer (a) promotion opportunities, (b) mentoring, and (c) perquisites that symbolize status (e.g., prestigious job titles, corner offices, company cars). One reason for this is that those with high levels of power distance may find jobs desirable that offer opportunities for advancement and status. Although some research has examined the relation between power distance and job choice preferences, to our knowledge no research has examined the degree to which power distance is related to preferences for jobs offering opportunities for advancement and status attainment. As a result, we make the following prediction to guide future research.

H8: Individuals with high levels of power distance values will be more likely than those with low levels of power distance to believe that jobs offering opportunities for advancement and status attainment are desirable.

**Power distance and beliefs about the
desirability of recruitment sources.**

Our modified model of the job application process also suggests that power distance cultural values may influence beliefs about the desirability of recruitment sources. In particular, it can be argued that individuals with high levels of power distance should be more likely to view high status recruitment sources as more desirable than those sources viewed as having low status. For instance, those with high power distance may view public employment agencies or newspaper advertisements as less desirable than private or executive-oriented employment agencies. The primary reason for this is that public employment agencies are often used to attract individuals for low level jobs and may be viewed as having less status than private employment agencies. Similarly, newspaper advertisements may be viewed as low status recruitment sources because they are often used to attract all qualified people in the workforce rather than just a subset of those with high status. In spite of these arguments, we know of no research on the relation between power distance or other cultural values and the desirability of various recruitment sources. Therefore, we offer the following hypothesis.

H9: The relation between individuals' power distance cultural values and the desirability of recruitment sources will be moderated by the degree to which the recruitment source is perceived to have high levels of status.

The relation between power distance and subjective norms.

Our model also suggests that individual differences in power distance cultural values should affect the extent to which individuals are influenced by subjective norms or the opinions of referent others. For instance, individuals who are high in terms of power distance values should be more influenced by the views of high status referent others than those who are low in power distance values. One reason for this is that those who emphasize power distance are more likely to believe they should be deferent or respectful of those in authority than those who do not stress power distance. Similarly, individuals who are high in power distance are also more likely to expect that authority figures will protect them in organizations and influence others on their behalf than are those who are low in power distance (Stone et al., 2006). As a result, those high in power distance should be more likely to comply with the views of high status referents and recruiters. Although these arguments seem plausible, we know of no research that has examined the relation between individual differences in power distance and compliance with the views of recruiters or high status referent others. Therefore, we propose the following hypothesis.

H10: The views of high status (a) referent others and (b) recruiters will have more influence on the job application intentions of those high in power distance values than on those who are low in terms of these values.

The relation between power distance and perceived control in the application process.

We also maintain that individual differences in power distance should be related to perceptions of control in the application process. More specifically, we believe that those who place emphasis on power distance should perceive they have less control when applying for jobs in some types of organizations than others. For instance, they may be less likely than those low in power distance to perceive they fit in highly egalitarian or participative organizations. As a result, they should be less likely to perceive they will be selected for jobs in these types of organizations. However, those high in power distance values should perceive they are more likely to fit in hierarchical organizations than would those who are low in power distance. Similarly, they are likely to perceive they will gain power or respect in hierarchical organizations more so than in egalitarian organizations. Thus, they should perceive they have greater levels of control when applying for positions in hierarchical, as opposed to egalitarian, organizations. As a consequence, they should have greater intentions of applying for jobs in the former rather than latter type of organization. Despite these arguments, we know of no research on these predictions. Therefore, we present the following hypothesis.

H11: The relation between individual differences in power distance values and perceived control in the application process will be moderated by (a) the values of the organization or (b) the design of the organization.

Time Orientation

Another cultural value that may affect job application intentions and behaviors is time orientation. Cross-cultural researchers (Kluckholn & Strodtbeck, 1961) have long argued that cultures vary considerably in time orientation, or the emphasis they place on the past, present, or future. For example, members of Hispanic cultures often emphasize a present time orientation and typically have a more flexible attitude toward time than do Anglos. For instance, they are less likely to stress punctuality, and lateness is often associated with success and likeableness (Okun, Fried, & Okun, 1999). Not surprisingly, this flexible view of time allows them to place more emphasis on the quality of interpersonal relationships (Marin & Marin, 1991). In contrast, Anglos are typically more future oriented than Hispanics and emphasize punctuality and delay in gratification (Trice & Beyer, 1993). One notable example of the Anglo orientation toward time is the quote by Benjamin Franklin that "time is money," which suggests that time should not be wasted and efficiency should be emphasized. Given these differences, we believe that individual differences in time orientation should influence beliefs about the desirability of job attributes and attitudes toward jobs. These relations are considered in the following subsections.

The relation between time orientation and beliefs about job attributes.

Given that there may be cultural differences in time orientation, our model suggests that these differences in values should influence beliefs about the desirability of job attributes. For instance, it can be argued that individuals with a present time orientation should find jobs with flexible hours and personal time off as more desirable than would those with a future time orientation. Similarly, those with a present time orientation should prefer jobs that offer short-term outcomes (e.g., on the spot bonuses) as opposed to long-term outcomes (e.g., retirement benefits). Although these predictions seem plausible, research by Stone and colleagues (2006) did not find that individual differences in time orientation were related to preferences for jobs with flexible work hours or considerable personal time off from work. The lack of relations in this study could be due to the fact that the measure of time orientation lacked construct validity. Therefore, we suggest that additional research is needed to examine the relation between time orientation and the beliefs about the desirability of job attributes. As a result, we offer the following hypothesis to guide future research.

H12: Individuals with a present time orientation, as opposed to a future time orientation, will be more likely prefer jobs with (a) flexible work hours, (b) considerable personal time off, and (c) short-term outcomes.

SUMMARY OF RELATIONS BETWEEN CULTURAL VALUES AND JOB APPLICATION PROCESSES

In summary, we have argued that cultural differences in collectivism, familism, power distance, and time orientation are likely to affect a number of elements in our model, including (a) beliefs about the desirability of job attributes, (b) beliefs about the desirability of recruitment sources, (c) attitudes toward jobs, (d) compliance with subjective norms, and (e) perceived control in the application process. In addition, attitudes toward jobs, coupled with subjective norms and perceptions of control, should influence individuals' intentions to apply for jobs and actual job application behaviors. Thus, we believe that our modified model should provide a better understanding of job application intentions and behaviors than existing models of the recruitment process (e.g., Breaugh & Starke, 2000; Rynes, 1991). Furthermore, we believe that an explicit recognition of cultural differences should enable multicultural organizations to attract and retain the broad array of talented employees in today's workforce.

IMPLICATIONS FOR THEORY, RESEARCH, AND PRACTICE

We also believe that our model of individuals' job application intentions and behaviors has important implications for theory, research, and practice. As a result, each of these issues is considered in the sections that follow.

Theoretical Implications

It is clear that extant models of the recruitment process (e.g., Breaugh & Starke, 2000; Rynes, 1991; Vroom, 1966) have provided us with considerable capacity to understand, explain, and predict individuals' attraction to organizations. However, given the growing levels of diversity in organizations and the increasing globalization of business, we believe, as do others (e.g., Erez, 1994; Erez & Earley, 1993; Triandis, 1994), that current models of recruitment need to be modified to explicitly recognize the influence that cultural values have on job application processes. Although organizational researchers have begun to consider the impact of cultural values on many aspects of behavior in organizations (e.g., Erez & Earley, 1993; Triandis, 1994), they have not directly addressed the influence of culture on the recruitment process. As a result, we modified Rynes' (1991) model of recruitment to reflect the key role that cultural values might have on job application intentions and behaviors. As suggested by our modified model, individual differences in cultural values are thought to influence (a) beliefs about job attributes and/or recruitment sources, (b) attitudes toward jobs, (c) compliance with the views of referent others (e.g., family, recruiters), (d) perceptions of control, (e) intentions to apply for jobs, and (f) actual job application behaviors. Thus, we believe our model should help organizations identify key factors that will help attract and retain individuals from diverse cultures and subcultures (e.g., African Americans, Asian Americans, Hispanic Americans, Native Americans).

Research Implications

Directions for research.

Research has examined the impact of national culture on organizational culture (e.g., Hofstede, 1980, 1991; Stone-Romero & Stone, 1998; Trice & Beyer, 1993) and on behavior in organizations (Erez & Earley, 1993; Triandis, 1994). Furthermore, researchers have begun to assess the relations between individuals' values, personality, and job choice preferences (e.g., Bretz & Judge, 1994; Judge & Bretz, 1992; Judge & Cable, 1997; Tom, 1971). However, little research has examined the relations between cultural values and job choice preferences for members of ethnic minority groups (e.g., Gomez, 2003; Stone et al., 2006; Thomas & Wise, 1999). This is surprising given the growing diversity and internationalization of the workforce. Thus, we believe that our model should foster research on the influence of cultural values on job application intentions and behaviors. However, research is needed to test the various linkages in our model (see Figure 2.1). For instance, research is needed to examine the extent to which cultural values affect (a) beliefs about the desirability of job attributes and recruitment sources, (b) attitudes toward jobs, (c) compliance with views of referent others and recruiters, and (d) perceptions of control in the job application process. Similarly, research is needed to assess the extent to which these factors (e.g., beliefs, attitudes, subjective norms, and perceptions of control) influence job application intentions and behaviors.

Methods issues in research.

To conduct the research mentioned in the previous paragraph, there are several key methodological issues that need to be addressed. First, researchers (Betancourt & Lopez, 1993) have argued that there is often construct confusion or confounding of the terms *ethnicity* and *culture*. For instance, the term *ethnicity* is typically used to refer to groups that are characterized by a common nationality, culture, or language (Betancourt & Lopez, 1993). In contrast, *culture* is often defined as "a set of collective, shared learned cultural values that represent a broad tendency to prefer certain states of affairs over others" (Hofstede, 1980, p. 25). Although cultural values are assumed to underlie ethnic group differences, this may not always be the case. Research shows that there is variation in cultural values within an ethnic group (Triandis, 1994). For example, although, on average, Hispanics may be more collective than Anglos, research shows that Hispanics vary in terms of collectivism. In particular, regardless of ethnicity, women and members of low socioeconomic groups are more likely to emphasize collective values than are men and high socioeconomic group members (Triandis, 1994). Thus, we believe, along with others (Betancourt & Lopez, 1993), that cultural values should be measured directly rather than relying on ethnic group membership as an indirect assessment of these values.

Second, research on cross-cultural issues has typically used typologies of cultural values (Hofstede, 1980, 1997; Kluckhohn & Strodtbeck, 1961) to explain behavior in organizations (e.g., career choice, preferences for outcome allocations). Although these frameworks provide an important first step in understanding the influence of culture on behavior in organizations, we believe that researchers should identify the specific cultural values associated with a given culture or subculture rather than use a standardized typology. For example, as noted previously in this chapter, research has shown that even though there is variability within Hispanic groups, they often share a common set of cultural values that include high levels of collectivism, familism, power distance, and a present time orientation (Marin & Marin, 1991). Thus, we believe that researchers should develop theoretical models and incorporate the values specific to a given culture in order to understand and predict behavior. This approach has been labeled the "top-down approach" to cross-cultural research (Betancourt & Lopez, 1993). The top-down approach is often contrasted with the "bottom-up approach," which identifies key cultural dimensions (e.g., individualism/collectivism) and assesses the degree to which these dimensions predict behavior. Despite these arguments, research is needed to examine the effectiveness of these alternative approaches to understanding the influence of cultural values on behavior in organizations.

Third, although there are numerous measures of cultural values, including (a) individualism/collectivism (e.g., Hui, 1988; Triandis, Chan, Bhawuk, Iwao, & Sinha, 1995), (b) familism (e.g., Villarreal, Blozis, & Widaman, 2005), and (c) power distance (e.g., Brockner et al., 2001; Earley & Erez, 1997; Maznewski & De Stefano, 1995), the construct validity of these measures has not always been assessed. Thus, the existing measures may not provide appropriate operational definitions of cultural values. Recently, the GLOBE project on cross-cultural leadership (House, Hanges, Ruiz-Quintanilla, Dorfman, & Gupta, 2004) has developed measures of many of these constructs. However, research is needed to assess the degree to which these new measures are reliable and valid.

Implications for Practice

In addition to its implications for theory and research, our model of job application intentions and behaviors has a number of important implications for attracting and retaining individuals in organizations. For example, it suggests that managers in multicultural organizations need to be aware of the fact that job applicants from different cultures may have very different job choice and reward preferences. As a result, multicultural organizations might adopt cafeteria-based reward and benefit systems that will enable them to attract and retain talented employees from all cultures. For instance, organizations could provide workers with a set amount of total compensation and allow workers to decide how to allocate these resources. In these systems, employees would be given a choice of rewards (e.g., a bonus or more time off with pay) to meet their needs.

In addition, our model suggests that referent others, including recruiters, may have more influence on some job applicants than on others. For example, our model hypothesizes that individuals who emphasize collectivistic values should be more influenced by family members and recruiters than would those who value individualism. Thus, organizations need to be aware that their choice of recruiters may have an meaningful impact on job application and job choice behaviors. As a result, they may want to ensure that their recruiters have backgrounds and values that are similar to their applicants' backgrounds. Likewise, our model suggests that the views of family members may be more important to applicants who emphasize high levels of familism than to those that do not stress familism values. Therefore, organizations may want to involve family members in the recruitment process for those applicants who stress familism values. These and other culturally sensitive recruitment strategies may help organizations attract and retain highly talented employees.

Furthermore, our model predicts that individual differences in cultural values may affect job applicants' perceptions of control and actual job application behaviors. Thus, organizations need to be aware that their image or organizational culture may affect the degree to which members of diverse cultures are attracted to organizations. As noted earlier, members of some subcultures may not perceive their values are congruent with the organization's culture or values. As a consequence, they may not believe they will be selected for jobs and may not apply for jobs in these organizations. Thus, organizations should take steps to ensure that they have human resource policies and practices that appeal not only to the dominant group but also to multicultural groups. In addition, when they advertise their job openings, they might promote the fact they have culturally sensitive human resource practices.

CONCLUSION

Throughout this chapter we have emphasized that individual differences in cultural values are likely to influence attraction to organizations and job choices. Thus, we developed a model of individuals' job application intentions and behaviors that explicitly considers the role that cultural values may have on these processes. It is our hope that the model will foster additional research on the influence of cultural values on the recruitment process. Furthermore, we believe that our model should enable organizations to attract and retain members of the new multicultural workforce. In addition, we hope that our model will enhance the employment opportunities of all members of our society and enable everyone to a enjoy a fulfilling work life.

REFERENCES

Ajzen, I. (1985). From intentions to actions: A theory of planned behavior. In J. Kuhl & J. Beckmann (Eds.), *Action control: From cognition to behavior* (pp. 11–39). New York: Springer-Verlag.

Bandura, A. (1986). *Social foundations of thought and action: A social cognitive theory.* Englewood Cliffs, NJ: Prentice Hall.

Barber, A. E., Daly, C. L., Giannantonio, C. M., & Phillips, J. M. (1994). Job search activities: An examination of changes over time. *Personnel Psychology, 47,* 739–766.

Betancourt, H., & Lopez, S. R. (1993). The study of culture, ethnicity, and race in American psychology. *American Psychologist, 48,* 629–637.

Blancero, D. M., & Blancero, D. A. (2001). Hispanic business professionals in corporate America: A profile and an analysis. In *Hispanic workforce: Hispanic Association on Corporate Responsibility corporate best practices.* Washington, DC: Hispanic Association on Corporate Responsibility (HACR).

Breaugh, J. A., & Starke, M. (2000). Research on employee recruitment: So many studies, so many recruiting questions. *Journal of Management, 26*, 405–434.

Bretz, R. D., Ash, R. A., & Dreher, G. G. (1989). Do people make the place? An examination of the attraction-selection-attrition hypothesis. *Personnel Psychology, 42*, 561–581.

Bretz, R. D., & Judge, T. A. (1994). The role of human resource systems in job applicant decision processes. *Journal of Management, 20*, 531–551.

Brockner, J., Ackerman, G., Greenberg, J., Gelfand, M. J., Francesco, A. M., Chen, Z. X., et al. (2001). Culture and procedural justice: The influence of power distance on reactions to voice. *Journal of Experimental Social Psychology, 37*, 300–315.

Cable, D. M., & Judge, T. A. (1996). Person-organization fit, job choice decisions, and organizational entry. *Organizational Behavior and Human Decision Processes, 67*, 294–311.

Chatman, J. A. (1989). Improving international organizational research: A model of person-organization fit. *Academy of Management Review, 14*, 333–349.

Cox, T. (1993). *Cultural diversity in organizations: Theory, research, and practice.* San Francisco: Berrett-Koehler.

Earley, P., & Erez, M. (1997). *New perspectives on international industrial/organizational psychology.* San Francisco: Jossey-Bass.

Erez, M. (1994). Toward a model of cross-cultural industrial and organizational psychology. In H. C. Triandis, M. D. Dunnette, & L. M. Hough (Eds.), *Handbook of industrial and organizational psychology* (Vol. 4, 2nd ed., pp. 559–607). Palo Alto, CA: Consulting Psychologists Press.

Erez, M., & Earley, P. C. (1993). *Culture, self-identity, and work.* New York: Oxford University Press.

Feldman, D. C., & Arnold, H. J. (1978). Position choice: Comparing the importance of organizational and job factors. *Journal of Applied Psychology, 63*, 706–710.

Fishbein, M., & Ajzen, I. (1975). *Belief, attitude, intention and behavior: An introduction to theory and research.* Reading, MA: Addison-Wesley.

Gomez, C. (2003). The relationship between acculturation, individualism/collectivism, and job attribute preferences for Hispanic MBAs. *Journal of Management Studies, 40*, 1089–1105.

Hofstede, G. (1980). *Culture's consequences: International differences in work-related values.* Beverly Hills, CA: Sage.

Hofstede, G. (1991). *Cultures and organizations.* New York: McGraw-Hill.

Hofstede, G. (1997). *Cultures and organizations: Software of the mind.* New York: McGraw-Hill.

House, R. J., Hanges, P. J., Javiclan, M., Dorfman, P. W., & Gupta, V. (Eds.). (2004). *Culture, leadership, and organizations. The GLOBE study of 62 societies.* Thousand Oaks, CA: Sage.

Hui, C. H. (1988). Measurement of individualism and collectivism. *Journal of Research in Personality, 22*, 17–36.

Huntington, S. P. (2004). *Who are we? The challenges of America's national identity.* New York: Simon & Schuster.

Huselid, M. A. (1995). The impact of human resource management practices on turnover, productivity, and corporate financial performance. *The Academy of Management Journal, 38*, 635–672.

Judge, T. A., & Bretz, R. D. (1992). Effects of work values on job choice decisions. *Journal of Applied Psychology, 77,* 261–271.

Judge, T. A., & Cable, D. M. (1997). Applicant personality, organizational culture and organization attraction. *Personnel Psychology, 50,* 359–394.

Jurgensen, C. E. (1947). Selected factors which influence job preferences. *Journal of Applied Psychology, 31,* 553–564.

Kluckhohn, F. R., & Strodtbeck, F. L. (1961). *Variations in value orientations.* Evanston, IL: Row, Peterson.

Kossek, E. E., & Lobel, S. A. (Eds.) (1996). *Managing diversity: Human resource strategies for transforming the workplace.* Cambridge, MA: Blackwell.

Kristof-Brown, A. L. (2000). Perceived applicant fit: Distinguishing between recruiters' perceptions of person-job and person-organization fit. *Personnel Psychology, 53,* 643–671.

Lacy, W. B., Bokemeier, J. L., & Shepard, J. M. (1983). Job attribute preferences and work commitment of men and women in the United States. *Personnel Psychology, 36,* 315–329.

Lobel, S. A., & Kossek, E. E. (1996). Human resource strategies to support diversity in work and personal lifestyles: Beyond the "family friendly" organization. In E. E. Kossek & S. A. Lobel (Eds.), *Managing diversity: Human resource strategies for transforming the workplace* (pp. 221–244). Cambridge, MA: Blackwell.

Madden, T. J., Ellen, P. S., & Ajzen, I. (1992). A comparison of the theory of planned behavior and the theory of reasoned action. *Personality and Social Psychology Bulletin, 18,* 3–9.

Marin, G., & Marin, B. V. (1991). *Research with Hispanic populations.* Newbury Park, CA: Sage.

Marin, G., & Triandis, H. C. (1985). Allocentrism is an important characteristic of the behavior of Latin Americans and Hispanics. In R. Diaz-Guerrero (Ed.), *Cross-cultural and national studies in social psychology* (pp. 85–104). Amsterdam: Elsevier.

Markus, H. R., & Kitayama, S. (1991a). Cultural variation and self-concept. In G. R. Goethals & J. Strauss (Eds.), *Multidisciplinary perspectives on the self* (pp. 18–48). New York: Springer.

Markus, H. R., & Kitayama, S. (1991b). Culture and the self: Implications for cognition, emotion, and motivation. *Psychological Review, 98,* 224–253.

Maznewski, M. L., & De Stefano, J. J. (1995). *Measuring culture in international management: The cultural perspectives questionnaire.* London, Ontario: University of Western Ontario.

McGoldrick, M., Giordano, J., & Pearce, J. K. (1996). *Ethnicity and family therapy* (2nd ed.). New York: Guilford Press.

McManus, M. A., & Ferguson, M. W. (2003). Biodata, personality, and demographic differences of recruits from threes sources. *International Journal of Selection and Assessment, 11,* 175–183.

Muniz, E. J. (2007). *The role of cultural values in organizational attraction.* Unpublished doctoral dissertation, University of Central Florida, Orlando.

Okun, B. F., Fried, J., & Okun, M. L. (1999). *Understanding diversity: A learning-as practice primer.* Pacific Grove, CA: Brooks/Cole.

Perloff, R. (1987). Self-interest and personal responsibility redux. *American Psychologist, 42,* 3–11.

Rynes, S. L. (1991). Recruitment, job choice, and post-hire consequences: A call for new research directions. In M. D. Dunnette & L. M. Hough (Eds.), *Handbook of industrial and organizational psychology* (2nd ed., pp. 399–444). Palo Alto, CA: Consulting Psychologists Press.

Schuler, R. S., Dowling, P. J., & De Cieri, H. (1993). An integrative framework of strategic international human resource management. *Journal of Management, 19*(2), 419–459.

Schwab, D. P., Rynes, S. L., & Aldag, R. J. (1987). Theories and research on job search and choice. In K. Rowland & G. R. Ferris (Eds.), *Research in personnel and human resource management* (Vol. 5, pp. 129–166). Greenwich, CT: JAI Press.

Spence, J. T. (1985). Achievement American style: The rewards and costs of individualism. *American Psychologist, 40,* 1285–1295.

Stone, D. L., Johnson, R. D., Stone-Romero, E. F., & Hartman, M. (2006). A comparative study of Hispanic-American and Anglo-American cultural values and job choice preferences. *Management Research, 4,* 8–21.

Stone, D. L., Lukaszewski, K. M., & Isenhour, L. C. (2005). E-recruiting: Online strategies for attracting talent. In H. G. Gueutal & D. L. Stone (Eds.). *The brave new world of eHR: Human resources management in the digital age* (pp. 22–53). San Francisco: Jossey-Bass.

Stone-Romero, E. F. (2005). Personality-based stigmas and unfair discrimination in organizations. In. R. L. Dipboye & A. Colella (Eds.), *Discrimination at work: The psychological and organizational bases* (pp. 255–280). Mahwah, NJ: Erlbaum.

Stone-Romero, E. F., & Stone, D. L. (1998). Religious and moral influences on work-related values and work quality. In D. B. Fedor & S. Ganoush (Ed.), *Advances in the management of organizational quality* (Vol. 3, pp. 185–285). Greenwich, CT: JAI Press.

Stone-Romero, E. F., Stone, D. L., & Salas, E. (2003). The influence of culture on role conceptions and role behaviors in organizations. *Applied Psychology: An International Review, 52,* 328–362.

Thomas, K. M., & Wise, P. G. (1999). Organizational attractiveness and individual differences: Are diverse applicants attracted by different factors? *Journal of Business and Psychology, 13,* 375–390.

Tom, V. R. (1971). The role of personality and images in the recruiting process. *Organizational Behavior and Human Performance, 6,* 573–592.

Triandis, H. C. (1994). Cross-cultural industrial and organizational psychology. In H. C. Triandis, M. D. Dunnette, & L. M. Hough (Eds.), *Handbook of industrial and organizational psychology* (2nd ed., pp. 103–172). Palo Alto, CA: Consulting Psychologists Press.

Triandis, H. C., Chan, D. K.-S., Bhawuk, D. P. S., Iwao, S., & Sinha, J. B. P. (1995). Multimethod probes of allocentrism and idiocentrism. *International Journal of Psychology, 30,* 461–480.

Triandis, H. C., Dunnette, M. D., & Hough, L. M. (Eds.) (1994). *Handbook of industrial and organizational psychology* (2nd ed). Palo Alto, CA: Consulting Psychologists Press.

Triandis, H. C., Marin, G., Hui, C. H., Lisansky, J., & Ottati, V. (1984). Role perceptions of Hispanic young adults. *Journal of Cross-Cultural Psychology, 15,* 297–320.

Trice, H. M., & Beyer, J. (1993). *The cultures of work organizations.* Englewood Cliffs, NJ: Prentice Hall.

Turban, D. B., Eyring, A. R., & Campion, J. E. (1993). Job attributes: Prefer-
    ences compared with reasons given for accepting and rejecting job offers.
    Journal of Occupational and Organizational Psychology, 66, 71–81.
Turban, D. B., & Keon, T. L. (1993). Organizational attractiveness: An interac-
    tionist perspective. *Journal of Applied Psychology, 78,* 184–193.
United Nations Conference on Trade and Development. (2004). *Transnational
    corporations and foreign affiliates* (chap. 3). Retrieved November 8, 2006,
    from http://www.unctad.org/en/docs/gdscsir20041c3_en.pdf
U.S. Census Bureau. (2000). *Population reports.* Retrieved March 18, 2007,
    from http://www.census.gov/prod/1/pop/p25-1130.pdf
Villarreal, R., Blozis, S. A., & Widaman, K. F. (2005). Factorial invariance of a
    pan-Hispanic familism scale. *Hispanic Journal of Behavioral Sciences, 27,*
    409–425.
Vroom, V. H. (1966). Organizational choice: A study of pre and post deci-
    sion processing. *Organizational Behavior and Human Performance, 1,*
    212–225.

3

The Clash between "Best Practices" for Selection and National Culture

ROBERT L. DIPBOYE AND
STEFANIE K. JOHNSON
University of Central Florida and Colorado State University

The primary knowledge base for human resource management (HRM) is the work of North American and Western European scholars. As noted by Rousseau and Tinsley (1997), "little explicit attention is given to location (i.e., region or country) and how it might impact the ways organizations obtain and manage people" (p. 39). Given this narrow research base, it is surprising that distinguished organizational scientists confidently proclaim "best practices" in HRM with little or no consideration of cultural limitations (Marchington & Grugulis, 2000). This chapter focuses on the implications of cultural differences for one of the practices that Pfeffer (1998) and others describe as a key to competitive success: the selective hiring of employees.

The amount of research on hiring would seem to justify the identification of best practices. Indeed, employee selection is arguably the most researched topic in HRM. Despite the technical sophistication of the scholarly literature, however, selection is typically depicted as a collection of methods, divorced from the larger organizational and cultural context. In this chapter we begin by describing how selection practices vary as a function of country, and we illustrate these variations by comparing selection in the United States to Mexico and China. Our message throughout this chapter is that national culture plays an important role in shaping the HRM systems in a country and, specifically, the methods and processes of employee selection. We compare patterns of selection in different cultures by locating them on a continuum anchored by the rational/analytic and the social/intuitive models. HRM in the United States promotes the rational/analytic model as the universal ideal, but we argue that this is a culturally naïve position that overemphasizes fit to the job and ignores the many other functions that the selection process serves. We conclude by arguing for a hybrid approach, in which elements of the rational/analytic and the social/intuitive are integrated to fit the culture and the multiple objectives of the selection process.

THE SELECTION PROCESS

The selection of employees moves implicitly or explicitly through several stages. First, agents of the organization identify the attributes (physical, intellectual, personality, temperament, appearance, demographics) that define the requirements of the position and the ideal applicant. The second stage involves the gathering of information about applicants to determine the individuals who best fit the requirements of the job. In the third and fourth stages, applicants are judged on the requirements of the position, and a hiring decision is made. The final stage of selection is the evaluation of the selection process to determine whether it is effective. A variety of criteria can enter into this phase to guide the evaluation, including the validity, fairness, and the utility of the procedures.

We would venture to conclude from the cross-national research that there are indeed large differences among countries around the world in how each phase of the selection process is handled. Unfortunately, with the possible exception of the research on judgment/decision making, the cross-national comparisons of selection practices are atheoretical, scattered, and based on opportunistic samples. A meaningful pattern of results is difficult to discern on the basis of this motley collection of studies.

Another reason that the results are not readily interpretable is the focus in much of the research on specific content of the selection process. In other words, the research question is typically framed in terms of such questions as how countries differ in their use of specific selection techniques and what specific applicant attributes they stress. The problem with this approach is that two organizations using the same techniques and focusing on the same attributes may still differ considerably in "how" they implement the selection process. We suggest that a clearer pattern of cross-cultural differences result if the underlying processes, not the specific techniques, are the focus of the examination. To this end, we propose that cross-national comparisons of selection focus on the distinction between rational/analytic and social/intuitive approaches.

RATIONAL/ANALYTIC AND SOCIAL/ INTUITIVE APPROACHES TO SELECTION

The ideal set forth in the United States, and to some extent in Western Europe, is a formal, planned, and scientifically based approach that we call the rational/analytic approach. By contrast, the ideal that dominates in many non-Western countries is informal, unplanned, and intuitive, an approach that we call the social/intuitive. The two decision processes models outlined here correspond to similar distinctions made in other dual process theories of information processing and thought. These include the distinctions between analytic versus intuitive (Hammond, 1996), experiential versus rational (Epstein, Pacini, & Denes-Raj, 1996), piecemeal versus categorical (Fiske, Neuberg, Beattie, & Milberg, 1987), and heuristic versus analytical (Evans & Curtis-Holmes, 2005). The rational/analytic end of these continua is equivalent to scientific approaches that are rule-based, controlled, independent of context, asocial, effortful, and acquired through education. The intuitive end of the continua is associative, holistic, automatic, effortless, fast, highly contextualized, personalized, social, and acquired through experience.

The rational/analytic approach to selection is basically the application of science to determining the means of screening and selecting from among applicants. This approach consists of the following steps:

1. Formal job analyses identifying the knowledge, skills, abilities, and other characteristics (KSAOs) required in the job
2. Gathering of information on applicant qualifications using validated, structured, and standardized instruments of selection, including mental tests, interviews, personality inventories, biographical data (biodata), work samples, assessment centers, and job simulations, among others
3. Quantitative assessment of the applicants on each KSAO and decisions based on the fit of the applicant to the profile of the ideal applicant
4. Empirical validation of judgments against job criteria and an emphasis on economic success. The underlying goal of selection is to maximize economic gain (Schmidt & Hunter, 1981; Schmidt, Hunter, McKenzie, & Muldrow, 1979).

The selection practices in many other countries diverge from this ideal in the direction of the social/intuitive approach. Here we see a reliance on unstructured procedures that experience has led the employer to believe work in the selection of employees.

1. Job requirements are based on personal beliefs of decision makers rather than explicit job analyses. Moreover, the fit to the KSAOs of the position are less important than fit to the context of the job, including the group and organizational culture.

2. There is an unstandardized search for information that is personal and idiosyncratic to the applicant. Decision makers follow their intuitions and ask for information that fits the particular applicant. Relationships often guide the process more than formal techniques.
3. Assessment of applicants is based on categorical judgments and general impressions, and choices among applicants are based on noncompensatory and intuitive judgments of general fit. To the extent that there is a holistic approach to judgment and problem solving, the whole is much more than the sum of the parts. In this case, intuition, overall impression, and clinical judgment are preferred over the impersonal, mechanical process characterized by statistical approaches.
4. Finally, evaluation of the selection system is based on noneconomic criteria. Although no organization in any culture can totally ignore economic success, some cultures place a higher priority on criteria such as maintaining harmony over competitive economic advantage.

In future research, we suggest that cross-national comparisons of selection and other HRM systems focus more on *how* the selection process differs in terms of this model than on *what* specific method is used to select employees. In these comparisons, we would further suggest that we compare various countries on the extent to which they are rational/analytic, as opposed to social/intuitive, in determining qualifications, implementing information gathering, judging applicants and making decisions, and evaluating the success of the selection (Dipboye, 1994). We propose that selection processes in the United States and Western Europe resemble the analytical/rational approach more, and the social/intuitive approach less, than in Far Eastern, Mediterranean, and Latin American nations. We first review the research on cross-national variations in selection practices that provide support for these propositions. We then examine the cultural factors that determine whether one or the other approach is dominant.

CROSS-NATIONAL VARIATIONS IN SELECTION PRACTICES

In the section that follows we provide evidence of how selection practices around the world vary as a function of national culture. These differences are described for each of several stages of the selection process. Employers in different countries differ in their views of the knowledge, skills, abilities, and other characteristics required in jobs. There are international differences in the selection techniques that are used to evaluate applicants. Finally, there are also variations in the design, evaluation, and implementation of selection procedures, and the criteria used to evaluate the success of selection.

Cross-National Variation in Job Specifications

Surveys of what is important to look for in an applicant show that the attributes employers see as most important for positions vary as a function of the country in which the survey is conducted (Ali, 1989; Cassens, as cited in Barrett & Bass, 1976; Hatvany & Pucik, 1981; Kamoche, 1993; Nagore, as cited in Tixier, 1996; Segalla, Sauquet, & Turati, 2001; Sinha, 1997). For instance, managers in the United States and Western Europe are more likely to identify adaptability/ flexibility as among the most important attributes required of applicants than are managers in Japan, where "managerial talent," technical knowledge of the business, and experience with the company are rated as the most important (Tung, 1990). Other attributes that managers identify as more important outside the United States and most Western European countries are moderate views and harmonious personality in Japan (Hatvany & Pucik, 1981), agreeableness, interpersonal relations, and trustworthiness in Islamic/Arab countries (Ali, 1989), membership in the same group as the employer in India (Sinha, 1997), integrity, loyalty, and attachment to one's family in Spain (Nagore, as cited in Tixier, 1996), and community values in Africa (Kamoche, 1993). Variations are also observed when the comparisons are limited to Western nations. In a survey of financial institutions in England, France, Germany, Italy, and Spain, Segalla et al. (2001) report that age, assessment test scores, references, training in foreign languages, academic background, graduate rank, international work experience, and professional experience are rated as among the most important factors. Some factors appear unique to specific countries. For instance, English managers stress applicant skills that fit the job and are willing to hire a qualified foreigner if they possess these skills. On the other hand, the Italians, Spanish, and French stress the candidate's nationality. The German respondents are not concerned with nationality but instead emphasize technical skills and personal network or contacts. According to Segalla et al. (2001), the emphasis of the Spanish respondents is harder to discern, but they appear to prefer Spanish applicants over foreign applicants.

Cross-National Variation in Techniques of Selection

Cross-national comparisons of the specific techniques of selection reveal large differences across nations in the use of selection procedures to gather information about applicants (Lévy-Leboyer, 1994; Robertson & Makin, 1986; Ryan, McFarland, Baron, & Page, 1999). These studies show that many of the standardized selection practices that are identified as "best practices" in Western research are used infrequently in many other cultures.

Applications, References, Unstructured Interviews

Some procedures seem almost universal in their use. These include the application form (Lévy-Leboyer, 1994; Robertson & Makin, 1986; Ryan et al., 1999; Shackleton & Newell, 1991; Smith & Abrahamsen, 1992; Tixier, 1996) and unstructured interviews (Eleftheriou & Robertson, 1999; Lévy-Leboyer, 1994; Robertson & Makin, 1986; Ryan et al., 1999; Shackleton & Newell, 1994). Among Western nations, France seems to stand out as a country that makes less use of the interview than others with only 45 percent reporting their use in one survey (Shackleton & Newell, 1994). Another exception is China, where employers seldom use the interview (Von Glinow & Chung, 1989). Even among countries where the use of the interview, application, and references is widespread, there are large variations in the information asked of the applicants. Questions about personal background and family are allowed in many countries but are often considered illegal or inappropriate in the United States. In some countries, such as China and Mexico, informal and unwritten referrals from friends and family are common. By contrast, in the United States, employers prefer impersonal, job-relevant information from previous employers.

Structured, Quantitative Selection Procedures

Even larger variations emerge when we examine the cross-national variations in the use of the standardized procedures that are the products of psychometric research. These include structured interviews, cognitive ability tests, personality inventories, and assessment centers, which are often seen as best practices in selection in the United States and some Western European nations. Despite this claim, the receptivity to these technically sophisticated procedures varies widely among nations.

One example is the structured interview, which is held up as a best practice in the United States and Western Europe but is not easily transported to other countries (Clark, 1993; Tixier, 1996). Ryan et al. (1999) conclude that in some cultures structured interviews are "antithetical to beliefs about how one should conduct an interpersonal interaction or the extent to which one should trust the judgment of the interviewer" (p. 386). Differences are also found in cognitive ability testing. Such tests are used more frequently in New Zealand, Belgium, and the United States than in Germany, United Kingdom, Italy, Russia, and France (Arminas, 1998; Clark, 1993; Lévy-Leboyer, 1994; Ryan et al., 1999; Salgado & Anderson, 2002). Large cross-national variations also are reported in the use of personality inventories (McCulloch, 1993; Ryan et al., 1999; Shackleton & Newell, 1991; Tixier, 1996).

The use of some selection techniques appears limited to a small subset of nations. Drug and integrity tests are used almost exclusively in the United States (Ryan et al., 1999; Shackleton & Newell, 1994), and graphology is used almost exclusively in France (Lévy-Leboyer, 1994; Ryan et al., 1999; Shackleton & Newell, 1991). Assessment centers are more frequently used in the United Kingdom, Germany, and the Netherlands than in France and Belgium (Lévy-Leboyer, 1994; Shackleton & Newell, 1991). Another rarely used, but well-researched and quantitatively sophisticated approach, is scored biodata. Although subjective judgments of application material are common, scored biographical data are mostly used in the United Kingdom and the United States and infrequently in most other countries (Robertson & Makin, 1986; Shackleton & Newell, 1991).

There is impressive evidence for the criterion related validity of the selection practices that are considered best practices in the United States, such as cognitive ability tests, assessment centers, structured interviews, and biodata (Schmidt & Hunter, 1998). Do these validities generalize across countries? So far the only convincing support is for the cross-national generalizability of cognitive ability testing (Salgado & Anderson, 2002; Salgado et al., 2003). There is much less support for the cross-cultural generalizability of procedures that measure attitudes, temperaments, integrity, personality traits, and interpersonal skills. The research is, at best, mixed in support of the cross-cultural generalizability of the criterion-related validity of personality tests (e.g., Nelson, Robertson, Walley, & Smith, 1999; Salgado, 1997; Stone & Ineson, 1997). Although there is support for the cross-national generalizability of the five-factor model when analyses are at the individual level (McCrae & Costa, 1997), there is little support for the universality of this model when the data are analyzed at the country level (Poortinga, Van de Vijver, & Van Hemert, 2002). Also, there is minimal support for the metric and full scale equivalence of personality measures (Fortmann, Leslie, & Cunningham, 2002; Grimm & Church, 1999; Kurman & Sriram, 1997; Middleton & Jones, 2000; Poortinga et al., 2002; Sandal & Inger, 2002; Smith, 2004).

CROSS-NATIONAL VARIATION IN THE CRITERIA FOR EVALUATING SELECTION

How do we know when a selection system works? Again, there is limited research on cross-national differences, but our general impression from the literature is that countries differ dramatically in what they consider important in the evaluation of a selection process.

Can Selection Enhance Performance of the Core Tasks of the Job?

The ultimate objective of selection practices in the United States is the achievement of financial results (Ferner & Quintanilla, 1998).

Carried to the extreme this could translate into hiring workers who are "obtained cheaply, used sparingly, and developed and exploited as fully as possible in accordance with the demands determined by the overall business strategy" (Sparrow & Hiltrop, 1994, p. 7). Economic utility is not the priority in many other countries. For instance, in India and Eastern Europe employers may view combating poverty as a more important consideration in hiring than minimizing labor costs (Herriot & Anderson, 1997; Sinha, 1997).

Is the Selection System Legal?

The structured selection systems used in the United States are heavily influenced by legal considerations (Rowe, Williams, & Day, 1994). In other words, employers in the United States not only select the best individuals to maximize profits but to avoid the loss of profit and reputation associated with violations of laws and government guidelines. Other countries do not have the same pressure of lawsuits, and many lack formal laws protecting individuals against discrimination in selection. Indeed, the legal pressure on employers to show the job relatedness and business necessity in their selection practices is perhaps the most important reason that U.S. employers adopt scientifically sound selection procedures. Chao and Nguyen (2005) note that there is a clear trend around the world to follow the lead of the United States and implement laws against discrimination, but that the definition of discrimination and the remedies available to victims vary widely across countries.

Do Applicants Accept the Selection Procedures?

An important consideration in the choice among alternative selection procedures is how applicants perceive these practices. Procedures that are viewed negatively by applicants may adversely impact recruiting and the firm's image, hinder the socialization of the new hire into the firm, and provoke lawsuits. The perceived fairness of selection as judged against norms of distributive and procedural justice receives the most current attention from researchers. The findings show large cross-national variations in what is seen as fair and what is seen as unfair (Marcus, 2003; Phillips & Gully, 2002; Steiner & Gilliland, 1996). For instance, Marcus (2003) and Phillips and Gully (2002) compare fairness reactions to selection techniques in Singapore and the United States. Perhaps as a result of their greater acceptance of authority, Singaporeans are more accepting of most selection techniques than is typically found of respondents in the United States. Moreover, Singaporeans view interpersonal warmth and respect for privacy as less important in judging process fairness than do respondents from the United States.

Cross-National Variations in Selection Practices as a Reflection of the Rational/ Analytic and Social/Intuitive Models

Based in part on our review of cross-national variations in selection, we propose that these variations reflect differences in the extent to which HRM in these countries conforms to a rational/analytic or to a social/ intuitive model. We propose that the ideal approach to selection conforms more to a rational/analytic model in the United States and Western Europe than in Latin American, Far Eastern, and Mediterranean countries. On the other hand, the ideal approach to selection is more likely seen as conforming to a social/intuitive model in non-Western countries. We base this proposition not only on the previous review of cross-national differences in selection, but also on research showing cross-national differences in judgments and decision making. Most of the latter research focuses on comparisons of East Asian and Western countries and provides evidence that judgment and decision making are more analytical and less holistic in Western cultures than in Eastern cultures (Choi, Dalal, Kim-Prieto, & Park, 2003; Fong & Wyer, 2003; Masuda & Nisbett, 2001; Miyamoto & Kitayama, 2002; Nisbett, Peng, Choi, & Norenzayan, 2001; Wallsten & Gu, 2003; Yi & Park, 2003).

Cross-national differences in judgment are shown in the information to which persons attend and the interpretation of that information. Respondents from the United States, relative to those from East Asia, are less likely to take into account the context and more likely to use trait attributions in describing and interpreting what they observe (Choi et al., 2003; Masuda & Nisbett, 2001). The correspondent bias (i.e., the inference of an attitude from a statement of position without taking into account pressures to make the statement) appears stronger among persons from East Asian countries than from Western nations (Miyamoto & Kitayama, 2002). Participants from Asian nations also seem to tolerate contradiction and require less information to form an impression than participants from Western nations (Nisbett et al., 2001).

Cross-cultural differences are found for decision making as well as in judgment. Participants from East Asian countries appear more skilled than those from the United States at collective decision making and show a stronger preference for group decision making by consensus compared to the United States where participants prefer decision making by majority vote (Yi & Park, 2003). Fong and Wyer (2003) find that Chinese students, in comparison to students from the United States, are more likely to make decisions on the basis of what others decide and less likely to base their decisions on the anticipated consequences of actions. Fong and Wyer also find that students from the United States are most influenced in their decisions by the happiness that they anticipate experiencing if they take a risk and benefit. Chinese students are more influenced by the regret they imagine having if they do not take the risk and miss out on the chance to benefit. In general, respondents from the United States anticipate more intense reactions to *both* favorable and unfavorable decision consequences than the Chinese respondents. Wallsten and Gu (2003) found that when choosing between two competing alternatives, individuals from Western cultures commonly focus on one or the other as more likely true, whereas those from Eastern cultures look for ways in which both may be true.

There is much less research comparing judgment and decision making in Western cultures with Latin American or Mediterranean cultures. Nevertheless, we speculate that the rational/analytic modes of thinking are more dominant in the Western countries, whereas social/ intuitive modes are more dominant in non-Western countries. Taking this speculation one step further, we propose that similar cross-cultural differences occur for selection practices. In Western cultures, the ideal approach to selection is more likely to conform to a rational/analytic model, whereas in non-Western cultures the ideal is more likely to conform to a social/intuitive model.

Cross-National Variations in Selection Practices as a Reflection of Culture

National culture is one of several forces that influence whether the selection process of an organization aligns more with a rational/analytic or a social/intuitive model (Dipboye, 1994). On the basis of a survey of 116,000 IBM employees across 66 countries, Hofstede (1991) proposed four dimensions of national culture: (a) individualism/collectivism, (b) power distance, (c) uncertainty avoidance, and (d) masculinity/femininity. Trompenaars and Hampden-Turner (1998) identify, on the basis of a study of 15,000 managers from 28 countries, several additional cultural dimensions: (a) universalistic versus particularistic, (b) affective versus neutral, (c) specific versus diffuse, (d) ascription versus achievement, (e) sequential versus synchronous, and (f) internal versus external control. We review the relation of each of these cultural factors to selection practices. On the basis of this review, we propose that the cross-national differences in the adherence to rational/analytic and social/intuitive approaches to selection reflect differences on these cultural dimensions. Specifically, we propose that the social/intuitive approach is more likely found in cultures that are collective, feminine, uncertainty avoidant, particularistic, diffuse, affective, ascriptive, synchronic, and external. A rational/analytic approach is more likely found in cultures that are individualistic, masculine, universalistic, specific, neutral, achievement oriented, sequential, internal, and low on uncertainty avoidance.

Individualism–collectivism.

In Hofstede's (1991) assessment of 40 countries, highly individualistic countries include the Czech Republic, United States, Australia, and the United Kingdom, whereas the most collectivistic countries include Colombia, Venezuela, Egypt, Japan, China, and Mexico. Trompenaars' assessment is similar, with the exception that Mexico is identified in his original research as individualistic rather than collectivist, possibly as the result of using top executives as respondents. Consistent with that explanation, Thompson and Phua (2005) find that national differences in the Hofstede model do not appear to generalize to senior managers.

The essence of the distinction between individualism and collectivism is whether persons are seen as interdependent or as autonomous entities in the society (Triandis & Bhawuk, 1997). In an individualistic culture, ties among individuals are loose; people look out for themselves and their immediate families. Personal autonomy is highly valued as are the self-fulfillment and personal rights of the individual. An individualistic society emphasizes rationality in which there is a computation of the costs and benefits of relationships. By contrast, in a collectivist society individuals define the self in terms of their memberships in groups and interdependency is at the core of how people identify themselves. Although persons within an in-group may relate to each other on the basis of norms of equality, even at the cost of personal gain, relationships with those outside the group are often more adversarial and competitive.

Collectivist cultures value treating everyone the same within the in-group, rather than differentiating among in-group members on the basis of performance or potential (McFarlin & Sweeney, 2001; Steiner & Gilliland, 2001). As a consequence, one could argue that employers in collectivist cultures are not as likely to compare and rank order individuals in the process of selection decisions (Love, Bishop, Heinisch, & Montei, 1994). Moreover, Rousseau and Tinsley (1997) propose that employee selection in collectivist cultures is person-centered, focuses on the fit of the recruit with the rest of the company, and is based on "socially constructed methods (meetings, unstructured interviews, dinners, etc.) and word-of-mouth recruitment" (p. 47). In individualistic cultures, though, employers are more likely to select applicants on the basis of whether they have the necessary task skills and to choose measures on the basis of their validity in assessing these attributes (Rousseau & Tinsley, 1997). Similarly, Triandis and Bhawuk (1997) speculate that employers in collectivist societies select employees by determining whether they can be trusted and are loyal, whereas employers in individualistic societies look for task competence. This difference between collectivist and individualistic cultures probably applies more to the selection from among in-group persons than from among out-group persons. For instance, the Japanese appear more likely to screen American workers through extensive use of test batteries than they are Japanese workers.

Peppas and Peppas (1999) find that enthusiasm is rated first in importance by a sample from the United States. Enthusiasm is rated only 12th in importance by the Chinese sample, which possibly is indicative of the greater value placed on maintaining harmony with the group. Also reflective of collectivist values, Peppas, Peppas, and Jin (2001) report that knowledge of the company is ranked in a Chinese sample as third in importance but is only 18th in a U.S. sample. Contrary to expectations, initiative is judged important in both the China and the United States samples (Peppas et al., 2001). The authors suggest that Chinese respondents interpret initiative as actions by the group, whereas the respondents in the United States interpret initiative as actions of individuals. Finally, seniority is more important in Taiwan and China than the United States, perhaps as a consequence of the veneration of age in China (Chen, 1995; Rusbult, Insko, & Lin, 1995).

Structured interview procedures appear to fit more with individualistic cultures than with collective cultures. Spence and Petrick (2000) compare interviews in the United Kingdom and the Netherlands with the less individualistic country of Germany. They find that highly structured, bureaucratic interviews are more likely in the individualistic countries of United Kingdom and the Netherlands than in the more collectivistic country of Germany.

Triandis and Bhawuk (1997) speculate that vertical collectivist cultures prefer the use of interviews and informal communication to convey information about jobs and to select employees. Moreover, when written tests are used for selection in a collectivist culture, a third party is more likely used "to avoid in-group pressure on the tester and compromising the selection" (p. 43). In horizontal collectivist and in individualist cultures, however, the written test and formal channels of communication for advertising job vacancies are the preferred methods. Finally, in collectivist cultures, group promotions are preferred, whereas individual promotions are preferred in individualistic societies.

Power distance.

This dimension refers to the degree to which members of a society are accepting of large status and power differences between individuals and groups. Organizations in countries lower in power distance de-emphasize differences in individuals' power and wealth, whereas countries higher in power distance focus on those differences. A high power distance country is more likely to have centralized authority, tall organizations with a larger proportion of supervisors, and autocratic and paternalistic leaders. Countries high in power distance include Japan, South Korea, Philippines, Mexico, Venezuela, India, and Singapore. The United States, Israel, Australia, Denmark, Ireland, and Sweden are among the countries scoring on the lower end of the power distance scale.

Ahlstrom et al. (2005) report that in China, "workers from state-owned enterprises still think that the factory boss should be their uncle; responsible for any and every personal problem they have" (p. 266). Similarly, in Mexico there is an emphasis on hierarchy in both the family, where the father is dominant, as well as at work, where good management is seen as paternalistic but dictatorial (Kras, 1995; Schuler, Jackson, Jackofsky, & Slocum, 1996).

Ryan et al. (1999) find that cultures high in power distance use more hierarchical selection in decision making and are less likely to use peers as interviewers than in organizations low in power distance. But contrary to expectations, they find that in high power distance cultures peers are more likely to participate in the final hiring decisions than in low power distance cultures. They speculate that strong labor unions emerge in countries high in power distance (e.g., Mexico) to represent workers. The greater involvement of employees in hiring reflects the influence of these unions. Ryan et al. (1999) also find that employers in Hong Kong, Malaysia, and Singapore, all high power distance countries, rely more on educational qualifications in hiring possibly because of the emphasis those countries place on status.

Uncertainty avoidance.

Persons in cultures higher in uncertainty avoidance are threatened by the unknown and are more likely to shun ambiguity and risk. As a consequence, individuals in these cultures want clear instructions and the guidance that comes from knowing what others will do. Countries high in uncertainty avoidance include Mexico, Japan, Taiwan, Greece, Portugal, and Belgium, and those low in uncertainty avoidance include the United Kingdom, India, Philippines, and the United States (Hofstede, 2001).

In high-uncertainty avoidance cultures, we find that organizations use more structured selection practices; in low-uncertainty avoidance cultures, organizations are more tolerant of spontaneity in selection (Stohl, 1993). It logically follows that organizations in high-uncertainty avoidance cultures use more thorough selection procedures to avoid risk. Ryan et al. (1999) find support for this hypothesis insofar as respondents in high-uncertainty avoidance cultures report more contact in interviews with candidates, greater use of fixed sets of interview questions, and greater use of audits. Contrary to the hypotheses, however, they find less extensive selection processes and less use of procedures to verify applicant backgrounds. A possible explanation for the inconsistent results is that high-uncertainty avoidance cultures trust the use of social connections and relationships in assessing applicants more than scientifically validated and impersonal selection procedures.

Masculinity–femininity.

Countries high in masculinity have strong gender stereotypes for men and women and value material success, assertiveness, heroism, and strength. Feminine cultures have more overlap in the social roles of men and women and value to a greater extent quality of life, relationships, caring for the weak, and modesty. In the high-masculinity (low femininity) cultures men are more likely to describe themselves as competitive, and women are more likely to describe themselves as gentle and feminine. Hofstede (1980) reports the highest levels of masculinity in Japan (ranked 1). The United States is also high in masculinity (rank of 15), as are Austria, Venezuela, Italy, and Mexico. Netherlands, Sweden, Norway, Denmark, Portugal, and Thailand rank low on masculinity.

The goal of selection procedures in feminine cultures is to hire individuals who have positive relationships with others (Nagore, as cited in Tixier, 1996). This partially explains why employers in Spain, a feminine country, use personality tests more frequently in selection than cognitive ability tests, whereas in the United States, a masculine culture, the reverse is true (Ryan et al., 1999). Spence and Petrick (2000) find greater use in masculine countries of highly structured interviews with uniform guidelines, little personal interaction, and the same questions asked of each candidate.

Universalism–particularism.

This dimension concerns the extent to which individuals follow standardized rules across situations, or prefer a flexible approach to dealing with situations. In universalistic cultures, individual beliefs about what is right and wrong are stable across situations, and individuals are expected to conform to these principles. If stealing is perceived as immoral, it is perceived as immoral regardless of the situation. In a particularistic culture, individuals' perceptions about right and wrong are contingent on the situation. Australia, Portugal, Switzerland, Canada, and the United States are universalistic countries, whereas Russia, Greece, Italy, China, and India are particularistic countries.

In a universalistic culture such as the United States, the primary goal of selection is to pick the best person for the job. Consequently, employers in these cultures are more likely to use a systematic approach with objective methods and more likely to check on the accuracy of information provided by the applicant. Applicants who fit the position are preferred regardless of personal relationships, likability, status, kinship, gender, or ethnicity. These factors are given more weight than objective qualifications in particularistic countries. In a particularistic culture, employers want to know the applicant as an individual, and this leads to a preference for more flexible and less standardized selection procedures. Indeed, the selection process is more likely framed in a particularistic culture as a conversation between two individuals, and attempts to impose structure are seen as inappropriate. Nyfield and Baron (2000) find that only 20% of the particularistic countries in their sample use structured interviews, whereas in more universalistic countries, such as Australia and Canada, 50% of respondents claim to use structured interviews. Respondents from universalistic countries are more likely to use panel interviews and objective evidence such as education qualifications. They are also more likely to rank order candidates and conduct formal audits of the selection process. The desire to know the applicant as an individual perhaps explains why in China, a very particularistic culture, employers rely on applicants' personal background more than on their job skills in their selection procedures decisions (Wang, 1997).

Neutral–affective.

Neutral–affective is the difference between cultures where emotions are controlled versus cultures where emotions are displayed openly. Neutral cultures, such as China, Japan, United States, and Canada, emphasize the rational side of business and value reserved and restrained behavior in business transactions. In an attempt to remain cool, calm, and collected at all times in their interactions, persons in neutral countries are less likely than those in affective countries to reveal what they are thinking and feeling. Persons in affective cultures, such as Mexico, Spain, the Philippines, and Venezuela, are more likely to use expressive and animated verbal and nonverbal behavior to reveal their thoughts and feelings. In support of this cultural difference, Soto, Levenson, and Ebling (2005) find that Chinese Americans report experiencing significantly less emotion than Mexican Americans in response to startle conditions in a laboratory experiment. Nyfield and Baron (2000) suggest that affective cultures are less likely to use paper-and-pencil testing but more likely to use interpersonal procedures that allow for more emotional expression, such as the unstructured interviews.

Specific–diffuse.

Persons in specific cultures are more concerned with efficiency and structure when doing business than those in diffuse cultures. Specific cultures, such as the United States, are concerned with efficiency and structure and, as a consequence, are more likely to use impersonal selection procedures. Interactions in these cultures are generally blunt and to the point and unconcerned with creating relationships. Diffuse cultures place strong emphasis on personal relationships. The United States, Sweden, Denmark, and the United Kingdom are specific, compared to diffuse countries such as Mexico, China, and Indonesia.

    The goal of selection procedures in diffuse cultures is to find individuals who have interpersonal skills. For example, in Arab/Islamic countries such as Egypt, there is a heavy emphasis on agreeableness, interpersonal relations, and trustworthiness (Ali, 1989). In Korea, also a diffuse country, individuals are often selected based on personal connections (Von Glinow & Chung, 1989). Diffuse countries should also use more interpersonal selection procedures, such as interviews, than impersonal selection procedures such as testing (Ryan et al., 1999).

    At the same time, because they blur the line between work and nonwork, employers and employees in diffuse cultures are more open to invasive selection procedures. For example, Ryan et al. (1999) find that organizations in Greece, a diffuse culture, report greater use of biodata than in the Netherlands and Sweden, both specific cultures where this procedure is probably seen as more invasive.

Achievement–ascription.

Achievement–ascription refers to whether status in a given culture is earned through achievements or attributed to people as a consequence of their background, personal characteristics, or birth. Ascriptive societies, such as Mexico, China, Cuba, Austria, and South Korea, judge individuals on the basis of their families, their belongings, and their backgrounds, and it is uncommon to question the qualifications of someone of higher status. Achievement-oriented societies, such as the United States, United Kingdom, Norway, and Canada, judge individuals on their merits and their actions.

Consistent with the achievement orientation of the United States, the preferred approach to selection is one that allows and requires applicants to demonstrate their individual accomplishments. In ascriptive cultures, such as Mexico and China, employers are more likely to choose applicants based on their family background and whether they are in the employer's in-group. In such cultures, word of mouth recruitment is favored over impersonal advertising (Aycan, 2000). Employers from ascriptive cultures also care more about the prestige of the universities that applicants attend than their academic performance (Nyfield & Baron, 2000). Selection procedures that require applicants to demonstrate their achievements are less accepted in ascriptive cultures. Similar to employers in countries that are high in Hofstede's power-distance dimension, employers from ascriptive countries prefer to hire persons of status who belong to their in-group (Sinha, 1997).

Sequential–synchronic.

The sequential–synchronic dimension refers to individuals' attitudes about time. In sequential cultures, people complete tasks one at a time, focus on the present, see time as linear, and follow schedules. Sequential countries include the United States, Philippines, Ireland, and India. In synchronic cultures, individuals are more likely to take on multiple tasks at once, focus more on the past than the present, and perceive the past, present, and future as overlapping. Synchronic counties include Hong Kong, Portugal, and South Korea.

In sequential countries, such as the United States, time is seen as linear, and as a consequence, there is more concern with applicants' performance in recent jobs. Ryan et al. (1999) find that employers in Sweden, a synchronic culture, are less likely to contact an applicant's previous employer than in Ireland, a sequential culture. In synchronic cultures, organizations are more concerned about applicants' overall past performances, whereas in sequential cultures they are more likely to evaluate applicants on the basis of their most recent performances.

Internal–external.

Internal–external refers to whether individuals feel that they have control over their situation (internal locus) or instead focus on the external environment and feel that their situation is beyond their control (external locus). The United States, Canada, Norway, and New Zealand are among the countries with a higher internal locus of control. Individuals in these countries have more dominating and aggressive attitudes toward winning and are comfortable with conflict. Individuals in countries with a higher external locus of control, such as Egypt, Oman, and Kuwait, are more concerned with harmony and maintaining relationships than they are with winning. Aycan, Kanungo, Mendonca, Yu, Deller, Stahl, and Kurshid (2000) find that managers from India, Pakistan, China, Turkey, Russia, and Romania score highest on fatalism (a cultural dimension similar to external control); managers from Israel and Germany score in the middle; managers from Canada and the United States score the lowest on fatalism. Countries with a high internal locus of control are more likely to prefer applicants who are aggressive and competitive, whereas cultures higher in external locus of control, such as Japan, prefer applicants who have moderate views and harmonious personalities (Hatvany & Pucik, 1981).

The Influence of Culture on Reactions to Selection Procedures

Whether applicants and employers accept or reject a selection process reflects to some extent the degree to which the selection fits the cultural dimensions that Hofstede and others identify. There is some evidence that individuals in collectivist and high power distance societies are not as sensitive to inequities as those in individualistic and low power distance societies (Nie, Hopkins, & Hopkins, 2002; Phillips & Gully, 2002; Wheeler, 2002). Perhaps indicative of the greater power distance in Eastern cultures, Phillips and Gully (2002) find that Singaporeans, relative to respondents from the United States, are more accepting of all selection methods and less likely to reject even the least liked procedures.

Employers in universalistic, specific, individualistic, internal control, and low power distance cultures emphasize merit. Selection procedures are used that provide applicants with the opportunity to demonstrate their individual competencies and that identify the most qualified applicants (McFarlin & Sweeney, 2001; Steiner & Gilliland, 2001). On the other hand, employers from collectivistic, high power distance, and external control cultures emphasize equality or need in deciding among applicants. McFarlin and Sweeney (2001) suggest that individuals in masculine and achievement-oriented countries prefer clear, job-related job performance standards, and the consistent application of these standards, more than do people in feminine countries (e.g., Arabic countries). In particularistic, feminine cultures, the structural aspects of the selection procedures are not as important as the interpersonal aspects of the selection procedure, and as a consequence, a face-to-face interview is preferred over written tests (Steiner & Gilliland, 2001). Persons in particularistic, collectivist cultures expect employers to explain selection procedures and to treat all applicants with the same respect (McFarlin & Sweeney, 2001; Steiner & Gilliland, 2001). In contrast to low-uncertainty avoidance cultures, applicants in high-uncertainty avoidance cultures want to know what and why for every aspect of the selection process and desire to know how well they perform in this process. Applicants in diffuse cultures are more concerned with interpersonal and informational justice than job relatedness or the opportunity to perform. Individuals in diffuse cultures see criticism as less appropriate and are less likely than those from specific cultures to respond favorably to feedback on their performance in the selection process.

Caveat: Culture Is Not the Only Determinant of Selection

A variety of forces are at work, in addition to culture, in determining the extent to which selection practices in a country conform more to a rational/analytic or the social/intuitive approach. Several theorists propose multilevel models in attempting to explain variations across cultures in HRM. The most distal of the causal influences are the national culture (the focus of this chapter), the business environment, other institutions, and the political and legal climate. Rousseau and Tinsley (1997) suggest that the three primary local factors shaping recruitment and selection practices are constraints on the relevant labor pool, legal requirements, and broader institutional forces such as educational practices and local culture. These local factors may overwhelm any influence of the national culture.

Occurring at a more proximal level are the culture and subcultures of the organization; the job and associated technologies, size, ownership, structure; and HRM strategies. We would add to these layers the most proximal influence, the personal orientations of the individual decision makers who are involved in implementing the selection process. The approach to selection is likely to vary as a function of all these factors. So far, most of the research focuses on the influence of job characteristics (Colarelli, 1996; Wilk & Cappelli, 2003) and organizational characteristics such as size (Colarelli, 1996; Lockyer & Scholarios, 2004; Lockyer & Scholarios, 1999; Shackleton & Newell, 1991; Wilk & Cappelli, 2003). A common finding is that larger firms use a more systematic approach to selection and rely more on standardized, validated procedures (Colarelli, 1996; Shackleton & Newell, 1991).

Despite the reality of multiple influences, there is some evidence that culture influences HRM practices even after taking into account these other factors. For instance, Huo and Von Glinow (1995) compared samples from the United States, Taiwan, and the People's Republic of China, and concluded that there were differences in HRM practices that reflect differences in culture independent of political or economic systems. This type of study is rare, however, and the best we can conclude at this time is that all of these forces are intertwined in their influence on whether an organization adopts a rational/analytic approach to selection or a more social/intuitive approach.

MEXICO, CHINA, AND THE UNITED STATES AS EXAMPLES

As an illustration of international variations in selection practices, we compare three countries that appear representative of major segments of the world economy: Mexico, the United States, and China (including the People's Republic of China, Taiwan, Hong Kong, and Chinese nationals in Singapore). We propose that the rational/analytic approach is perceived as the ideal approach to selection in the United States, but that the social/intuitive approach is perceived as the ideal in China and in Mexico. In turn, the differences in selection practices among these three nations appear consistent with the emphasis on the rational/analytic in United States and the emphasis on the social/intuitive in China and Mexico.

These differences reflect the national culture of these three countries. Using a scale anchored by 0 (low) and 100 (high), the United States is, in terms of Hofstede's dimensions, very high on individualism (91), low on power distance (40) and uncertainty avoidance (46), and high on masculinity (62). China is low on individualism (20), high on power distance (80), moderate on masculinity (50), and high on uncertainty avoidance (60). Mexico is low on individualism (30), high on power distance (81), high on masculinity (69), and very high on uncertainty avoidance (82). In terms of Trompenaars' dimensions, the United States is internal, universalistic, neutral, achievement oriented, sequential, and specific. China is external, particularistic, neutral, ascriptive, diffuse, and synchronic, and Mexico is external, particularistic, affective, ascriptive, and synchronic. Consistent with these cultural differences, the rational/analytic approach is more common in the United States, whereas the social/intuitive approach is more common in China and Mexico.

The Social, Economic, and Political Contexts

The cultural influences in these three countries are intertwined with social, political, and economic forces that also shape selection practices. Although the People's Republic of China (PRC) is one of the few remaining communist countries, there are dramatic reformations underway that are moving it closer to a more competitive market system. Even with these reforms, employer and employee alike are still highly controlled by central government. There is little employment-at-will, and layoffs and firings are rare (Von Glinow & Teagarden, 1988). In comparison to both the United States and Mexico, China has a much stronger social welfare system, and the government oversees virtually every aspect of workers' lives. Confucian principles permeate the way all aspects of business are approached in China, including employee selection. Confucianism stresses respect for work, discipline, thrift, protecting face (i.e. avoidance of conflict and maintenance of harmony), ordering relationships by status (and respecting the order of that status), duty to family, and economic egalitarianism (Bond & Kwang-Kuo, 1986; Hofstede & Bond, 1988; Von Glinow & Teagarden, 1993). China lacks the rational-legal tradition of the United States. Traditionally, civil and criminal law are not emphasized in maintaining order, but rather, there is a reliance on "rule by man" in which "officials assumed to be of good character judge each case on its special merits" (Jacobs, Guopei, & Herbig, 1995, p. 30). The morality of actions is judged less on the rights of the individual than on the needs and interests of the family and clan. Another crucial component of Confucian thought is *guanxi*, or the use of informal relationships to achieve personal objectives (Jacobs, Guopei, & Herbig, 1995, p. 33).

Mexico is closer to the United States than to China in its political-economic system but resembles China in several other respects. Employers in the United States enjoy employment-at-will, but there is far less employment-at-will in Mexico and China. In China, where enterprises are typically assigned workers by the central government, layoffs and firings are rare (Von Glinow & Teagarden, 1988). The Mexican Federal Labor Law governs all employment matters with state labor boards made up of government, union, and management representatives. According to this law, an employer has 28 days after hiring to evaluate the employee's work ethics, after which, dismissal becomes very difficult. A recent World Bank report ranked Mexico 125th out of the 155 countries on difficulty of doing business in the category of hiring and firing (O'Grady, 2005). For instance, it costs a firm in Mexico almost 75 weeks of wages to fire a worker.

An important aspect of Mexico is the emphasis on family (Fadil, Seg-rest-Purkiss, Hurley-Hanson, Knudstrup, & Stepina, 2004). The devotion to family contributes to nepotism in hiring as well as absenteeism and turnover. Similar to China, persons in Mexico value face, respect for status differences, duty to family, and relationships (de Forest, 1994). According to some observers, workers in Mexico do not consider their work as central to their life but are hard working out of loyalty to their employers (Kras, 1995; Paik & Teagarden, 1995). Rivera, Anderson, and Middleton (1999) describe Mexicans as "(a) living in harmony, (b) as emphasizing the present, (c) 'being' rather than 'doing' and (d) identifying individual goals as subordinate to group goals" (pp. 95–96). In contrast to the United States, employees in Mexico are more casual in their attention to rules and regulations and more likely to obey their boss than obey a rule. Pelled and Xin (1997) hypothesize that employees in the United States, compared to employees in China and Mexico, value to a greater extent hard work, job earnings, promotion, and vertical job involvement.

Differences Among Mexico, United States, and China in Employee Selection

We have already stated that a rational/analytic model of HRM strongly influences selection practices in the United States. By comparison, the selection practices in China and in Mexico appear to conform to a greater extent to the social/intuitive model.

Yan (2003) compared Anglo-Saxon cultures, Continental Europe, Japan, and China's selection procedures and found that Anglo-Saxon cultures had more formal recruitment processes than those found in China. Several other surveys show that Chinese employers in the PRC and Hong Kong use informal and nonsystematic selection procedures and make little use of testing (Björkman & Lu, 1999; Latham & Napier, 1989; Ryan et al., 1999; Shen & Edwards, 2004; Von Glinow & Chung, 1989). Even the interview, a crucial step in recruiting personnel in the United States, is often omitted in the PRC and Taiwan (Huo & Von Glinow, 1995). Instead of formal selection procedures, there is a heavy reliance in these countries on *guanxi* or the use of informal relationships and contacts. Connections certainly influence hiring in the United States as well, but hiring because of the people the applicant knows rather than personal attributes is usually seen as inappropriate. By contrast, hiring on the basis of contacts or *guanxi* is an explicit factor for consideration in China. Chinese employers frequently hire for the relationships that applicants bring to the organization (Huo & Von Glinow, 1995; Shen & Edwards, 2004). *Guanxi* often begins with a letter of introduction in which a respected authority supports the character and reliability of the person being introduced. Hiring itself is part of the process in which employers form relationships with others. An example is provided by Ahlstrom, Foley, Young, and Chan (2005), who found that hiring more employees than needed is a tactic that employers use to maintain good relations with the local government. Law, Wong, and Leong (2001) provide evidence that some tests used in the United States may need to be modified to take into account *guanxi*. In a test of Holland's hexagonal structure on vocational interests, they find a stronger social-enterprising link in a sample of Hong Kong respondents than is typically found in the United States; they attribute this difference to the influence of *guanxi*.

There are also differences between decision makers in China and the United States in their gathering of information about applicants and their hiring decisions. Peppas et al. (1999) compare samples from the United States and China on the extent to which different applicant attributes are perceived as important to selection. In the Chinese sample, respondents perceive most of the factors as more important in selecting among applicants than do participants in the United States sample (age, company knowledge, community involvement, grades in school, hobbies, leadership, marital status, school-age children, school reputation, sex, willingness to relocate, and work experience). Indeed, assertiveness is the only attribute in this study that is more important in the United States sample than the Chinese sample. The authors suggest that in the United States, individuals prefer to shorten a variable list by eliminating what they feel is least important and focusing on a subset, one variable at a time. In contrast, decision makers in Eastern cultures prefer to consider many variables all at the same time. The Eastern approach seems confusing to Westerners, and the Western approach seems overly simplistic to Asians, but neither is necessarily the correct approach.

Similar to China, selection and other HRM procedures in Mexico are marked by informality (Greer & Stephens, 1996). Also similar to China is the emphasis in Mexico on personal contacts and relationships. Recruitment in Mexico is often done primarily by approaching people and asking them to apply (Teagarden, Butler, & Von Ginlow, 1992; Schuler et al., 1996). Rothstein (2004) describes how managers from plants "drove around the small villages (or *ranchos*) dotting the countryside, in a cab with a megaphone on the roof advertising to young women the availability of jobs paying twice the minimum wage" (p. 217). Mexican employers tend to hire and recruit people they know and can trust, but are not as comfortable as employers in the United States in hiring those they do not know (Geringer & Frayne, 1990; Teagarden et al., 1992). As a consequence, nepotism is common, and many family members often work in the same plant (Schuler et al., 1996).

A Warning: Avoid Overgeneralization

Any attempt to understand selection in terms of national differences in culture runs the risk of oversimplification and even stereotyping. Although this chapter focuses on the potential clashes between the rational/analytic model of selection and national cultures other than the United States, this does not mean that the rational/analytic model is wholeheartedly accepted in the United States. To the contrary, the typical selection procedure in the United States often strays far from the rational/analytic ideal. Nevertheless, one can still argue that the rational/analytic approach is more compatible with the national culture of the United States than with the cultures of China and Mexico. Also, one could argue that despite the deviations from the ideal, there is a consensus in the United States that the rational/analytic model "should" be the approach to selection.

IMPLICATIONS FOR THE FUTURE
OF EMPLOYEE SELECTION

Research in HRM conducted in the United States and Western Europe promotes the superiority of a rational/analytic model over social/

intuitive approaches to selection. With the globalization of commerce, the spread of multinational corporations, and the increased education of non-Western managers in the rational-analytic model, we can expect increased efforts to implement the findings of this research in non-Western countries. What will happen as this model clashes with the social/intuitive approaches more prevalent in other cultures?

One possibility is that selection practices around the world will converge around a rational/analytic model (Farley, Hoenig, & Yang, 2004; Fisher & Härtel, 2004; Peng & Luo, 2000; Robertson & Makin, 1986; Ryan et al., 1999; Schlevogt, 2000; Shackleton & Newell, 1991; Smith & Abrahamsen, 1992; Tixier, 1996). One might predict from this perspective that an increasing number of firms around the world will derive job qualifications based on rigorous job analyses, gather information on these qualifications from applicants using structured and validated selection procedures, and reach judgments and decisions based on a careful mapping of measured applicant qualifications to job requirements. Moreover, we would expect firms to continue these selection practices or modify them based on a scientific evaluation of the extent to which they accomplish the economic objectives of the firm. If a convergence hypothesis is correct, then the main issue is one of implementation, that is, the rational/analytic approach will work; it's just a matter of convincing those who must implement the procedures that they can work and then fully implementing the procedure as it should be implemented.

Although there is evidence of some convergence, the prevailing conclusion is that nations around the world continue to show remarkable diversity in their selection practices. This leads us to the divergence hypothesis, which states that the cultural forces at work in various countries remain strong and clash with attempts to impose a common, rational/analytic model of selection. Huo, Huang, and Napier (2002) examine the hiring practices in 10 different countries and find that, despite some convergence in recruitment, selection criteria are driven by each country's prevalent cultural values. Even though the authors find some inching toward global convergence on what "is" used, there are large differences in respondents' descriptions of what "should be" used. Others have warned that attempts to transport Western practices to other nations where the culture is incompatible with the practices are likely to fail (Gomez-Mejia & Palich, 1997). The suggestion is that only those selection practices that fit the culture of the host country prove effective.

A third possible scenario is hybridization in which there is a blending of cultures (Fisher & Härtel, 2004). According to this view, Western management methods are neither rejected nor wholeheartedly accepted but are, instead, adapted to fit with the culture and local conditions of the host country (Ahlstrom, Bruton, & Chan, 2001; Björkman & Lu, 1999; Huo, Huang, & Napier, 2002; Lockett, 1988; Wong & Law, 1999). Likewise, Western selection practices may benefit from the adoption of practices in other cultures. Evidence of this benefit is the increased attention being given in the United States to hiring for fit of the person to the organization's values, an approach that seems more in tune with a social/intuitive approach and Eastern thinking (Von Glinow, Drost, & Teagarden, 2002). A rational/analytical approach to selection has something to learn from a social/intuitive approach to selection (Horwitz, Kamoche, & Chew, 2002; Maruyama, 1984). Von Glinow et al. (2002) go so far as to argue that what constitutes good scientific research needs to change: "The rigorous execution of a research design and instrument that masks the derived etic in favor of the imposed etic is simply error of the third kind or, solving the wrong problem well!" (p. 127).

We agree with this statement to the extent that most of the phases of selection are culturally bound. One cannot assume the universal effectiveness of a structured, systematic approach to determining requirements of a position, gathering information on these requirements, judging applicants against these requirements, and choosing from among applicants. Moreover, it is fundamentally flawed to propose a set of best practices, such as cognitive ability testing, structured interviews, and biodata, based on research in North America and Western Europe. We would claim universality, however, for the final phase of the rational/analytic model, where the effectiveness of the selection process is evaluated using scientifically rigorous methods. The scientific model *is* the one best approach to evaluating the effectiveness of selection procedures. But contrary to the rational/analytic model, we argue that scientific evaluation will show that practices normally thought of as violations of a rational/analytic model and "irrational" are, in fact, superior in some cultural contexts to "rational" selection practices.

The basic suggestion here is that selection practices must be evaluated scientifically against the criteria of effectiveness that make the most sense in the culture in which they are embedded. In the United States and Western Europe, the criterion is most often how well the employee performs on the core tasks of the job. When evaluated on the basis of this criterion, the rational/analytic model does quite well. However, selection practices serve other functions in addition to providing the best fit to the job. When we consider these various functions and the wide range of criteria associated with them, a synthesis of the rational/analytic and the social/intuitive makes more sense. Along these lines, Colarelli (1996) concluded that hiring practices that violate best practices are warranted and even preferred if one distinguishes between the manifest functions of a selection practice as opposed to the latent functions. The manifest functions are those that are the intended and generally accepted reasons for the practice (e.g., use tests to select the person with the best skills and abilities), whereas the latent functions are usually less visible but very important (e.g., use an unstructured interview to convey the values of the organization and socialize the applicant into the organization). Colarelli (1996) argues that "establishments may retain practices that do not have scientific support because they serve important functions *other than* their intended functions" and that "there may be good, functional reasons why establishments do not use a scientifically valid technology" (p. 174). Similarly, Huo and Von Glinow (2005) argue that rather than being "shocked by the 'irrational' way of doing things in Asian nations . . . the word 'rationality' ought to be interpreted in a specific cultural context, for culture influences how people define a problem, how they go about trying to solve the problem and how the actual solution is reached" (p. 13).

Rather than advocating one model over the other, sufficient flexibility is needed to allow a blending of approaches. We are convinced that the rational/analytical approach is needed to actually evaluate the effectiveness of the selection process. We also believe that these scientific evaluations will demonstrate that what is effective varies with the criterion and the culture. A highly quantitative and structured approach, such as suggested by a rational/analytic approach, is probably superior in most cases if the objective is an accurate assessment of the applicant's fit to the core tasks of the job. But if we evaluate a selection system against other criteria, such as the impact on recruiting applicants, building commitment, and conveying the values of the organization to the outside world, we may well find that the "best practices" are informal procedures, such as those suggested by a social/intuitive approach. In a global economy in which organizations must deal with diversity, the challenge is finding the combinations of the two approaches that allow us to achieve both sets of objectives.

REFERENCES

Ahlstrom, D., Bruton, G. D., & Chan, E. S. (2001). HRM of foreign firms in China: The challenge of managing host country personnel. *Business Horizons, 44*, 59–68.

Ahlstrom, D., Foley, S., Young, M. N., & Chan, E. S. (2005). Human resource strategies in post-WTO China. *Thunderbird International Business Review, 47*, 263–285.

Albright, L., Malloy, T. E., Dong, Q., Kenny, D. A., Fang, X., Winquist, L., et al. (1997). Cross-cultural consensus in personality judgments. *Journal of Personality and Social Psychology, 72*, 558–569.

Ali, A. J. (1989). A comparative study of managerial beliefs about work in the Arab states. In B. Prasad (Ed.), *Advances in International Comparative Management.* (Vol. 4, pp. 95–112). Greenwich, CT: JAI Press.

Aluja, A., Rossier, J., Garcia, L. F., & Verardi, S. (2005). The 16PF5 and the NEO-PI-R in Spanish and Swiss Samples: A cross-cultural comparison. *Journal of Individual Differences, 26*, 53–62.

Arminas, D. (1998, July 16). Staffing problems tax Russian minds. *Personnel Today*, 11–12.

Aycan, Z. (2000). Cross-cultural industrial and organizational psychology: Contributions, past developments, and future directions. *Journal of Cross-Cultural Psychology, 31*, 110–128.

Aycan, Z., Kanungo, R. N., Mendonca, M., Yu, K., Deller, J., Stahl, G., & Kurshid, A. (2000). Impact of culture on human resource management practices; A 10-country comparison. *Applied Psychology: An International Review, 49*, 192–221.

Barrett, G. V., & Bass, B. M. (1976). Cross-cultural issues in industrial and organizational psychology. In M. D. Dunnette (Ed.), *Handbook of industrial and organizational psychology* (pp. 1639–1686). Chicago: Rand McNally.

Björkman, I., & Lu, Y. (1999). The management of human resources in Chinese-Western joint ventures. *Journal of World Business, 34*, 306–324.

Bond, M. H., & Kwang-Kuo, H. (1986). The social psychology of Chinese people. In M. H. Bond (Ed.), *The psychology of the Chinese people* (pp. 213–266). New York: Oxford University Press.

Bowen, D. E., Galang, C., & Pillai, R. (2002). The role of human resource management: An exploratory study of cross-country variance. *Human Resource Management, 41*, 103–122.

Chao, G. T., & Nguyen, H.-H. D. (2005). International employment discrimination: A review of legal issues, human impacts, and organizational implications. In R. L. Dipboye & A. Colella (Eds.), *Discrimination at work: The psychological and organizational bases* (pp. 379–409). Mahwah, NJ: Erlbaum.

Chen, M. (1995). *Asian management systems.* London: Routledge.

Choi, I., Dalal, R., Kim-Prieto, C., & Park, H. (2003). Culture and judgment of causal relevance. *Journal of Personality and Social Psychology, 84*, 46–59.

Clark, T. (1993). Selection methods used by executive search consultancies in four European countries: A survey and critique. *International Journal of Selection and Assessment, 1*, 41–49.

Colarelli, S. M. (1996). Establishment and job context influences on the use of hiring practices. *Applied Psychology: An International Review, 45*, 153–176.

de Forest, M. E. (1994). Thinking of a plant in Mexico? *Academy of Management Executive, 8*, 33–40.

Dipboye, R. L., (1994). Structured and unstructured interviews: Beyond the job-fit model. In G. R. Ferris (Ed.), *Research in personnel and human resources management* (Vol. 12, pp. 79–124). Greenwich, CT: JAI Press.

Eleftheriou, A., & Robertson, I. (1999). A survey of management selection practices in Greece. *International Journal of Selection and Assessment, 7*, 203–208.

Epstein, S., Pacini, R., Denes-Raj, V., & Heier, H. (1996). Individual differences in intuitive-experiential and analytical-rational thinking styles. *Journal of Personality and Social Psychology, 71*, 390–405.

Evans, J. S. B. T., & Curtis-Holmes, J. (2005). Rapid responding increases belief bias: Evidence for dual-process theory of reasoning. *Thinking and Reasoning, 11*, 382–389.

Fadil, P., Segrest-Purkiss, S. L., Hurley-Hanson, A. E., Knudstrup, M., & Stepina, L. (2004). Distributive justice in northern Mexico and the US: A cross-cultural comparison. *Cross Cultural Management, 11*, 3–24.

Farley, J. U., Hoenig, S., & Yang, J. Z. (2004). Key factors influencing HRM practices of overseas subsidiaries in China's transition economy. *International Journal of Human Resource Management, 15*, 688–704.

Ferner, A., & Quintanilla, J. (1998). Multinationals, national business systems and HRM: The enduring influence of national identity or a process of "Anglo-Saxonization." *International Journal of Human Resource Management, 9*, 710–731.

Fisher, G. B., & Härtel, C. E. J. (2004). Evidence of crossvergence in the perception of task and contextual performance: A study of Western expatriates working in Thailand. *Cross-Cultural Management: An International Journal, 11,* 3–15.

Fiske, S., Neuberg, S., Beattie, A. E., & Milberg, S. J. (1987). Category-based and attribute-based reactions to others: Some informational conditions of stereotyping and individuating processes. *Journal of Experimental Social Psychology, 23,* 399–427.

Fong, C. P. S., & Wyer, R. S. (2003). Cultural, social, and emotional determinants of decisions under uncertainty. *Organizational Behavior and Human Decision Processes, 90,* 304–322.

Fortmann, K., Leslie, C., & Cunningham, M. (2002). Cross-cultural comparisons of the Reid Integrity scale in Latin America and South Africa. *International Journal of Selection and Assessment, 10,* 98–108.

Geringer, J. M., & Frayne, C. A. (1990). Human resource management and international joint venture control: A parent company perspective. *Management International Review, 30,* 103–120.

Geringer, J. M., Frayne, C. A., & Milliman, J. F. (2002). In search of "best practices" in international human resource management: research design and methodology. *Human Resource Management, 41,* 5–30.

Gomez-Mejia, L. R., & Palich, L. E. (1997). Cultural diversity and the performance of multinational firms. *Journal of International Business Studies, 27,* 309–335.

Greer, C., & Stephens, G. (1996). Employee relations issues in U.S. companies in Mexico. *California Management Review, 38,* 121–137.

Grimm, S. D., & Church, A. T. (1999). A cross-cultural study of response biases in personality measures. *Journal of Research in Personality, 33,* 415–441.

Hammond, K. (1996). *Human judgment and social policy.* New York: Oxford Press.

Hatvany, N., & Pucik, V. (1981). Japanese management: Practices and productivity. *Organizational Dynamics, 10,* 5–21.

Herriot, P., & Anderson, N. (1997). Selecting for change: How will personnel and selection psychology survive? In N. Anderson & P. Herriot (Eds.), *International handbook of selection and assessment* (pp. 1–38). Chichester, UK: John Wiley.

Hofstede, G. (1980). Motivation, leadership, and organization: Do American theories apply abroad? *Organizational Dynamics, 9,* 42–63.

Hofstede, G. (1991). *Cultures and organizations: Software of the mind.* London: McGraw-Hill.

Hofstede, G. (2001). *Culture's consequences: Comparing values, behaviors, institutions, and organizations across nations* (2nd ed.). London: Sage.

Hofstede, G., & Bond, M. H. (1988). The Confucius connection: From cultural roots to economic growth. *Organizational Dynamics, 16,* 4–21.

Horwitz, Fr. M., Kamoche, K., & Chew, I. (2002). Looking east: Diffusing high performance work practices in the southern Afro-Asian context. *International Journal of Human Resource Management, 13,* 1019–1041.

Huo, Y. P., Huang, H. J., & Napier, N. K. (2002). Divergence or convergence: A cross national comparison of personnel selection practices. *Human Resource Management, 41,* 31–44.

Huo, Y. P., & Von Glinow, M. A. (1995). On transplanting human resource practices to China: A culture-driven approach. *International Journal of Manpower, 16,* 3–16.

Jacobs, L., Guopei, G., & Herbig, P. (1995). Confucian roots in China: A force for today's business. *Management Decision, 33,* 29–35.

Kamoche, K. (1993). Toward a model of HRM in Africa. *Research in Personnel and Human Resources Management, 3,* 259–278.

Kras, E. S. (1995). *Management in two cultures: Bridging the gap between US and Mexican managers.* Yarmouth, ME: Intercultural Press.

Kurman, J., & Sriram, N. (1997). Self-enhancement, generality of self-evaluation, and affectivity in Israel and Singapore. *Journal of Cross-Cultural Psychology, 28,* 421–441.

Latham, G. A., & Napier, N. K. (1989). Chinese human resource management practices in Hong Kong and Singapore: An exploratory study. *Research in Personnel and Human Resource Management, 1,* 173–199.

Law, K. S., Mobley, W. H., & Wong, C. (2002). Impression management and faking in biodata scores among Chinese job-seekers. *Asia Pacific Journal of Management, 19,* 541–546.

Law, K. S., Wong, C.-S., & Leong, F. (2001). The cultural validity of Holland's model and its implications for human resource management: The case of Hong Kong. *International Journal of Human Resource Management, 12,* 484–496.

Lévy-Leboyer, C. (1994). Selection and assessment in Europe. In H. C. Triandis, M. D. Dunnette, & L. M. Hough (Eds.), *Handbook of industrial and organizational psychology* (2nd ed., Vol. 4, pp. 173–190). Palo Alto, CA: Consulting Psychologists Press.

Lockett, M. (1988). Culture and the problems of Chinese management. *Organization Studies, 9,* 475–496.

Lockyer, C. & Scholarios, D. (2004). Selecting hotel staff: Why best practice does not always work. *International Journal of Contemporary Hospitality Management, 16,* 125–135.

Love, K. G., Bishop, R. C., Heinisch, D. A., & Montei, M. S. (1994). Selection across two cultures: Adapting the selection of American assemblers to meet Japanese job performance demands. *Personnel Psychology, 47,* 837–846.

Marchington, M., & Grugulis, I. (2000). Best practice human resource management: Perfect opportunity or dangerous illusion? *International Journal of Human Resource Management, 11,* 1104–1124.

Marcus, B. (2003). Attitudes towards personnel selection: A partial replication and extension in German sample. *Applied Psychology: An International Review, 52,* 515–532.

Markus, H. R., & Kitayama, S. (1991). Culture and the self: Implications for cognitive, emotion, and motivation. *Psychological Review, 98,* 224–253.

Maruyama, M. (1984). Alternative concepts of management: Insights from Asia and Africa. *Asia Pacific Journal of Management, 1,* 100–111.

Masuda, T., & Nisbett, R. E. (2001). Attending holistically versus analytically: Comparing the context sensitivity of Japanese and Americans. *Journal of Personality and Social Psychology, 81,* 922–934.

McCrae, R. R., & Costa, P. T., Jr. (1997). Personality trait structure as a human universal. *American Psychologist, 52,* 509–516.

McCulloch, S. (1993). Recent trends in international assessment. *International Journal of Selection and Assessment, 1,* 59–61.

McFarlin, D. B., & Sweeney, P. D. (2001). Cross-cultural applications of organizational justice. In R. Cropanzano, (Ed.), *Justice in the workplace* (Vol. 2, pp. 67–95). Mahwah, NJ: Erlbaum.

Middleton, K. L., & Jones, J. L. (2000). Socially desirable response sets: The impact of country and culture. *Psychology and Marketing, 17,* 149–163.

Miyamoto, Y., & Kitayama, S. (2002). Cultural variation in correspondence bias: The critical role of attitude diagnosticity of socially constrained behavior. *Journal of Personality and Social Psychology, 83,* 1239–1248.

Nelson, A., Robertson, I. T., Walley, L., & Smith, M. (1999). Personality and work performance: Some evidence from small- and medium-sized firms. *Occupational Psychologist, 12,* 28–36.

Nie, W., Hopkins, W. E., & Hopkins, S. A. (2002). Gender-based perceptions of equity in China's state-owned enterprises. *Thunderbird International Business Review, 44,* 353–377.

Nisbett, R. E., Peng, K., Choi, I., & Norenzayan, A. (2001). Culture and systems of thought: Holistic versus analytic cognition. *Psychological Review, 108,* 291–310.

Nyfield, G., & Baron, H. (2000). Cultural context in adapting selection practices across borders. In J. F. Kehoe (Ed.), *Managing selection strategies in changing organizations* (pp. 242–268). San Francisco: Jossey-Bass.

O'Grady, M. A. (2005, November 25). Americas: Why Latin nations are poor. *Wall Street Journal,* p. A11.

Paik, Y., & Teagarden, M. B. (1995). Strategic international human resource management approaches in the maquiladora industry: A comparison of Japanese, Korean, and US firms. *The International Journal of Human Resource Management, 6,* 568–587.

Peng, K., Nisbett, R. E., & Wong, N. Y. C. (1997). Validity problems comparing values across cultures and possible solutions. *Psychological Methods, 2,* 329–344.

Peng, M. W., & Luo, Y. (2000). Managerial ties and firm performance in a transition economy: The nature of a micro-macro link. *Academy of Management Journal, 43,* 486–501.

Peppas, S. C., Peppas, S. R., & Jin, K. (1999). Choosing the right employee: Chinese vs U.S. preferences. *Management Decision, 37,* 7–13.

Peppas, S. C., Peppas, S. R., & Jin, K. (2001). Choosing the right employee: Chinese vs. US preferences. *Career Development International, 6,* 100–106.

Pfeffer, J. (1998). *The human equation: Building profits by putting people first.* Boston: Harvard Business School Press.

Phillips, J. M., & Gully, S. M. (2002). Fairness reactions to personnel selection techniques in Singapore and the United States. *International Journal of Human Resource Management, 13,* 1186–1205.

Poortinga, Y. H., Van de Vijver, F. J. R., & Van Hemert, D. A. (2002). Cross-cultural equivalence of the Big Five: A tentative interpretation of the evidence. In R. R. McCrae & J. Allik (Eds.), *The five-factor model of personality across cultures* (pp. 281–302). New York: Kluwer Academic.

Rivera, A. A., Anderson, S. K., & Middleton, V. A. (1999). A career development model for Mexican-American women. *Journal of Career Development, 26,* 91–106.

Robertson, I. T., & Makin, P. J. (1986). Management selection in Britain: A survey and critique. *Journal of Occupational Psychology, 59,* 45–57.

Rothstein, J. S. (2004). Creating lean industrial relations: General Motors in Silao, Mexico. *Competition and Change, 8,* 203–221.

Rousseau, D. M., & Tinsley, C. (1997). Human resources are local: Society and social contracts in a global economy. In N. Anderson & P. Herriot (Eds.), *International handbook of selection and assessment* (pp. 39–61). Chichester, UK: John Wiley.

Rowe, P. M., Williams, M. C., & Day, A. L. D. (1994). Selection procedures in North America. *International Journal of Assessment and Selection, 2,* 74–79.

Rusbult, C. E., Insko, C. A., & Lin, Y.-H. W. (1995). Seniority-based reward allocation in the United States and Taiwan. *Social Psychology Quarterly, 58,* 13–30.

Ryan, A. M., McFarland, L., Baron, H., & Page, R. (1999). An international look at selection practices: Nation and culture as explanations for variability in practice. *Personnel Psychology, 52,* 359–391.

Salgado, J. F. (1997). The five factor model of personality and job performance in the European Community. *Journal of Applied Psychology, 82,* 30–43.

Salgado, J. F., & Anderson, N. (2002). Cognitive and GMA testing in the European Community: Issues and evidence. *Human Performance, 15,* 75–96.

Salgado, J. F., Anderson, N., Moscoso, S., Bertua, C., de Fruyt, F., & Rolland, J. P. (2003). A meta-analytic study of general mental ability validity for different occupations in the European Community. *Journal of Applied Psychology, 88,* 1068–1081.

Sandal, G. M., & Inger, M. E. (2002). Sensitivity of the CPI Good Impression scale detecting "Faking Good" among Norwegian students and job applicants. *International Journal of Selection and Assessment, 10,* 304–311.

Schlevogt, K. (2000). China II. Investing and managing in China: How to dance with the dragon. *Thunderbird International Business Review, 42,* 201–226.

Schmidt, F. L., & Hunter, J. E. (1981). Employment testing: Old theories and new research findings. *American Psychologist, 36,* 1128–1137.

Schmidt, F. L., & Hunter, J. E. (1998). The validity and utility of selection methods in personnel psychology: Practical and theoretical implications of 85 years of research findings. *Psychological Bulletin, 124,* 262–274.

Schmidt, F. L., Hunter, J. E., McKenzie, R. C., & Muldrow, T. W. (1979). Impact of valid selection procedures on work-force productivity. *Journal of Applied Psychology, 64,* 609–626.

Scholarios, D., & Lockyer, C. (1999). Recruiting and selecting professionals: Context, qualities, and methods. *International Journal of Selection and Assessment, 7,* 142–156.

Schuler, R. S., Jackson, S. E., Jackofsky, E., & Slocum, J. W. (1996). Managing human resources in Mexico: A cultural understanding. *Business Horizons, 39*(3), 55–61.

Segalla, M., Sauquet, A., & Turati, C. (2001). Symbolic vs. functional recruitment: Cultural influences on employee recruitment policy. *European Management Journal, 19,* 32–43.

Shackleton, V., & Newell, S. (1994). European management selection methods: A comparison of five countries. *International Journal of Selection and Assessment, 2,* 91–102.

Shackleton, V., & Newell, S. (1994). Management selection: A comparative survey of methods used in top British and French companies. *Journal of Occupational Psychology, 64,* 23–36.

Shen, J., & Edwards, V. (2004). Recruitment and selection in Chinese MNEs. *International Journal of Human Resource Management, 15,* 814–835.

Sinha, J. B. P. (1997). A cultural perspective on organizational behavior in India. In P. C. Earley & M. Erez (Eds.), *New perspectives on international industrial/ organizational psychology* (pp. 53–74). San Francisco: New Lexington Press.

Smith, P. B. (2004). Acquiescent response bias as an aspect of cultural control. *Journal of Cross-cultural Psychology, 35,* 50–61.

Smith, M., & Abrahamsen, M. (1992, May). Patterns of selection in six countries. *The Industrial Psychologist,* 205– 207.

Soto, J., Levenson, R. W., & Ebling, R. (2005). Cultures of moderation and expression: Emotional experience, behavior, and physiology in Chinese Americans and Mexican Americans. *Emotion, 5,* 154–165.

Sparrow, P., & Hiltrop, J. M. (1994). *European human resource management in transition.* New York, NY: Prentice Hall.

Spence, L. J., & Petrick, J. A. (2000). Multinational interview decisions: Integrity capacity and competing values. *Human Resource Management Journal, 10,* 49–67.

Steiner, D. D., & Gilliland, S. W. (2001). Procedural justice in personnel selection: International and cross-cultural perspectives. *International Journal of Selection and Assessment, 9,* 124–137.

Steiner, D. D., & Gilliland, S. W. (1996). Fairness reactions to personnel selection techniques in France and United States. *Journal of Applied Psychology, 81,* 134–142.

Stohl, C. (1993). European managers' interpretations of participation: A semantic network analysis. *Human Communication Research, 20,* 97–117.

Stone, G. J., & Ineson, E. M. (1997). An international comparison of personality differences between hospitality and other service sector managers. *International Journal of Selection and Assessment, 5,* 215–228.

Teagarden, M. B., Butler, M. C., & Von Ginlow, M. A. (1992). Mexico's maquiladora industry: Where strategic human resource management makes a difference. *Organizational Dynamics, 20,* 34–47.

Thompson, E. R., & Phua, T. T. F. (2005). Are national cultural traits applicable to senior firm managers? *British Journal of Management, 16,* 59–68.

Tixier, M. (1996). Employers recruitment tools across Europe. *Employee Relations, 18,* 67–79.

Triandis, H. C., & Bhawuk, D. P. S. (1997). Culture theory and the meaning of relatedness. In P. C. Earley & M. Erez (Eds.), *New perspectives on internatonal industrial/organizational psychology* (pp. 13–52). San Francisco: Pfeiffer.

Trompenaars, F., & Hampden-Turner, C. (1998). *Riding the waves of culture: Understanding cultural diversity in global business.* (2nd edition). New York: McGraw-Hill.

Tung, R. L. (1990). International human resource management policies and practices: A comparative analysis. *Research in Personnel and Human Resource Management, 2,* 171–186.

Von Glinow, M. A., Drost, E. A., & Teagarden, M. B. (2002). Converging on IHRM best practices: Lessons learned from a globally distributed consortium on theory and practice. *Human Resource Management, 41*, 123–140.

Von Glinow, M. A., & Chung, B. J. (1989). Comparative human resource management practices in the United States, Japan, Korea, and the People's Republic of China. *Research in Personnel and Human Resource Management, 1*, 153–171.

Von Glinow, M. A., & Teagarden, M. B. (1988). The transfer of human resource technology in Sino-US cooperative ventures: Problems and solutions. *Human Resource Management, 27*, 201–229.

Von Glinow, M. A., & Teagarden, M. B. (1993). *Contextual determinants of human resource management effectiveness in international cooperative alliances: Evidence from the People's Republic of China.* Los Angeles: University of Southern California, School of Business Administration, Center for Effective Organizations.

Wallsten, T. S., & Gu, H. (2003). Distinguishing choice and subjective probability estimation processes: Implications for theories of judgment and for cross-cultural comparisons. *Organizational Behavior and Human Decision Processes, 90*, 111–123.

Wang, Z. M. (1997). Integrated personnel selection, appraisal, and decisions: A Chinese approach. In N. Anderson & P. Herriot (Eds.), *International handbook of selection and assessment* (pp. 63–81). New York: Wiley.

Wheeler, K. G. (2002). Cultural values in relation to equity sensitivity within and across cultures. *Journal of Managerial Psychology, 17*, 612–678.

Wilk, S. L., & Cappelli, P. (2003). Understanding the determinants of employer use of selection methods. *Personnel Psychology, 56*, 103–124.

Wong, C.-S., & Law, K. S. (1999). Managing localization of human resources in the PRC: A practical model. *Journal of World Business, 34*, 26–40.

Wong, I. F. H., & Phooi-Ching, L. (2000). Chinese cultural values and performance at job interviews: A Singapore perspective. *Business Communication Quarterly, 63*, 9–22.

Yan, Y. (2003). A comparative study of human resource management practices in international joint ventures: The impact of national origin. *International Journal of Human Resource Management, 14*, 487–510.

Yi, J.-S., & Park, S. (2003). Cross-cultural differences in decision-making styles: A study of college students in five countries. *Social Behavior and Personality, 31*, 35–48.

4

Culture and Human Resource Management Practices:

Personnel Selection Based on Personality Measures

EUGENE F. STONE-ROMERO AND
CAROL A. THORNSON
University of Texas at San Antonio and University of Central Florida

INTRODUCTION

The U.S. workforce is becoming increasingly diverse in terms of a number of individual difference variables, including culture, sex, ethnicity, and sexual orientation (e.g., Konrad, Prasad, & Pringle, 2006; Stockdale & Crosby, 2004). Nevertheless, a review of the human resource management (HRM) literature shows that relatively little attention has been paid to a number of dimensions along which workers vary. For example, relative to other issues considered by the same literature, there is very little research on the degree to which HRM processes and practices (e.g., recruitment, selection, compensation, training) are influenced by the cultural backgrounds of job applicants and job incumbents. Thus, we consider this issue with respect to employee selection. More specifically, we illustrate how selection is influenced by individuals' responses to personality measures.

Our focus on personality is based on two important considerations. First, research shows that there are systematic differences in personality across individuals from different cultural (e.g., national, ethnic) backgrounds (e.g., Hofstede, 1980, 1991; Triandis, 1994; Triandis & Wasti, 2007). Among the many reasons for this is that personality is shaped by the socialization practices of cultures (e.g., national) and subcultures. Second, during the past three decades, interest has increased markedly in the use of personality measures for various HRM purposes (e.g., selection, placement, training). This raises a number of important concerns, one of which is the potential for the use of such measures for HRM purposes to discriminate unfairly against individuals from cultures other than the one that is dominant in an organization. Arguments central to this point are considered below.

The extant literature offers many possible justifications for the use of personality measures for HRM purposes, one of which is the seemingly widely accepted view that various so-called traits (e.g., agreeableness, dominance, introversion, conscientiousness, emotional stability) either have main effects on criteria relevant to organizations and their members (e.g., individual, group, and organizational performance, job attitudes, person–organization fit, and person–job fit) or interact with situational variables to affect such criteria (e.g., Barrick & Mount, 1991; Hogan, 1991; Hough, Oswald, & Ployhart, 2001; Tett, Jackson, & Rothstein, 1991). Nevertheless, the use of personality measures for various HRM purposes has not gone unchallenged (e.g., Guion & Gottier, 1965; Stone-Romero, 1994, 2005). In fact, more than four decades ago, Guion and Gottier (1965) cautioned against the use of such measures for personnel selection (hereinafter selection) purposes, concluding that "it is difficult in the face of this summary to advocate with a clear conscience the use of personality measures in most situations as a basis for making employment decisions" (p. 160). Subsequently, Guion (1991) noted that there are serious flaws in the research evidence associated with the use of personality measures for selection purposes in that much of it comes from concurrent (as opposed to predictive) criterion-related validity studies. In addition, the findings of many studies have not been replicated. As a consequence, he argued that "the evidence does not exist to justify the use of personality measures, without specific research for specific purposes, as the basis for employment decisions" (p. 343). Moreover, several critics of personality assessment in organizational contexts (e.g., for selection purposes) have noted how such measures may invade the privacy of individuals who are asked to complete them (e.g., Stone & Stone, 1990; Stone-Romero and Stone, 2007; Stone-Romero, Stone, & Hyatt, 2003). Moreover, Stone-Romero (1994, 2005) noted how inferences stemming from measures of personality may serve to stigmatize certain individuals, especially those in protected groups. As a result, they may be treated unfairly in organizational contexts (Stone-Romero & Stone, 2005). In spite of these and other concerns, during the past several decades, interest in the use of personality measures for various HRM purposes seems to have increased.

PURPOSES OF CHAPTER

In view of the above-noted issues concerning the use of personality measures for HRM purposes, the major purposes of this chapter are to describe the personnel selection process and to specify the dysfunctional consequences of using various measures of personality (hereinafter personality measures) for HRM purposes. Our focus is on the use of personality measures for selection. However, given our view that the use of personality measures for selection may have dysfunctional consequences, the chapter also considers several other important and related issues, including (a) the construct of personality, (b) environmental determinants of personality (e.g., socialization, exposure to stressors, job-related experiences), (c) dispositional versus situational determinants of behavior, (d) personality as a basis for the stigmatization of job applicants and job incumbents, (e) the influence of implicit and explicit measures of personality on selection and other HR practices, and (f) a set of conclusions about the use of personality measures for HRM purposes.

THE PERSONALITY CONCEPT

In this section, we provide a general definition of the personality concept. Following this, we offer perspectives on personality that pertain to several fields of psychology.

Basic Nature of Personality

A consideration of the relevant literature reveals a number of definitions of personality. For example, Carver and Scheier (2004) view it as "a dynamic organization inside the person, of psychophysical systems that create the person's characteristic patterns of behavior, thoughts, and feelings" (p. 15). Hogan (1991) provides a similar definition, noting that personality has to do with a person's inner nature, in terms of "the structures, dynamics, processes, and propensities that explain why he or she behaves in a characteristic way" (p. 875). However, he notes that personality is often viewed from the perspective of a person's social reputation; that is, the way the person is viewed by others in terms of such traits as agreeableness, dominance, extroversion, conscientiousness, and risk-taking. Consistent with both of the just-noted perspectives, many theorists and researchers use *measures* of hypothesized traits as the operational definition of personality (Wiggins & Pincus, 1992). In this chapter, we adopt this measurement-based approach to personality. The principal reason for this is that formal and informal measures of personality are used in organizations for various HRM purposes (e.g., selection).

However, there is a nontrivial distinction between actual traits and measures of such traits. The distinction is important because a person's score on a personality measure may not be a valid reflection of his or her standing on some trait. As such, personality measures may lack construct validity (Stone-Romero, 1994, 2005). We elaborate on this issue below.

Perspectives on Personality

The trait perspective is common to conceptions of personality found in several fields of psychology (e.g., personality, social, and industrial and organizational) and various other disciplines (e.g., organizational behavior, HRM). Thus, we next consider illustrative trait views that are found in the literature of such fields as personality psychology, vocational psychology, and organizational psychology.

Personality psychology.

One of the most popular contemporary approaches to both the conceptualization and measurement of personality is the Big Five approach (Digman, 1990). It views personality in terms of five major dimensions: (a) agreeableness or likability, (b) conscientiousness or conformity, (c) extraversion or surgency, (d) intelectance or openness to experience, and (e) neuroticism or emotional stability. Not only has this approach gained a considerable following among personality psychologists, but it also has been widely used in industrial and organizational psychology and allied disciplines (e.g., Barrick & Mount, 1991; Tett, Jackson, & Rothstein, 1991). There are, however, conflicting views on the number of dimensions (traits) necessary to conceptualize and measure personality. For example, Jackson's (1984) measure deals with 20 traits, and Cattell, Eber, and Tatsuoka's (1977) measure considers 16 factors.

Vocational and occupational psychology.

The view that job applicants and/or job incumbents have occupational or work-related personalities dates back several decades (e.g., Roe, 1956; Strong, 1943; Super & Bohn, 1970). In the overlapping fields of vocational and occupational psychology, the major foci of theory and research on occupational personalities were interests, values, and needs. Of particular importance to vocational psychologists was the way in which these variables (along with job-related aptitudes and abilities) influenced occupational choice and occupational success. Illustrative of this perspective, Lofquist and Dawis (1969) view personality as having to do with the stable characteristics of individuals, including their job-related abilities and needs. Needs are conceived of as the reinforcement values that individuals attach to various stimulus conditions in organizations. As such, their concept of needs is similar to the valence concept of Expectancy Theory (Vroom, 1964).

Organizational psychology.

Kahn, Wolfe, Quinn, Snoek, and Rosenthal (1964) offered a seminal model of individual adjustment to role-taking in organizations, which served as a basis for the well-known role-taking model of Katz and Kahn (1978). Kahn et al. viewed personality as a function of all of the factors that serve to influence a person's propensities to behave in certain ways, including the person's motives, values, fears, sensitivities, and habits. In the role-taking model of Katz and Kahn (1978), personality is reflected in the "attributes of the person" element.

All of the just-noted conceptions of personality make explicit or implicit reference to individuals' values. Note, in addition, that values are important elements in many other theories in industrial and organizational psychology and related disciplines. For example, they are components of Expectancy Theory (Vroom, 1964), the Theory of Planned Behavior (Ajzen, 1988), and the Theory of Reasoned Action (Fishbein & Ajzen, 1975).

Summary.

As should be obvious from the previous sections, broadly conceived, personality refers to both traits (e.g., needs, values, interests) and aptitudes and abilities. However, unless otherwise noted, in this chapter our focus is on the use of measures of what are often regarded as traits for selection purposes.

THE ORIGINS OF PERSONALITY

Three major perspectives on the origins of personality are briefly described in this section. They are important because they influence the inferences that are made about individuals on the basis of their scores on personality measures. As a result, they affect selection decisions and other HRM processes.

Perspectives on the Origins of Personality

The *nature* (biological, genetic, dispositional) perspective holds that personality traits are a function of an individual's genetic endowment (e.g., Eysenck & Eysenck, 1985). It argues that people have relatively stable traits (dispositions) that vary little across different environments (situations). Such traits are seen as largely immutable.

In contrast to the nature view, the *nurture* perspective considers personality to be a byproduct of such environmental influences as learning, reinforcement history, and socialization. As such, appropriate changes in an individual's environment will lead to changes in his or her personality. This is an especially important issue because culture has well-established relations with various measures of personality. For instance, as is noted below, individuals from different cultures (and subcultures) differ from one another on measures of such variables as individualism–collectivism, introversion, tolerance of ambiguity, familism, openness to experience, masculinity, acceptance of power differentials across individuals, and universalism (Hofstede, 1980, 1991; Trompenaars & Hampden-Turner, 1998).

Which of the previously noted personality perspectives one adopts has profound implications for the way in which individuals are treated in social systems, including work organizations. To the degree that one adopts the biological view, traits will be regarded as largely unchangeable. Thus, an individual's potential to succeed in any social system will be largely a function of his or her genetic endowment. On the other hand, to the extent that one subscribes to the learning perspective, an individual's traits will be viewed as modifiable. Thus, it will be possible to alter the person's standing in a social system through such environmental influences as socialization, education, and training.

The *interactionist* perspective regards personality as a function of the interaction between traits and the situations in which individuals find themselves (e.g., Mischel, 1977). It posits that the degree to which traits influence behaviors varies across situations. As a result, behavior may not be as consistent across situations as one would predict on the basis of a trait approach. Thus, for example, a person might appear to be outgoing at social gatherings, but quite reserved at work or highly conscientious at work, but rather neglectful of his or her responsibilities at home.

Relation to HRM Practices

In a widely used HRM textbook, Cascio (1998) states that "the evidence now indicates that scores on well-developed measures of normal personality (1) are stable over reasonably long periods of time, (2) predict important occupational outcomes, . . . [and] . . . (3) do not discriminate unfairly against any ethnic or national group" (p. 228). The view that scores on personality measures are stable over time seems to be predicated on an endorsement of the trait perspective. And the acceptance of this perspective can have profound implications for HRM practices. For example, because the nature perspective views traits as largely immutable, personnel selection systems that use personality predictors will be structured so as to screen out individuals who have "dispositions" that make them less suitable for work than others. Unfortunately, the trait perspective largely ignores two highly important determinants of personality, that is, environmental stressors and the socialization that is experienced by individuals who are members of specific subcultures. We consider both such influences below.

THE SELECTION PROCESS

In this section, we provide a brief description of the selection process. In addition, we indicate how personality measures may come into play at various stages of the process.

The General Purpose of Selection

Research shows that there are often considerable differences among job applicants and incumbents on measures of such predictors of job success (hereinafter "predictor measures" or "predictors") as abilities, aptitudes, and personality (e.g., values, interests). Scores on such predictor measures are often used to predict various criteria, including job performance, absenteeism, counterproductive behavior, and turnover.

Selection systems have utility to the degree that a number of conditions exist. Among these are that (a) there is a high degree of correlation between predictor measures and criteria, (b) there is a low degree of correlation between (among) the predictors, (c) job applicants differ greatly from one another on the predictors, (d) the selection ratio is low, and (e) the cost of testing (i.e., measuring the predictors) is low (Cascio & Aguinis, 2005; Guion, 1991).

Predictors that may be used in selection include interviews, references, recommendation letters, application blanks, biographical inventories, honesty tests, job experience, cognitive ability tests, personality inventories, work samples, and biodata. Any given selection system may consider one or more of these predictors.

The Assessment of Personality

There are two common strategies for measuring personality in selection contexts, that is, interviews and standardized measures of personality.

Interviews.

Whether structured or unstructured, interviews are almost always used in selection (Moscoso, 2000). They often serve as a basis for the inferences that personnel decision makers (hereinafter "decision makers") generate about the personality of job applicants (hereinafter "applicants"). In general, interviews (especially those of the unstructured variety) are indirect or informal measures of personality. Interviewers often use them to generate inferences about the standing of an applicant on a number of dimensions of personality (e.g., agreeableness, aggressiveness, conscientiousness, neuroticism). One such personality-based inference is the degree to which the applicant is likely to *fit* in a job, work group, and organization. A commonly used indicator of fit (explained below) is the degree to which an applicant has values that are congruent with those of other organizational members (Cable & Judge, 1997).

Standardized personality measures.

Personality also can be assessed using any one of a number of standardized measures. These include the 16 Personality Factor Questionnaire (16 PF), the California Personality Inventory (CPI), the Guilford-Zimmerman Temperament Survey (GZTTS), and the Personality Research Form (PRF).

Personality-Based Stigmatization

As a result of their responses to personality measures, applicants may be stigmatized in the eyes of decision makers or computerized decision-making systems. A *stigma* is a negative (discrediting) discrepancy between a person's actual social identity and his or her virtual social identity (Goffman, 1963). A *virtual social identity* represents what the decision maker expects of a job applicant in terms of such attributes as abilities, personality, appearance, morality, attitudes, and behavioral propensities. In organizations, virtual social identities are based on such factors as job descriptions, job analyses, organization-specific views about the ideal job incumbent, and the idiosyncratic views of specific decision makers (Stone-Romero & Stone, 2007). For example, among other attributes, a decision maker may view the ideal job incumbent as a white male who is agreeable, conscientious, achievement-oriented, and open-minded.

In contrast to a person's virtual social identity, his or her *actual social identity* represents the way the applicant is seen, or is capable of being seen, by a decision maker (Goffman, 1963; Stone-Romero & Stone, 2007). An actual social identity may be based on such factors as the applicant's appearance, verbal and nonverbal responses to employment interview questions, scores on standardized measures (e.g., ability, aptitude, and personality), and responses to items on an employment application. On the basis of this and other information, for example, a decision maker may view a given applicant as argumentative, irresponsible, not achievement-oriented, and closed-minded. As a result, the applicant's actual social identity would be negatively discrepant from the virtual social identity, and he or she would be stigmatized.

Influence of in-group membership on virtual social identities.

It is important to note that members of dominant groups in organizations are typically in the position of being able to specify the characteristics of the ideal job applicant and to make judgments about the degree to which an applicant's actual social identity is consistent with the virtual social identity of an incumbent in a specific job (Stone-Romero & Stone, 2007). Thus, for example, decision makers in a Japanese organization would be likely to view a job applicant with collective values as more suitable for a job than a person with individualistic values. And, in the typical U.S. organization, decision makers would be prone to regard an applicant who was extroverted more favorably than one who was introverted.

Because virtual social identities are determined largely by the views of decision makers who are members of organizational in-groups (e.g., whites, males, Protestants), in many cases, members of out-groups (e.g., Mexican Americans, females, Catholics) will be seen as having reduced odds of succeeding on a job (i.e., not having good fit). One reason for this is that stereotypes about out-group members may influence the way that they are viewed and treated by in-group members at various stages of the selection process (Stone-Romero & Stone, 2007). In terms of the focus of this chapter, formal or informal assessments of personality may lead decision makers to view selected applicants as out-group members. For example, a Gulf War veteran suffering from post-traumatic stress disorder (PTSD) may likely be viewed as *not* having a high degree of fit with a job and/or an organization. We consider person–job and person–organization fit issues more fully below.

Influence of culture on virtual social identities.

There are two major reasons for the just-noted arguments. One is that national culture influences organizational culture (Hofstede, 1980, 1991; Stone & Stone-Romero, 1994, 1998, 2007; Stone-Romero, Stone, & Salas, 2003; Trice & Beyer, 1993). The second is that organizational culture affects conceptions of virtual social identities (Stone-Romero & Stone, 2007). U.S. organizations tend to have cultures that promote rationality, efficiency, practicality, individual achievement, competition, and freedom (Hofstede, 1980, 1991; Stone-Romero & Stone, 1998, 2002; Trice & Beyer, 1993). As a result, the selection systems of U.S. organizations tend to favor individuals who have personalities that are viewed as having a good fit with extant organizational cultures (Schneider, 1987). Stated somewhat differently, selection systems promote person–organization fit. Note, in addition, that potential applicants who do not perceive a high degree of fit between their values and those of an organization (e.g., as outlined in a job description), will likely have a low level of motivation to apply for openings in the organization. Moreover, those who *do* apply, despite a lack of fit, often are weeded out at a later stage of the selection process.

PERSONALITY AND THE SELECTION PROCESS

As noted above, applicants may be stigmatized in the selection process on the basis of informal and formal personality measures. Although our focus is on selection, personality measures also may influence a number of other HRM processes, including recruitment, placement, training and development, performance management, and retention.

The Use of Personality Measures for Selection

Interest in the use of personality measures for selection has increased over the last two decades. Much of this is attributable to the development and popularization of the five-factor conception of personality (e.g., Digman & Inouye, 1986; McCrae & Costa, 1985, 1987) and unduly optimistic reports of meta-analytic research on the validity of personality measures for predicting job performance (e.g., Barrick & Mount, 1991; Tett, Jackson, & Rothstein, 1991).

Validity evidence.

Interestingly, the just-noted meta-analyses reveal only weak evidence of criterion-related validity. Average corrected correlation coefficients were .12 for extroversion, .12 for emotional stability, .07 for agreeableness, .22 for conscientiousness, and .05 for openness to experience (Barrick & Mount, 2003). Overall, what the evidence shows quite clearly is that personality measures explain very low proportions of the variance in various measures of job success. Thus, their utility for selection purposes appears quite suspect (Guion, 1991; Guion & Gottier, 1965; Stone-Romero, 1994, 2005).

It is noteworthy that the five-factor approach to the conceptualization and measurement of personality has been the target of considerable criticism (Block, 1995; Eysenck, 1992; McAdams, 1992; Pervin, 1994; Tellegen, 1993; Zuckerman, 1992). Big Five measures of personality have been criticized as not being comprehensive enough and lacking in construct validity. For instance, Hough, Paunonen, and their colleagues argued that the Big Five measures (a) are too heterogeneous and (b) reflect confounded constructs. Thus, they obscure relations between personality variables and the criteria of interest (e.g., Ashton, Jackson, Paunonen, Helmes, & Rothstein, 1995; Hough, 1992, 1997; Hough, Eaton, Dunnette, Kamp, & McCloy, 1990; Hough & Schneider, 1996; Paunonen, 1998). In spite of these criticisms, personality inventories continue to be used to predict employee performance and other criteria (Cascio & Aguinis, 2005). In addition, the developers of personality measures that are used primarily for selection purposes (e.g., Hogan, 1991) argue that not only are such measures quite useful for this purpose, but the validity problems cited by Ghiselli (1973) and Guion and Gottier (1965) are mythical and unfounded.

Standardized and unstandardized personality measurement.

As noted earlier, inferences about personality stem from not only the use of standardized personality measures but also the verbal and nonverbal behaviors of job applicants during employment interviews. For example, such personality dimensions as empathy (Cliffordson, 2002) and personal initiative (Fay & Frese, 2001) may be assessed during interviews. In fact, a review of 388 characteristics that were rated in 47 employment interview studies revealed that personality traits and applied social skills were rated *more often* in interviews than any other type of construct (Huffcutt, Conway, Roth, & Stone, 2001). This is a nontrivial matter for two reasons. One is that research suggests that personality impressions influence hiring decisions (Sears & Rowe, 2003). The other is that interviewers typically have little or no training in the assessment of personality. Thus, their assessments may be contaminated by a host of biases, including those stemming from the age, sex, nationality, race, and appearance of the interviewee (Stone-Romero & Stone, 2007).

Fit issues.

As noted above, scores on personality measures are often used to make inferences about the degree to which an applicant will fit into a job, group, and/or organization (Kristof-Brown, 2007a, 2007b, 2007c). The first of these, *person–job (P–J) fit*, involves congruence between a person's knowledge, skills, abilities, and other characteristics (KSAOs) and the requirements of a job and reinforcers available to the job incumbent. Thus, for example, there would be a lack of P–J fit if an applicant had needs that could not be met by the reinforcer system associated with a job for which he or she had applied or had interests that were incongruent with those of the same job. *Person–organization (P–O) fit* exists when there is correspondence between the individual's values and those of the organization. For instance, there would be poor P–O fit if an applicant had collective values, but the culture of the organization stressed rugged individualism. Finally, *person–group (P–G) fit* exists when an applicant is similar to members of the group in which he or she is likely to work with respect to such variables as demographic characteristics and personality variables. As such, there would be poor fit if, for example, an applicant was low on agreeableness but would have to work in a group whose members were all high on this dimension.

The concept of fit is important because a job applicant's scores on personality measures may signal a lack of one or more types of fit (P–J, P–O, P–G). As a result, he or she may be unfairly stigmatized and not offered a job. Indeed, research shows that decision makers are more likely to recommend hiring applicants who share an organization's values than those who don't (Chatman, 1989; Schein, 1990). One reason for this is that fit is assumed to result in a strong organizational culture, which is thought to contribute to individual, group, and organizational performance (Schein, 1990).

Trait Versus State Issues

Consistent with the just-noted fit perspectives, a review of the literature shows clear advocacy for the view that individuals who have certain personality traits are more suitable for jobs than others. For example, numerous authors have written about the dysfunctional consequences of having employees who score high on measures of negative affectivity (e.g., Brief, Burke, George, Robinson, & Webster, 1988; Burke, Brief, & George, 1993; Levin & Stokes, 1989). A clear assumption is that the same scores reflect the existence of a trait (disposition) and that people with certain traits are unlikely to fit in jobs, teams, and organizations. Representative of this trait-oriented perspective, George and Jones (2004) argued that "individuals who are high in neuroticism [a supposed marker of negative affectivity] are more likely to experience negative moods at work, feel stressed, and have a negative orientation to the work situations" (p. 9). In addition, DuBrin (2004) wrote that "people with negative affectivity are often distressed even when working under conditions that coworkers perceive as interesting and challenging" (p. 164). For reasons detailed below, to the degree that such views influence selection practices, individuals in various groups (e.g., African Americans, Mexican Americans) may experience unfair discrimination (Stone-Romero, 2005).

Unfortunately, the dispositional view seems to have been accepted *uncritically* by many HRM scholars (e.g., Cascio, 1998). This is regrettable because a considerable body of research shows that what are widely regarded as dispositions (e.g., negative affectivity, neuroticism, self-esteem, subjective well-being) vary considerably across environmental conditions, including the characteristics of roles in organizations (Kohn & Schooler, 1983). This is aptly illustrated by research and theory on social causation models of mental health (or psychological well-being). This work shows that environments have a profound effect on personality and because of this, measured levels of what many believe to be traits (e.g., emotional stability, negative affectivity, depression, anxiety) may very well reflect the effects of stressors and other factors that are found in the work and nonwork environments of individuals (Dohrenwend, 1975, 2000; Dohrenwend & Dohrenwend, 1970, 1974; Kohn & Schooler, 1983; Link, Dohrenwend, & Skodol, 1986; Link, Lennon, & Dohrenwend, 1993; Taylor, Repetti, & Seeman, 1997; Stone-Romero, 2005; Williams & Collins, 1995; Yu & Williams, 1999). The effects of stressors on numerous measures of physical and mental well-being have been demonstrated in both experimental and nonexperimental research. See Stone-Romero (2005) for more on this issue.

The effects of stressors on individuals is especially problematic vis-à-vis the use of personality measures for selection and other HRM purposes because individuals in several minority groups (e.g., blacks, Latinos, American Indians) are exposed to stressors at much greater rates than are Anglos (Cohn, 2000; Kerbo, 1983; Stone-Romero, 2005;

Williams & Williams-Morris, 2000; Yu & Williams, 1999). For example, data from the 2000 U.S. Census (Bishaw & Iceland, 2003) showed that the percentages of individuals living below the poverty level were 9.1 for Whites, 24.9 for Blacks, 22.6 for Hispanics or Latinos, and 25.7 for American Indians. These data are extremely important because there is clear and consistent evidence of a negative relation between socioeconomic status (SES) and the degree to which individuals are exposed to environmental stressors (Contrada et al., 2000; Dohrenwend et al., 1992; Kessler, Price, & Wortman, 1985; Link et al., 1986, 1993; Taylor et al., 1997; Williams, 1990; Williams & Collins, 1995; Yu & Williams, 1999). Thus, rather than being a reflection of traits, scores on personality measures may very well index states that remain invariant to the degree that environmental variables (e.g., stressors) remain unchanged. A clear illustration is the stress and strain experienced by soldiers involved in combat (e.g., Vietnam, Iraq, Afghanistan). For example, recent data (Army Medicine, 2006) suggest that approximately 15% of soldiers serving in Iraq have symptoms of acute stress, 8% suffer from anxiety, and a comparable percentage show signs of depression.

What these and other studies reveal quite clearly is that environmental variables can have a profound effect on scores derived from personality measures. Therefore, to the degree that a person is exposed to stressors on a continual basis, he or she will show relatively constant signs of stress and psychological strain. Thus, the fact that scores on personality measures remain constant over time may very well *not* be evidence of the existence of a trait (e.g., negative affectivity). Instead, it may be a function of the ongoing effects of stressors on a person's states. As a result, it may prove impossible to determine the degree to which scores on such measures reflect the existence of traits or states.

Similarity Biases in Selection

The degree to which an applicant is viewed as having adequate fit with a job, group, or organization is often a function of the extent to which he or she is similar to other individuals in the organization. Several theoretical perspectives are consistent with this argument. We consider three of them below. In addition, we specify how similarity effects may influence both the conduct of interviews and interview-based inferences.

Similarity-attraction paradigm.

The similarity-attraction paradigm suggests that similarity leads to liking and increased attraction between individuals (Byrne, 1971). Therefore, recruiters and decision makers will have better interactions with, and be more attracted to, applicants with personalities that are similar to themselves and others in an organization (Dipboye, 1992). As a consequence, the more similar an applicant is to current organizational members, the more likely he or she will be offered employment.

The attraction-selection-attrition framework.

Schneider's (1987) attraction-selection-attrition (ASA) framework suggests that recruiters and decision makers prefer applicants whose dispositional characteristics are compatible with the culture of an organization (Kristof-Brown, 2000). Thus, individuals who are not viewed as having appropriate attributes (e.g., traits) are unlikely to be selected for jobs. In addition, even if they are selected, their lack of fit often results in organizational experiences that lead to their attrition.

Relational demography.

The relational demography perspective posits that decision makers assess the degree of similarity between themselves and an applicant on the basis of such demographic variables as race, sex, educational level, or SES (Sacco, Scheu, Ryan, & Schmitt, 2003). The same perspective has clear ties to both the P–O fit and the similarity-attraction paradigm literatures (Byrne, 1971; Newcomb, 1956). To the degree that applicants are similar to members of organizational in-groups in terms of their demographic characteristics, they will be favored by decision makers. Thus, individuals who are stigmatized by lacking such similarity will be unlikely to be made job offers (Stone-Romero & Stone, 2007).

The ideal-employee stereotype.

Consistent with the above-described views on stigmatization, Dalessio and Imada (1984) argue that the degree to which a decision maker is attracted to an applicant is a function of the extent to which the applicant is similar to an "ideal-employee" (equivalent to a virtual social identity). Stated somewhat differently, the decision maker compares each applicant to an ideal-employee stereotype, and the greater the similarity, the greater the odds of the applicant being offered a job. Their research provided evidence of the existence of an ideal-employee stereotype. In addition, it showed that the effect of similarity on interview judgments was most likely when interviewers felt they themselves possessed the competencies required for the job (i.e., they perceived themselves as being an ideal employee).

Interviews and similarity effects.

The employment interview (hereinafter "the interview") is the most prevalent of all selection techniques (Harris, 1989), and is a stage in the selection process at which similarity effects are very likely to manifest themselves. For example, research shows that interviewers accord more favorable ratings to candidates who are similar to themselves in terms of such factors as demographic variables (e.g., age, race), personality characteristics (Sears & Rowe, 2003), attitudes (e.g., Baskett, 1973; Griffitt & Jackson, 1970; Peters & Terborg, 1975), biographical variables (e.g., Rand & Wexley, 1975), and race (e.g., Lin, Dobbins, & Farh, 1992). In addition, the less structured the interview is, the greater the likelihood is of there being similarity effects.

Cultural and Subcultural Differences in Personality Measures

In view of the importance of fit between an applicant and a job, group, or organization to personnel decision makers, we next consider how several variables that vary across cultures and subcultures may lead them to view an applicant as having a lack of fit. These variables include nationality, race (or ethnicity), sex, SES, and values.

National culture and socialization.

Responses to personality measures (e.g., measures of values) may be influenced considerably by culture-based differences in socialization. Thus, in this subsection, we consider the concept of culture, the effects of culture on personality, and evidence of cultural differences in personality.

Culture may be viewed as "a set of collective, shared, learned values which represent a broad tendency to prefer certain states of affairs over others" (Hofstede, 1980, p. 25). There is considerable evidence that the cultures of various nations differ from one another in terms of a host of culture-based values, including individualism, masculinity, uncertainty avoidance, achievement orientation, familism, power distance, and long-term planning (e.g., Hofstede, 1980, 1991; Triandis, 1995; Trompenaars & Hampden-Turner, 1998). For example, research by Hofstede (1980, 1991) showed very large differences in the degree to which individualism was valued by workers in 50 countries. National averages on this value were very low in such nations as Taiwan, Singapore, Hong Kong, and Japan and very high in such countries as Canada, Great Britain, Australia, and the United States. Within any given culture (e.g., national), there are likely to be many different subcultures. These may be a function of such variables as ethnicity, race, religion, sex, sexual orientation, age, and disability. In fact, a number of studies have shown evidence of within-nation, subculture-based differences on a host of culture-relevant variables.

Individuals are exposed to and learn important aspects of their culture(s) and subculture(s) through socialization (e.g., Erez & Earley, 1993; Triandis, 1989). Such socialization practices result in differences in the degree to which members of cultures and subcultures subscribe to such values as achievement, individualism, masculinity, conformity, self-reliance, and familism. Therefore, individuals from different cultures and subcultures will likely differ in terms of their responses to measures of different dimensions of personality. As noted below, this is a very important issue, because if personality measures are used for selection, individuals who have scores that differ from what the organization views as the ideal (i.e., the virtual social identity) on one or more dimensions will have reduced odds of being offered a job.

One very important culture-based value is individualism versus collectivism. As a result of socialization experiences, people of various nations differ greatly from one another on the extent to which they endorse individualistic versus collectivistic values (Hofstede, 1980; Hui & Triandis, 1986; Markus & Kitayama, 1991; Triandis, 1995). Those from many Western nations (e.g., Great Britain, Australia, Canada, and the United States) tend to endorse individualism and are idiocentric, whereas those from numerous non-Western countries (e.g., Japan, South Korea, Hong Kong, China) tend to endorse collectivism and are allocentic.

Idiocentric people assume that every individual is a self-contained entity who should remain independent in dealing with others (Markus & Kitayama, 1991; Oyserman, Coon, & Kemmelmeier, 2002; Sampson, 1988; Triandis, 1989). Thus, idiocentric people tend to value independence, autonomy, self-reliance, uniqueness, achievement, and competition. In contrast, allocentric people stress the importance of (a) maintaining harmonious relationships with others through interpersonal interdependence and conformity with group norms, (b) viewing the self as interdependent with others (Heine, Lehman, Markus, & Kitayama, 1999; Markus & Kitayama, 1991; Triandis, 1989), and (c) respecting one's superiors (Hwang, 2000, 2001; Liu, 1986). As a result, the behaviors and attitudes of people in collective cultures are determined largely by norms or demands of such in-groups as the extended family and the community (Green, Deschamps, & Páez, 2005). Research shows that the value of individualism versus collectivism is related to differences in a number of other variables, including other values, attitudes, behaviors, cognitions, communication styles, attributional tendencies, and self-concepts (Green et al., 2005).

As a result of socialization, individuals from collectivistic and individualistic cultures also are likely to differ from one another on extroversion. More specifically, Asians and Native Americans typically have lower levels of extroversion than Anglo Americans (Iwawaki, Eysenck, & Eysenck, 1980; Leighton & Kluckholn, 1947; Loo & Shiomi, 1982). Thus, to the degree that personnel decisions are based on measures of extroversion, they may unfairly discriminate against individuals who are members of several groups, including Native Americans and Asian Americans. For example, the values, beliefs, and behaviors of allocentric people (e.g., viewing the self as interdependent and respecting one's superiors) may lead idiocentric (e.g., U.S., Anglo) decision makers to view allocentric applicants as obsequious during a job interview. In addition, the decision makers may incorrectly infer that such applicants have low self-esteem and self-efficacy and do not have the interpersonal skills needed to succeed in leadership positions.

Ethnicity.

There is evidence of systematic relations between personality measures and membership in ethnicity-based subgroups. As noted above, several studies show relations between and among SES, race, and psychological strain. For example, based upon the analysis of data derived from a large set of primary studies, Hough, Oswald, and Ployhart (2001) reported that there were differences between blacks and whites on measures of adjustment. Interestingly, relative to whites, (a) blacks had lower scores on measures of affiliation, dependability, openness to experience, and managerial potential, (b) Hispanics had lower scores on measures of dependability, agreeableness, and openness to experience, (c) Native Americans had lower scores on measures of extroversion, surgency, dependability, and agreeableness, and (d) Asian Americans had lower scores on measures of extroversion, dependability, and openness to experience.

Research also shows that people from different ethnic groups within the United States differ from one another on individualism versus collectivism (Coon & Kemmelmeier, 2001; Gaines, Marelich, Bledsoe, & Steers, 1997; Oyserman et al., 2002; Singelis, 1994). For example, Hispanics are more collective than people of northern or western European ancestry (Triandis, 1989).

Moreover, a number of studies have shown value differences between blacks and whites. These may stem from a number of factors, including socialization experiences (Akbar, 1979; Boykin, 1983; Gay, 2000; Hilliard, 2001; Moemeka, 1998) and the effects of racism, oppression, and other discriminatory practices that have permeated the lives of many African Americans (Boykin, 1986; Tyler, Boykin, Boelter, & Dillihunt, 2005). For example, the cultural themes and values derived from West African worldviews and related experiences have led many blacks to value (a) *communalism*, defined as a predisposition toward the fundamental interdependence of people, and (b) *verve*, defined as a special receptiveness to high levels of sensory stimulation (Akbar, 1979; Tyler, Boykin, Boelter, & Dillihunt, 2005).

Interestingly, research shows that African American students hold preferences for and perform better in academic settings where communalism (as opposed to individualism and competition) and verve are salient during learning and instruction (Bailey & Boykin, 2001). Thus, it appears that African Americans are another group of individuals for whom the "cookie-cutter" ideal personality of the Westernized U.S. society does not apply. The same appears to be true for Native Americans, Hispanics, and Asian Americans. Consequently, as the proportion of whites in the United States continues to decline, it seems imprudent to define the ideal job incumbent as an idiocentric, extroverted, white male.

Sex.

Research shows evidence of sex-based differences in personality. For example, males typically score one-half of a standard deviation above females on measures of dominance (Sackett & Ellingson, 1997). In addition, there is considerable evidence of sex-based differences in individualism versus collectivism. Males tend to be more idiocentric than females, and females tend to be more allocentric than males (Bakan, 1966; Bem, 1974; Gilligan, 1982; Kashima et al., 1995; Lorenzi-Cioldi & Dafflon, 1998; Williams & Best, 1982). Moreover, there are sex-based differences on various scales of such personality measures as the California Personality Inventory (CPI), the Guilford-Zimmerman Temperament Survey (GZTTS), the Personality Research Form (PRF), and the 16 Personality Factor Questionnaire (16 PF; Sackett & Wilk, 1994).

Age.

There are generational differences in personality (Matsumoto et al., 1996; Mishra, 1994). For example, research by Matsumoto et al. showed that older individuals are more collective than younger people. Thus, maintaining the ideal job candidate as one who is individualistic may lead to unfair age-based discrimination.

Socioeconomic status.

There are differences in personality that relate to SES (Freeman, 1997; Marshall, 1997; Wink, 1997). For instance, the higher their SES, the greater the degree to which people endorse the value of individualism. An important implication of this is that those who most need jobs are least likely to get them.

The finding of personality differences across individuals in various SES strata is not surprising. One reason for this is that the lower a person's SES, the more likely it is that he or she will be exposed to environmental stressors, and, as a result, show signs of stress and strain (Taylor et al., 1997). This would be reflected in higher scores on measures of neuroticism, depression, and similar constructs (Stone-Romero, 1994, 2005).

Effects of Cultural and Subcultural Differences on Selection Decisions

The foregoing makes it clear that a number of factors other than traits influence scores on personality measures. Thus, to the extent that selection systems rely on the use of such measures, there is the potential for individuals who are members of various groups or subgroups to be screened out on the basis of their scores on such measures. Unfortunately, this discrimination is often of the unfair variety (Stone-Romero & Stone, 2005, 2007).

Interestingly, on the basis of meta-analytic research, some authors have argued that the use of personality measures in selection does *not* result in adverse impact (e.g., Hough & Furnham, 2003). However, given the above-noted differences, this conclusion seems highly questionable for a number of reasons. For example, in highly competitive hiring situations, even small differences on personality measures might have a large impact on the likelihood of an offer being made to a job applicant (Stone, Stone, & Dipboye, 1992).

The Legality of Using Personality Measures for Selection Purposes

A number of laws and guidelines that relate to employment practices are relevant to the use of personality measures for selection. Below we consider two of these, that is, the Uniform Guidelines on Employee Selection Procedures (1978) and the Americans With Disabilities Act (1990).

The Uniform Guidelines specify principles on the use of employee selection procedures, including the use of tests. One is that it is inappropriate to use a test or selection procedure that creates *adverse impact*, unless the procedure has demonstrated validity (e.g., criterion related validity). Adverse impact occurs when the selection rate for individuals in one group (e.g., females, blacks, war veterans) is less than 80% that of individuals in another group (e.g., males, whites, nonveterans). Adverse impact is an important issue because of the fact that there are well-established cultural and subcultural differences in personality. Thus, to the degree that selection systems screen out individuals on the basis of their scores on personality measures for which there are group or subgroup differences, there may be adverse impact. For example, because members of several minority groups have higher scores on neuroticism (and its correlates) than whites, they may be denied employment. In addition, war veterans who manifest signs of post traumatic stress disorder (PTSD) may be screened out at higher rates than nonveterans. In view of the fact that measures of neuroticism (and related constructs) explain negligible proportions of the variance in job success criteria (Stone-Romero, 1994, 2005), their use for selection purposes appears to fly in the face of the principles contained in the Uniform Guidelines.

The Americans with Disabilities Act.

Under the Americans with Disabilities Act (ADA), qualified individuals with disabilities must be given equal opportunity in all aspects of employment. Disability, defined broadly, includes *any physical or mental impairment* that substantially limits one or more of an individual's major life activities, such as caring for oneself, walking, talking, hearing, or seeing. Of note here is the fact that the authors of one of the most popular personality inventories used in personnel and management selection, the Neuroticism-Extroversion-Openness Personality

Inventory (NEO-PI), stated: "The five-factor model developed in studies of normal personality is fully adequate to account for the dimensions of abnormal personality as well" (Costa & McCrae, 1992, p. 347).

It is neither appropriate nor legal under the ADA to include items in a selection battery that may disclose an applicant's mental condition (Camara & Merenda, 2000), including items in the NEO-PI and/or other measures of neuroticism or emotional stability. Under the ADA, employers are permitted only to inquire about an applicant's abilities to perform essential job functions. Further, the ADA stipulates that employers only may ask disability-related questions and require an applicant to submit to a medical examination *after* he or she has been given a conditional job offer. These issues are, for example, specifically addressed in 42 U.S.C. §12112(d)(2), C.F.R. 1630.13(a), and 1630.14(a)(b).

The Equal Employment Opportunity Commission (EEOC) has issued guidelines concerning what constitutes a medical examination under the ADA (October 10, 1995). Most telling is the statement that "psychological examinations are medical if they provide evidence that would lead to identifying a mental disorder or impairment (for example, those listed in the American Psychiatric Association's most recent version of the Diagnostic and Statistical Manual of Mental Disorders [DSM])" (EEOC, 1995, p. 16). This is highly relevant because (a) one of the scales the NEO-PI is designed to assess is emotional stability/neuroticism, (b) neuroticism is very strongly related to depression (Duggen et al., 1995; Kendler et al., 1993; Sen, Nesse, & Stoltenberg, 2003; Watson & Clark, 1984), and (c) the DSM regards depression as a psychiatric disorder. Because the NEO-PI and similar measures have the capacity to reveal the presence of a disability (e.g., mental illness), it would appear that their use constitutes a medical inquiry that is prohibited prior to a conditional job offer. Thus, their use appears to fly in the face of extant laws and guidelines.

Use of Subgroup Norms in Selection

One way of reducing the potential for personality measures to produce adverse impact is to consider an applicant's scores in terms of subgroup (e.g., race- or sex-based) norms. Quite telling is that the use of subgroup norms is standard practice in clinical and personality research, where it is commonly believed that the only meaningful way to interpret an individual's score is in terms of his or her standing within a given group. However, Title I of the Civil Rights Act (CRA) of 1991, Section 106, specifies that *in employment settings* it unlawful to adjust scores based on sex, race, and so on. As a result, in industrial and organizational psychology and allied fields, there is a "conflict between law and science" (Arthur, Woehr, & Graziano, 2001). Therefore, until selection practices rely more heavily on sound science rather than laws regarding subgroup norms, it would seem imprudent to use personality measures for selection purposes in cases where (a) there are subgroup differences on measured variables (e.g., neuroticism, agreeableness, extroversion) and (b) there are prohibitions against the use of subgroup norms in the interpretation of scores derived from such measures. A case in point here is the use of personality measures for selection purposes.

CONCLUSIONS

In view of the fact that individuals' responses to personality measures are often influenced by situational variables, it would appear prudent not to interpret them solely in trait terms. To the degree that individuals' states (e.g., anxiety) are erroneously viewed as traits (e.g., negative affectivity), job applicants and incumbents may suffer from unfair discrimination (Stone-Romero, 1994, 2005). Thus, we urge caution in the use of such variables as neuroticism for selection purposes. In addition, we believe that HRM practitioners should greatly limit the use of other personality measures for such purposes. For example, the use of measures of extroversion for selection purposes may lead to unfair discrimination against individuals who have been socialized not to behave in an extroverted manner (e.g., Asians, Native Americans). Moreover, even if scores on personality measures were not a function of such factors as socialization and various environmental variables, they would appear to have very little value for selection purposes. A key reason for this is that because of their very low levels of criterion-related validity (Guion, 1991; Guion & Gottier, 1965; Stone-Romero, 2005) most such measures have little or no value as predictors of job success. Thus, it would appear prudent for HRM practitioners to base selection decisions on predictors of job success that have higher levels of criterion-related validity than personality measures.

REFERENCES

Ajzen, I. (1988). *Attitudes, personality, and behavior.* Chicago: Dorsey Press.
Akbar, N. (1979). African roots of black personality. In W. D. Smith, K. Burlew, W. Whitney, & M. Mosley (Eds.), *Reflections on black psychology.* Washington, DC: University Press of America.
Americans with Disabilities Act of 1990, 42 U.S.C. §12101 *et seq.*
Army Medicine. (2006). Mental Health Advisory Team III Information. Retrieved on June 1, 2006 from http:www.armymedicine.army.mil/news/mhat/mhat_iii/mhat_iii.cfm
Arthur, W., Jr., Woehr, D. J., & Graziano, W. G. (2001). Personality testing in employment settings: Problems and issues in the application of typical selection practices. *Personnel Review, 30,* 657–676.
Ashton, M. C., Jackson, D. N., Paunonen, S. V., Helmes, E., & Rothstein, M. G. (1995). The criterion validity of broad factor scales versus specific facet scales. *Journal of Research in Personality, 29,* 432–442.

Bailey, C., & Boykin, A. W. (2001). The role of task variability and home contextual factors in the academic performance and task motivation of African American elementary school children. *Journal of Negro Education, 70,* 84–95.

Bakan, D. (1966). *The duality of human existence.* Chicago: Rand McNally.

Barrick, M., & Mount, M. (1991). The Big Five personality dimensions and job performance: A meta-analysis. *Personnel Psychology, 44,* 1–26.

Barrick, M. R., & Mount, M. K. (2003). Impact of meta-analysis on understanding personality and performance relations. In K. Murphy (Ed.), *The impact of validity generalization methods on personnel selection* (pp. 197–221). Mahwah, NJ: Erlbaum.

Baskett, G. (1973). Interview decisions as determined by competency and attitude similarity. *Journal of Applied Psychology, 57,* 343–345.

Bem, S. L. (1974). The measurement of psychological androgyny. *Journal of Consulting and Clinical Psychology, 42,* 155–162.

Bishaw, A., & Iceland, J. *Poverty: 1999, Census 2000 Brief (C2KBR–19).* Washington, DC: U. S. Department of Commerce, U.S. Census Bureau.

Block, J. (1995). A contrarian view of the five-factor approach to personality description. *Psychological Bulletin, 117,* 187–215.

Boykin, A. W. (1983). The academic performance of Afro-American children. In J. Spence (Ed.), *Achievement and achievement motives* (pp. 323–371). San Francisco: Freeman.

Boykin, A. W. (1986). The Triple Quandary and the schooling of Afro-American children. In U. Neisser (Ed.), *The school achievement of minority children.* Hillsdale, NJ: Erlbaum.

Brief, A. P., Burke, M. J., George, J. M., Robinson, B. S., & Webster, J. (1988). Should negative affectivity remain an unmeasured variable in the study of job stress? *Journal of Applied Psychology, 73,* 193–198.

Burke, M. J., Brief, A. P., & George, J. M. (1993). The role of negative affectivity in understanding relations between self-reports of stressors and strains: A comment on the applied psychology literature. *Journal of Applied Psychology, 78,* 402–412.

Byrne, D. (1971). *The attraction paradigm.* New York: Academic Press.

Cable, D. M., & Judge, T. A. (1997). Interviewers' perceptions of person–organization fit and organizational selection decisions. *Journal of Applied Psychology, 82,* 546–561.

Camara, W. J., & Merenda, P. F. (2000). Using personality tests in preemployment screening: Issues raised in Soroka v. Dayton Hudson Corporation. *Psychology, Public Policy, and Law, 6*(4), 1164–1186.

Carver, C. S., & Scheier, M. F. (2004). *Perspectives on personality* (5th ed.). Boston: Pearson.

Cascio, W. F. (1998). *Applied psychology in human resource management* (5th ed.). Upper Saddle River, NJ: Prentice Hall.

Cascio, W. F., & Aguinis, H. (2005). *Applied psychology in human resource management* (6th ed.). Upper Saddle River, NJ: Pearson Prentice Hall.

Cattell, R. B., Eber, H. W., & Tatsuoka, M. M. (1977). *Handbook for the 16 personality factor questionnaire.* Champaign, IL: Institute for Personality and Ability Testing.

Chatman, J. A. (1989). Improving interactional organizational research: A model of person–organization fit. *Academy of Management Review, 14,* 333–349.

Cliffordson, C. (2002). Interviewer agreement in the judgment of empathy in selection interviews. *International Journal of Selection and Assessment, 10,* 198–205.

Cohn, S. (2000). *Race and gender discrimination at work.* Boulder, CO: Westview Press.

Contrada, R. J., Ashmore, R. D., Gary, M. L., Coups, E., Egeth, J. D., Sewell, A., et al.. (2000). Ethnicity-related sources of stress and their effects on well-being. *Current Directions in Psychological Science, 9,* 136–139.

Coon, H. M., & Kemmelmeier, M. (2001). Cultural orientations in the United States. (Re)examining differences among ethnic groups. *Journal of Cross-Cultural Psychology, 32,* 348–364.

Costa, P. T., Jr., & McCrae, R. R. (1992). The five-factor model of personality and its relevance to personality disorders. *Journal of Personality Disorders, 6,* 343–359.

Dalessio, A., & Imada, A. (1984). Relationships between interview selection decisions and perceptions of applicant similarity to an ideal employee and self: A field study. *Human Relations, 37,* 67–80.

Digman, J. M. (1990). Personality structure: Emergence of the five-factor model. *Annual Review of Psychology, 41,* 417–440.

Digman, J. M., & Inouye, J. (1986). Further specification of the five robust factors of personality. *Journal of Personality and Social Psychology, 50,* 116–123.

Dipboye, R. L. (1992). *Selection interviews: Process perspectives.* Cincinnati, OH: Southwestern.

Dohrenwend, B. P. (1975). Sociocultural and social-psychological factors in the genesis of mental disorders. *Journal of Health and Social Behavior, 16,* 365–392.

Dohrenwend, B. P. (2000). The role of adversity and stress in psychopathology: Some evidence and its implications for theory and research. *Journal of Health and Social Behavior, 41* (March), 1–19.

Dohrenwend, B. P., & Dohrenwend, B. S. (1970). Class and race as status-related sources of stress. In S. Levine & N. A. Scotch (Eds.), *Social stress* (pp. 111–140). Chicago: Aldine.

Dohrenwend, B. P., & Dohrenwend, B. S. (1974). Social and cultural influences on psychopathology. *Annual Review of Psychology, 25,* 417–452.

Dohrenwend, B. P., Levav, I., Shrout, P. E., Schwartz, S., Naveh, G., Link, B. G., et al. (1992). Socioeconomic status and psychiatric disorders: The causation–selection issue. *Science, 255,* 946–952.

DuBrin, A. J. (2004). *Applying psychology: Individual and organizational effectiveness* (6th ed.). Upper Saddle River, NJ: Prentice Hall.

Duggan, C., Sham, P., Lee, A., Minne, C., & Murray, R. (1995). Neuroticism: A vulnerability marker for depression evidence from a family study. *Journal of Affective Disorders, 35,* 139–143.

Erez, M., & Earley, P. C. (1993). *Culture, self-identity, and work.* New York: Oxford University Press.

Eysenck, H. J. (1992). Four ways five factors are not basic. *Personality and Individual Differences, 6,* 667–673.

Eysenck, H. J., & Eysenck, M. W. (1985). *Personality and individual differences: A natural science approach.* New York: Plenum.

Fay, D., & Frese, M. (2001). The concept of personal initiative: An overview of validity studies. *Human Performance, 14,* 97–124.

Fishbein, M., & Ajzen, I. (1975). *Belief, attitude, intention, and behavior: An introduction to theory and research.* Reading, MA: Addison-Wesley.

Freeman, M. A. (1997). Demographic correlates of individualism and collectivism: A study of social values in Sri Lanka. *Journal of Cross-Cultural Psychology, 28,* 321–341.

Gaines, S. O. J., Marelich, W. D., Bledsoe, K. L., & Steers, W. N. (1997). Links between race/ethnicity and cultural values as mediated by racial/ethnic identity and moderated by gender. *Journal of Personality and Social Psychology, 72,* 1460–1476.

Gay, G. (2000). *Culturally responsive teaching.* New York: Teachers College Press.

George, J. M., & Jones, G. R. (2004). Individual differences: Personality and ability. In B. M. Staw (Ed.), *Psychological dimensions of organizational behavior* (3rd ed., pp. 3–23). Upper Saddle River, NJ: Prentice Hall.

Ghiselli, E. E. (1973). The validity of occupational aptitude tests in personnel selection. *Personnel Psychology, 26,* 461–477.

Gilligan, C. (1982). *In a different voice.* Cambridge, MA: Harvard University Press.

Goffman, E. (1963). *Stigma: Notes on the management of spoiled identity.* Englewood Cliffs, NJ: Prentice-Hall.

Green, E. G. T., Deschamps, J. C., & Páez, D. (2005). Variation of individualism and collectivism within and between 20 countries: A typological analysis. *Journal of Cross-Cultural Psychology, 36,* 321–339.

Griffitt, W., & Jackson, T. (1970). Influence of information about ability and non-ability on personnel selection decisions. *Psychological Reports, 27,* 959–962.

Guion, R. M. (1991). Personnel assessment, selection, and placement. In M. D. Dunnette & L. M. Hough (Eds.), *Handbook of industrial and organizational psychology* (2nd ed., Vol. 2, pp. 327–397). Palo Alto, CA: Consulting Psychologists Press.

Guion, R. M., & Gottier, R. F. (1965). Validity of personality measures in personnel selection. *Personnel Psychology, 18,* 135–164.

Harris, M. (1989). Reconsidering the employment interview: A review of recent literature and suggestions for future research. *Personnel Psychology, 42,* 691–726.

Heine, S. J., Lehman, D. R., Markus, H. R., & Kitayama, S. (1999). Is there a universal need for positive self-regard? *Psychological Review, 106,* 766–794.

Hilliard, A. (2001). "Race," identity, hegemony, and education: What do we need to know now? In W. Watkins, J. Lewis, & V. Chou (Eds.), *Race and education.* Boston: Allyn & Bacon.

Hofstede, G. (1980). *Culture's consequences: International differences in work-related values.* Beverly Hills: Sage.

Hofstede, G. (1991). *Cultures and organizations: Software of the mind.* London: McGraw-Hill.

Hogan, R. T. (1991). Personality and personality measurement. In M. D. Dunnette & L. M. Hough (Eds.), *Handbook of industrial and organizational psychology* (2nd ed., Vol. 2, pp. 873–919). Palo Alto, CA: Consulting Psychologists Press.

Hough, L. M. (1992). The "Big Five" personality variables–construct confusion: Description versus prediction. *Human Performance, 5,* 139–155.

Hough, L. M. (1997). The millennium for personality psychology: New horizons or good old daze. *Applied Psychology: An International Review, 47,* 233–262.

Hough, L. M., Eaton, N. K., Dunnette, M. D., Kamp, J. D., & McCloy, R. A. (1990). Criterion-related validities of personality constructs and the effect of response distortion on those validities. *Journal of Applied Psychology, 75,* 581–595.

Hough, L. M., & Furnham, A. (2003). Use of personality variables in work settings. In W. C. Borman, D. R. Ilgen, & R. J. Klimoski (Eds.), *Handbook of psychology: Industrial and organizational psychology* (Vol. 12, pp. 131–169). Hoboken, NJ: Wiley.

Hough, L. M., Oswald, F. L., & Ployhart, R. E. (2001). Determinants, detection, and amelioration of adverse impact in personnel selection procedures: Issues, evidence, and lessons learned. *International Journal of Selection and Assessment, 9,* 152–194.

Hough, L. M., & Schneider, R. J. (1996). Personality traits, taxonomies, and applications in organizations. In K. Murphy (Ed.), *Individual differences and behavior in organizations* (pp. 31–88). San Francisco: Jossey Bass.

Huffcutt, A. I., Conway, J. M., Roth, P. L., & Stone, N. J. (2001). Identification and meta-analytic assessment of psychological constructs measured in employment interviews. *Journal of Applied Psychology, 86,* 897–913.

Hui, C. H., & Triandis, H. C. (1986). Individualism–collectivism: A study of cross-cultural researchers. *Journal of Cross-Cultural Psychology, 17,* 225–248.

Hwang, K. K. (2000). Chinese relationalism: Theoretical construction and methodological considerations. *Journal for the Theory of Social Behavior, 30,* 155–178.

Hwang, K. K. (2001). The deep structure of Confucianism: A social psychological approach. *Asian Philosophy, 11,* 179–204.

Iwawaki, S., Eysenck, S. B., & Eysenck, H. J. (1980). Japanese and English personality structure: A cross-cultural study. *Psychologia: An International Journal of Psychology in the Orient, 23,* 195–205.

Jackson, D. N. (1984). *Personality Research Form Manual* (3rd ed). Port Huron, MI: Research Psychologists Press.

Jackson, D. N., Paunonen, S. V., Fraboni, M., & Goffin, R. D. (1996). A Five-Factor versus Six-Factor model of personality structure. *Personality and Individual Differences, 20,* 33–45.

Kahn, R. L., Wolfe, D. M., Quinn, R. P., Snoek, J. D., & Rosenthal, R. A. (1964). *Organizational stress: Studies in role conflict and ambiguity.* New York, NY: Wiley.

Kashima, Y., Yamaguchi, S., Kim, U., Choi, S.-C., Gelfand, M. J., & Yuki, M. (1995). Culture, gender, and self: A perspective from individualism–collectivism research. *Journal of Personality and Social Psychology, 69,* 925–937.

Katz, D., & Kahn, R. L. (1978). *The social psychology of organizations* (2nd ed.). New York: Wiley.

Kendler, K. S., Neale, M. C., Kessler, R. C., Heath, A. C., & Eaves, L. J. (1993). A longitudinal twin study of personality and major depression in women. *Archives of General Psychiatry, 50,* 843–852.

Kerbo, H. R. (1983). *Social stratification and inequality: Class conflict in the United States.* New York: McGraw-Hill.

Kessler, R. C., Price, R. H., & Wortman, C. B. (1985). Social factors in psychopathology: Stress, social support, and coping processes. *Annual Review of Psychology, 36*, 531–572.

Kohn, M., & Schooler, C. (1983). *Work and personality: An inquiry into the impact of social stratification*. Norwood, NJ: Ablex.

Konrad, A. M., Prasad, P., & Pringle, K. K. (2006). *Handbook of workplace diversity*. Thousand Oaks, CA: Sage.

Kristof-Brown, A. L. (2000). Perceived applicant fit: Distinguishing between recruiters' perceptions of person–job and person–organization fit. *Personnel Psychology, 53*, 643–671.

Kristof-Brown, A. L. (2007a). Person–environment fit. In S. G. Rogelberg (Ed.), *Encyclopedia of industrial and organizational psychology* (Vol. 2, pp. 615–618). Thousand Oaks, CA: Sage.

Kristof-Brown, A. L. (2007b). Person–job fit. In S. G. Rogelberg (Ed.), *Encyclopedia of industrial and organizational psychology* (Vol. 2, pp. 618–620). Thousand Oaks, CA: Sage.

Kristof-Brown, A. L. (2007c). Person–organization fit. In S. G. Rogelberg (Ed.), *Encyclopedia of industrial and organizational psychology* (Vol. 2, pp. 620–621). Thousand Oaks, CA: Sage.

Leighton, D., & Kluckholn, C. (1947). *Children of the people*. Cambridge, MA: Harvard University Press.

Levin, I., & Stokes, J. P. (1989). Dispositional approach to job satisfaction: Role of negative affectivity. *Journal of Applied Psychology, 74*, 752–758.

Lin, T., Dobbins, G. H., & Farh, J. (1992). A field study of race and age similarity effect on interview ratings in conventional and situational interviews. *Journal of Applied Psychology, 77*, 363–371.

Link, B. G., Dohrenwend, B. P., & Skodol, A. E. (1986). Socio-economic status and schizophrenia: Noisome occupational characteristics as a risk factor. *American Sociological Review, 51*, 242–258.

Link, B. G., Lennon, M. C., & Dohrenwend, B. P. (1993). Socioeconomic status and depression: The role of occupations involving direction, control, and planning. *American Journal of Sociology, 98*, 1351–1387.

Liu, I. (1986). Chinese cognition. In M. H. Bond (Ed.), *The psychology of the Chinese people* (pp. 73–105). New York: Oxford University Press.

Lofquist, L. H. & Dawis, R. V. (1969). *Adjustment to work*. New York: Appleton-Century-Crofts.

Loo, R., & Shiomi, K. (1982). The Eysenck personality scores of Japanese and Canadian undergraduates. *Journal of Social Psychology, 118*(1), 3–9.

Lorenzi-Cioldi, F., & Dafflon, A.-C. (1998). Norme individuelle et norme collective, I: Representations du genre dans une société individualiste [Individual norms and collective norms, I: Representations of gender in an individualist society]. *Swiss Journal of Psychology, 57*, 124–137.

McAdams, D. P. (1992). The five-factor model in personality: A critical appraisal. *Journal of Personality, 60*, 329–361.

McCrae, R. R., & Costa, P. T., Jr. (1985). Updating Norman's "adequate taxonomy": Intelligence and personality dimensions in natural language and in questionnaires. *Journal of Personality and Social Psychology, 49*, 710–721.

McCrae, R. R., & Costa, P. T., Jr. (1987). Validation of the five-factor model across instruments and observers. *Journal of Personality and Social Psychology, 52*, 81–90.

Markus, H. R., & Kitayama, S. (1991). Culture and the self: Implications for cognition, emotion, and motivation. *Psychological Review, 98,* 224–253.

Marshall, R. (1997). Variances in levels of individualism across two cultures and three social classes. *Journal of Cross-Cultural Psychology, 28,* 430–495.

Matsumoto, D., Kudoh, T., & Takeuchi, S. (1996). Changing patterns of individualism and collectivism in the United States and Japan. *Culture and Psychology, 2,* 77–107.

Mischel, W. (1977). The interaction of person and situation. In D. Magnusson & N. S. Endler (Eds.), *Personality at the crossroads: Current issues in interactional psychology* (pp. 333–352). Hillsdale, NJ: Erlbaum.

Mishra, R. C. (1994). Individualist and collectivist orientation across generations. In U. Kim, H. C. Triandis, C. Kagitçibasi, S.-C. Choi, & G. Yoon (Eds.), *Individualism and collectivism: Theory, method, and applications* (pp. 225–238). Thousand Oaks, CA: Sage.

Moemeka, A. A. (1998). Communalism as a fundamental dimension of culture. *Journal of Communication, 48,* 118–141.

Moscoso, S. (2000). A review of validity evidence, adverse impact, and applicant reactions. *International Journal of Selection and Assessment, 8,* 237–247.

Newcomb, T. M. (1956). The prediction of interpersonal attraction. *American Psychologist, 11,* 575–586.

Oyserman, D., Coon, H. M., & Kemmelmeier, M. (2002). Rethinking individualism and collectivism: Evaluation of theoretical assumptions and meta-analyses. *Psychological Bulletin, 128,* 3–72.

Paunonen, S. V. (1998). Hierarchical organization of personality and prediction of behavior. *Journal of Personality and Social Psychology, 74,* 538–556.

Pervin, L. A. (1994). A critical analysis of current trait theory. *Psychological Inquiry, 5,* 103–113.

Peters, L., & Terborg, J. (1975). The effects of temporal placement of unfavorable information and of attitude similarity on personnel selections decisions. *Organizational Behavior and Human Performance, 13,* 279–293.

Rand, T., & Wexley, K. (1975). Demonstration of the effects, "similar to me," in simulated employment interviews. *Psychological Reports, 36,* 535–544.

Roe, A. (1956). *The psychology of occupations.* New York: Wiley.

Sacco, J. M., Scheu, C. R., Ryan, A. M., & Schmitt, N. (2003). An investigation of race and sex similarity effects in interviews: A multilevel approach to relational demography. *Journal of Applied Psychology, 88,* 852–865.

Sackett, P. R., & Ellingson, J. E. (1997). The effects of forming multi-predictor composites on group differences and adverse impact. *Personnel Psychology, 50,* 707–721.

Sackett, P. R., & Wilk, S. L. (1994). Within-group norming and other forms of score adjustment in preemployment testing. *American Psychologist, 49,* 929–954.

Sampson, E. E. (1988). The debate on individualism: Indigenous psychologies of the individual and their role in personal and societal functioning. *American Psychologist, 43,* 15–22.

Schein, E. (1990). *Organizational culture and leadership.* San Francisco: Jossey-Bass.

Schneider, B. (1987). The people make the place. *Personnel Psychology, 40,* 437–453.

Sears, G. J., & Rowe, P. M. (2003). A personality-based similar-to-me effect in the employment interview: Conscientiousness, affect-versus competence-mediated interpretations, and the role of job relevance. *Canadian Journal of Behavioural Science, 35,* 13–24.

Sen, S., Nesse, R. M., & Stoltenberg, S. F. (2003). A BDNF coding variant associated with the NEO personality inventory domain neuroticism: A risk factor for depression. *Neuropsychopharmacology, 28,* 397–401.

Singelis, T. M. (1994). The measurement of independent and interdependent self-construals. *Personality and Social Psychology Bulletin, 20,* 580–591.

Stockdale, M. S., & Crosby, F. J. (2004). *The psychology and management of workplace diversity.* Malden, MA: Blackwell.

Stone, E. F., & Stone, D. L. (1990). Privacy in organizations: Theoretical issues, research findings, and protection strategies. In G. R. Ferris & K. M. Rowland (Eds.), *Research in personnel and human resources management,* Vol. 8 (pp. 349–411) Greenwich, CT: JAI Press.

Stone, D. L., & Stone-Romero, E. F. (2004). The influence of culture on role-taking in culturally diverse organizations. In M. S. Stockdale & F. J. Crosby (Eds.), *The psychology and management of workplace diversity* (pp. 78–99). Malden, MA: Blackwell.

Stone, E. F., Stone, D. L., & Dipboye, R. L. (1992). Stigmas in organizations: Race, handicaps, and physical attractiveness. In K. Kelley (Ed.), *Issues, theory, and research in industrial/organizational psychology* (pp. 385–457). Amsterdam: Elsevier Science.

Stone-Romero, E. F. (1994). Construct validity issues in organizational behavior research. In J. Greenberg (Ed.), *Organizational behavior: The state of the science* (pp. 155–179). Hillsdale, NJ: Erlbaum.

Stone-Romero, E. F. (2005). Personality-based stigmas and unfair discrimination in work organizations. In R. L. Dipboye & A. Colella (Eds.), *Discrimination at work: The psychological and organizational bases* (pp. 255–280). Mahwah, NJ: Erlbaum.

Stone-Romero, E. F., & Stone, D. L. (1998). Religious and moral influences on work-related values and work quality. In D. Fedor & S. Ganoush (Eds.), *Advances in the management of organizational quality* (Vol. 3, pp. 185–285). Greenwich, CT: JAI Press.

Stone-Romero, E. F., & Stone, D. L. (2002). Cross-cultural differences in responses to feedback. *Research in Personnel and Human Resource Management, 21,* 275–331.

Stone-Romero, E. F., & Stone, D. L. (2005). How do organizational justice concepts relate to discrimination and prejudice? In J. Greenberg & J. A. Colquitt (Eds.), *Handbook of organizational justice* (pp. 439–467). Mahwah, NJ: Erlbaum.

Stone-Romero, E. F., & Stone, D. L. (2007). Cognitive, affective, and cultural influences on stigmatization and its impact on human resource management processes and practices. *Research in Personnel and Human Resource Management, 26,* 117–167.

Stone-Romero, E. F., Stone, D. L., & Hyatt, D. (2003). Personnel selection procedures and invasion of privacy. *Journal of Social Issues, 59,* 343–368.

Stone-Romero, E. F., Stone, D. L., & Salas, E. (2003). The influence of culture on role conceptions and role behavior in organizations. *Applied Psychology: An International Review, 52,* 328–362.

Strong, E. K. (1943). *Vocational interests of men and women.* Stanford, CA: Stanford University Press.

Super, D. E., & Bohn, M. J. (1970). *Occupational psychology*. Belmont, CA: Wadsworth.

Taylor, S. E., Repetti, R. L., & Seeman, T. (1997). Health psychology: What is an unhealthy environment and how does it get under the skin? *Annual Review of Psychology, 48*, 411–447.

Tellegen, A. (1993). Folk concepts and psychological concepts of personality and personality disorder. *Psychological Inquiry, 4*, 122–130.

Tett, R., Jackson, D., & Rothstein, M. (1991). Personality measures as predictors of performance: A meta-analytic review. *Personnel Psychology, 44*, 703–742.

Triandis, H. C. (1989). The self and social behavior in different cultural contexts. *Psychological Review, 96*, 506–520.

Triandis, H. C. (1995). *Individualism & collectivism*. Boulder, CO: Westview Press.

Triandis, H. C., & Wasti, A. (2007). Culture. In D. Stone & E. F. Stone-Romero (Eds.), *The influence of culture on human resource management processes and practices* (pp. 1–24). New York: Taylor and Francis.

Trice, H., & Beyer, J. (1993). *The cultures of work organizations*. Upper Saddle River, NJ: Prentice-Hall.

Trompenaars, F., & Hampden-Turner, C. (1998). *Riding the waves of culture: Understanding cultural diversity in global business*. New York: McGraw-Hill.

Tyler, K. M., Boykin, A. W., Boelter, C. M., & Dillihunt, M. L. (2005). Examining Mainstream and Afro-Cultural Value Socialization in African American Households. *Journal of Black Psychology, 31*, 291–311.

U. S. Equal Employment Opportunity Commission, U. S. Civil Service Commission, U. S. Department of Labor, and U. S. Department of Justice. (1978). Uniform guidelines on employee selection procedures. *Federal Register, 43*(166), 38295–38309.

Vroom, V. H. (1964). *Work and motivation*. New York: Wiley.

Watson, D., & Clark, L. A. (1984). Negative affectivity: The disposition to experience aversive emotional states. *Psychological Bulletin, 96*, 465–490.

Wiggins, J. S., & Pincus, A. L. (1992). Personality: Structure and assessment. *Annual Review of Psychology, 43*, 473–504.

Williams, D. R. (1990). Socioeconomic differentials in health: A review and redirection. *Social Psychology Quarterly, 53*, 81–99.

Williams, D. R., & Collins, C. (1995). U.S. socioeconomic and racial differences in health: Patterns and explanations. *Annual Review of Sociology, 21*, 349–386.

Williams, D. R., & Williams-Morris, R. (2000). Racism and mental health: The African American experience. *Ethnicity & Health, 5*, 243–268.

Williams, J. E., & Best, D. L. (1982). *Measuring sex stereotypes: A thirty-nation study*. Beverly Hills, CA: Sage.

Wink, P. (1997). Beyond ethnic differences: Contextualizing the influence of ethnicity and individualism and collectivism. *Journal of Social Issues, 53*, 329–350.

Yu, Y., & Williams, D. R. (1999). Socioeconomic status and mental health. In C. S. Aneshensel & J. C. Phelan (Eds.), *Handbook of the sociology of mental health* (pp. 151–166). New York: Plenum.

Zuckerman, M. (1992). What is a basic factor and which factors are basic? Turtles all the way down. *Personality and Individual Differences, 13*, 675–682.

5

Designing and Delivering Training for Multicultural Interactions in Organizations

EDUARDO SALAS, KATHERINE A. WILSON, AND REBECCA LYONS
University of Central Florida

The United States has often been referred to as a melting pot, consisting of individuals from numerous cultures, backgrounds, and religions. With the expansion of over 10,000 companies worldwide to global markets (Adler, 1997), a multicultural workforce is inevitable. This shift is demonstrated by the growing popularity of new technologies such as distributed capabilities (e.g., telecommuting), which improve the chances of interaction of employees from different national cultures. To add further complexity, organizations' use of teams as a means of improving organizational outcomes is increasing. As such, the likelihood of multicultural teams (i.e., two or more individuals from at least two different national cultures who must work interdependently to reach the team's goals) being developed in organizations is greater than ever (Dwyer, Engardio, Schiller, & Reed, 1994).

Research abounds about training individuals and teams to be successful in the workplace (see Salas & Cannon-Bowers, 2001). We know what to do; we know what it takes to make such teams effective. Although this statement is true when referring to homogeneous interactions (i.e., interactions between employees of the same national culture), less is known about heterogeneous interactions (i.e., interactions between employees of multiple national cultures) and about training employees to overcome cultural challenges. Beyond the obvious external differences between employees from different cultures (e.g., physical appearance, verbal accent), there are also internal differences (e.g., cognitive, attitudinal) that will likely influence these interactions in positive or negative ways. The purpose of this chapter is to discuss how training should be designed and delivered to improve multicultural interactions. Our review of the literature indicated a number of terms used to describe teams consisting of members from multiple cultures—specifically, multicultural, multinational, and cross-cultural. For the purpose of this chapter, we consider these terms to be synonymous, and they may be used interchangeably throughout.

WHY SHOULD ORGANIZATIONS CARE ABOUT MULTICULTURALISM?

Culture provides a blueprint to show individuals how to perceive, think, and act in a social environment. Klein (2004) argues that individuals from different cultures view the world around them through different cultural lenses. The lens serves to filter and organize information received from others and perceived in the environment, helps make sense of that information, frames social interactions and communications, structures planning, and impacts adaptation to changing situations. Members of the same national culture often share the same lens, thus providing a common ground for social interactions (e.g., teams in organizations). When members of multiple cultures are organized together, how they see the situation will differ (sometimes greatly); this potentially leads to conflict, dissonance, and ultimately team process losses (see Table 5.1). For example, the importance of understanding multiculturalism in the workplace has also been emphasized by Stone-Romero, Stone, and Salas (2003), who state that individuals have differing work scripts (i.e., ideas about the appropriate sequence of events within a given situation) and behavioral expectations based on cultural differences. This will ultimately impact the organization in that goals may not be reached (e.g., loss of productivity and profits, accidents in the workplace, failed mergers). In this context, training can be applied to help individuals understand cultural differences that may be present in the work scripts and to help smooth differences in organizational expectations.

To best understand the impact of multiculturalism on an organization and the resultant need for training, let us first begin with several examples of how multiculturalism has affected performance in several different industries. On May 7, 1998, it was announced that America's third largest automobile manufacturer, Chrysler Corporation, and Germany's Daimler-Benz AG would merge to form Daimler-Chrysler, thus becoming the fifth largest automobile manufacturer in the world (Schulten, 1998). With combined annual revenues of around $130 billion and over 420,000 employees, the success of the merger was imperative. Successful integration of the two culturally different teams was the responsibility of upper-level managers from both companies (Kreitner & Kinicki, 2001). The process of becoming acquainted started across the waters, where in their homelands, each team began to learn about the other's culture. Teams took cultural awareness and language classes to better understand the other's language, business, and social behaviors. Initially, team meetings between the companies were strained due to differences in work habits—Germans preferred to lay out detailed plans before making decisions, and Americans preferred a quicker, trial-and-error method. From the start, the two teams began to understand each other's decision-making styles and even attempted to try each other's approaches. The merger of Daimler-Chrysler was, overall, a success. Credited to their success was that the teams surrounded themselves with each other's culture.

Although the merger of Daimler-Chrysler has seemed to encourage exploration of divergent cultures, interactions at the Russian space station Mir illustrate a contrasting case study. In 1997, nearly 2 years after the first American astronaut boarded Mir, the fourth astronaut assigned to the space station departed the Kennedy Space Center for his 4-month mission (Burrough, 1998). Unlike his predecessors, who remained deferential to the Russian crew members, this astronaut was more independent and not as "easygoing." His Russian counterparts described him as not being a "team player" and stated that he could not "work as a part of some collective family" (p. 15). It appeared that the collectivist values of the Russians clashed with the individualistic values of the American, creating strain among the crew members. This team was not prepared for their cultural differences, and thus performance was hindered.

Finally, the impact of culture on organizations can have catastrophic consequences. Consider Avianca Flight 52, which crashed because of fuel exhaustion and resulted in the deaths of 73 passengers and crew members. Failures in teamwork due in part to national culture were cited as probable causes of this accident (Helmreich, 1994). In other words, the cultural values of the Colombian crew (i.e., high collectivism and high power distance; Hofstede, 1980) may have put the flight in jeopardy. Barriers to communication resulted in the crew not properly stating the extent of the low fuel status to air traffic control. Specifically, those from collectivist cultures are not comfortable "standing out," and it is believed that for this reason the crew did not want to request that their aircraft be landed before others despite their low fuel state. Furthermore, the high power distance indicative of the Colombian crew may have prevented the first officer from expressing

TABLE 5.1 Process gains and losses of multicultural interactions (expanded from Adler, 1997)

Process Gains	Process Losses
Diversity results in:	**Diversity results in:**
Greater representation of cultural values (Ilgen et al., 1997)	Lack of cohesion (Jackson, 1992; Katz et al., 1958)
Greater creativity (Adler, 1997)	Mistrust
Wider range of perspectives (Watson et al., 1993)	• Lower interpersonal attractiveness
More and better ideas (Adler, 1991; Daily et al., 1996; Thomas, 1999)	• Use of inappropriate stereotyping (initially; Horenczyk & Bekerman, 1997)
Less groupthink (Ilgen et al., 1997; Janis, 1972)	• More within-culture conversations
Better problem definition (Adler, 1997)	• Less trusting (Triandis, 2000; Distefano & Maznevski, 2000)
More alternative ideas (Daily et al., 1996)	Difficulty communicating (Thomas, 1999; Steiner, 1972)
Better solutions (Hoffman & Maier, 1961)	• Less contribution from minorities (Kirchmeyer & Cohen, 1992)
Better/higher quality decisions (Hoffman & Maier, 1961)	• Lower communication competence (Kirchmeyer, 1993)
	Miscommunication
	• Slower speech: Nonnative speakers and translation problems (Adler, 1997)
	• Decreased accuracy (Adler, 1997)
	• Less information shared/transmitted (Ilgen et al., 1997; Li, 1999)
	• 50% of information lost in transmission (Li, 1999)
	Increased stress
	• More counterproductive behavior (Hayles, 1982 as cited in Adler, 1997)
	• Less disagreement on content
	• Tension
	Difficulty leading (Salas et al., 2004)
	• Status hierarchy (Harrison, McKinnon, Wu, & Chow, 2000)

Diversity requires understanding others':
Ideas (Adler, 1997)
Meanings (Adler, 1997)
Arguments (Adler, 1997)
Outgroup members perceived as more similar
(Horenczyk & Bekerman, 1997)

Teams succeed at: (Watson et al., 1993)
Simple tasks
• Increased effectiveness and productivity
Complex tasks if established for some time
(Thomas, 1999)

Teams have difficulty:
Validating ideas and people (Adler, 1997)
Agreeing when agreement is needed (Adler, 1997)
Gaining consensus on decisions (Argote & McGrath, 1993; Watson et al., 1993)
Taking concerted action (Adler, 1997)
Overcoming stereotypes (Nachbar & Lause, 1992)
Coordinating and cooperating (Argote & McGrath, 1993)
Identifying problems (Ilgen et al., 1997)
Creating a shared view of a situation/problem (Ilgen et al., 1997)
On complex tasks
• Process loss, at least initially (Thomas, 1999; Watson et al., 1993)
• Decreased efficiency, effectiveness, and productivity (Adler, 1997)

Note. Expanded from Adler, N. J. (1997). International dimensions of organizational behavior (3rd ed.). Cincinnati, OH: International Thomson.

concerns over the low fuel state of the aircraft and encouraging the captain to declare an emergency.

Although the decisions and actions made by teams in many organizations may not be life-and-death as in the last example, the barriers for multicultural team members (e.g., communication, cooperation) are similar. Their impact on organizational outcomes, such as profitability and safety, make the need to prepare team members (e.g., through training) for multicultural interactions imperative.

If the challenges faced by multicultural teams can be overcome (e.g., communication barriers), and team members can see the world more similarly (or at a minimum understand and respect where others are coming from), there are many advantages to using multicultural teams to achieve organizational outcomes (e.g., expanded pool of skills, values, and perspectives; see Table 5.1). But Helmreich and Merritt (1998) found that team members feel that multicultural interactions are challenging and frustrating more often than they are rewarding. It is further stated that multicultural teams result in difficulties communicating, misunderstandings, and conflict, and additional effort to be understood (Helmreich, 2000). But this is not always the case. At least initially, multicultural teams may result in a process loss (e.g., Thomas, 1999), and it is likely the case that the effectiveness of multicultural teams depends on the task at hand. For example, it has been argued that multicultural teams performing complex tasks suffer from process losses (Adler, 1997; Thomas, 1999; Watson, Kumar, & Michaelsen, 1993). Researchers suggest that there is a loss of productivity, efficiency, and effectiveness. Conversely, research has indicated that multicultural teams develop more and better ideas covering a wider range of perspectives than do homogeneous teams, suggesting that multicultural teams may be more suitable for tasks requiring creativity (Adler, 1997; Daily, Whatley, Ash, & Steiner, 1996; Thomas, 1999; Watson et al., 1993).

HOW ARE ORGANIZATIONS PREPARING THEIR WORKFORCES?

Training in organizations is big business; some estimate it to be a $250 billion industry (American Society for Training and Development, 2005). Since the 1970s, diversity has been addressed in many organizations, primarily through training (Caudron, 1993). Based on the literature, a majority of the training programs offered in organizations focuses on training the individual, not the team (Bhawuk & Brislin, 2000; Deshpande & Viswesvaran, 1992). Additionally, diversity training efforts are very broad and teach employees about a multitude of individual differences in the organization (e.g., age, gender, race, ethnicity). All these characteristics may impact performance in organizations, but a much larger issue is that of national culture, which should be individually addressed. Furthermore, training tends to focus on changing the knowledge and attitudes of employees (e.g., awareness training, culture assimilator training) rather than providing the skills needed to effectively perform in a multicultural/national environment (Scott & Meyer, 1991).

Cross-cultural training is the most common strategy used by organizations to prepare their workforces for multicultural operations. Littrell and colleagues (2005, 2006) recently conducted a review of 25 years of cross-cultural training in organizations. They found that a great number of studies focused on expatriate preparation for overseas operations and that successful training programs used multiple strategies (i.e., attribution training, interaction training, language training, etc.) incorporating various combinations of informational and experiential (i.e., practice-based) learning opportunities. However, it has been estimated that U.S. organizations lose more than $2 billion each year as a result of failed overseas assignments (e.g., expatriates; Noe, 2002). One of the primary reasons cited for these failures is a lack of cultural preparation. Organizations spend more time and effort providing employees with technical skills rather than the interpersonal skills they will need to interact with multicultural personnel.

In addition, multicultural training typically focuses on Hofstede's (1980) cultural dimensions (i.e., individualism–collectivism, high–low power distance, high–low uncertainty avoidance, and masculinity–femininity). A recent review found 180 studies that used Hofstede's cultural values framework; however, the authors of the review argue that this framework is "fragmented, redundant, and overly reliant on certain levels of analysis and direction of effects" (Kirkman, Lowe, & Gibson, 2006). Furthermore, a number of dimensions tap the more cognitive functions of individuals (e.g., analytic–holistic reasoning, Ji, Peng, & Nisbett, 2000; high–low context, Hodgetts & Luthans, 2000; Triandis, 2000) that also likely influence multicultural interactions.

Further complicating the issue is that many consultants claim to be experts in diversity and training for diversity and offer to improve the issues caused by diversity in organizations (Caudron, 1993). However, many of these consultants apply "quick fixes" to the diversity problems in these organizations. In an effort to overcome the difficulties faced in many organizations, several large U.S. companies have determined that "diversity is a long-term process, not a program" (Caudron, 1993, p. 54). In addition to developing diversity training programs, these organizations developed strategies such as diversity councils to monitor the company's diversity efforts, employee networks to address concerns of employees and to support them, and accountability techniques to hold managers accountable for hindering diversity efforts. However, like the diversity training programs mentioned previously, a majority of these diversity strategies have focused on the individual worker, not the team.

We did find one company that integrated team building strategies within its current diversity training program and another that developed self-managed, cross-functional work teams to handle issues more directly. But the bottom line is that organizations are not addressing multicultural issues appropriately—especially when coordination is needed among individuals from diverse cultures (Caudron, 1993). Individual training is a first step, but it is not enough to improve the competencies important for multicultural interactions. Furthermore, the design and delivery of training needs to be based on the science of training and learning. It cannot be put together in a day or taken off the shelf. Multicultural training must be designed (like any other training system) systematically and with specific, multicultural, and multilevel outcomes in mind. Until then, multicultural training and subsequent multicultural interactions in organizations are not likely to be efficient or effective. We next discuss how to design training systems to improve multicultural interactions.

HOW SHOULD TRAINING BE DESIGNED TO IMPROVE MULTICULTURAL INTERACTIONS?

The first problem we have identified is that organizations do not define clearly the purpose or learning outcomes of multicultural training. The most common focus is on training expatriates about the foreign culture's beliefs and values, helping the expatriate and his or her family become accustomed to the new country, and teaching them the appropriate behaviors for adapting to that culture. Instead, multicultural training should focus beyond awareness of a country's culture to ways that expatriates might best interact, behave, think, and feel in a collaborative environment. We found one such definition that encompassed a more complete picture. Paige and Martin (1983) best define cross- or multicultural training as "those educative processes that are designed to promote intercultural learning, by which we mean the acquisition of behavioral, cognitive and affective competencies associated with effective interaction across cultures" (p. 36). Therefore, the goal of multicultural training should be more than just the acquisition of information, it should include changing trainees' attitudes towards different cultures, which ultimately affects their behaviors (Bhagat & Prien, 1996).

Once multicultural training is appropriately defined, it must be designed, developed, implemented, and evaluated appropriately. A host of such training literature is available to organizations. A thorough explanation of this is beyond the scope of this chapter, so we encourage the reader to seek several outside resources—namely, Goldstein (1993), Goldstein and Ford (2002), and Salas and Cannon-Bowers (1997, 2000, 2001). We note that though these resources apply to designing and developing training programs in general, not multicultural training specifically, the steps are the same. What differs, of course, is the content, the delivery mechanisms, and the learning outcomes incorporated into the training program. In general, when designing a training program, whether multicultural or other, it is important, as noted, that the science of learning and training be used as guidance. Using sound theoretical underpinnings, instructional strategies should be developed using available tools (e.g., needs analysis), incorporating delivery methods (i.e., information- and/or practice-based), and focusing on relevant content (i.e., multicultural competencies) specific to the needs of an organization (see Salas & Cannon-Bowers, 1997, 2001, for more information). We cannot forget that learning is a behavioral and cognitive event. Therefore, training is optimized when multiple methods are used in the process (Salas & Cannon-Bowers, 1997). Specifically, trainees learn when they are (a) presented with information about the task, (b) shown demonstrations (i.e., examples) of effective and ineffective performance, (c) provided opportunities to practice applying knowledge and skills learned, and (d) given constructive, timely, and diagnostic feedback during and after task performance (Salas & Cannon-Bowers, 2000). Next, multicultural training needs to create a learning environment where trainees acquire the necessary knowledge (i.e., what and how to think), skills (i.e., what and how to do), and attitudes (i.e., what to feel); practice applying the learned knowledge, skills, and attitudes (KSAs); and receive feedback regarding their performance so that they can interact appropriately in a multicultural work environment. Third, in line with Paige and Martin's (1983) definition of cross-cultural training, training must prepare individuals to not only work in a different cultural setting but also to interact with others within their own cultural environment who are culturally different. We think this is important, and more organizations should broaden the purpose of their multicultural training programs. The next sections focus on developing the necessary competencies to improve multicultural interactions in organizations as well as how to maintain these competencies over time.

PRACTICE-BASED APPROACHES

Germans are rude. Americans are arrogant. Asians are nerds. These are just a few of the stereotypes that individuals may hold towards members of other cultures. However, not all Germans are rude, Americans arrogant, or Asians nerds. Each of us carries stereotypes, whether consciously or subconsciously, based on our previous experiences or media-based cultural portrayals, and these stereotypes can potentially impact our interactions with other cultures. The examples discussed at the beginning of this chapter illustrate the importance of understanding diverse cultures and overcoming stereotypes in organizations. For multicultural interactions to be successful, it is important that we understand the culture, its norms, and what is acceptable and what is not.

To develop the knowledge, skills, and attitudes necessary for multicultural interactions, training must first take us back to the basics—defining the culture(s), learning about our own culture and others, helping us understand our own feelings, concerns, emotions, and unconscious responses to culture, and helping us recognize similarities and differences between our culture and others (Bennet, 1986; Bussema & Nemec, 2006). This discussion will help individuals to develop a common understanding of cultural similarities, differences, and biases (i.e., cultural awareness), leading to greater tolerance and behavioral flexibility. Once a common understanding has been developed, training can begin to focus on aspects of culture that relate to the organization's needs specifically (e.g., cultures involved in an upcoming merger).

It should be no surprise that education is critical in overcoming biases. Although it may not be possible to strip individuals of all their biases, providing them with an accurate and complete knowledge base from which to make their judgments is a step in the right direction. It is important when providing cultural knowledge that the correct and most appropriate delivery methods be used. Common delivery methods include lectures, workbooks, slide presentations, computer-based instruction, and demonstration videos (Salas & Cannon-Bowers, 1997). These methods of presentation are easy to implement, flexible, and affordable, but they can be criticized for restricting the learner to a passive role (Bhawuk & Brislin, 2000). Therefore, we next discuss practice-based strategies that might be used to improve multicultural interactions.

As noted, providing employees with the knowledge about cultural differences and challenges is not enough. Employees must also be provided with the skills—acquire a behavioral repertoire—to overcome these challenges. Necessary (but not sufficient) for learning is the ability to practice the needed KSAs. Practice provides trainees with the opportunity to apply the knowledge and skills learned. As practice alone is not enough, it must be guided (by feedback) to help trainees understand, organize, and assimilate culturally focused KSAs.

A number of practice strategies can be used to prepare trainees for multicultural interactions (e.g., simulations, role-play exercises, critical incidents). One of the most common training strategies used to allow trainees to develop requisite competencies through practice is scenario-based training (SBT). (SBT has not often been applied in multicultural training.) Unique to this approach is that learning opportunities are embedded within the scenarios (e.g., based on critical incidents) where "trigger events" elicit the targeted behaviors and thus provide trainees with a meaningful framework by which to learn (Fowlkes, Dwyer, Oser, & Salas, 1998; Salas & Cannon-Bowers, 2000). Practice opportunities can range from low-fidelity role-playing exercises (e.g., reenactment of a multicultural interaction) to computer-based games or simulations to high-fidelity simulations (e.g., simulators). Simulations (sometimes characterized as synthetic learning environments) are often used as an instructional strategy as they offer a safe environment in which to practice complex and dynamic KSAs necessary for otherwise stressful environments. For example, Fowler (1994) conducted a review of diversity training and found that simulations (i.e., computer-based games) were

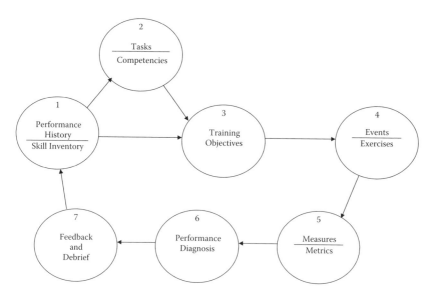

Figure 5.1   Life cycle of scenario-based training (adapted from Oser et al., 1999).

useful at training practical skills necessary for multicultural interactions. One of the benefits of SBT, especially for fostering multicultural interactions, is that it provides instructional designers with a valuable, principled tool set to achieve training goals. It offers a systematic way to learn through scenario generation, "trigger events", performance metrics, performance assessment, and feedback. In SBT, the scenario is the "curriculum" and creates an environment such that the trainee is guided, informed, diagnosed, and given feedback related to the learning outcomes. Thus, the cycle presented here is built around developing these scenarios and providing feedback to improve performance. Figure 5.1 provides a graphical depiction of the SBT cycle (see Oser, Cannon-Bowers, Salas, & Dwyer, 1999, and Cannon-Bowers, Burns, Salas, & Pruitt, 1998, for a more detailed discussion).

As previously mentioned, the presentation of critical incidents to trainees is a form of practice within scenario-based training. These incidents depict a number of real-world, multicultural interactions that have led to a negative outcome (Bhawuk & Brislin, 2000). Trainees review the incidents and then apply their knowledge and skills to respond to a particular question related to the incident (e.g., What would the appropriate response have been to this conflict? What would you have done differently?). To appropriately respond, trainees must reflect on the incident to ensure understanding before making a response. Trainees can be given two options to respond—they can generate their own response or they can be provided with a number of potential response choices from which they can choose the best one. After trainees make their decision, feedback and explanations are provided as to why each choice was correct or incorrect. This feedback is critical, because it is likely that individuals from different cultures will choose different responses.

In addition to critical incidents, scenario-based training can encompass role playing exercises to help trainees practice what they have learned (Salas & Cannon-Bowers, 1997). Role playing begins with trainees observing situations where multicultural interactions were successful (e.g., successfully managed a conflict). Next trainees are provided the opportunity to participate in realistic situations similar to those that they have observed. Role playing can take place in the classroom or as a part of a simulation (e.g., computer-based; high-fidelity).

Finally, storytelling is a form of practice that is useful in training for multicultural interactions. Storytelling is an interactive technique that involves the trainer or trainees sharing their stories surrounding a given topic (Denning, 2004; 2006) (in this case, multicultural interactions). The events are then discussed as a group—what went well, what went wrong, what should have been done. Storytelling is beneficial in that trainees are able to envision themselves in a situation and can relate to the information presented, which is important to retention. This technique can also, for example, be combined with scenario-based training in that the story told could lead to a role-playing exercise. Unlike the scenario-based training techniques discussed above, storytelling is not scripted. Therefore, it is important that the trainer be able to keep the training focused (don't let stories stray far off topic). It is also important that certain rules be established. For example, as multicultural issues may be a sensitive topic, trainees must be respectful when telling a story, avoiding the use of harsh or derogatory language.

HOW DO WE ENSURE MULTICULTURAL KSAS ARE MAINTAINED AT WORK?

Designing an effective multicultural training program and ensuring the transfer of trained competencies to the work environment is essential to effective multicultural development, but these are not the only necessary solutions. Multicultural training should not be a one time event. Despite effective initial training, trainees undergo skill decay over time. Skill decay is the gradual loss of trained skills or knowledge over extended periods of nonuse. Despite an organization's best efforts, some degree of skill decay is inevitable; however, a number of variables may moderate the relationship between time and skill loss. Arthur and Bennett (1998) summarized some of the most relevant moderators, including: the degree of overlearning (Driskell, Willis, & Copper, 1992; Schendal & Hagman, 1982), various task characteristics (e.g., closed-looped versus open-looped tasks, physical versus cognitive tasks), speed versus accuracy, methods of testing for original learning and retention, conditions, or retrieval, and individual differences. Furthermore, inadequate or absent feedback is further associated with skill or knowledge decay (Driskell et al., 1992; Farr, 1987; Hurlock & Montague, 1982). Thus, the rate and degree to which skill decay occurs (as discussed previously) is influenced by the amount of time since training relative to skill use and is additionally moderated by the above factors to either increase or decrease the rate of decay due to elapsed time alone.

To help remediate skill decay, follow-up training (ranging in degrees of formality) can be implemented. One example of a potential remediation is encouraging multicultural interactions through follow-up inter-cultural workshops. Such events provide employees an opportunity to interact with individuals of other cultures and learn/review cultural information. Similarly, remediation may occur less formally by building it into general work practices. For example, a team may briefly discuss culture and cultural issues/concerns as a component of weekly team meetings. Such discussions may help maintain employees' awareness of cultural issues and may encourage the development of skills by demonstrating that they are an important aspect of the team's work. Providing remediation and recurrent training sends the message to employees that successful multicultural interactions are important.

TRAINING FOR MULTICULTURAL INTERACTIONS: A BRIEF RESEARCH AGENDA

The perspective provided throughout this paper is Anglo. Furthermore, what we have presented relates to training in general rather than to specifically multicultural. This we cannot ignore. However, this is where much of the literature has been focused. We conclude this chapter with some future research needs. We note first that research into how to train multicultural interactions in complex and dynamic environments is in its infancy. Much more research needs to be done—from theory development to outlining appropriate metrics to how, when, and why to use certain instructional strategies.

In general, better culture-focused theories of individual and team performance are desperately needed—theories that provide testable propositions and offer some generalizability. Of course, we need better metrics to evaluate multicultural training, especially those that go beyond reaction data. This is a big challenge. Training can only help if we have a full understanding of the behavior, attitudes, and cognitions we need to improve in multicultural settings. Presented next are a few research questions that we feel would help the multicultural training arena move forward.

What Methodologies Can Be Used to Guide the Design and Delivery of Training for Different Cultures?

The design of training can only be as good as what is used to guide its development. The science of learning and training can help. We know a lot about the design and delivery of training, in general. We also rely on task/job analysis (Goldstein, 1993) or, as of recent, cognitive task analysis methodologies (Cooke, 1999). But the multicultural training domain still lacks a robust, credible, and useful approach to uncovering the key components, incidents, or events in multicultural interactions that matter. Certainly, cognitive task analysis approaches can be leveraged, but more research aimed at developing a reliable methodology where cultural incidents, competencies, and multicultural-based learning outcomes are derived is needed. Storytelling and knowledge elicitation approaches need to be adapted, tested, and improved for guiding the design and delivery of multicultural training.

How Do We Design and Deliver Training for Different Cultures?

What works for one culture may not work for another. It is not enough to offer a generic, off-the-shelf multicultural training program. As individuals from different backgrounds think and act differently, it is likely the case that they will think and act differently regarding training. Therefore, training needs to be tailored according to the cultures in the organization. But how? Research needs to explore how to provide training to individuals with differing cultural backgrounds. For example, experiential training methods (i.e., learning by doing) are commonly used in the United States (an individualistic, low power distance culture; Sarkar-Barney, 2004). However, trainees who are highly collectivist (and prefer to save face) may be uncomfortable with this type of training, as they prefer a more passive role. For example, role-playing exercises, in which individuals are asked to act out scenarios in front of the class, may work for some cultures but not for others. Similarly, trainees from high power distance cultures may find it difficult to speak up in training, either to ask a question or respond to an instructor's request. One study found that as a result of some Chinese students taking this passive approach to communicating with their Australian instructor, the instructor rated them as less talented and was less willing to help them (Gallois et al., 1990, as cited in Sarkar-Barney, 2004). These examples indicate the importance of not only the delivery methods by which training is presented but also how instructors interact with trainees (Sarkar-Barney, 2004).

Another obstacle when designing and delivering training is that not all KSAs are universally accepted. The aviation community has studied the impact of Westernized crew resource management training for cockpit crews on non-Western cultures. In a study conducted by Helmreich and Merritt (1996), it was suggested that many cultures agree on issues such as the importance of crew communication and coordination and the importance of preflight briefings. However, these same cultures disagree on issues regarding junior crew member assertiveness to speak up or question authority, the influence of personal problems on performance, and the likelihood of making errors in judgment during emergency situations. These differences may have serious consequences for organizational outcomes (e.g., safety, productivity). More research is needed to understand how different cultures relate to these KSAs so that these differences can be incorporated into training.

Another big challenge is how to represent cultural nuances in scenarios. When a diverse group of individuals is brought together, for training or otherwise, a number of subtleties may influence their behavior and thinking. For example, people from different cultures will (not surprisingly) have differing assumptions, expectations, and underlying traditions (recall Klein's cultural lens model discussed previously). These will thus impact how they communicate (i.e., verbally or nonverbally), how they perceive gestures (e.g., eye contact is considered disrespectful by Asians), and how they approach conflict. The challenge then is how do we represent these different subtleties in training?

What Organizational Strategies Are Needed to Ensure Transfer of Training?

Just as training needs to be developed for different cultures, so do the strategies used to ensure that the learned competencies are transferred to the job. Research is mixed as to what motivates individuals from different cultures to transfer what they have learned to the job—is it supervisor support? Peer support? Rewards? For example, Sarkar-Barney (2004) argues that peer support is more critical in egalitarian (e.g., Great Britain) than hierarchical (e.g., Belgium) cultures, due to egalitarian cultures being low power distance and having a more interdependent nature in organizational work. In terms of reward systems, too, differences have been found between cultures. Wheeler (2001) found that cultures high in collectivism and femininity prefer reward systems that "emphasize intrinsic outcomes, including meaningful, challenging work, and a sense of accomplishment" (p. 625), as well as those involving the whole team. In contrast, those low in collectivism and femininity prefer tangible benefits (e.g., pay or benefits) that are based on individual performance. To look at this another way, collectivist cultures prefer rewards based on equality (each person gets the same reward), whereas individualistic cultures prefer rewards based on equity (each person rewarded for extent of contribution; Bond, Leung, & Wan, 1982; Leung & Bond, 1984; Sarkar-Barney, 2004). The relationship between culture, supervisor support, and reward/compensation strategies needs to be considered in organizations. Furthermore, more research is needed to explore how these support and reward systems can be integrated into the organization to ensure effective transfer of training.

CONCLUDING REMARKS

Multicultural interactions are inevitable and cannot be ignored. The purpose of this paper was to explore the training and culture literature to better understand how to prepare employees of different cultures to work together through the systematic design of training. We found a lot of literature on training and a lot of literature on multicultural issues. What was lacking was a discussion of how to improve multicultural inter-actions through training. What we do know is that multicultural differences exist. To improve its effectiveness, multicultural training must be integrated with other training programs and focus beyond the individual (i.e., multilevel). What we provide here is just the beginning, and we cannot stress more that further exploration is needed. We need to deter-mine what works and what doesn't for various cultures and how training should be designed to compensate for these differences. We have some initial research to guide us and can begin to hypothesize how training should look, but again more is needed. We hope that we have raised inter-est in this area that will serve to broaden the research being conducted.

REFERENCES

Adler, N. (1991). *International dimensions of organizational behavior* (2nd ed.). Boston: PWS-Kent.

Adler, N. J. (1997). *International dimensions of organizational behavior* (3rd ed.). Cincinnati, OH: International Thomson.

American Society for Training & Development (ASTD). (2005). *ASTD 2005 state of the industry report*. Alexandria, VA: Author.

Argote, L., & McGrath, J. E. (1993). Group processes in organisations: Continuity and change. In C. L. Cooper & I. T. Robertson (Eds.), *International review of industrial and organisational psychology* (Vol. 8, pp. 333–389). New York: Wiley.

Arthur, W., Jr., & Bennet, W., Jr. (1998). Factors that influence skill decay and retention: A quantitative review and analysis. *Human Performance, 11*(1), 57–101.

Bennett, J. M. (1986). Modes of cross-cultural training: Conceptualizing cross-cultural training as education. *International Journal of Intercultural Relations, 10,* 117–134.

Bhagat, R., & Prien, K. O. (1996). Cross-cultural training in organizational contexts. In D. Landis & R. S. Bhagat (Eds.), *Handbook of intercultural training* (2nd ed., pp. 216–230). Thousand Oaks, CA: Sage.

Bhawuk, D. P. S., & Brislin, R. W. (2000). Cross-cultural training: A review. *Applied Psychology: An International Review, 49*(1), 162–191.

Bond, M. H., Leung, K., & Wan, K. C. (1982). How does cultural collectivism operate? The impact of task and maintenance contributions on reward allocation. *Journal of Cross-Cultural Psychology, 13,* 186–200.

Burrough, B. (1998). *Dragonfly: NASA and the crisis aboard the MIR.* New York: Harper Collins.

Bussema, E., & Nemec, P. (2006). Training to increase cultural competence. *Psychiatric Rehabilitation Journal, 30*(1), 71–73.

Cannon-Bowers, J. A., Burns, J. J., Salas, E., & Pruitt, J. S. (1998). Advanced technology in scenario-based training. In J. A. Cannon-Bowers & E. Salas (Eds.), *Making decisions under stress: Implications for individual and team training* (pp. 365–374). Washington, DC: American Psychological Association.

Caudron, S. (1993). Training can damage diversity efforts. *Personnel Journal, 72*(4), 51–62.

Cooke, N. J. (1999). Knowledge elicitation. In F. T. Durso, R. S. Nickerson, R. W. Schvaneveldt, S. T. Dumais, D. S. Lindsay, & T. H. Chi (Eds.), *Handbook of applied cognition* (pp. 479–509). New York: Wiley.

Daily, B., Whatley, A., Ash, S. R., & Steiner, R. L. (1996). The effects of a group decision support system on culturally diverse and culturally homogeneous group decision making. *Information & Management, 30*, 281–289.

Denning, S. (2004). Telling tales. *Harvard Business Review, 82*(5), 122–153.

Denning, S. (2006). Effective storytelling: Strategic business narrative techniques. *Strategy & Leadership, 34*(1), 42–48.

Deshpande, S. P., & Viswesvaran, C. (1992). Is cross-cultural training of expatriate managers effective: A meta-analysis. *International Journal of Intercultural Relations, 16*(3), 295–310.

Distefano, J. J., & Maznevski, M. L. (2000). Creating value with diverse teams in global management. *Organizational Dynamics, 29*(1), 45–63.

Driskell, J. E., Willis, R. P., & Copper, C. (1992). Effect of overlearning on retention. *Journal of Applied Psychology, 77*, 615–622.

Dwyer, P., Engardio, P., Schiller, S., & Reed, S. (1994). The new model: Tearing up today's organization chart. *Business Week*, 80–90.

Farr, M. J. (1987). *The long-term retention of knowledge and skills: A cognitive and instructional perspective.* New York: Springer.

Fowler, S. M. (1994). Two decades of using simulation games for cross-cultural training. *Simulation & Gaming, 25*(4), 464–476.

Fowlkes, J., Dwyer, D. J., Oser, R. L., & Salas, E. (1998). Event-based approach to training (EBAT). *International Journal of Aviation Psychology, 8*(3), 209–221.

Goldstein, I. L. (1993). *Training in organizations* (3rd ed.). Pacific Grove, CA: Brooks/Cole.

Goldstein, I. L., & Ford, J. K. (2002). *Training in organizations: Needs assessment, development, and evaluation* (4th ed.). Belmont, CA: Wadsworth.

Harrison, G. L., McKinnon, J. L., Wu, A., & Chow, C. W. (2000). Cultural influences on adaptation to fluid workgroups and teams. *Journal of International Business Studies, 31*(3), 489–505.

Helmreich, R. L. (1994). Anatomy of a system accident: The crash of Avianca Flight 052. *International Journal of Aviation Psychology, 4*(3), 265–284.

Helmreich, R. L. (2000). Culture and error in space: Implications from analog environments. *Aviation, Space, and Environmental Medicine, 71*(9 Suppl), 133–139.

Helmreich, R. L., & Merritt, A. C. (1996). Cultural issues in crew resource management training. Paper presented at the ICAO Global Human Factors Seminar, Auckland, New Zealand, April, 1996. Retrieved July 13, 2007 from: http://homepage.psy.utexas.edu/homepage/grove/HelmreichLAB/Publications/Pub%20Project/254.doc

Helmreich, R. L., & Merritt, A. C. (1998). *Culture at work in aviation and medicine: National, organizational, and professional influences.* Aldershot, UK: Ashgate.

Hodgetts, R. M., & Luthans, F. (2000). *International management: Culture, strategy, and behavior.* New York: McGraw-Hill.

Hoffman, L. R., & Maier, N. R. F. (1961). Quality and acceptance of problem solutions by members of homogeneous and heterogeneous groups. *Journal of Abnormal Psychology, 62*(2), 48–61.

Hofstede, G. (1980). *Culture's consequences: International differences in work related values.* Beverly Hills, CA: Sage.

Horenczyk, G., & Berkerman, Z. (1997). The effects of intercultural acquaintance and structured intergroup interaction on ingroup, outgroup, and reflected ingroup stereotypes. *International Journal of Intercultural Relations, 21*(1), 71–83.

Hurlock, R. E., & Montague, W. E. (1982). *Skill retention and its implications for navy tasks: An analytical review* (NPRDC Special Rep. No. 82-21). San Diego, CA: Navy Personnel Research and Development Center.

Ilgen, D. R., LePine, J. A., & Hollenbeck, J. R. (1997). Effective decision making in multinational teams. In P. C. Earley & M. Erez (Eds.), *New perspectives on international industrial/organizational psychology* (pp. 377–409). San Francisco: New Lexington Press/Jossey-Bass.

Jackson, S. E. (1992). Team composition in organizational settings: Issues in managing a diverse workforce. In S. Worchel, W. Wood, & J. Simpson (Eds.), *Group process and productivity* (pp. 138–173). Thousand Oaks, CA: Sage.

Janis, I. L. (1972). *Victims of groupthink.* New York: Houghton Mifflin.

Ji, L., Peng, K., & Nisbett, R. E. (2000). Culture, control, and perception of relationships in the environment. *Journal of Personality and Social Psychology, 78*(5), 943–955.

Katz, I., Goldston, J., & Benjamin, L. (1958). Behavior and productivity in biracial work groups. *Human Relations, 11,* 123–141.

Kirchmeyer, C. (1993). Multicultural task groups. *Small Group Research, 24*(1), 127–148.

Kirchmeyer, C., & Cohen, A. (1992). Multicultural groups. *Groups & Organization Management, 17*(2), 153–170.

Kirkman, B. L., Lowe, K. B., & Gibson, C. B. (in press). A quarter century of *Culture's Consequences*: A review of empirical research incorporating Hofstede's cultural values framework. *Journal of International Business Studies.*

Klein, H. A. (2004). Cognition in natural settings: The cultural lens model. In M. Kaplan (Ed.), *Cultural ergonomics* (pp. 249–280). Amsterdam: Elsevier.

Kreitner, R., & Kinicki, A. (2001). International OB: Managing across cultures. In *Organizational behavior* (4th ed., pp. 84–113). Columbus, OH: McGraw-Hill.

Leung, K., & Bond, M. H. (1984). The impact of cultural relativism on reward allocation. *Journal of Personality and Social Psychology, 47,* 793–804.

Li, H. Z. (1999). Communicating information in conversations: A cross-cultural comparison. *International Journal of Intercultural Relations, 56,* 1–23.

Littrell, L. N., & Salas, E. (2005). A review of cross-cultural training: Best practices, guidelines, and research needs. *Human Resource Development Review, 4*(3), 305–334.

Littrell, L. N., Salas, E., Hess, K. P., Paley, M., & Riedel, S. (2006). Expatriate preparation: A critical analysis of 25 years of cross-cultural training research. *Human Resources Developmental Review*, 5(3), 355–388.

Nachbar, J., & Lause, K. (1992). *Popular culture: An introductory text*. Chicago: Popular Press.

Noe, R. A. (2002). *Employee training and development* (2nd ed.). New York: McGraw-Hill.

Oser, R. L., Cannon-Bowers, J. A., Salas, E., & Dwyer, D. J. (1999). Enhancing human performance in technology-rich environments: Guidelines for scenario-based training. In E. Salas (Ed.), *Human/technology interaction in complex systems* (Vol. 9, pp. 175–202). Stamford, CT: JAI Press.

Paige, R. W., & Martin, J. N. (1983). Ethical issues and ethics in cross-cultural training. In D. Landis & R. Brislin (Eds.), *Handbook of intercultural training* (Vol. 1, pp. 36–60). New York: Pergamon Press.

Salas, E., & Cannon-Bowers, J. A. (1997). Methods, tools, and strategies for team training. In M. A. Quiñones & A. Ehrenstein (Eds.), *Training for a rapidly changing workplace: Applications of psychological research* (pp. 249–279). Washington, DC: American Psychological Association.

Salas, E., & Cannon-Bowers, J.A. (2000). The anatomy of team training. In S. Tobias & J. D. Fletcher (Eds.), *Training & retraining: A handbook for business, industry, government, and the military* (pp. 312–335). New York: Macmillan.

Salas, E., & Cannon-Bowers, J. A. (2001). The science of training: A decade of progress. *Annual Review of Psychology*, 52, 471–499.

Salas, E., Burke, C. S., Fowles, J. E., & Wilson, K. A. (2004). Challenges and approaches to understanding leadership efficacy in multi-cultural teams. In M. Kaplan (Ed.), *Advances in Human Performance and Cognitive Engineering Research* (Vol. 4, pp. 341–384). Oxford, UK: Elsevier.

Sarkar-Barney, S. (2004). The role of national culture in enhancing training effectiveness: A framework. In E. Salas (Ed.), *Advances in human performance and cognitive engineering research* (Vol. 4, pp. 183–213). Amsterdam: Elsevier.

Schendal, J. D., & Hagman, J. D. (1982). On sustaining procedural skills over a prolonged retention interval. *Journal of Applied Psychology*, 67, 605–610.

Schulten, T. (1998). Industrial relations aspects of the Daimler-Chrysler merger. Retrieved August 22, 2003, from http://www.eiro.eurofound. eu.int

Scott, W. R., & Meyer, J. W. (1991). The rise of training programs in firms and agencies: An institutional perspective. In B. Staw & L. L. Cummings (Eds.), *Research in organizational behavior* (Vol. 13, pp. 297–326). Greenwich, CT: JAI Press.

Steiner, I. D. (1972). *Group process and productivity*. New York: Academic Press.

Stone-Romero, E. F., Stone, D. L., & Salas, E. (2003). The influence of culture on role conceptions and role behavior in organisations. *Applied Psychology: An International Review*, 52(3), 328–362.

Thomas, D. C. (1999). Cultural diversity and work group effectiveness. *Journal of Cross-cultural Psychology*, 30(2), 242–263.

Triandis, H. C. (2000). Culture and conflict. *International Journal of Psychology*, 35(2), 145–152.

Watson, W. E., Kumar, K., & Michaelsen, L. K. (1993). Cultural diversity's impact on interaction process and performance: Comparing homogeneous and diverse task groups. *Academy of Management Journal, 36*(3), 590–602.
Wheeler, K. G. (2001). Cultural values in relation to equity sensitivity within and across cultures. *Journal of Managerial Psychology, 17*(7), 612–627.

AUTHOR NOTE

This work was supported by funding from the U.S. Army Research Laboratory's Advanced Decision Architecture Collaborative Technology Alliance (Cooperative Agreement DAAD19-01-2-0009). All opinions expressed in this paper are those of the authors and do not necessarily reflect the official opinion or position of the University of Central Florida, the U.S. Army Research Laboratory, or the Department of Defense.

6

Culture Diversity and Performance Appraisal Systems

GERALD R. FERRIS* AND DARREN C. TREADWAY†

Florida State University and State University of New York at Buffalo

There is perhaps no more central and foundational human resource system than performance appraisal. However, even after decades of research on how to design and implement effective performance appraisal systems, there remains considerable dissatisfaction by organizations with such systems. Add to this the additional challenges of effectively managing an increasingly diverse workforce in U.S. organizations and the design of performance appraisal systems in overseas operations for multinational companies, and we have a broad array of issues that need to be addressed in order to successfully manage performance in organizations worldwide today and in the future.

In this chapter, we examine both traditional issues concerning the measurement and evaluation of performance, in addition to more recently investigated process issues in performance appraisal. Further-

---

* Gerald R. Ferris, Department of Management, College of Business, Florida State University, Tallahassee, FL 32306-1110, Ph: (850) 644-3548, Fax: (850) 644-7843, E-mail: gferris@cob.fsu.edu
† Darren C. Treadway, Department of Organization and Human Resources, State University of New York at Buffalo, 280B Jacobs Management Center, Buffalo, NY 14260-4000, Ph: (716) 645-3244, Fax: (716) 645-2863, E-mail: darrent@buffalo.edu

more, we consider how social influence or political perspectives on performance appraisal can highlight some important considerations for the process of performance measurement, evaluation, and management, and also how recent work on accountability needs to be integrated into this area in order to develop a more informed understanding of the performance appraisal process and system dynamics as they operate in both domestic and global organizations.

PERFORMANCE APPRAISAL AS A MECHANISM OF ACCOUNTABILITY

Human resources management systems, like performance appraisal systems, provide organizations mechanisms by which to monitor and manage the behaviors of its employees. As such, these systems are formal accountability mechanisms because they hold employees answerable for their work behavior (i.e., performance), and thus channel and shape behavior in directions prescribed by the organization. Therefore, performance appraisal systems provide an important control mechanism (Eisenhardt, 1985; Ouchi & Macguire, 1975) for organizations, which can increase performance and effectiveness (Ferris, Mitchell, Canavan, Frink, & Hopper, 1995). When setting up performance appraisal systems, it is necessary to consider a number of important issues and to make decisions that will have implications for the nature of accountability reflected by such systems. Below, we discuss some of these key issues and their implications.

Performance appraisal systems, fundamentally, need to address issues of defining performance, engaging in systematic evaluations of that performance on a regular basis (e.g., once a year), and providing feedback to employees regarding how they are performing so needed action can be taken to reward effective performance or provide remedial steps so low performance can be improved. Hall et al. (2003) suggested that accountability could be perceived as a mechanism for linking all three of these elements. They argued that "by articulating the standards by which individuals will be judged, evaluating individuals by those standards, and providing information to employees regarding their achievement of these standards, organizations can direct and monitor the behaviors of employees" (p. 9). However, within these three fundamental areas, there are several additional specific issues that need to be adequately addressed in developing effective performance appraisal systems, which we deal with in the next sections.

FOCUS OF APPRAISAL: ACCOUNTABILITY FOR WHAT?

Formal accountability systems are defined by two elements: process accountability and outcome accountability (Siegel-Jacobs & Yates,

1996). Process accountability reflects the degree to which an individual is responsible for the correct implementation of procedures and processes during a task event. In contrast, outcome accountability refers to being held accountable for the quantity and/or quality of only the outcomes of an assignment. Research indicates that outcome accountability often results in dysfunctional decision making, whereas process accountability has been linked to more effective decisions (Lerner & Tetlock, 1999). Accordingly, scholars have argued that organizations should integrate both process and outcome accountability considerations in their performance appraisal systems (cf. Bowen, 1987).

Specificity is an important criterion for a performance appraisal system. For example, a performance evaluation system should provide information concerning for what one is accountable. The nature of job performance has fascinated organizational scientists for decades from both a scientific and practical standpoint. However, as Campbell (1990) noted, amazingly little work has focused on the theoretical delineation of job performance compared to the degree of attention devoted to the conceptualization of predictor measures. He proposed a higher-order conceptualization of job performance that included dimensions focusing on the execution of substantive or technical tasks, as well as elements focusing on interpersonal and motivational aspects. This suggestion distinguished formally prescribed performance from aspects of job performance that are neither formally designated nor required but that are valued by the organization.

Murphy and Cleveland (1995) addressed the issue of performance criterion development and noted the difficulty of equating task performance to overall job performance (an assumption that has frequently been made in the field, at least implicitly). In response, they argued that two dimensions of job performance are relevant across a broad variety of jobs: (a) task performance, which includes the formally prescribed tasks and duties typically provided in job descriptions; and (b) those aspects of performance defined or dictated by the social context of the job and organization. They suggested that one ubiquitous aspect of social contextual performance is interpersonal effectiveness, or the extent to which employees can maintain good interpersonal relations with others in the organization (e.g., supervisors, coworkers, etc.). Furthermore, work on job analysis by Ilgen and Hollenbeck (1991) differentiated job elements from role elements, which essentially makes the same distinction noted above between task and contextual performance.

However, it has been the work of Borman, Motowidlo, and their colleagues that has theoretically and empirically substantiated the distinction between task performance and contextual performance as critical and pervasive dimensions of job performance across virtually all types of jobs (Borman, 1991; Borman & Brush, 1993; Borman & Motowidlo, 1993, 1997a, 1997b; Motowidlo, Borman, & Van Scotter, 1997; Motowidlo & Van Scotter, 1994; Van Scotter & Motowidlo, 1996). Task performance is the set of core substantive tasks and duties central to a particular job, and essentially, it represents the activities that differentiate one occupation from another. Borman and colleagues referred to contextual performance as behaviors not formally prescribed by any specific job but rather inherent in all jobs and behaviors that support the social fabric of the organization. Borman and Motowidlo (1993) originally considered contextual performance to represent behaviors including volunteering, helping, cooperating, following rules, persisting, and so forth, which bear strong similarity to organizational citizenship behaviors (Organ, 1997).

Recent research has demonstrated that contextual performance actually separates into two dimensions of job dedication and interpersonal facilitation (Van Scotter & Motowidlo, 1996), which uniquely reflect significant positive paths to overall job performance (Conway, 1999). Van Scotter and Motowidlo defined *job dedication* as "self disciplined behaviors such as following rules, working hard, and taking the initiative to solve a problem at work" (p. 526). Conway elaborated on the components of job dedication to also include taking initiative, demonstrating commitment and motivation, and putting forth a certain amount of effort. *Interpersonal facilitation* was defined by Van Scotter and Motowidlo as "interpersonally oriented behaviors that contribute to organizational goal accomplishment" (p. 526). Taken one step further, Conway emphasized "building and mending relationships; compassion and sensitivity; putting people at ease; cooperation; consideration; interpersonal relations" (p. 6).

Research by Suliman (2001) extends this multidimensional concept of performance to the international context. Using a sample of 1,000 Jordanian managers, this research indicated that performance is composed of five interrelated factors: work enthusiasm, readiness to innovate, work skills, understanding work duties, and job performance. Unfortunately, the authors explained their contribution in terms of the dimensionality of performance appraisal rather than cultural aspects that may serve to define the fundamental meaning of the performance criterion. Furthermore, this research indicated that the importance of the specific performance dimension was dependent upon the source of the performance appraisal. Specifically, the dominant performance dimension for self-rated performance was work skills, whereas supervisor ratings indicated that readiness to innovate was the dominant performance dimension. The variability in ratings due to rating source would thus appear to be a universal aspect of performance appraisal systems.

SOURCE OF APPRAISAL: ACCOUNTABILITY TO WHOM?

It also is very important to clearly specify to whom one is accountable, thereby making clear the source of appraisal. For many years, the source of appraisal issue was effectively a nonissue, because it was the case that one's immediate supervisor was the person given the responsibility of conducting the performance appraisal on some regular basis. However, changing work contexts and an interest in providing a wider set of inputs into an individual's performance review have identified additional sources of appraisal. There are three general sources of performance evaluation data: self, peer, and 360-degree feedback.

Self-Appraisal

The use of self-appraisals has been resisted by practitioners for many years out of the fear that individuals would simply inflate their own performance ratings. To that point, some research has concluded that individuals have a different opinion of their performance than do other raters (Thornton, 1980). More recent research has indicated that these concerns are not wholly unfounded. Indeed, Harris and Schaubroeck (1988) found modest correlations between self- and peer ratings (.36) and self–supervisor ratings (.35). Accordingly, most organizations employing self-ratings of performance typically do not use these ratings as the sole indicator of performance but rather in conjunction with immediate supervisor's appraisal.

Research indicates that the application of self-rating in performance appraisal may be sensitive to cultural influences. In a comparison of self- versus other ratings, Farh, Dobbins, and Cheng (1991) found that Taiwanese workers actually rated their performance lower than their supervisors rated them. This effect was later replicated in relation to Chinese workers (Yu & Murphy, 1993). This "modesty bias" has been explained as demonstrating cultural differences in relation to collectivism and individualism. Indeed, these authors suggested that cultural pressure to subsume individual interests to the group results in a biasing of ratings downward.

Peer Appraisal

As work contexts have changed to incorporate more team-based work structures, it makes more sense to incorporate coworker or team member evaluations of each other into the overall rating scheme. Thus, organizations have begun to implement peer ratings as an integral facet of their performance appraisal systems. Whereas some scholars have asserted that peer ratings are the most accurate indicator of employee behavior (Wexley & Kilmoski, 1984), meta-analytic results indicate that peer ratings are most valid when raters have interacted with ratees long enough to understand their qualifications, objective criteria are used for evaluation, and raters believe the data will be used for only research purposes (Norton, 1992).

As with other rating formats, peer ratings are sensitive to the functional and demographic similarity among the rater and ratee. For example, Fox, Ben-Nahum, and Yinon (1989) found that Israeli soldiers were less accurate in rating others that were dissimilar in relation to general, course achievement, and background. Similarly, Antonioni and Park (2001) found that similarity between peer dyads in relation to conscientiousness was positively related to peer ratings of contextual work behaviors. Therefore, one might suggest that difficulties may arise when peer rating is used in contexts where the members of the dyad are from different cultures.

360-Degree Appraisal

Multisource or 360-degree feedback incorporates all of the above sources of performance information in addition to ratings from the ratee's immediate supervisor and, when applicable, subordinates. The objective of this type of rating scheme is to establish convergence across the various sources. To the degree that convergence is obtained, these ratings are believed to be a more accurate representation of an employee's actual job performance. Perhaps in light of the promise of these types of appraisal designs, the use of these types of formats has become widespread (London & Smither, 1995).

Unfortunately, academicians have been unable to provide conclusive support for the improvement in ratings from 360-degree feedback that justifies the costs of implementing such programs (Wood, Allen, Pillinger, & Kohn, 1999). Indeed, some researchers have concluded that 360-degree systems are susceptible to halo effects that hinder the instrument's ability to distinguish among performance categories (Beehr, Ivanitskaya, Hansen, Erofeev, & Guganowski, 2001). As such, these ratings are relatively useless for developmental purposes. To this point, Atkins and Wood (2002) found that within a 360-degree feedback system, supervisor ratings often underestimated the performance of moderate performers, peer ratings overestimated the performance of substandard performers, and self-ratings were inversely related to performance. These researchers suggested that the inaccuracy of self-ratings make 360-degree systems problematic because the self-rating components often are used to benchmark other ratings.

Despite the use of multiple sources of rating information, 360-degree feedback systems may still be sensitive to cultural considerations. For example, authors have identified the context (Hall, 1988) and Confucianism (Rowson, 1998) as cultural value sets that may affect the implementation of 360-degree systems internationally. In low-context cultures (e.g., the United States), communication is direct and explicit. In such cultures, value is placed on identifying "true" performance regardless of the interpersonal consequences. However, in high-context cultures (e.g., Japan), communication is less open and confrontational. Therefore, confidentiality regarding performance is important and the performance data obtained may be seen as intrusive. Similarly, Confucian values of absolute loyalty and obedience to authority may result in higher upward appraisal ratings within the context of 360-degree systems.

PERFORMANCE APPRAISAL AS AN INFLUENCE ARENA

Mintzberg (1983) argued that organizations are inherently "political arenas," and as such, one needs political will and political skill to survive and be effective. That is, one must possess the motivation to engage in influence and politics as well as to hone the skills necessary to engage in such activities in effective ways. Although some might characterize such a view of organizations as unduly cynical, others embrace such a perspective as an accurate way of depicting organizations (e.g., Pfeffer, 1981). Indeed, Fernandez (1993) characterized organizations as follows:

> Corporations are arenas in which individuals compete and struggle for limited commodities such as authority, power, status, money, promotion, and recognition. A fundamental characteristic of corporate thought is that it treats problems as administrative rather than as political. Behind all the rational laws and rules of corporations, though, are the socially fashioned interests of specific groups. Order, therefore, is based not on reason but on socially conflicting, irrational forces that become reconciled in the "rational" order—in short, a very political process. (p. 277)

Accepting this premise, then, has implications for the way we see performance appraisal systems and processes operating in organizations. The political perspective has been contrasted to the rational perspective of appraisal by both Ferris and Judge (1991) and Cardy and Dobbins (1994).

Indeed, the issues of to whom and for what one is accountable can provide the context, if not adequately addressed, for politics and social influence processes operating in performance appraisal systems. As noted by Nemeth and Staw (1989), where criteria are vague regarding performance appraisal and/or promotion systems, surrogate criteria can emerge that take the form of conformity to the particular preferences or tastes of one's supervisor or of organization norms. When performance criteria are not easily measured objectively, employee behavior, rather than actual results, typically becomes the focus of appraisal. Furthermore, Pfeffer (1981) even argued that as the ambiguity of the work context increases, employees are evaluated on the basis of attitudes, beliefs, values, and even effort, all of which are highly subjective and certainly prone to manipulation and image management.

The qualitative work of Longenecker, Sims, and Gioia (1987) helped researchers to finally understand the very subjective, even political, nature of the performance evaluation process. These researchers found that performance appraisal was only objective to a degree. Supervisors often had to balance the needs of future objectives with the reality of pay and performance decisions. As they noted:

> Although academicians have been preoccupied with the goal of accuracy in appraisal, executives reported that accuracy was not their primary concern. Rather, they were much more interested in whether their

ratings would be effective in maintaining or increasing the subordinates' future level of performance. (p. 187)

The subjective nature of performance evaluation is echoed in definitions of political behavior in organizations. For example, Ferris, Fedor, and King (1994) described political behavior as focusing on the

management of shared meaning, which focuses on the subjective evaluations and interpretations of meaning rather than the view that meanings are inherent, objective properties of situations. . . . [T]he objective is to manage the meaning of situations in such a way to produce desired, self-serving responses or outcomes. (p. 4)

Ferris and Judge (1991) proposed a political influence perspective on human resources systems, and thus characterized how such social influence and political processes can operate in performance appraisal systems. They proposed a model of the influence process that identified antecedents, intermediate linkages, and outcomes, and empirical tests of parts of this model have provided support for the conceptualization (e.g., Ferris, Judge, Rowland, & Fitzgibbons, 1994; Wayne, Liden, Graf, & Ferris, 1997). This work, combined with a recent review and discussion of influence tactics in performance appraisal, sheds light on the tactics and strategies employed, as well as the effectiveness of different tactics (Frink, Treadway, & Ferris, 2005).

WHAT IS INFLUENCE BEHAVIOR?

The foundation of scholarly work on politics or influence behavior in organizations is addressed by French and Raven (1959). These authors identified the manner in which personal influence is wielded in organizations. Their work identified five bases of personal power: referent; expert; legitimate; reward; and coercive. Inherently based on conceptualizations of organizational leadership, these five bases of power offer a view of how leaders may act toward subordinates, and why subordinates may follow these supervisors.

Kipnis, Schmidt, and Wilkinson (1980) suggested that early conceptualizations were plagued by their lack of distinctiveness between the categories of influence. To address this concern, their work defined eight dimensions of personal influence. Subsequent research refined these categorizations into six types of behaviors that are relatively consistent across target and context. The first of these dimensions, rationality, represents individuals who use factual information to support their case for action. Ingratiatory behaviors attempt to place the target in a good mood or to sway the target to think favorably of the actor before asking for support for their initiative. Individuals who circumvent the chain of command and go "above the head" of the target to obtain support are engaging in upward appeals behavior. Individuals engaging in the bartering of favors are applying exchange influence tactics. Individuals using coalition building tactics develop relationships with others to present a united front toward a course of action. Finally, individuals who demand their course of action be taken are demonstrating assertive influence behaviors.

Whereas the Kipnis et al. (1980) research focused on the utilization of single influence behaviors, other scholars argued that individuals engage in clusters or strategies of influence behavior (e.g., Farmer, Maslyn, Fedor, & Goodman, 1997; Kelly, 1988; Perreault & Miles, 1978). Consistent with this argument, Kipnis and Schmidt (1983) defined influence strategies by both the frequency and type of influence behavior used. Their work suggested that the styles of downward influence could be classified into three distinct groupings: shotgun, tactician, and bystander. Shotgun managers use a greater degree of influence behavior with their subordinates, and primarily focus their tactics on assertiveness and bargaining. Tactician managers influence their subordinates through influence behaviors that emphasize reasoning. Bystander managers use little, if any, influence behavior with their subordinates. Later research (Kipnis & Schmidt, 1988) identified that an additional strategy was used when behavior was directed upwardly. This style represents those that are more likely to use ingratiatory behaviors and thus was labeled the ingratiatory influence style.

One issue that was neglected in the area of social influence and politics until quite recently is the style with which one demonstrates the influence attempt. Indeed, Jones (1990) argued that whereas we have built a sizable knowledge base regarding influence tactics, we know virtually nothing about the interpersonal style component that largely explains the success of the influence attempt. Furthermore, Ferris et al. (2005) concluded that more than a decade after Jones' appeal, we still saw relatively little work being done in this area. An exception to this has been the work on political skill, which Mintzberg (1983, 1985, p. 127) discussed as one of the two important aspects of survival in political arenas. Ferris et al. (2005) defined political skill as "the ability to effectively understand others at work, and to use such knowledge to influence others to act in ways that enhance one's personal and/or organizational objectives" (p. 4), and they developed an 18-item, 4-dimension political skill inventory to measure the construct. So, in future research on influence attempts in organizations, and performance appraisal systems in particular, we need to include political skill as a potential moderator of the relationships between influence tactics and performance outcomes.

HOW DOES INFLUENCE AFFECT PERFORMANCE RATINGS?

As an arena for influence, the performance appraisal context has generated a great deal of research activity. Research has suggested that influence tactics affect performance ratings by modifying the affect or liking the supervisor feels toward the subordinate. Specifically, subordinate use of assertiveness and reasoning has been found to positively relate, and bargaining and self-promotion to inversely relate, to the managers' perceptions of the subordinates' interpersonal skills. Similarly, exchange behaviors are positively related to both manager perceptions of similarity and manager liking of the subordinate (Wayne et al., 1997). Similarly, assertive tactics are less likely to result in perceptions of liking by supervisors (van Knippenberg, van Knippenberg, Blaauw, & Vermunt, 1999).

In a recent meta-analysis of 23 articles published from 1967 to 2000, Higgins, Judge, and Ferris (2003) evaluated the relationship between influence tactics and work-related outcomes. The results of this study demonstrated that ingratiation and rationality had positive effects on both performance evaluations and extrinsic success, and these tactics had stronger effects on performance assessments than on extrinsic success. Self-promotion showed a weak relationship with the outcome measures, and assertiveness exhibited a negative effect on performance assessments and a positive effect for extrinsic success. Although not as abundant in the literature, some research has investigated the relation between influence behavior and performance ratings from an influence strategy perspective. From this perspective, Kipnis and Schmidt (1988) found that individuals engaging in shotgun styles of upward influence were rated less favorably than those utilizing tactician styles were.

WHAT IS CULTURE?

Definitions of culture are diverse and vague (Kelley & Worthley, 1981). In its simplest form, it might be said that "culture is to a society what memory is to a person" (Triandis, 1989, p. 510). More explicitly, culture can be viewed as "patterns of thought and manners that are widely shared. The boundaries of the social collectivity within which this sharing takes place are problematic so that it may make as much sense to refer to a class or regional culture as to a national culture" (Child & Kieser, 1977, p. 2). Hofstede (1980) extended the most widely used conceptualization of culture in the research literature. He described culture as the collective programming of the mind, which resulted in the production of closely shared cultural values.

Whereas several scholars have articulated various frameworks of national values (e.g., Hofstede, 1980; Rokeach, 1973; Schwartz, 1992, 1994), Triandis (1979) was the first to discuss the specific impact of the role that culture plays in generating individual behavior. Triandis (1979) distinguished between subjective and objective culture and defined subjective culture as "a group's characteristic way of perceiving its social environment" (Bhagat & McQuaid, 1982). Attitudes, beliefs, and feelings can be attributed to subjective culture to the degree that they are shared by those who speak a common language and interact because of their close geographical location during a particular historical time period (Triandis, 1972). Subjective culture manifests itself in norms, roles, and values. Members of a particular culture interpret their subjective culture through the lens of their own personality. Together these two forces impact the interpretation of social factors and the affect toward and perceived consequences of action. In turn, these expectancies serve to create intention toward behavior.

CULTURE IN PERFORMANCE APPRAISAL

Within the global marketplace, Laurent (1986) argued that human resource systems are the business practices most likely to be affected by the cultural context within which they are applied. Indeed, it has been argued that cultural differences significantly affect, among other business practices, "performance appraisals in a diverse workplace" (Li & Karakowsky, 2001, p. 501). Unfortunately, organizational researchers have all but forgotten about the cultural context of performance appraisal systems. The few studies that have addressed the issue have focused almost explicitly on the facets of the performance appraisal system rather than the interpersonal dynamics of the performance appraisal process. The current chapter provides an initial step toward integrating social influence processes in organizations and culture in the performance appraisal context.

Performance appraisal systems are artifacts built upon the underlying assumptions of a national culture (Schneider, 1988). For example, Japanese firms are more likely concerned with integrity, morality, and loyalty than they are with sales. Given the subjective nature of culture, it is curious that research has not attempted to understand the mechanisms through which culture affects the interpretation, acceptance, and enactment of influence behaviors in the performance appraisal context. Indeed, Li and Karakowsky (2001) argued that language and mental models may affect the effectiveness of performance rating formats.

The research on culture and performance appraisal is limited. The abundance of published work on culture and performance appraisal addresses the role of developing performance appraisal systems for expatriates (e.g., Gregerson, Hite, & Black, 1996; Martin & Bartol, 2003; Suutari & Brewster, 2001). Unfortunately, this literature focuses little on cultural differences or interaction and almost exclusively on the nature and context of the job. However, domestic research on demographic subgroups suggests that the characteristics of raters and employees affect the performance appraisal process. Specifically, in samples where there is a small minority population, minority status affects the ratings received by the subordinate (Kraiger & Ford, 1985).

In a limited cultural context, Li and Karakowsky (2001) used a laboratory experiment to assess the role of culture in performance ratings of Asian Americans and Caucasian Americans. Performance criteria were selected to reflect contextual-type performance dimensions upon which the researchers believed that culture would create differences between the groups. Their research concluded that culture should be a factor in the selection of raters and that culture affects the observational accuracy of raters.

Perhaps the (in)effectiveness of these formats is the product of the manner in which these instruments have been utilized. Indeed, scholars have argued that objective criteria are used for evaluation in same-race rating dyads, whereas more subjective criteria are used for evaluation of cross-race dyads (Cox & Nkomo, 1986). It can be argued that because subjective rating scales have greater potential to be affected by social influence behavior (Ferris et al., 1994; Wayne & Ferris, 1990), the fact that minorities tend to obtain lower ratings may be as much the product of political skill deficiency (Ferris, Frink, & Galang, 1993) as it is an actual performance decrement.

The importance of choosing and applying appropriate rating criteria is echoed in the geocentric work of Entrekin and Chung (2001). In their evaluation of the perceptions of Hong Kong Chinese and American executives working in Hong Kong toward performance evaluation systems, they sought to evaluate the affect of peer evaluations, subordinate ratings, and 360-degree feedback on executives' acceptance of the performance appraisal system. Their findings indicated that Hong Kong Chinese managers were less supportive of performance appraisal, focused on group more than individual, and had a greater willingness to evaluate nonjob, or subjective, criteria. Consistent with these findings, authors have suggested that 360-degree rating systems are less likely to be accepted in high-context cultures (Rowson, 1998).

DOES CULTURE AFFECT SOCIAL INFLUENCE BEHAVIOR?

Culture affects the meaning employees place on and the meaning they derive from the performance evaluation process. However, little, if any, research has been conducted that assesses the impact of culture on the perception and enactment of social influence behavior in organizations. Furthermore, no research has been conducted that evaluates the cultural elements of influence behavior in the performance evaluation context. Some research has investigated differences in impression management strategies across demographic subgroups within an individual population. Whereas these studies may indicate that meaningful differences may exist between subcultures within a country, scholars still know very little about demographic distinctions and influence behavior (Ferris et al., 2002).

Allison and Herlocker (1994) argued that individuals' identity as a minority affects their attributions of, and thereby their subsequent impression management behavior toward, a person with majority status.

Majority group members often harbor stereotypical images of minority groups and often reward impression management behavior that is consistent with these notions. Perhaps as a result of this phenomenon, research has demonstrated that underrepresented minorities often engage in socially desirable impression management behavior (Rosenfeld, Booth-Kewley, Edwards, & Alderton, 1994).

Engaging in stereotypical or socially desirable influence behavior does not always demonstrate the assertive qualities that are valued by organizations in evaluating career potential. Therefore, in order to succeed in an organizational context, minorities often are expected to engage in influence behaviors that echo the patterns of behaviors in the dominant coalition. Unfortunately, while predicting career success, these influence patterns often result in social sanctions. Rudman (1999) articulated the impact of this phenomenon by suggesting that females are often victims of their own counter-stereotypical impression management behavior. She argued that although women demonstrating aggressive and assertive behaviors in the workplace were often rewarded with promotions, they were viewed unfavorably in relation to social aspects of the work relationship. Thus, women who play the political game to achieve career success often pay the price of reduced friendships and affection.

From an alternative viewpoint, it has been argued that underrepresented minorities in organizations often lack the political skill necessary to achieve organizational success (Ferris et al., 1993; Ferris & King, 1992). Indeed, it is suggested that ethnic/racial minorities and women are placed at a decided disadvantage because they are never "taught the rules of the game," so to speak, in terms of being taken aside and educated in the informal aspects and politics of the organization. Such treatment typically is reserved for those similar in qualities and characteristics as the dominant coalition, or as typically the case in U.S. organizations, other white males.

Therefore, such a process places minorities and women at a disadvantage from the beginning that is hard to overcome—that of operating in political arenas without knowing the game or the rules. Empirical examination of these notions has received some support in recent years (Ferris, Frink, Bhawuk, Zhou, & Gilmore, 1996). Furthermore, in his critical analysis of race issues in corporate America today, Fernandez (1993) quoted an African American employee who described some of the challenges he faced, which seem to reflect accurately on political skill deficiency: "Lack of interpersonal skills: Do not know how to play politics with peers or supervisor. Do not know how to sell myself" (p. 261).

Few empirical studies have directly assessed differences in influence behavior usage and national culture. However, three studies have provided information that begins to explain cultural variation in influence behavior. Although not specifically an assessment of cultural differences in influence behavior, Kipnis, Schmidt, Swaffin-Smith, and Wilkinson (1984) found no differences in influence behavior among managers in three English-speaking countries (United States, United Kingdom, and

Australia). In a more appropriately designed test of cultural differences, Hirokawa and Miyahara (1986) found that Japanese managers relied primarily on rational influence tactics, whereas their American counterparts relied most heavily on strategies that most closely demonstrated their reward power in their organizations. A third study found that managers in Hong Kong were more likely to use assertive and less likely to use ingratiation influence tactics than were their American counterparts (Schermerhorn & Bond, 1991).

Domestically, research has indicated that Hispanics and Asian Americans are particularly sensitive to personal criticism. As a response to criticism, these individuals are more likely to withdraw from the situation than are their Caucasian counterparts (Kras, 1989). Similarly, Hispanics are less likely to use self-promotion in performance appraisal contexts (Theiderman, 1991). In these studies, we see the general tendency of Hispanic culture to devalue calling attention to oneself affecting individual influence behaviors.

CULTURE, INFLUENCE, AND PERFORMANCE APPRAISAL: NEEDED RESEARCH DIRECTIONS

Although we have witnessed the increased globalization of business in the past two decades, scholarship on international and cross-cultural business practices and employee reactions has lagged considerably behind practice. Therefore, recent literature reviews, after lamenting the lack of work published to date on culture and human resources management, have provided suggestions for future work. Schuler and Florkowski (1996) suggested that there is a need to move beyond descriptive case studies and utilize more rigorous research designs. They argued that international human resources management research "is still at a point where published findings raise more questions than they answer" (p. 388).

Arvey, Bhagat, and Salas (1991) pointed to such ambiguity as perhaps resulting from the lack of a strong theoretical perspective which could be used to drive predictions and explanations for behavior in organizations. Finally, and somewhat consistent with the sentiments expressed by Arvey et al., Ferris, Hochwarter, Buckley, Harrell-Cook, and Frink (1999) suggested that serious efforts need to be devoted to the development of an integrative paradigm of the international human resources management research process, which also incorporates key environmental factors that might play important roles in understanding differences across cultures.

It is with this general backdrop that we consider research directions for future work on cultural diversity and performance appraisal processes and systems. First, we desperately need to know about how different performance appraisal design features (e.g., methods of appraisal, sources of appraisal, performance criteria used, etc.) are reacted to by employees in different countries. That is, we are not sure how much the design features are driven by the local values, beliefs, and customs, or by the organizations' idealized sense of what looks appropriate and therefore would legitimize the practices or system (Galang, Elsik, & Russ, 1999). For example, upward appraisals might be an effective source of performance appraisal in U.S. firms and appear to be quite progressive, but they might not work at all in Japanese firms where they might be perceived as undermining authority.

Arvey et al. (1991) reviewed some work on the nature of performance appraisal practices across cultures and arrived at several conclusions. First, they concluded that appraisal systems are reasonably objective, focused, and geared toward accomplishing specific purposes only in the United States (and perhaps some western European countries). Instead, in many other cultures, appraisal practices are very subjective and informal and usually reserved only for management-level personnel. Also, they found that there exist cultural differences regarding the appropriateness of differentiating employees on the basis of performance differences and then using such differential performance ratings as the basis for allocation of rewards, punishments, and so forth.

It seems of interest to investigate the extent to which the nature and dimensions of job performance from U.S.-based research translates to organizations in other cultures. Borman and Motowidlo (1993) and their colleagues have developed a quite interesting program of research over the past decade. It focuses on the distinction between task performance and contextual performance, where contextual performance refers to such extra-role behaviors as helping, volunteering, and facilitating, which transcend specific jobs and should be exhibited on all jobs. We might find that such behaviors are not viewed as aspects of job performance in some cultures but perhaps are in others. To the extent that we can view contextual performance behaviors as similar in nature to human relations and interpersonal aspects of performance, we might see applicability through research reported by Ali (1988) on performance appraisal in Arab countries. Ali studied appraisal systems in five Arab countries and found they tended to be informal, subjective, and placed considerable emphasis on interpersonal interaction aspects of job performance.

Future research needs to more systematically investigate influence processes in the performance appraisal context, with specific reference to cross-cultural differences in interpretation and effectiveness. Although there has been some research conducted on influence processes in performance appraisal in different cultures, as noted in an earlier section of this chapter, most of the research in this area is U.S. based (e.g., Ferris & Judge, 1991; Frink, Treadway, & Ferris, 2005). The use of ingratiation, self-promotion, assertiveness, and other tactics might be perceived, interpreted, and reacted to quite differently in different cultures.

Additionally, as the topic of emotions in organizations has gained great interest in recent years, Ferris et al. (2002) argued that the strategic display of emotion should be investigated as yet another specific behavior or set of behaviors in the arsenal of influence tactics to be examined within the context of human resources practices. Arvey, Renz, and Watson (1998) proposed a model of emotionality in the workplace; in their conceptualization, displayed emotion was predicted to affect both perceived and actual job performance. Because there appear to be great differences worldwide concerning the appropriateness of emotion demonstration, particularly in work contexts, it would be quite interesting to examine the cross-cultural implications of demonstrated emotion at work on performance appraisal processes and outcomes.

REFERENCES

Ali, A. (1988). A cross-national perspective of managerial work value systems. In R. N. Farmer & E. G. McGowen (Eds.), *Advances in international comparative management* (pp. 151–165). Greenwich, CT: JAI Press.

Allison, S. T., & Herlocker, C. E. (1994). Constructing impressions in demographically diverse organizational settings. *American Behavioral Scientist, 37,* 637–652.

Antonioni, D., & Park, H. (2001). The effects of personality similarity on peer ratings of contextual work behaviors. *Personnel Psychology, 54,* 331–359.

Arvey, R. D., Bhagat, R. S., & Salas, E. (1991). Cross-cultural and cross-national issues in personnel and human resources management. In G. R. Ferris & K. M. Rowland (Eds.), *Research in personnel and human resources management* (Vol. 9, pp. 367–407). Greenwich, CT: JAI Press.

Arvey, R. D., Renz, G. L., & Watson, T. W. (1998). Emotionality and job performance: Implications for personnel selection. In G. R. Ferris (Ed.), *Research in personnel and human resources management* (Vol. 16, pp. 103–147). Greenwich, CT: JAI Press.

Atkins, P. W., & Wood, R. E. (2002). Self- versus others' ratings as predictors of assessment center ratings: Validation evidence for 360-degree feedback programs. *Personnel Psychology, 55,* 871–904.

Beehr, T. A., Ivanitskaya, L., Hansen, C. P., Erofeev, D., & Guganowski, D. M. (2001). Evaluation of 360-degree feedback ratings: Relationships with each other and with performance and selection predictors. *Journal of Organizational Behavior, 22,* 775– 788.

Bhagat, R. S., & McQuaid, S. J. (1982). Role of subjective culture in organizations: A review and directions for future research. *Journal of Applied Psychology, 67,* 653–684.

Borman, W. C. (1991). Job behavior, performance, and effectiveness. In M. D. Dunnette & L. M. Hough (Eds.), *Handbook of industrial and organizational psychology* (2nd. ed., Vol. 2, pp. 271–326). Palo Alto, CA: Consulting Psychologists Press.

Borman, W. C., & Brush, D. H. (1993). More progress toward a taxonomy of managerial performance requirements. *Human Performance, 6,* 1–21.

Borman, W. C., & Motowidlo, S. J. (1993). Expanding the criterion domain to include elements of contextual performance. In N. Schmitt & W. C. Borman (Eds.), *Personnel selection* (pp. 71–98). San Francisco: Jossey-Bass.

Borman, W. C., & Motowidlo, S. J. (1997a). Introduction: Organizational citizenship behavior and contextual performance. *Human Performance, 10,* 67–69.

Borman, W. C., & Motowidlo, S. J. (1997b). Task performance and contextual performance: The meaning for personnel selection research. *Human Performance, 10,* 99–109.

Bowen, M. G. (1987). The escalation phenomenon reconsidered: Decision dilemmas or decision errors? *Academy of Management Review, 12,* 52–66.

Campbell, J. P. (1990). Modeling the performance prediction problem in industrial and organizational psychology. In M. D. Dunnette & L. M. Hough (Eds.), *Handbook of industrial and organizational psychology* (2nd ed., Vol. 1, pp. 687–732). Palo Alto, CA: Consulting Psychologists Press.

Cardy, R. L., & Dobbins, G. H. (1994). *Performance appraisal: Alternative perspectives.* Cincinnati, OH: South-Western Publishing.

Child, J., & Kieser, A. (1977). *Contrasts in British and West German management practice: Are recipes for success culture bound?* Paper presented at the conference on Cross-Cultural Studies on Organizational Functioning, Honolulu, Hawaii.

Conway, J. M. (1999). Distinguishing contextual performance from task performance for managerial jobs. *Journal of Applied Psychology, 84,* 3–13.

Cox, T., & Nkomo, S. M. (1986). Differential performance appraisal criteria: A field study of black and white managers. *Group and Organization Studies, 11,* 101–119.

Eisenhardt, K. M. (1985). Control: Organizational and economic approaches. *Management Science, 31,* 134–149.

Entrekin, L., & Chung, Y. H. (2001). Attitudes toward different sources of executive appraisal: A comparison of Hong Kong Chinese and American managers in Hong Kong. *International Journal of Human Resource Management, 12,* 965–987.

Farh, J., Dobbins, G. H., & Cheng, B. S. (1991). Cultural relativity in action: A comparison of self-ratings made by Chinese and U.S. workers. *Personnel Psychology, 44,* 129–147.

Farmer, S. M., Maslyn, J. M., Fedor, D. B., & Goodman, J. S. (1997). Putting upward influence strategies in context. *Journal of Organizational Behavior, 18,* 17–42.

Fernandez, J. P. (1993). *The diversity advantage: How American business can outperform Japanese and European companies in the global marketplace.* New York: Lexington Books.

Ferris, G. R., Fedor, D. B., & King, T. R. (1994). A political conceptualization of managerial behavior. *Human Resource Management Review, 4*(1), 1–34.

Ferris, G. R., Frink, D. D., Bhawuk, D. P. S., Zhou, J., & Gilmore, D. C. (1996). Reactions of diverse groups to politics in the workplace. *Journal of Management, 22,* 23–44.

Ferris, G. R., Frink, D. D., & Galang, M. C. (1993). Diversity in the workplace: The human resources management challenges. *Human Resource Planning, 16,* 41–51.

Ferris, G. R., Hochwarter, W. A., Buckley, M. R., Harrell-Cook, G., & Frink, D. D. (1999). Human resources management: Some new directions. *Journal of Management, 25,* 385–415.

Ferris, G. R., Hochwarter, W. A., Douglas, C., Blass, R., Kolodinsky, R. W., & Treadway, D. C. (2002). Social influence processes in organizations and human resources systems. In G. R. Ferris & J. J. Martocchio (Eds.), *Research in personnel and human resources management* (Vol. 21, pp. 65–127). Oxford, UK: JAI Press.

Ferris, G. R., & Judge, T. A. (1991). Personnel/human resources management: A political influence perspective. *Journal of Management, 17,* 447–488.

Ferris, G. R., Judge, T. A., Rowland, K. M., & Fitzgibbons, D. E. (1994). Subordinate influence and the performance evaluation process: Test of a model. *Organizational Behavior and Human Decision Processes, 58,* 101–135.

Ferris, G. R., & King, T. R. (1992). The politics of age discrimination in organizations. *Journal of Business Ethics, 11,* 341–350.

Ferris, G. R., Mitchell, T. R., Canavan, P. J., Frink, D. D., & Hopper, H. (1995). Accountability in human resource systems. In G. R. Ferris, S. D. Rosen, & D. T. Barnum (Eds.), *Handbook of human resource management* (pp. 175–196). Oxford, UK: Blackwell.

Ferris, G. R., Treadway, D. C., Kolodinsky, R. W., Hochwarter, W. A., Kacmar, C. J., Douglas, C., et al. (2005). Development and validation of the political skill inventory. *Journal of Management.*

Fox, S., Ben-Nahum, Z., & Yinon, Y. (1989). Perceived similarity and accuracy of peer ratings. *Journal of Applied Psychology, 74,* 781–786.

French, J. R. P., & Raven, B. H. (1959). The bases of social power. In D. Cartwright (Ed.), *Studies in social power.* Ann Arbor: University of Michigan Press.

Frink, D. D., Treadway, D. C., & Ferris, G. R. (2005). Social influence in the performance evaluation process. In S. Cartwright (Ed.), *Blackwell encyclopedic dictionary of human resource management.* (pp. 346–349). Oxford, UK: Blackwell.

Galang, M. C., Elsik, W., & Russ, G. S. (1999). Legitimacy in human resource management. In G. R. Ferris (Ed.), *Research in personnel and human resources management* (Vol. 17, pp. 41–79). Greenwich, CT: JAI Press.

Gregerson, H. B., Hite, J. M., & Black, J. S. (1996). *Journal of International Business Studies, Fourth Quarter,* 711–738.

Hall, E. T. (1988). *Understanding cultural differences.* Yarmouth, Maine: Entercultural Press.

Hall, A. T., Frink, D. D., Ferris, G. R., Hochwarter, W. A., Kacmar, C. J., & Bowen, M. G. (2003). Accountability in human resources management. In C. A. Schriesheim & L. Neider (Eds.), *New directions in human resource management* (pp. 29–63). Greenwich, CT: Information Age.

Harris, M. M., & Schaubroeck, J. (1988). A meta-analysis of self-supervisor, self-peer, and peer-supervisor ratings. *Personnel Psychology, 41,* 43–62.

Higgins, C. A., Judge, T. A., & Ferris, G. R. (2003). Influence tactics and work outcomes: A meta-analysis. *Journal of Organizational Behavior, 24,* 89–106.

Hirokawa, R.Y., & Miyaha, A. (1986). A comparison of influence strategies utilized by managers in American and Japanese organizations. *Communication Quarterly, 34,* 250–265.

Hofstede, G. (1980). *Culture's consequences: International differences in work-related values.* Beverly Hills: Sage.

Ilgen, D. R., & Hollenbeck, J. R. (1991). The structure of work: Job design and roles. In M. D. Dunnette & L. M. Hough (Eds.), *Handbook of industrial and organizational psychology* (Vol. 2, pp. 165–207). Palo Alto, CA: Consulting Psychologists Press.

Jones, E. E. (1990). *Interpersonal perception.* New York: Freeman.

Kelley, L., & Worthley, R. (1981). The role of culture in comparative management: A cross-cultural perspective. *Academy of Management Journal, 24,* 164–173.

Kelly, C. (1988). *The destructive achiever.* Reading, MA: Addison-Wesley.

Kipnis, D., & Schmidt, S. M. (1983). An influence perspective on bargaining in organizations. In M. H. Bazerman & J. L. Roy (Eds.), *Bargaining inside organizations* (pp. 303–319). Beverly Hills, CA: Sage.

Kipnis, D., & Schmidt, S. M. (1988). Upward-influence styles: Relationship with performance evaluations, salary, and stress. *Administrative Science Quarterly, 33,* 528–542.

Kipnis, D., Schmidt, S. W., Swaffin-Smith, C., & Wilkinson, I. (1984). Patterns of managerial influence: Shotgun managers, tacticians, and bystanders. *Organizational Dynamics, 12,* 58–67.

Kipnis, D., Schmidt, S. M., & Wilkinson, I. (1980). Intraorganizational influence tactics: Explorations in getting one's way. *Journal of Applied Psychology, 65*(4), 440–452.

Kraiger, K., & Ford, J. K. (1985). A meta-analysis of rate race effects in performance ratings. *Journal of Applied Psychology, 70,* 56–65.

Kras, E. S. (1989). *Management in two cultures.* Yarmouth, ME: Intercultural Press.

Laurent, A. (1986). The cross-cultural puzzle of international human resource management. *Human Resource Management, 25,* 91–102.

Lerner, J. S., & Tetlock, P. E. (1999). Accounting for the effects of accountability. *Psychological Bulletin, 125,* 255–275.

Lewin, K. (1936). *Principles of topological psychology.* New York: McGraw-Hill.

Li, J., & Karakowsky, L. (2001). Do we see eye to eye? Implications of cultural differences for cross-cultural management research and practice. *The Journal of Psychology, 135,* 501–517.

London, M., & Smither, J. W. (1995). Can multi-source feedback change perceptions of goal accomplishment, self-evaluations, and performance related outcomes? *Personnel Psychology, 48,* 803–839.

Longenecker, C. O., Sims, H. P., & Gioia, D. A. (1987). Behind the mask: The politics of employee appraisal. *Academy of Management Executive, 1,* 183–193.

Martin, D. C., & Bartol, K. M. (2003). Factors affecting expatriate performance appraisal system success: An organizational perspective. *Journal of International Management, 9,* 115–132.

Mintzberg, H. (1983). *Power in and around organizations.* Englewood Cliffs, NJ: Prentice-Hall.

Motowidlo, S. J., & Van Scotter, J. R. (1994). Evidence that task performance should be distinguished from contextual performance. *Journal of Applied Psychology, 79,* 475–480.

Motowidlo, S. J., Borman, W. C., & Van Scotter, J. R. (1997). A theory of individual differences in task and contextual performance. *Human Performance, 10,* 71–83.

Murphy, K. R., & Cleveland, J. N. (1995). *Understanding performance appraisal: Social, organizational, and goal-based perspectives.* Thousand Oaks, CA: Sage.

Nemeth, C. J., & Staw, B. M. (1989). The tradeoffs of social control and innovation in groups and organizations. In L. Berkowitz (Ed.), *Advances in experimental social psychology* (Vol. 12, pp. 175–210). New York: Academic Press.

Norton, S. M. (1992). Peer assessments of performance and ability: An exploratory meta-analysis of statistical artifacts and contextual moderators. *Journal of Business and Psychology, 6,* 387–399.

Ouchi, W. G., & Macguire, M. A. (1975). Organizational control: Two functions: *Administrative Science Quarterly, 20,* 559–569.

Organ, D. W. (1997). Organizational citizenship behavior: It's construct clean-up time. *Human Performance, 10,* 85–97.

Perreault, W. D., & Miles, R. H. (1978). Influence strategy mixes in complex organizations. *Behavioral Science, 23,* 86–98.

Pfeffer, J. (1981). Management as symbolic action: The creation and maintenance of organizational paradigms. In L. L. Cummings & B. M. Staw (Eds.), *Research in organizational behavior* (Vol. 3, pp. 1–52). Greenwich, CT: JAI Press.

Rokeach, M. (1973). *The nature of human values.* New York: Free Press.

Rosenfeld, P., Booth-Kewley, S., Edwards, J. E., & Alderton, D. L. (1994). Linking diversity and impression management: A study of Hispanic, black, and white navy recruits. *American Behavioral Scientist, 37,* 672–681.

Rowson, A. M. (1998). Using 360 degree feedback instruments up, down and around the world: Implications for global implementation and use of multi-rater feedback. *International Journal of Selection and Development, 6,* 45–48.

Rudman, L. A. (1999). To be or not to be self-promoting: The consequences of counterstereotypical impression management behavior. In R. M. Kramer & M. A. Neale (Eds.), *Power and influence in organizations* (pp. 287–310). Thousand Oaks, CA: Sage.

Schermerhorn, J. R., Jr., & Bond, M. H. (1991). Upward and downward influence tactics in managerial networks: A comparative study of Hong Kong Chinese and Americans. *Asia Pacific Journal of Management, 8,* 147–158.

Schneider, S. C. (1988). National vs. corporate culture: Implications for human resource management. *Human Resource Management, 27,* 231–246.

Schuler, R. S., & Florkowski, G. W. (1996). International human resources management. In B. Punnett & O. Shenkar (Eds.), *Handbook for international management research* (pp. 351–390). Cambridge, MA: Blackwell.

Schwartz, S. H. (1992). Universals in the content and structure of values: Theory and empirical tests in 20 countries. In M. Zanna (Ed.), *Advances in experimental social psychology* (Vol. 25, pp. 1–65). New York: Academic Press.

Schwartz, S. H. (1994). Are there universals in the content and structure of values? *Journal of Social Issues, 50,* 19–45.

Siegel-Jacobs, K., & Yates, J. F. (1996). Effects of procedural and outcome accountability on judgment quality. *Organizational Behavior and Human Decision Processes, 65,* 1–17.

Suliman, A. M. T. (2001). Work performance: Is it one thing or many things? The multidimensionality of performance in a Middle Eastern context. *International Journal of Human Resource Management, 12,* 1049–1061.

Suutari, V., & Brewster, C. (2001). Expatriate management practices and perceived relevance: Evidence from Finnish expatriates. *Personnel Review, 30,* 554–577.

Theiderman, S. (1991). *Profiting in America's multicultural marketplace.* New York: Lexington Books.
Thornton, G. C. (1980). Psychometric properties of self-appraisals of job performance. *Personnel Psychology, 33,* 263–271.
Triandis, H. C. (1972). *The analysis of subjective culture.* New York: Wiley.
Triandis, H. C. (1979). Values, attitudes, and interpersonal behavior. *Nebraska Symposium on Motivation* (pp. 195–259). Lincoln: University of Nebraska Press.
Triandis, H. C. (1989). The self and social behavior in differing cultural contexts. *Psychological Review, 96,* 506–520.
van Knippenberg, B., van Knippenberg, D., Blaauw, E., & Vermunt, R. (1999). Relational considerations in the use of influence tactics. *Journal of Applied Social Psychology, 29*(4), 806–819.
Van Scotter, J. R., & Motowidlo, S. J. (1996). Interpersonal facilitation and job dedication as separate facets of contextual performance. *Journal of Applied Psychology, 81*(5), 525–531.
Wayne, S. J., & Ferris, G. R. (1990). Influence tactics, affect, and exchange quality in supervisor-subordinate interactions: A laboratory experiment and field study. *Journal of Applied Psychology, 75,* 487–499.
Wayne, S. J., Liden, R. C., Graf, I. K., & Ferris, G. R. (1997). The role of upward influence tactics in human resource decisions. *Personnel Psychology, 50,* 978–1006.
Wexley, K. N., & Klimoski, R. (1984). Performance appraisal: An update. In K. M. Rowland & G. R. Ferris (Eds.), *Research in personnel and human resources management* (Vol. 2, pp. 35–79). Greenwich, CT: JAI Press.
Wood, R. E., Allen, J., Pillinger, T., & Kohn, N. (1999). 360-feedback: Theory, research and practice. In A. Travaglione & V. Marshall (Eds.), *Human resource strategies: An applied approach* (pp. 209–228). Sydney: McGraw-Hill.
Yu, J., & Murphy, K. R. (1993). Modesty bias in self-ratings of performance: A test of the cultural relativity hypothesis. *Personnel Psychology, 46,* 357–363.

7

Culture, Feedback, and Motivation

ROBERT D. PRITCHARD AND
SATORIS S. YOUNGCOURT
University of Central Florida and Kansas State University

This chapter focuses on the effects of culture on feedback. A motivational perspective is used to explore the potential influences of culture on motivation and feedback and thereby performance. Motivational variables that are most likely to be influenced by cultural differences are identified. Based on this motivational perspective and other literature on feedback, implications are presented on how to give feedback to improve performance in different cultures. Finally, cross-cultural data are presented on the effectiveness of one results-oriented feedback intervention designed to improve performance through increasing motivation. Findings suggest that the feedback system was equally effective in all four of the cultures examined; however, the reasons for the success of the feedback system differed substantially across cultures.

INTRODUCTION

The importance of cultural influences in human resources practices is becoming increasingly evident as organizations become more global and the workforce more culturally diverse. As Cascio (2003) noted, "cross-cultural exposure, if not actual interaction, has become the norm" (p. 404). However, although this cross-cultural contact is increasing, we still know little about cultural influences on various human resources practices (Erez, 1994; Erez & Earley, 1993; Milliman et al., 1998; Triandis, Dunnette, & Hough, 1994).

Human resources practices ultimately are designed to ensure employees behave in a way that is consistent with business strategy and external environment in order to achieve an organization's objectives and sustain its competitiveness (Cascio, 1998; Huselid, Jackson, & Schuler, 1997; Lee, MacDermid, & Buck, 2000; Lepak & Snell, 1999; Wright & McMahan, 1992). This focus on behavior is an issue of motivation. *Motivation* is defined as the process whereby people allocate their energy to different actions or tasks (Naylor, Pritchard, & Ilgen, 1980). Put another way, motivation is how much energy (intensity) is applied to which actions (direction) for how long (persistence). Thus, motivation includes the intensity, direction, and persistence components of behavior (Campbell & Pritchard, 1976; Cofer & Appley, 1964; Vroom, 1964). To change behavior so it is optimally aligned with organizational objectives, one must influence motivation. One way to influence motivation, and thereby behavior, is through feedback.

A primary question, however, is whether current models of motivation and approaches to feedback, which are based on Western cultures, apply to other cultures. There is little doubt that reward systems and the values people place on rewards differ by culture (Cascio, 2003; Erez, 1994, 1997; Stone-Romero & Stone, 2002). Furthermore, such cultural differences should affect the way feedback is given (Levy, Silverman, Norris-Watts, Diefendorff, & Ramakrishnan, 2003; Sully de Luque & Sommer, 2000). However, this does not necessarily mean that the fundamental motivation concepts and relationships will also differ across cultures.

STRUCTURE OF THE CHAPTER

This chapter is divided into four sections. The first three are conceptual and the last is empirical. We first define culture and briefly describe several dimensions that differentiate cultures. The next section is an attempt to include formal theory in the study of cultural differences, as suggested by Alderfer and Sims (2003). Specifically, we examine one theory of motivation and identify the components of the theory that are most likely to be influenced by cultural differences. In the next section we explore implications from this motivation theory and other work on feedback for how to give feedback in different cultures. In the final section of the chapter, we present empirical results that compare the effects of feedback in different cultures.

CULTURE

Culture has been defined in many ways. In fact, some have suggested that the search for a single definition of culture is futile (Segall, 1984). Nevertheless, Hofstede (1991) offered a frequently used definition of culture as "the collective programming of the mind which distinguishes the members of one group or category of people from another" (p. 5). To examine cultural differences, we use the framework presented by Hofstede (1980, 1991, 2001).

Although we acknowledge there are numerous other cultural frameworks with different underlying dimensions (e.g., Douglas, 1970; Fiske, 1992; Schwartz, 1992; Trompenaars, 1993), in the interest of brevity we chose only to examine differences based on Hofstede's framework. Despite criticisms of his work, including concerns that five dimensions are not sufficient to distinguish among the intricacies of various cultures and that findings from survey data are not altogether generalizable, Hofstede's cross-cultural work remains the most widely used, cited, and replicated cultural framework to date. Hofstede describes the dimensions of individualism versus collectivism, power distance, masculinity versus femininity, uncertainty avoidance, and long-term orientation.

Perhaps the most widely studied dimension is that of individualism versus collectivism. Essentially, it describes the degree to which individuals within a culture rely on, and have allegiance to, the self (individualism) or to a group (collectivism). According to Hofstede and Bond (1988), power distance, the second dimension, is defined "as the extent to which the less powerful members of institutions and organizations accept that power is distributed unequally" (p. 419). The third dimension, masculinity versus femininity, also called the achievement-nurturance dimension, refers to the degree to which individuals in a culture value such behaviors as assertiveness, achievement, acquisition of wealth or value caring for others, social supports, and the quality of life. Uncertainty avoidance, the fourth dimension, refers to how comfortable people feel toward ambiguity, with individuals in low uncertainty avoidance cultures feeling relatively comfortable with the unknown and individuals in high uncertainty avoidance cultures preferring formal rules and having less tolerance for ambiguity. The final dimension, long-term orientation, focuses on the extent to which individuals in the culture are oriented toward the future, focusing on savings and persistence, or oriented toward the past or present, focusing on tradition and fulfilling social obligations (Hofstede & Bond, 1988).

MOTIVATIONAL THEORY

A central tenet of this chapter is that feedback influences performance through motivation and that one important issue is how differences in culture are reflected in motivation. To do this analysis, we use a single motivation theory and examine how cultural differences might influence the components of this theory. The theory to be used is one recently proposed by Pritchard and Ramstad (2003) and summarized in Pritchard and Payne (2003). We are not arguing this is the only theory that could be used for such an analysis. However, we do feel it is a useful one. This theory is based on the motivational components of the theory proposed by Naylor et al. (1980), also known as NPI theory, and is an example of an expectancy theory. Expectancy theories posit that people are motivated by the anticipation or expectancy of how their actions will lead to future positive or negative affect (e.g., Campbell & Pritchard, 1976; Heckhausen, 1991; Vroom, 1964).

The Pritchard and Ramstad motivational theory is shown in Figure 7.1. The first row of the figure reflects an assumption of the theory that at any given time, people have a certain amount of energy. This energy is known as the *Energy Pool*, and varies across people and within people over time. People also have *Needs*, the satisfaction of which creates positive affect. To satisfy these needs, an individual draws from his or her energy pool. This is shown by the arrow from Energy Pool to Needs. This arrow is not meant to suggest that the Energy Pool somehow causes Needs, rather that energy is used to satisfy needs. As the second row of the figure indicates, motivation is the process of allocating this energy to meet one's needs. The motivation process is the mechanism for using energy to meet needs.

The third row of Figure 7.1 shows the components of this motivation process. The first box on the left indicates that people allocate energy to *Actions*, or behaviors. A police officer's actions, for example, include patrolling neighborhoods, writing traffic tickets, filing reports, and meeting with members of the community. When an officer applies energy toward these actions, *Results* are generally produced. For example, an officer may stop a driver (an action) he or she believes is under the influence of alcohol. This stop may lead to an arrest (a result).

When results are observed by different individuals, *Evaluations* are made. Evaluations occur when one or more evaluators, such as supervisors, peers, subordinates, and/or the self, place the measured result on an evaluative continuum ranging from good to bad. The officer's arrest report (a result) may be evaluated by the officer him- or herself, as well as by superiors or staff in the district attorney's office.

After these evaluations are made, *Outcomes* occur that can be self-administered or externally administered. Outcomes can be intrinsic, such as feelings of accomplishment, or can be extrinsic, such as forms of recognition or pay raises. The officer may feel a sense of pride in making

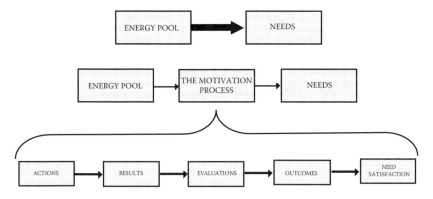

Figure 7.1 The Motivation Model

the roads safer and for completing an error-free report (a self-administered outcome), or he or she may receive praise from superiors for doing a good job (an externally administered outcome).

Outcomes get their motivating power because of their ties to *Need Satisfaction.* When needs are satisfied, positive affect occurs; when needs are not satisfied, negative affect occurs. It is the anticipation of this need satisfaction that influences the motivational process. This anticipated satisfaction may or may not match the actual satisfaction that occurs when the outcome is actually received.

The different components of the theory (actions, results, evaluations, outcomes, and need satisfaction) together determine *motivational force.* Motivational force is the degree to which a person believes that changes in energy devoted to a given action will result in changes in need satisfaction. Actions with high motivational force are predicted to have large amounts of energy allocated to them. Little or no energy will be allocated to actions with low motivational force.

Motivational Theory Connections and Cultural Influences

The Pritchard and Ramstad theory is about *relationships.* The overall theory focuses on the relationships between amount of energy allocated to various acts and the expected levels of need satisfaction. Each of the separate components of the theory is also connected by relationships, which are symbolized in Figure 7.1 by the arrows connecting the boxes. For example, the arrow connecting results and evaluations refers the degree of relationship between the level of results produced and the favorableness of the evaluation. These relationships, known as "connections" in the theory, are where culture is expected to have the most influence on motivation and, ultimately, performance. In this section we define these connections and describe how they can be influenced by culture.

Action-to-Result Connections

Action-to-result connections describe a person's perceived relationship between the amount of effort directed toward an action and the amount of a result that is expected to occur. The person may see a very close relationship between the two, or perceive a much weaker relationship. Continuing with the police officer example, the officer may see a strong relationship between the amount of effort devoted to meeting with community members (the action) and the number of community members contacted (the result). However, effort devoted to patrolling (the action) may have a weaker relationship with the number of arrests (the result) because the number of violators varies due to factors beyond the officer's control.

Cultural Influences on Action-to-Result Connections

Individualism versus collectivism. Employees in collectivist cultures, because they are motivated by such things as deference, affiliation, and abasement (Markus & Kitayama, 1991), may approach a problem using teamwork and cooperative acts in the hopes of achieving results that benefit the group (Hofstede, 1991). Conversely, as Stone-Romero and Stone (2002) noted, employees from individualistic cultures, because they are motivated by their own wants, needs, and motives, will be more likely to take actions that will lead to results that benefit themselves in terms of providing them more pay, prestige, or power. This could influence action-to-result connections in that the actions people take can vary depending on whether they value the individual above the collective or the collective above the individual. At the very least, the focus of action-to-result connections in collective cultures will focus more heavily on the group's results rather than the individual's results. Also, if actions are dictated by the organization that are not consistent with the individual's values (e.g., actions must be highly interdependent, but the individual is highly individualistic), the individual's action-to-result connections will likely be weak, and therefore motivation will likely be low.

Uncertainty avoidance.

Uncertainty avoidance is another dimension that could impact action-to-result connections. Specifically, individuals from cultures where ambiguity is not tolerated well will more likely prefer a strong relationship between their actions and their results. In these high uncertainty avoidance cultures, individuals will most likely seek to obtain feedback in order to decrease the ambiguity, thus making the connection stronger and motivation subsequently greater. If action-to-result connections are weak, individuals from such cultures may find this more aversive than would individuals from cultures where ambiguity is more tolerated.

Masculinity versus femininity and power distance.

Two other cultural dimensions that could influence action-to-result connections are masculinity versus femininity and power distance. People in masculine cultures value assertiveness more readily than do people in feminine cultures. Therefore, individuals in a masculine culture may be more likely to assert themselves and take actions that are not assigned to them in order to achieve desired results. Similarly, people from low power distance cultures, who tend to consider themselves more equal with their supervisors than do people from high power distance cultures, may be more likely to take actions that they do not have the authority to take. Thus, masculinity and low power distance could increase one's action-to-results connections because individuals believe they have the authority to make changes to improve how the work is done. This produces changes in work strategies and thus action-to-results connections. Furthermore, individuals in such cultures would tend to find low action-to-result connections more demotivating than would individuals in feminine or high power distance cultures.

Result-to-Evaluation Connections

The result-to-evaluation connections reflect perceived relationships between the amount of the result that is produced and the level of the evaluation that is expected to occur. Such a connection exists for each different result and for each evaluator. For example, the number of drug-related arrests an officer makes may be highly related to a sergeant's evaluation of the officer as well as the officer's self-evaluation. The number of parking tickets written, however, may have a much weaker relationship to level of the evaluation.

Cultural Influences on Result-to-Evaluation Connections

Individualism versus collectivism.

The extent to which certain results are valued by a culture will likely influence the type of evaluation that will result. For example, collectivistic cultures value results that benefit the group. Therefore, in these cultures, results that further the goals of the work group or organization may be evaluated more favorably (by all evaluators, including the self) than will results that simply promote the individual.

Uncertainty avoidance.

Just as individuals from high uncertainty avoidance cultures would need to know how actions lead to results, they also need to know the connections between results and evaluations. However, high uncertainty avoidance cultures, being less tolerant of others' differing opinions, would be less likely to seek out or accept feedback, particularly if it is negative (Sully de Luque & Sommer, 2000). Such individuals, not knowing what results are needed to achieve a desired evaluation, will likely experience anxiety and the negative effects that accompany stress. Conversely, the effects of a weak result-to-evaluation connection will be less negative in cultures that have a high tolerance for ambiguity. That is, individuals from low uncertainty avoidance cultures are less threatened by opinions and behaviors that differ from their own (Berger, 1979) and therefore are more likely to seek the necessary feedback that will strengthen this connection.

Evaluation-to-Outcome Connections

Evaluation-to-outcome connections represent the perceived relationships between the level of the evaluation and the level of an outcome that will result. If pay raises are entirely contingent on supervisor evaluations, there will be a strong evaluation-to-outcome connection between the evaluation and the size of the pay raise. If raises are equal for everyone regardless of performance, there will be a weak evaluation-to-outcome connection for raises.

Cultural Influences on Evaluation-to-Outcome Connections

Individualism versus collectivism.

Evaluation-to-outcome connections could differ for individualistic versus collectivistic individuals. Specifically, rewards (outcomes) in collectivistic cultures are likely to be more group-based, whereas rewards in individualistic cultures are likely to be individually based.

Power distance.

Different evaluators may have different importance in different cultures. For example, individuals in high power distance cultures may be more likely to accept both positive and negative feedback from superiors because they accept the power distance more readily than do individuals from a low power distance culture. The importance of an evaluator is dependent on the outcomes he or she controls (Naylor et al., 1980). So a greater power distance would be associated with control over more powerful outcomes. This would make evaluation-to-outcome connections stronger in high power distance settings.

Masculinity versus femininity and long-term orientation.

The humility or modesty of people within a culture could also influence the evaluation-to-outcome connection. For example, the preference for modesty in feminine cultures and humility in high long-term orientation cultures could lead evaluators from such cultures to be less likely to provide recognition (in the form of verbal praise or material recognition) to individuals who receive good evaluations, even if they have the authority to provide such outcomes. Therefore, individuals whose managers subscribe to such values, but they themselves do not (i.e., their values are more in line with masculine and low long-term orientation cultures), likely will have weaker evaluation-to-outcome connections and therefore lower motivation. They may believe that regardless of their evaluation, they will not receive an outcome they value. This implies that managers should tailor at least some outcomes (e.g., praise, recognition) based on the values held by the subordinate.

Outcome-to-Need Satisfaction Connections

The final set of relationships in the motivation theory is the perceived relationships between the amount of outcomes received and the resulting degree of need satisfaction. If increases in the size of a monetary bonus result in increased need satisfaction, then outcome-to-need satisfaction connections are high and indicate that monetary bonuses are important to that person. If larger bonuses do not lead to greater feelings of need satisfaction, then the connection is considered weaker and is indicative that bonuses are not as important for that person.

Cultural Influences in Outcome-to-Need Satisfaction Connections

Individualism versus collectivism.

Just as rewards can vary by culture, the values placed on such rewards likely will vary as well. That is, individuals from individualistic cultures are likely to value individual-based rewards more strongly than group-based rewards. Conversely, individuals from collectivist cultures are more apt to value group-based rewards.

Power distance.

In high power distance cultures, outcomes that maintain or encourage a status differential, such as promotions, will more likely be more valued than in low power distance cultures. This should also be true for outcomes that involve outward forms of recognition.

Long-term orientation and masculinity versus femininity.

Value placed on rewards can be expected to vary based on individuals' long-term orientation and masculinity (vs. femininity) as well. Specifically, individuals from high long-term orientation cultures, because of their emphasis on humility and the importance of relationship-building, may not value praise or recognition as much as individuals from a low long-term orientation culture. In these cases, such outcomes could backfire as means for improving motivation because the link between the outcome and need satisfaction is low or even negative. Likewise, individuals from masculine cultures, valuing achievement and success, may have a greater need for recognition than would individuals from a feminine culture, who value modesty above achievement.

FEEDBACK

One means for influencing motivation, and thereby behavior, is feedback. As such, each connection of the motivational theory is influenced by feedback processes. Feedback can provide information on what the organization considers desirable results, what actions will lead to such results, what level of results will lead to a particular evaluation, and what outcomes are associated with those evaluations, they rely on feedback from others in the organization. This feedback can be solicited by the individual or can be provided without the individual having to seek it. Furthermore, the individual can react to the feedback in ways that may influence future feedback and performance. Just as the components of the motivational theory were influenced by cultural differences, feedback seeking, feedback giving, and feedback reactions undoubtedly are affected by culture as well.

Feedback Seeking

Several researchers have noted that context is an important factor in feedback-seeking behavior (Ashford & Cummings, 1985; Levy, Albright, Cawley, & Williams, 1995; Northcraft & Ashford, 1990). Sully de Luque and Sommer (2000) presented a cross-cultural model of feedback-seeking behavior. They provided several propositions as to how the various cultural values might influence feedback providing, feedback-seeking behavior, cost of seeking feedback, strategy for seeking feedback, and source for seeking feedback.

How people seek feedback could influence subsequent motivation. For example, if, as Sully de Luque and Sommer (2000) proposed, individuals from high uncertainty avoidance cultures engage in more feedback seeking, each of the motivation connections should be stronger. Feedback can influence task strategies (action-to-results connections), add clarity to what results or outputs are valued (results-to-evaluation connections), help in understanding the reward system (evaluation-to-outcome connections), and provide additional valued outcomes such as recognition (evaluation-to-need satisfaction connections). Individuals from low uncertainty avoidance cultures might not seek as much feedback, which would result in less clear connections and lower motivation.

Feedback Giving

Numerous researchers have acknowledged the influence of culture on feedback giving (e.g., Brutus, Leslie, & McDonald-Mann, 2001; Earley, Gibson, & Chen, 1999; Levy et al., 2003; Milliman et al., 1998; Sully de Luque & Sommer, 2000). For example, Milliman et al. (1998) examined the impact of culture on the performance appraisal process. Hofstede (1980, 1991) presents several propositions for how individualism versus collectivism, power distance, and long-term orientation might affect the delivery of feedback to employees.

Individuals from various cultures will likely differ in not only how they give feedback (e.g., directly vs. indirectly) but also what type of feedback they provide (e.g., results-oriented vs. relationship-oriented or team-based vs. individual-based). We propose that the more feedback agents provide feedback that is consistent with the recipients' cultural values, the more the motivational connections will be strengthened. For example, managers from individualistic cultures will more likely emphasize personal achievement, whereas managers from collectivistic cultures will emphasize team-based achievement. To the extent employees receiving feedback hold the same values as the manager—for example, both employee and manager hold individualistic values, or both hold collectivistic values—the relevant connections will be stronger than if they hold different values. This match of values is particularly salient in multicultural organizations where subordinates and supervisors may come from different cultures.

Feedback Reactions

Stone-Romero and Stone (2002, 2003) recently developed the Cross-Cultural Feedback Model (CCFM), which takes into account the effects of culture on individuals' responses to feedback. The CCFM posits that the cultural backgrounds of the feedback agent (i.e., the individual giving the feedback) and the intended receiver of the feedback cause, in part, the values to which the agent and feedback receiver subscribe. Their cultural backgrounds also influence the way each of the selves is construed and the behavioral scripts (Shank & Abelson, 1977) available.

In their description of the CCFM, Stone-Romero and Stone (2002) primarily discussed differences between idiocentric individuals (i.e., people subscribing to individualistic values) and allocentric individuals (people subscribing to collectivist values). Because idiocentric individuals tend to view the self as an independent, autonomous entity and focus on implications of the feedback that concern their own welfare, they will tend to react to negative feedback in self-enhancing, often dysfunctional ways. Specifically, idiocentric individuals tend to acquire, process, and use information in ways that will benefit themselves (Greenwald, 1980; Taylor & Brown, 1988). This self-serving, self-enhancing tendency will likely lead individuals from individualistic cultures to make internal attributions for good outcomes, such as taking credit for good performance, and make external attributions for bad outcomes, such as denying responsibility for poor performance (Stone-Romero & Stone, 2002; Weiner, 1985).

Allocentric individuals, conversely, tend to construe the self as being highly interdependent and focus on implications of the feedback that concern the welfare of their group. Allocentric individuals, according to Stone-Romero and Stone (2002), tend to be more self-critical and will be more likely to respond to negative feedback in functional ways that will lead to improvement. This self-critical nature would lead individuals from collectivist cultures to be more likely to make internal attributions for poor performance (Stone-Romero & Stone, 2002).

CROSS-CULTURAL EFFECTS AND A MOTIVATION/FEEDBACK INTERVENTION

This chapter has so far focused on conceptual issues relating culture to motivation and feedback. In this final section, we focus on empirical results of using a feedback intervention in different cultures. The intervention is the Productivity Measurement and Enhancement System, or ProMES (Pritchard, 1990, 1995; Pritchard, Jones, Roth, Stuebing, & Ekeberg, 1989). ProMES uses results-oriented feedback to influence the various components of the Pritchard and Ramstad motivational theory. The ProMES process is described in detail in Pritchard (1990), and an overview is in Pritchard, Paquin, DeCuir, McCormick, and Bly (2002). In this final empirical section, we are not attempting to test the implications discussed in the first three sections of the chapter, but rather see if differences in response to feedback occur across cultures and if those differences can be related to cultural factors.

The ProMES Process

Essentially, ProMES is a formal, step-by-step process that identifies organizational objectives, develops a measurement system to assess how well the work group is meeting those objectives, and develops a feedback system that gives people in the work group and their management information on how well the work group is performing. This intervention typically is done on a group but can be done on individuals as well. It has been used in approximately 150 applications in different types of organizations, for different levels of organizational personnel from entry level to top management, in seven different countries (Pritchard, 1995; Pritchard et al., 2002).

The process of ProMES begins with the formation of a design team comprised of individuals responsible for completing the job requirements, one or two supervisors, and a facilitator to guide the process. These individuals collectively determine the group's three to six major objectives. Examples of objectives include such things as "Provide Excellent Customer Service" and "Maintain a Knowledgeable and Trained Staff." The design team then develops quantitative measures, termed indicators, to show how well the team is meeting the objectives. For example, possible indicators could include scores on a customer service survey for the first objective and percentage of individual training goals attained for the second objective.

Once the design team has established the objectives and developed the indicators for each objective, the team formally operationalizes the NPI and Pritchard and Ramstad result-to-evaluation connections in what are termed *contingencies*. These contingencies are graphs that relate the amount of the result produced to the value that amount of result contributes to the overall organization. The horizontal axis of a contingency is the level of output and the vertical axis expresses value to the organization, termed *Effectiveness*. Effectiveness typically ranges from -100 (well below expectations) through 0 (meeting minimum expectations) to +100 (well above expectations). The completed contingency is a graph of the relationship between level of output and the effectiveness of that level of output. There is one contingency for each indicator. Contingencies are described more fully in Pritchard et al. (2002).

Contingencies have a number of advantages. They capture the relative importance of each indicator by their slope or range. They also allow for both descriptive and evaluative information to be fed back because they translate the amount of each indicator (description) into how valuable that amount is to the organization (evaluation). Contingencies rescale each indicator into a common metric of effectiveness, the value created for the organization. Because levels of all measures are converted to this common scale, scores on individual measures can be combined into an overall effectiveness score.

The entire system, including the objectives, indicators, and contingencies, are known to all personnel and are approved by higher management to ensure they accurately capture value to the organization. Next, data are collected on each indicator, and a feedback report is prepared and given to the work group on a regular basis, usually monthly. This feedback report shows how the work group did on each measure and, using the contingencies, translates this level on each measure into its corresponding effectiveness score: the value to the organization. These effectiveness scores are also summed to produce an overall effectiveness score. At each performance period, which can range from one to several months depending on the nature of the work, the work group meets with management to review the feedback report and make plans for improvements. These feedback reports and the feedback meetings continue over time in a continuous improvement model. The system is monitored over time with changes to the system made as needed.

ProMES and the Pritchard and Ramstad Motivation Theory

The ProMES intervention addresses each of the motivational components of the Pritchard and Ramstad motivational theory. The result-to-evaluation connections, for example, are operationalized through the contingencies in the development of the system. Therefore, ProMES contingencies literally are the result-to-evaluation connections. The action-to-result connections are influenced by the discussions during the feedback meetings involving the development and evaluation of new ways of doing the work and by the forming of strategies for making these improvements. By discussing steps the group can take to improve performance, the action-to-result connections are improved and clarified. ProMES can also change the evaluation-to-outcome connections. If by doing ProMES, the evaluation system is clearer, the connections between evaluations and outcomes become clearer. Finally, the outcome-to-need satisfaction connections could be affected by ProMES. For example, if people in the work group have more confidence in the accuracy of the evaluation system, a pay raise based on that evaluation system could lead to satisfaction of needs for achievement in addition to needs for money.

Thus, between development of the system, receipt of feedback by work group personnel, and the use of feedback to make improvements, there are direct connections between ProMES components and the entire Pritchard and Ramstad motivational chain. This suggests that ProMES can be used to increase motivation. Furthermore, because each of the motivational connections is influenced by culture, and because various parts of the feedback process are also influenced by culture, we next consider previous ProMES projects that have been conducted in different cultures in order to make cross-cultural comparisons in feedback and motivation.

Method

ProMES projects have been developed in numerous organizations in several different countries. Information is available on many of these projects, including characteristics of the organization, such as the initial state of the organization, and the target work group and initial attitudes toward productivity and ProMES. Other information describes the nature of the developed system, reactions to the system, and performance data for baseline and feedback periods. Using the ProMES database, descriptive information on feedback usage and acceptance was compared across different countries.

Participants: Country and Cultural Differences

Countries where a sufficient number of ProMES projects had been completed for meaningful comparisons included the United States ($N = 12$),

Sweden ($N = 7$), the Netherlands ($N = 10$), and Germany/Switzerland ($N = 8$). Because the Swiss projects ($N = 3$) were conducted in the German-speaking part of Switzerland, they were combined with the German projects ($N = 5$). Furthermore, these country groupings are in line with Ronen and Shenkar's (1985) country clusters.

As Smith and Bond (1998) noted, researchers often erroneously report country differences as being analogous with cultural differences. Therefore, rather than simply imply there are cultural differences because we have different countries, we must first indicate on which cultural variables these countries differ. Furthermore, whereas individuals within a national culture can vary on their cultural values, Hofstede's dimensions are typically thought of in terms of the countries/cultures as a whole.

To determine how the countries differed in terms of culture, we referred to Hofstede's (2001) country classification ratings. The top row of Table 7.1 indicates the five culture dimensions we are using, along with their means and standard deviations across all the countries reported by Hofstede. The next four rows show the individual country scores and standard scores for each dimension by country. These standard scores compare the individual country to all countries on each culture dimension. They are the score for that country minus the mean across all countries divided by the standard deviation across all countries. Cultural differences between the countries can be seen by examining the differences in the standard scores on the dimensions.

It is not surprising that these countries do not represent anywhere near the entire range of possible culture scores, because they are all Western cultures. However, there are still meaningful differences between them. The range of standard scores across the four countries is .95 for individualism versus collectivism, .42 for power distance, 3.39 for masculinity versus femininity, 1.51 for uncertainty avoidance and .52 for long-term orientation. If we assume that a .5 standard deviation difference is a moderate difference (Cohen, 1977), the differences across countries exceed this value on four dimensions and are close on the fifth. Nevertheless, it is important to note that most of these differences in culture are rather small compared with the different cultures that exist, and one must bear this in mind while interpreting the results.

Measures

Comparisons focused on three variables: initial appeal of the ProMES intervention, reactions to the system after experience, and the strength of the effects of feedback on performance. Initial appeal refers to the primary purposes of implementing ProMES and the anticipated benefits seen by managers and those decision makers who initially approved using the system. The purposes and anticipated benefits can be classified as either management-focused or employee-focused. That is, initial appeal is either directed more at benefiting or aiding management's

TABLE 7.1 Classifications, Dimension Scores, and Strength of Cultural Dimension for Country Comparisons

	Individualism vs. Collectivism (M = 43.7; SD = 25.2)	Power Distance (M = 56.3; SD = 21.5)	Masculinity vs. Femininity (M = 50.1; SD = 18)	Uncertainty Avoidance (M = 65; SD = 23.9)	Long-term Orientation (M = 46.7; SD = 28.5)
Germany/Switzerland* (Germanic)	Raw score = 67 z score = .93	Raw score = 35 z score = -.99	Raw score = 66 z score = .88	Raw score = 65 z score = -.00	Raw score = 31 z score = -.55
Netherlands (Nordic)	Raw score = 80 z score = 1.44	Raw score = 38 z score = -.85	Raw score = 14 z score = -2.01	Raw score = 53 z score = -.50	Raw score = 44 z score = -.10
Sweden (Nordic)	Raw score = 71 z score = 1.08	Raw score = 31 z score = -1.17	Raw score = 5 z score = -2.51	Raw score = 29 z score = -1.51	Raw score = 33 z score = -.48
United States (Anglo)	Raw score = 91 z score = 1.88	Raw score = 40 z score = -.75	Raw score = 62 z score = .66	Raw score = 46 z score = -.80	Raw score = 29 z score = -.62

Notes: Values in the row are for Germany only because Hofstede did not separate the German, French, and Italian parts of Switzerland when determining country scores. Ronen and Shenkar's (1985) country clusters are in parentheses beneath each country.

role in the organization (management-focused) or is directed more at helping employees develop or fulfill their role within the organization (employee-focused).

The management-focused scale consisted of four items: the ability to monitor work groups more accurately, the ability to evaluate productivity, the use of the feedback for identifying and communicating to top management, and the use of the feedback as a management information system. These four dichotomous items were scored with a 1, indicating endorsement of the statement, or 0, indicating lack of endorsement. This scale exhibited good internal consistency reliability (KR-20 = .91). The final measure used in the analyses was the percentage of items endorsed for each project. The mean percentage endorsement was then calculated for the projects in each country.

The employee-focused scale of initial appeal included four similarly scored dichotomous items: more employee participation, reduced stress, improved quality, and the ability to help groups manage themselves. This scale also exhibited good internal consistency reliability (KR-20 = .82). Percentage of endorsement by country was determined in the same manner as the management-focused scale.

The second area of comparison is reactions to ProMES. Reactions of management and people in the work groups were examined. These reactions were separated into reactions reflecting uncertainty avoidance and reactions reflecting a tendency to be nurturing. The uncertainty avoidance scale included 12 items, with 6 items assessing management endorsement and 6 assessing endorsement of people in the work group. Items included positive reactions for clarification of what is important, clarification of priorities, giving the work group information to know how to improve, giving management more control (for management only), giving the work group more control (for work group personnel only), giving personnel better feedback, and allowing personnel to participate in decision making. Items were dichotomous, scored with either a 1 indicating endorsement or a 0 indicating lack of endorsement. This scale demonstrated good internal consistency reliability (KR-20 = .96). Percentage of endorsement by country was calculated in the same manner as the management-focused and employee-focused scales.

The nurturing scale consisted of 12 dichotomous items with an equal number of items for management and for work group endorsement. Items focused on positive reactions for reducing stress, reducing wasted effort, allowing personnel to fix problems before they became serious, allowing personnel the chance to make improvements, providing information/recognition for good work, and improving attitudes of personnel. This scale also exhibited good internal consistency reliability (KR-20 = .92). The percentage of endorsement by country was calculated just as the other dichotomous scales were calculated.

The final comparison between the countries concerns the strength of effects of the intervention. Recall that ProMES provides an overall effectiveness score for each time period, including both baseline and feedback time periods. The effect of the intervention on improving productivity was assessed by the effect size (d score) comparing performance during baseline to performance during feedback. This effect size was calculated for each project by taking the average overall effectiveness score at baseline and subtracting it from the average overall effectiveness score at feedback and dividing by the pooled standard deviation of the overall effectiveness scores.

Results and Discussion

Figure 7.2 shows the results comparing endorsement of the scales by country. Analyses indicated differences between countries consistent with their cultural values. Specifically, as shown in the upper graph in Figure 7.2, projects completed in the United States, a country high in individualistic values, had decision makers who endorsed management-focused benefits with greater frequency than they endorsed employee-focused benefits, $t(11) = 3.55, p < .05$. The European countries, although also relatively individualistic, are more collective in their values compared with the United States. Whereas there were no significant differences in each European country between management-focused and employee-focused benefits, the direction of the means in each country showed employee-focused benefits endorsed with greater frequency than management-focused purposes. Furthermore, there were differences in endorsement of management-focused benefits by country, $F(3, 33) = 5.24, p < .05$. Specifically, post hoc analyses using Bonferroni adjustments to account for inflated Type I error rates indicated that U.S. endorsement of management-focused items were significantly greater than management-focused endorsement in the Netherlands projects.

The initial appeal findings can also be explained by the different levels of masculinity of the countries. Sweden, for example, has been characterized as a predominantly feminine culture. Such cultures tend to be relationship-oriented or nurturing, whereas masculine cultures tend to be task-focused. This tendency to be nurturing could explain why projects completed in Sweden tended to have decision makers who endorsed employee-focused items with greater frequency than did decision makers in any of the other three country categories, $F(3, 33) = 35.49, p < .01$. Post hoc analyses using Bonferroni adjustments indicated significant differences between Sweden and each of the other countries, as well as between the United States and Germany/Switzerland, with the United States endorsing significantly fewer employee-focused purposes. This finding, although logically explained through individualism–collectivism, is counterintuitive when using masculinity–femininity as the explanatory cultural variable.

For both the nurturing and uncertainty avoidance scales, complete information was not available for all projects. Therefore, fewer projects per country were available for comparisons. Specifically, eight of the

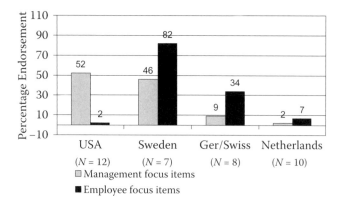

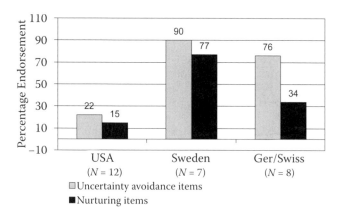

Figure 7.2 Percentage endorsement by country.

Netherlands projects were missing relevant information (resulting in $N = 2$). Therefore, results concerning the Netherlands are not reported.

Regarding the uncertainty avoidance items, results indicated differences between countries in endorsement, $F(2,24) = 14.91$, $p < .01$. Post hoc analyses using Bonferroni adjustments indicated the United States endorsement of uncertainty avoidance items was significantly less than that of Sweden and Germany/Switzerland, whereas differences between Sweden and Germany/Switzerland were not significant. This finding is surprising given that Sweden has the lowest level of uncertainty avoidance compared with the other countries, as shown by the individual country scores in Table 7.1. However, it is clear that, in general, the Swedish decision makers endorsed more items across the board.

In terms of nurturing items, results indicated significant differences by country, $F(2, 24) = 15.26$, $p < .01$. Post hoc analyses using Bonferroni adjustments revealed differences between Sweden and each of the other countries but not among the remaining countries. Specifically, management and work group personnel in Sweden reported significantly greater endorsement of nurturing items compared with the other countries' management and work group personnel. This can be explained by Sweden's higher level of femininity, which is characterized by relationship-oriented, nurturing behaviors and preferences. Furthermore, consistent with Hofstede's findings that German/Swiss individuals are more masculine than feminine, their endorsement of uncertainty avoidance items was greater than their endorsement of nurturing items, $t(7)$ = 5.40, $p < .01$.

The final comparison is strength of effects of the intervention. Effect sizes ranged from −1.11 to 5.31, with a mean of 1.96 (SD = 1.64). Mean effect sizes by country were 2.18 for the United States (N = 12); 2.20 for Sweden (N = 7); 2.18 for Germany and Switzerland (N = 8); and 1.36 for the Netherlands (N = 10). The mean effect sizes by country were all large, and there were no significant differences among the countries, $F(3,33)$ = .60, p = .62. These effect sizes, ranging from 1.36 to 2.20, indicate that in each of these countries, the smallest increase in productivity under ProMES feedback is almost one and a half standard deviations higher than productivity during baseline. Cohen (1977) indicated that an effect size of .2 is small, .5 is medium, and .8 is large. Clearly, these effect sizes are large. This suggests that ProMES, which follows the same basic steps regardless of the culture in which it is implemented, has a strong effect on productivity for all these countries.

One interesting note concerning the success of ProMES in each of these countries is the fact that ProMES is a results-oriented feedback system, which, according to Milliman et al. (1998), would be expected to be more successful in cultures that embrace high long-term orientation than in cultures with a low long-term orientation. As indicated in Table 7.1, the only country that would be categorized as a high long-term orientation culture is the Netherlands, whereas the remaining countries would be classified as being low long-term orientation cultures. Our results, therefore, do not support the Milliman et al. position.

SUMMARY AND CONCLUSIONS

Our conceptual analysis suggests that culture can affect many of the determinants of motivation and thus performance. It is certainly interesting to speculate on what these differences among cultures might be, as we have done here. However, one key implication is that when organizations combine individuals from different cultures, the ideal measurement, feedback, and reward systems may well be different. Understanding the potential for such differences should lead to a careful analysis of how these systems are designed so that cultural differences can be identified and incorporated.

The empirical part of this chapter shows that one feedback system designed to influence motivation and performance is equally effective across countries that vary on several cultural dimensions. That is, the effect sizes are the same. However, the countries examined are all Western cultures that do not differ as much as some other cultures in areas such as collectivism and concern with tradition. Future research should examine such differences in a wider range of cultures. Although the overall effects of the feedback system were similar across the four culture groups, the reasons for success of the feedback intervention seem to be quite different. This suggests that feedback systems can be designed to be successful in multiple cultures.

REFERENCES

Alderfer, C. P., & Sims, A. D. (2003). Diversity in organizations. In I. B. Weiner (Editor in Chief) & W. C. Borman, D. R. Ilgen, & R. J. Klimoski (Vol. Eds.), *Handbook of psychology: Vol. 12. Industrial and organizational psychology* (pp. 595–614). Hoboken, NJ: Wiley.

Ashford, S. J., & Cummings, L. L. (1985). Proactive feedback seeking: The instrumental use of the information environment. *Journal of Occupational Psychology, 58,* 67–79.

Berger, C. R. (1979). Beyond initial understanding: Uncertainty, understanding, and the development of interpersonal relationships. In H. Giles & R. N. St. Clair (Eds.), *Language and social psychology* (pp. 122–144). Oxford, UK: Blackwell.

Brutus, S., Leslie, J. B., & McDonald-Mann, D. (2001). Cross-cultural issues in multisource feedback. In D. W. Bracken & C. W. Timmreck (Eds.), *The handbook of multisource feedback: The comprehensive resource for designing and implementing MSF processes* (pp. 433–446). San Francisco: Jossey-Bass.

Campbell, J. P., & Pritchard, R. D. (1976). Motivation theory in industrial and organizational psychology. In M. D. Dunnette (Ed.), *Handbook of industrial and organizational psychology* (pp. 63–130). Chicago: Rand-McNally.

Cascio, W. F. (1998). *Applied psychology in human resource management* (5th ed.). Upper Saddle River, NJ: Prentice Hall.

Cascio, W. F. (2003). Changes in workers, work, and organizations. In I. B. Weiner (Editor in Chief) & W. C. Borman, D. R. Ilgen, & R. J. Klimoski (Vol. Eds.), *Handbook of psychology: Vol. 12. Industrial and organizational psychology* (pp. 401–422). Hoboken, NJ: Wiley.

Cofer, C. N., & Appley, M. H. (1964). *Motivation: Theory and research.* Oxford, UK: Wiley.

Cohen, J. (1977). *Statistical power analysis for the behavioral sciences.* (Rev. ed.). New York: Academic Press.

Douglas, M. (1970). *Natural symbols.* London: Barrie & Rockliffe.

Earley, P. C., Gibson, C. B., & Chen, C. (1999). How did I do versus how did we do? Intercultural contrasts of performance feedback search and self-efficacy in China, Czechoslovakia, and the United States. *Journal of Cross Cultural Psychology, 30,* 594–619.

Erez, M. (1994). Towards a model of cross-cultural I/O psychology. In H. C. Triandis, M. D. Dunnette, & L. M. Hough (Eds.), *Handbook of industrial and organizational psychology* (2nd ed., Vol. 4, pp. 559–608). Palo Alto, CA: Consulting Psychologists Press.

Erez, M. (1997). A culture-based model of work motivation. In P. C. Earley & M. Erez (Eds.), *New perspectives on international industrial and organizational psychology* (pp. 193–242). San Francisco: New Lexington Press.

Erez, M., & Earley, P. C. (1993). *Culture, self-identity, and work.* New York: Oxford University Press.

Fiske, A. P. (1992). The four elementary forms of sociality: Framework for a unified theory of social relations. *Psychological Review, 99,* 689–723.

Greenwald, A. G. (1980). The totalitarian ego: Fabrication and revision of personal history. *American Psychologist, 35,* 603–618.

Heckhausen, H. (1991). *Motivation and action.* Berlin: Springer.

Hofstede, G. (1980). *Culture's consequences: International differences in work-related values.* Newbury Park, CA: Sage.

Hofstede, G. (1991). *Cultures and organizations: Software of the mind.* London: McGraw-Hill.

Hofstede, G. (2001). *Culture's consequences: Comparing values, behaviors, institutions, and organizations across nations* (2nd ed.). Thousand Oaks, CA: Sage.

Hofstede, G., & Bond, M. H. (1988). Confucius and economic growth: New trends in culture's consequences. *Organizational Dynamics, 16*(4), 4–21.

Huselid, M. A., Jackson, S. E., & Schuler, R. S. (1997). Technical and strategic human resource management effectiveness as determinants of firm performance. *Academy of Management Journal, 40,* 171–188.

Lee, M. D., MacDermid, S. M., & Buck, M. L. (2000). Organizational paradigms of reduced-load work: Accommodation, elaboration, and transformation. *Academy of Management Journal, 43,* 1222–1226.

Lepak, D. P., & Snell, S. A. (1999). The human resource architecture: Toward a theory of human capital allocation and development. *Academy of Management Review, 24,* 31–48.

Levy, P. E., Albright, M. D., Cawley, B. D., & Williams, J. R. (1995). Situational and individual determinants of feedback seeking: A closer look at the process. *Organizational Behavior and Human Decision Processes, 62,* 23–37.

Levy, P. E., Silverman, S. B., Norris-Watts, C., Diefendorff, J., & Ramakrishnan, M. (2003, April). Differences across cultures in developmental feedback. In L. W. Porter (Chair), *Cross-cultural perspectives on the feedback giving and responding process.* Symposium conducted at the meeting of the Society for Industrial and Organizational Psychology, Orlando, FL.

Markus, H. R., & Kitayama, S. (1991). Culture and the self: Implications for cognitive, emotion, and motivation. *Psychological Review, 98,* 224–253.

Milliman, J., Nason, S., Gallagher, E., Huo, P., Von Glinow, M. A., & Lowe, K. B. (1998). The impact of national culture on human resource management practices: The case of performance appraisal. *Advances in International Comparative Management, 12,* 157–183.

Naylor, J. C., Pritchard, R. D., & Ilgen, D. R. (1980). *A theory of behavior in organizations.* New York: Academic Press.

Northcraft, G. B., & Ashford, S. J. (1990). The preservation of self in everyday life: The effects of performance expectations and feedback context on feedback inquiry. *Organizational Behavior and Human Decision Processes, 47,* 42–64.

Pritchard, R. D. (1990). *Measuring and improving organizational productivity: A practical guide*. New York: Praeger.

Pritchard, R. D. (Ed.). (1995). *Productivity measurement and improvement: Organizational case studies*. New York: Praeger.

Pritchard, R. D., Jones, S. D., Roth, P. L., Stuebing, K. K., & Ekeberg, S. E. (1989). The evaluation of an integrated approach to measuring organizational productivity. *Personnel Psychology, 42*, 69–115.

Pritchard, R. D., Paquin, A. R., DeCuir, A. D., McCormick, M. J., & Bly, P. R. (2002). Measuring and improving organizational productivity: An overview of ProMES, The Productivity Measurement and Enhancement System. In R. D. Pritchard, H. Holling, F. Lammers, & B. D. Clark (Eds.), *Improving organizational performance with the Productivity Measurement and Enhancement System: An international collaboration* (pp. 3–50). Huntington, NY: Nova Science.

Pritchard, R. D., & Payne, S. C. (2003). Motivation and performance management practices. In D. Holman, T. D. Wall, C. W. Clegg, P. Sparrow, & A. Howard (Eds.), *The new workplace: People, technology and organisation: A handbook and guide to the human impact of modern working practices* (pp. 219–244). Chichester, UK: Wiley.

Pritchard, R. D., & Ramstad, P. M. (2003). *Managing motivation*. Unpublished manuscript.

Ronen, S., & Shenkar, O. (1985). Clustering countries on attitudinal dimensions: A review and synthesis. *Academy of Management Review, 10*, 435–454.

Schwartz, S. (1992). Universals in the content and structure of values: Theoretical advances and empirical tests in 20 countries. In M. P. Zanna (Ed.), *Advances in experimental social psychology* (Vol. 25, pp. 1–65). New York: Academic Press.

Segall, M. H. (1984). More than we need to know about culture but are afraid not to ask. *Journal of Cross-Cultural Psychology, 15*, 153–162.

Smith, P. B., & Bond, M. H. (1998). *Social psychology across cultures* (2nd ed.). New York: Harvester Wheatsheaf.

Stone-Romero, E. F., & Stone, D. L. (2002). Cross-cultural differences in responses to feedback: Implications for individual, group, and organizational effectiveness. *Research in Personnel and Human Resources Management, 21*, 275–331.

Stone-Romero, E. F., & Stone, D. L. (2003, April). A model of cross-cultural differences in responses to feedback. In L. W. Porter (Chair), *Cross-cultural perspectives on the feedback giving and responding process*. Symposium conducted at the meeting of the Society for Industrial and Organizational Psychology, Orlando, FL.

Sully de Luque, M. F., & Sommer, S. M. (2000). The impact of culture on feedback-seeking behavior: An integrated model and propositions. *Academy of Management Review, 25*, 829–849.

Taylor, S. E., & Brown, J. D. (1988). Illusions and well-being: A social psychological perspective on mental health. *Psychological Bulletin, 103*, 193–210.

Triandis, H. C., Dunnette, M. D., & Hough, L. M. (Eds.). (1994). *Handbook of industrial and organizational psychology* (2nd ed., Vol. 4). Palo Alto, CA: Consulting Psychologists Press.

Trompenaars, F. (1993). *Riding the waves of culture: Understanding cultural diversity in business*. London: The Economist Press.

Vroom, V. H. (1964). *Work and motivation.* New York: Wiley.
Weiner, B. (1985). An attribution theory of achievement motivation and emotion. *Psychological Review, 92,* 548–573.
Wright, P. M., & McMahan, G. C. (1992). Theoretical perspectives for strategic human resource management. *Journal of Management, 18,* 295–320.

AUTHOR NOTE

We thank Melissa J. Sargent for her helpful comments on earlier drafts of this chapter. Requests for reprints should be sent to Robert D. Pritchard, Department of Psychology, University of Central Florida, P.O. Box 161390, Orlando, FL 32816-1390. Phone: (407) 823-2560; Fax: (407) 823-5862. E-mail: rpritcha@pegasus.cc.ucf.edu.

8

Compensation and Reward Systems in a Multicultural Context

APARNA JOSHI* AND JOSEPH J. MARTOCCHIO†

University of Illinois at Urbana-Champaign

COMPENSATION AND REWARD SYSTEMS IN A MULTICULTURAL CONTEXT

Management scholars as well as practitioners frequently acknowledge the need to harness the benefits of a culturally diverse workforce. In the United States, creating and sustaining multicultural organizations are both challenges and business necessities (Cox, 1996; Cox & Tung, 1997). This is a reality now more than ever. Over the past decade, an average of 1 million immigrants entered the United States annually, and new immigrants account for nearly 50% of the population growth in this period (Hanson, Scheve, Slaughter, & Spilimbergo, 2001). Because

* Institute of Labor and Industrial Relations, 109 LIR Building, 504 East Armory Avenue, Champaign, IL 61820; Ph: 217-333-1483, Fax: 217-244-9290, E-mail: aparnajo@ilir.uiuc.edu
† Institute of Labor and Industrial Relations, 111 LIR Building, 504 East Armory Avenue, Champaign, IL 61820; Ph: 217-244-4098, Fax: 217-244-9290, E-mail: martocch@uiuc.edu

a majority of immigrants are of working age, these population trends have had a significant impact on U.S. labor markets (Little & Triest, 2002). Legal immigrants in the United States contributed to approximately 40% of the growth in the U.S. labor force in the 1990s (Little & Triest, 2002). The demographic shifts in the U.S. labor force have significant implications for the design and implementation of managerial practices.

Researchers in the fields of human resource management and industrial-organizational psychology clearly agree that a singular method for managing diverse workforces is simply not feasible (Adler & Jelinek, 1986; Goodstein, 1981; Hofstede, 1980b, 1983, 1993; Newman & Nollen, 1996), despite the potential operating efficiencies of doing so. Clearly, researchers recognize that variations in cultural values may enhance or diminish the impact of managerial practices on job attitudes (Hofstede, 1991) and behaviors (Earley, 1989, 1993; Erez, 1994). Logically, the effectiveness of managerial practices may partly rest on an appropriate fit between the assumptions, values, and beliefs inherent in any given managerial practice and the culturally based assumptions, values, and beliefs held by those who are being managed (Hofstede, 1993; Kirkman & Shapiro, 1997).

Following this reasoning, we maintain that compensation and reward systems play a critical role in aligning the interests of a culturally diverse workforce with organizational goals. Yet, the design and implementation of compensation and reward systems in U.S. companies generally rest on the assumption that the workforce is homogeneous with respect to cultural values, emphasizing individualistic values rather than collectivist values. Current population and labor market trends call for a revision of this assumption (Hanson et al., 2001; Little & Triest, 2002). At the time that U.S. compensation policies were developed in the first half of the 20th century, immigrants came from individualistic countries in Northern and Western Europe. Although the magnitude of immigrant inflow in the 1990s was close to that of the early 1900s, there has been a major shift in the national composition of the immigrant population (Little & Triest, 2002). A majority of working-age immigrants in the United States today come from collectivistic nations in Latin America and Asia (Hanson et al., 2001). Although the demographics of the U.S. labor force have undergone a major transformation in the 20th century, assumptions underlying compensation and reward policies remain unchanged.

Models of motivation (e.g., expectancy theory, equity theory, goal setting) have shown to be effective in explaining and predicting behavior in individualistic cultures or where the context has been held constant (Erez, 1994). However, given the rise of multiculturalism in organizations the context has changed, and many of the individualistic assumptions underlying our reward and motivation theories may not be applicable in all organizational contexts. Thus, it is possible that compensation and reward systems do not effectively motivate employees to strive for or attain first-rate job performance.

Given these changes in organizational contexts, the primary purpose of this chapter is to consider the role that cultural diversity plays in the development of reward and compensation systems for multicultural organizations. Specifically, we reexamine the individualistic assumptions underlying reward and motivation theories and undertake an analysis of cultural differences in employee responses to specific reward systems. Our analysis unfolds as follows. First, we present the main assumptions that guided our work. Second, we review the fundamentals of national cultural values and how these values relate to employee motivation, or the catalyst that prompts affective and cognitive reactions to compensation and reward systems. Third, we review the fundamentals of compensation practices in U.S. companies, emphasizing the elements that relate to cultural values. Fourth, we call on Affective Events Theory (AET; Weiss & Cropanzano, 1996) and the person–organization fit perspective to justify subsequent propositions about employees' reactions to compensation and reward systems. Finally, we conclude with suggestions for future research.

ASSUMPTIONS

Two main assumptions guide our work. First, following Robert and colleagues (Robert, Probst, Martocchio, Drasgow, & Lawler, 2000), we assume that the relationships between employees' attitudes and behaviors and various proximal events (i.e., the implementation of human resources practices such as an incentive pay system) are influenced by such distal contingency factors as national culture. Figure 8.1 contains

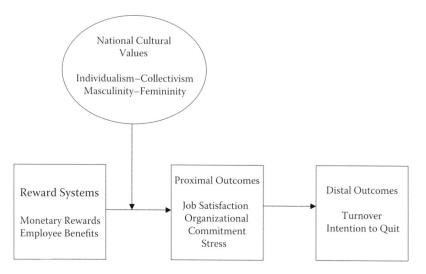

Figure 8.1   Model of the influence of national cultural values and reward systems on proximal and distal outcomes.

a general model that depicts these relationships. This general model draws on a contingency approach as a meta-theory to conceptualize the role of distal factors in our model (Schoonhoven, 1981). It suggests that managerial practices must be aligned or "fit" with environmental demands in order to promote desired work attitudes and behaviors (Schuler & Jackson, 1987).

Second, we expect that employees' reactions to aligned or misaligned compensation and reward practices may be characterized as both affective and cognitive in nature. We call on AET (Weiss & Cropanzano, 1996) to explain the affective process that ensues from perceptions of degree of fit. We draw on the concept of value congruence to describe the contingency mechanism that is a precursor to job attitudes and cognitions. Specifically, we suggest that met expectations, or the congruence between the values implicit in any given managerial practice and the values held by individuals who are subject to those practices, will result in job satisfaction (Locke, 1976; Mowday, Porter, & Steers, 1982). Congruence can be evaluated theoretically, by determining the degree to which national cultures and managerial practices are similar on underlying dimensions. Next, we describe the theoretical constructs of individualism–collectivism and masculinity–femininity, as well as typical compensation and reward practices.

LINKING CULTURAL VALUES
TO EMPLOYEE MOTIVATION

Culture Defined

Culture is defined as "the human-made part of the environment (Herskovits, 1955). It has both objective elements—tools, roads, appliances—and subjective elements—categories, associations, beliefs, attitudes, norms, roles, and values" (Triandis, 1994, p. 113). Cultural values shape work-related attitudes and behaviors (Triandis, 1994). Culture also influences the domain of normative behavior (e.g., behavior that is desirable versus condemned for members of the culture), defines roles for individuals in the social structure, and prescribes guiding principles and values in one's life. As a result, culture specifies how things in the environment—including an organization's practices, policies, and procedures—are to be evaluated and subsequent reactions to such procedures (Robert et al., 2000).

Hofstede's fourfold framework of cultural dimensions has been heralded as one of the "major landmarks of cross-cultural research for many years to come" (Triandis, 1994, p. 90) and has provided an enduring framework for understanding cultural differences in employee attitudes and behaviors. The four dimensions of culture—power distance, masculinity (femininity), uncertainty avoidance, and individualism (collectivism)—have been widely applied in cross-cultural research for more than two decades (Hofstede, 1980a; for a review see Triandis,

1994). These dimensions have been useful in revising current theories of motivation, leadership, and work values in organizations (Hofstede, 1983; Meindl, Hunt, & Lee, 1989).

We focus on two cultural dimensions that have received considerable research attention (Hofstede, 1980a, 1980b, 1991; Triandis, 1995): individualism–collectivism and masculinity–femininity. According to Triandis (1995), individualism is "a social pattern that consists of loosely linked individuals who view themselves as independent of collectives; are primarily motivated by their own preferences, needs, [and] rights, . . . and emphasize the rational analysis of the advantages and disadvantages to associating with others" (p. 2). On the other hand, collectivism may be defined as a cultural orientation where individuals "see themselves as parts of one or more collectives (family, co-workers, tribe, nation); are primarily motivated by the norms of, and duties imposed by, those collectives; . . . and emphasize their connectedness to members of these collectives" (p. 2).

More recent empirical refinements of the individualism–collectivism dimension suggest distinctions between horizontal and vertical individualism and collectivism (Triandis, 1995, 1998). This approach to the individualism–collectivism dimension corresponds with Hofstede's (1980a, 1980b) original research. Hofstede had reported a strong correlation as well as an empirical overlap between power distance and individualism–collectivism (Hofstede, 1980a). Triandis' recent work draws attention to an underlying horizontal–vertical dimension to the individualism–collectivism orientation (Triandis, 1995). A horizontal collectivist orientation refers to a focus on the group along with an assumption of equality among its members. Vertical collectivism, on the other hand, suggests an acceptance of inequality within the collectivistic framework. The individualistic orientation also differs based on the extent to which individuals accept inequality (vertical individualism) versus equality (horizontal individualism; Singelis, Triandis, Bhawuk, & Gelfand, 1995; Triandis, 1998).

A second cultural dimension relevant to our discussion is masculinity–femininity. Masculine cultures differentiate clearly between gender-based roles, whereas feminine cultures are characterized by minimal distinctions between men and women. (In this and in subsequent discussions, we use the terms *masculine* and *feminine* as adjectives to describe cultural values rather than biological sex, gender roles as addressed in the social psychology literature, or social movements such as feminism.) Research suggests that masculine cultures assume the centrality of work and focus on career advancement and achievement. Assertiveness and the "acquisition of money and things, and not caring for others, the quality of life, or people" are important characteristics of masculine cultures (Hofstede, 1980b, p. 46). In feminine cultures the focus is on quality of life rather than career advancement (Hofstede, 1980b, 1991). Individuals who are more feminine in their orientation believe that rewards should be distributed on the basis of need rather than achievement.

Cultural Values in Relation to Individual
Attitudes and Behaviors

Culture is a group concept and typically measured as the norm for a particular society or subgroup within a society (e.g., region, linguistic group, ethnic group, organization). Corresponding to the individualism and collectivism concepts at the cultural level are individual differences in values at the psychological level termed *idiocentrism* and *allocentrism* (Triandis, Bontempo, Villareal, Asai, & Lucca, 1988). There are numerous defining attributes of allocentrics and idiocentrics that are analogous to the cultural characteristics of collectivism and individualism (Triandis, 1995). Allocentrics define themselves in terms of the in-groups to which they belong. Therefore, in-group harmony is extremely valued, and the goals of the in-group have primacy over personal goals. On the other hand, idiocentrics view the individual as the most basic unit of social perception. Individual goals have primacy over in-group goals, in-group confrontation is acceptable, and behavior tends to be regulated by cost–benefit analyses and personal preferences rather than in-group status (Triandis, McCusker, & Hui, 1990).

Although cross-cultural researchers have focused extensively on individualism–collectivism, we maintain that the aforementioned rationale also applies to masculinity–femininity. Neither can we think of any rationale to preclude treatment of masculinity–femininity as individual differences in values, nor did we encounter contradictory reasoning or evidence in our review of the cross-cultural psychology literature.

Cross-cultural psychologists (e.g., Markus & Kitayama, 1991; Triandis, 1994) conjecture that culture influences individuals' preferences for certain things over others (values) and for some ways of doing things over others (norms). Erez (1994) suggests how culture influences preferences and norms. Specifically, she proposes that culture acts as a filter through which individuals interpret and react to managerial practices in the workplace. If people's values and norms are not congruent with the managerial practices they encounter in the workplace, they may become dissatisfied with those aspects of their jobs (Erez, 1994). Over time, organizational commitment is influenced by one's assessment of whether or not one is more consistently satisfied or dissatisfied with one's job. Similarly, organizational withdrawal tendencies are a response to negative attitudes and lack of commitment (Hulin, 1991). Thus, the fact that individuals may be satisfied by certain things over others is influenced by one's culturally determined values and norms.

Individualism–Collectivism in Relation
to Employment Practices

Cultural values act as a lens through which employees interpret and react to managerial decisions and employment practices (Erez, 1994). An extensive body of research has examined individualism–collectivism in relation to employees' attitudes and perceptions (for reviews, see Erez, 1994, and Erez & Early, 1993). Research indicates that individualism–collectivism determines the extent to which individuals display cooperative versus competitive behaviors in work groups (Cox, Lobel, & McLeod, 1991). Overall there is consistent evidence suggesting that individuals with a collectivistic orientation are more likely to cooperate with peers (Mann, 1980) and are more likely to prefer shared responsibility (Earley, 1989). Research has also shown that individualists prefer working alone, whereas collectivists prefer working with members of their in-groups (Earley, 1993).

Research on the relationship between leader behavior and group effectiveness suggests that individualistically oriented individuals also expect to participate more in decision making than collectivistic individuals (Ayman & Chemers, 1983). Further, collectivistic individuals expect greater social support from their leaders than do individualists (Orpen, 1982).

Cultural values also influence the extent to which certain management techniques and practices are accepted and implemented in organizations. For instance, management-by-objectives, a popular management practice in the United States, has failed to take root in several other countries such as France and Germany that score higher on cultural dimensions such as power distance and collectivism (Hofstede, 1980b). Managers in these countries find it harder to accept the practice of individual goal setting and egalitarian relationships with supervisors (Hofstede, 1980b). In addition, research has shown that work units reported higher levels of performance in individualistic settings when managers recognized individual employee contributions. Conversely, units in collectivistic settings reported lower performance when individual contributions were recognized (Newman & Nollen, 1996). These findings suggest that individualistic or collectivistic cultural orientation can determine expectations and attitudes regarding managerial practices.

Masculinity–Femininity in Relation to Employment Practices

In comparison to research on individualism–collectivism in cross-cultural settings, research examining the femininity–masculinity dimension in relation to employee attitudes and behaviors is fairly limited. Based on the logic developed earlier in this chapter, we can surmise that the femininity–masculinity cultural dimension should be an important influence on employee preferences and perceptions regarding employment practices. Early research has shown that employees in Scandinavian countries, with high scores on the femininity dimension, tend to favor job design practices that focus on the "humanization of work." These practices include job enrichment to allow a greater role for interpersonal relationships at work. On the other hand, employees in more masculine cultures, such as in the United States, prefer job designs that are oriented toward individual performance (Hofstede, 1980a, 1980b). Research also shows that in feminine cultures there is a greater expectation of leader support for quality of life and work–family balance (Newman & Nollen, 1996). Further, merit-based pay and promotions have been related to performance in masculine settings more so than in feminine work contexts (Newman & Nollen, 1996).

LINKING CULTURAL VALUES TO EMPLOYEE REACTIONS TO COMPENSATION AND REWARD PRACTICES

Compensation represents both the intrinsic and extrinsic rewards employees receive for performing their jobs (Martocchio, 2004). Intrinsic compensation reflects employees' psychological mind-sets that result from performing their jobs such as described in job characteristics theory (Hackman & Oldham, 1976). Extrinsic compensation includes both monetary and nonmonetary rewards. Examples of monetary rewards include base pay, merit pay, incentive pay, and competency-based pay. Nonmonetary rewards, referred to as employee benefits in professional practice, include protection programs (e.g., health insurance), paid time-off (e.g., vacations), and services (e.g., day care assistance). We limit our discussion to extrinsic compensation because our focus in this chapter is on the practices that are typically associated with compensation and reward systems in companies (Martocchio, 2004).

In this section we suggest how cultural values may map onto these practices by drawing on the main characteristics of individualism–collectivism and masculinity–femininity. For individualism, we consider the importance of an individual's preferences and the instrumental role of affiliation with others to facilitate the achievement of personal goals. Collectivism emphasizes the welfare of group to which an individual belongs and embracing the relations with other group members. For masculinity, we consider the centrality of work, career advancement, and importance of material things such as money. Quality of life and the importance of fulfilling personal needs rather than personal achievement represent the hallmarks of femininity. Next, we provide concise descriptions of monetary rewards and employment benefits, subsequently discussing issues of fit between cultural values and reward practices. Specifically, these descriptions offer an overview of the practice. Table 8.1 provides examples of which compensation and reward systems fit, based on particular values that define individualist–collectivist and feminine–masculine beliefs.

Monetary Rewards

Seniority pay.

Seniority pay systems reward employees with permanent increases to base pay according to employees' lengths of service performing their jobs. These pay plans assume that employees become more valuable to companies with time and that valued employees will leave if they do not have a clear idea that their wages will progress over time. This rationale comes from the human capital theory (Becker, 1975), which states that employees' knowledge and skills generate productive capital known as human capital. Employees can develop such knowledge and skills from formal education and training, including on-the-job experience. Over time, employees presumably refine existing skills or acquire new ones that enable them to work more productively. Thus, seniority pay rewards employees for acquiring and refining their skills as indexed by length of employment (years).

Base pay.

Each employee receives base pay, or money, for performing his or her job. Base pay is recurring; that is, employees will continue to receive base pay as long as they remain in their jobs. Companies disburse base pay to employees in either one of two forms, hourly pay (wage) or salary, based on the nature of work as set forth in the Fair Labor Standards Act. Employees earn hourly pay for each hour worked. Employees earn salaries for performing their jobs, regardless of the actual number of hours worked. Companies measure salary on an annual basis.

Companies typically set base pay amounts for jobs based on job content and market pay rates for the jobs. Compensable factors define the content of jobs on which the relative worth of jobs within an organization is determined. Job content is generally described based on the type and level of skill, effort, and responsibility required to perform the jobs and the severity of the working conditions. Once jobs have been evaluated in terms of worth, organizations survey the pay levels of competing organizations (on the basis of product/service or labor), which they use as a reference point for establishing pay rates.

Once base pay rates are set, monetary compensation periodically increases to reward job performance or the acquisition of job-relevant knowledge or skills. Merit and incentive pay programs recognize job performance, whereas competency-based pay rewards employees for the acquisition of job-relevant knowledge or skills. The former practices reward employees for promised fulfilled (i.e., merit and incentive rewards are contingent on attained job performance). The latter practice rewards employees simply on the basis of potential for positive job performance.

Merit pay.

Merit pay programs assume that employees' compensation over time should be determined by differences in job performance. Employees earn permanent increases to base pay according to their performance, which rewards excellent effort or results, motivates future performance, and helps employers retain valued employees.

TABLE 8.1   Examples of Fit between Individualism–Collectivism and Femininity–Masculinity Cultural Values and Compensation and Reward Practices

Individualism		Collectivism	
Cultural Values*	Reward Practices (VI = Vertical individualism; HI = Horizontal individualism)	Cultural Values*	Reward Practices (VC = Vertical collectivism; HC = Horizontal collectivism)
Everybody takes care of themselves. "I" consciousness Identity based on individual Emotional independence from organization Involvement with organization is calculative Individual initiative and achievement Leadership is the ideal Right to private life Autonomy, variety, pleasure, individual financial security Belief is placed in individual decisions	**Monetary Rewards** Merit pay programs (VI) Individual incentives (VI) Group incentives (HI) **Employee Benefits** Health insurance (POS plans) Disability insurance Defined contribution plans with employee responsibility for making investment choices Paid time-off Flexible work schedules Tuition reimbursements	People are born into families and clans which protect them in exchange for loyalty "We" consciousness Identity is based on a social system Emotional dependence on org. Involvement with organization is moral Membership is the ideal Private life may be invaded by the organization Expertise order, duty, and security are provided by the organization Belief in group decisions Values differ for in-group and out-groups	**Monetary Rewards** Base pay (seniority and geography based) (VC) Company-wide incentives (HC) Competency based pay (VC) **Employee Benefits** Health insurance (HMO or managed care) Health protection Defined benefit plans for retirement Family assistance programs Plans to manage employees' and families' mental and physical well-being

Femininity		Masculinity	
Cultural Values*	Reward Practices	Cultural Values*	Reward Practices
Men can be nurturing	**Monetary Rewards**	Men should be assertive and	**Monetary Rewards**
Sex roles are fluid	Group/Company-wide	women nurturing	Seniority-based pay
Equality between sexes	incentives	Sex roles are differentiated	Individual incentives
Quality of life is important		Men should dominate	Merit-based pay
Work in order to live	**Employee Benefits**	Performance counts	
People and environment are	Paternity leave	Live in order to work	**Employee Benefits**
important	Disability insurance	Money and things are	Defined contribution
Interdependence is ideal	Life insurance including	important	retirement plans
Service provides motivation	accidental death and	Independence is ideal	Health insurance with POS
Sympathy for the	dismemberment claims	Ambition provides drive	plan
unfortunate	Defined benefit plans for	Admiration for successful	
	retirement	achievers	
	Health protection for		
	employee and family		
	Paid time-off		
	Flexible work schedules		

* Based on Hofstede, G. (1980a). *Culture's consequences: International differences in work-related values.* Beverly Hills: Sage.

Incentive pay.

Incentive pay rewards employees for partially or completely attaining predetermined work objectives. Incentive pay is defined as compensation (other than base wages or salaries) that fluctuates according to employees' attainment of some standard based on a preestablished formula, individual or group goals, or company earnings. Individual incentive awards may be based on quality or quantity of output, customer satisfaction, safety record, or other measurable performance indicators. Group incentive awards may be based on the quantity or quality of output based on collaborative efforts or on cost savings through gainsharing programs. Company-wide incentive plans typically reward employees for the attainment of financial goals such as profits or increases in market value evident in gains in public stock prices.

At this point, it is necessary to clarify our reference to the term *group* for purposes of understanding the fit issues between cultural values and group-oriented compensation and rewards systems. Consistent with the literature (cf. Banker, Field, Schroeder, & Sinha, 1996), we recognize a distinction between traditional work groups and various work team configurations. Although researchers have used various criteria to distinguish between traditional work groups and teams, Banker et al.'s (1996) classification holds theoretical and practical appeal. Accordingly, teams can be classified on a continuum of autonomy. Traditional work groups possess the least autonomy, because workers perform relatively independent core production activities, and their activities are led by first-line managers. On the other end of the continuum, self-designing teams self-regulate work on their interdependent tasks, and they possess control over the design of the teams. Based on this distinction, we emphasize possible differences in fit.

Competency-based pay.

Competency-based pay rewards employees for successfully learning specific curricula. Skill-based pay, used mostly for employees who perform physical work, increases these workers' pay as they master new skills. This approach rewards employees for the range, depth, and types of skills or knowledge they are capable of applying productively to their jobs. Rewarding employees for the attainment of knowledge and skills distinguishes competency-based pay plans from merit pay and incentive pay, which reward employees based on the level or quality of attained job performance. That is, competency-based programs reward employees for their potential to make meaningful contributions on the job.

Propositions Linking Cultural Orientations to Monetary Reward Preferences

With regard to employee perceptions of reward systems in cross-cultural settings, researchers have drawn on three principles: equity, equality, and need (e.g., Deutsch, 1975; Mikula, 1980). Briefly restated, the equity principle dictates that employees should be rewarded based on individual contributions. The equality principle states that all employees should be rewarded equally, regardless of individual performance. Finally, based on the need principle, employee needs should determine rewards (Zhou & Martocchio, 2001). Because individualistic employees prefer to be recognized for their individual contributions and performance, these employees prefer reward systems that are based on equity. On the other hand, because a collectivistic orientation is characterized by a need to conform and maintain in-group harmony, collectivistically oriented employees prefer rewards based on equality (Zhou & Martocchio, 2001). We acknowledge that specific preferences for monetary rewards may be further tempered by the extent to which employees are horizontal or vertical in the individualism–collectivism orientation. However, we found limited empirical research to develop specific propositions in this regard. For the present we propose:

Proposition 1a: Employees with a highly individualistic orientation will prefer monetary rewards such as individual incentive-based pay or merit-based pay. Collectivistic individuals will prefer monetary rewards such as seniority-based pay and company-wide incentive plans.

Because empirical research relating masculinity–femininity to reward preferences is negligible, we draw on Hofstede's (1980a, 1980b) seminal work in this area to identify certain hallmark values representing this dimension and relate these values to specific monetary rewards and employee benefits. For instance, femininity represents an expectation of equality between sexes, sympathy for the less fortunate, and the importance of interpersonal relationships and quality of life (Hofstede, 1980b). These values may correspond to the *principle of need* in reward preferences. On the other hand, masculinity represents a focus on performance and achievement in the workplace, a predisposition toward materialistic rewards, and an overriding personal ambition (Hofstede, 1980b). The *equity principle* may drive the reward preferences of masculine employees. These individuals may prefer monetary rewards that drive employees toward higher levels of performance and visible acknowledgements of successful employees.

Proposition 1b: Employees with a masculine orientation will prefer monetary rewards such as individual incentive-based or merit-based pay. Feminine individuals will prefer monetary rewards such as group and company-wide incentive plans.

Employee Benefits

Employee benefits refer to compensation other than hourly wage or salary. Three fundamental roles characterize benefits: protection programs (income and health, respectively), paid time-off, and accommodation and enhancement benefits. Protection programs provide family benefits, promote health, and guard against income loss caused by catastrophic factors like unemployment, disability, or serious illnesses. Paid time-off policies compensate employees when they are not performing their primary work duties, such as during vacation, holidays, and bereavement. Accommodation and enhancement benefits promote opportunities for employees and their families. There is a wide variety of programs, including stress management classes, flexible work schedules, and tuition reimbursement.

There are two broad sources of employee benefits. The U.S. government requires that most employers provide particular sets of benefits to employees. We refer to these as legally required benefits. Such laws as the Social Security Act of 1935 mandate a variety of programs designed to provide income to retired workers, monetary benefits to the beneficiaries of deceased workers, and medical protection for older Americans. In addition, companies offer additional benefits on a discretionary basis. We refer to these benefits as discretionary benefits.

Different forces led to the rise of legally required and discretionary employee benefits. A brief review of these forces will provide a backdrop for considering fit issues. The U.S. government established programs to protect individuals from catastrophic events such as disability and unemployment. As highlighted earlier, legally required benefits are protection programs that attempt to promote worker safety and health, maintain family income streams, and assist families in crisis.

Historically, legally required benefits provided a form of social insurance. Prompted largely by the rapid growth of industrialization in the United States during the early part of the 20th century and the Great Depression of the 1930s, social insurance programs were designed to minimize the possibility that individuals who became severely injured while working or unemployed would become destitute. In addition, social insurance programs aimed to stabilize the well-being of dependent family members of injured or unemployed individuals. Further, early social insurance programs were designed to enable retirees to maintain subsistence income levels. These intents of legally required benefits remain intact today.

Discretionary benefits originated in the 1940s and 1950s, due in large part to federal government restrictions placed on increasing wage levels. Employee benefits were not subject to those restrictions. Companies expanded their discretionary benefits as an alternate to wage increases as a motivational tool. During that period, the term *welfare practices* described employee benefits. Welfare practices were "anything for the comfort and improvement, intellectual or social, of the employees, over and above wages paid, which is not a necessity of the industry nor required by law" (U.S. Bureau of Labor Statistics, 1919).

The opportunities available to employees through welfare practices varied. For instance, some employers offered libraries and recreational areas, whereas others provided financial assistance for education and home improvements. In addition, employers' sponsor of medical insurance coverage became common. Employee unions also directly contributed to the increase in employee welfare practices. One of the main aims of labor unions is to protect the interests of workers by negotiating with management over terms of employment, including wages, hours, and working conditions. The National Labor Relations Act of 1935 legitimized bargaining for employee benefits and seniority-based monetary compensation. Union workers tend to participate more in benefits plans than do nonunion employees (U.S. Department of Commerce, 2003). Unions also indirectly contribute to the rise in benefits offerings in nonunion settings. Nonunion companies tend to minimize the likelihood of unionization by offering their employees benefits that are comparable to the benefits received by employees in union shops (Solnick, 1985).

Employees typically view employer-sponsored benefits as entitlements (Weathington & Tetrick, 2000). Anecdotal evidence suggests that most employees still feel this way: Company membership entitles them to benefits. Until recently, companies have also treated virtually all elements of benefits as entitlements. They have not questioned their role as social welfare mediators. However, both rising benefits costs and increased foreign competition have led companies to question this entitlement ethic; some companies are trying to instill in employees that benefits are earned based on job performance (Salisbury, 1998).

Legally required benefits.

Legally required benefits are mandated by the following laws: the Social Security Act of 1935, various state workers' compensation insurance, and the Family and Medical Leave Act of 1993. All provide protection programs to employees and their dependents. The Social Security Act of 1935, amended in 1965, requires that employers contribute to funding three programs relevant to employees: OASDI, UI, and, in 1965, Medicare.

The term *old-age, survivor, and disability insurance* (OASDI) refers to the programs that provide retirement income, income to the survivors of deceased workers, and income to disabled workers and their family members. Medicare serves nearly all U.S. citizens aged 65 and older and disabled Social Security beneficiaries by providing insurance coverage for hospitalization, convalescent care, and major doctor bills. Employees earn eligibility to earn OASDI and Medicare benefits based on minimum monetary contributions paid through mandatory payroll taxes based on employee and employer contributions.

Workers' compensation insurance came into existence during the early decades of the 20th century, when industrial accidents were very common and workers suffered from occupational illnesses at alarming rates (Dulles & Dubofsky, 1993). There were no laws that required employers to ensure the health and safety of employees during the early years of industrialization of the U.S. economy. The seriously injured and ill workers were left with virtually no recourse because social insurance programs to protect the injured and ill workers were nonexistent. State compulsory disability laws created workers' compensation programs. Workers' compensation insurance programs are designed to cover expenses incurred in employees' work-related accidents or injuries regardless of fault. Employers pay insurance premiums on behalf of employees.

The Family and Medical Leave Act (FMLA) provides employees job protection in cases of family or medical emergency. The FMLA permits eligible employees to take up to a total of 12 work weeks of unpaid leave during any 12-month period. These employees possess the right to return to the position he or she left when the leave began or to an equivalent position with the same terms of employment, including pay and benefits. The passage of the FMLA reflects growing recognition that many employees' parents are becoming elderly, rendering them susceptible to a serious illness or medical condition.

Discretionary benefits.

Most employers offer discretionary benefits that serve four objectives as previously noted: income protection, health protection, paid time-off, and accommodation and enhancement programs. Income protection programs include disability insurance, life insurance, retirement, and health insurance. Disability insurance replaces income for employees who become unable to work on a regular basis because of any illness or injury. Employer-sponsored disability insurance is more encompassing than workers' compensation because these benefits generally apply to work- and nonwork-related illness or injury. Disability insurance typically takes two forms. The first, short-term disability insurance, provides benefits for limited periods of time, usually less than 6 months. The second, long-term disability insurance, provides benefits for extended periods of time, anywhere between 6 months and life. Disability insurance provides substantial income replacement, between one half and two thirds of predisability income.

Employer-sponsored life insurance protects family members by paying a specified amount to an employee's beneficiaries upon the employees' death. Most policies pay some multiple of the employee's salary; for instance, benefits paid equal the deceased employee's annual salary. Employees usually have the option of purchasing additional coverage. Frequently, employer-sponsored life insurance plans also include accidental death and dismemberment claims, which pay additional benefits if death was the result of an accident or if the insured incurs accidental loss of a limb.

Retirement plans, also known as pension plans, provide income to employees and beneficiaries. Companies may establish their retirement plans as defined contribution plans or defined benefit plans. Overall, retirement plans should promote a sense of security in current employees. However, the distinction between these plans may be relevant to cultural values because the extent of risk varies with each plan.

Defined contribution plans present the most risk for employees. Under defined contribution plans, an employer and employee make annual contributions to an account established on behalf of the employee. (Sometimes, it is only the employee or only the employer who makes the contributions; nevertheless, the defined contribution plans ultimately pose risk as we note shortly.) Defined contribution plans specify the amount an employee or employer sets aside. This type of retirement plan holds more risk for employees because the amount of money received during retirement depends upon how much money was contributed and how well these monetary contributions (through investment vehicles such as company stock or government bonds) perform during the employees' work years. In addition, defined contribution plans bestow the responsibility of actively choosing investment vehicles, regularly monitoring investment performance over time, and choosing different investment vehicles based on expectations of future performance.

Defined benefit plans are associated with relatively low risk, because the provisions of these plans guarantee retirement payments for an individual's life. Defined benefit plans are based on a specified percentage of an employee's annual pay in the years preceding retirement and on age and length of employment. In addition, many defined benefit plans regularly award increases (usually, annually) to retirement payments according to increases in the cost of living, helping retirees maintain their standard of living. Finally, the features of defined benefit plans do not require much employee discretion.

Health protection programs refer to a host of practices geared toward promoting sound health. Health protection programs subsume health insurance as well as a variety of additional programs designed to promote physical and mental health. Employers refer to these programs, often set up to promote healthier lifestyles, as wellness programs. Examples of wellness programs include ones that help employees to manage stress effectively, lose excess body weight, and quit smoking.

Health insurance covers the costs of a variety of services that promote sound physical and mental health, including physical examinations, diagnostic testing (x-rays), surgery, and hospitalization. Companies can choose from two broad classes of health insurance programs: fee-for-service plans or managed care plans. Fee-for-service plans reimburse individuals after they have received health care services. Managed care plans emphasize cost control by limiting an employee's choice of doctors and hospitals. Three common managed care arrangements include health maintenance organizations (HMOs), preferred provider organizations (PPOs), and point-of-service (POS) plans. These plans vary in the degree of choice given to employees with regard to selecting doctors and other health care professionals. HMOs give employees the least choice and POS plans provide the most choice.

Paid time-off.

Paid time-off policies compensate employees when they are not performing their primary work duties. Companies offer most paid time-
off as a matter of custom, particularly paid holidays, vacations, and
sick leave. In unionized settings, paid time-off provisions are specified
within the collective bargaining agreement. The paid time-off practices
that are most typically found in unionized settings are jury duty, funeral
leave, military leave, clean-up, preparation, travel time, rest period, and
lunch period.

Accommodation and enhancement programs.

These benefits promote opportunities for employees and family members. Five specific objectives of accommodation and enhancement benefits
include (corresponding benefit practice stated in parentheses): (a) employees' and family members' mental and physical well-being (e.g., stress
management), (b) family assistance programs (e.g., child care), (c) flexible
work schedules (e.g., telecommuting), (d) skills and knowledge acquisition through educational programs (e.g., tuition reimbursement), and (e)
opportunities to manage daily challenges (e.g., transportation services).

Propositions Linking Cultural Orientations to Employee Benefit Preferences

As discussed earlier, employee preferences for rewards based on principles of equity, equality, or need are related to their cultural orientation
(Zhou & Martocchio, 2001). Based on the logic used to outline propositions 1a and 1b, we can also develop propositions linking employees'
cultural orientation to benefit preferences. For instance, based on the
equity principle, individualistic employees may prefer benefits that
allow them autonomy and freedom of choice in their benefit options.
Collectivistic employees may prefer benefits that provide long-term
security and support for the family. Individuals with a feminine orientation would prefer reward systems that allow access to benefits that provide them with work–family balance and overall quality of life. On the
other hand, masculinity employees oriented toward material rewards
may prefer benefit plans that represent more tangible monetary gains.
Therefore we propose the following:

Proposition 2a: Individualistic employees will prefer benefits such as
POS health insurance plans, defined contribution plans, paid time-off, and
flexible schedules. Collectivistic employees will prefer health protection,
family assistance programs, and defined benefit plans for retirement.

Proposition 2b: Masculine employees will prefer employee benefits
such as POS health insurance plans and defined contribution plans.

Feminine employees will prefer health protection, family assistance programs, paid time-off, and flexible working schedules.

THE EFFECTS OF (MIS) FIT BETWEEN CULTURAL VALUES AND REWARD SYSTEMS

We call on two theoretical perspectives, AET and the Person–Organization (P–O) Fit perspective, to further enlighten the psychological processes that link cultural values and employee reactions to compensation and reward practices. Figure 8.1 depicts the framework for our discussion.

Affective Events Theory (AET)

AET posits that characteristics of the workplace and incidents at work constitute "discrete events" that influence transient moods and emotions (Ashkanasy, Hartel, & Daus, 2002). As stated by Weiss and Cropanzano (1996), job satisfaction is a "judgment" made by employees regarding their work environment based on specific affective experiences. AET also proposes that employee affective states such as fear, anger, pride, and happiness are reflections of specific components of the work environment such as the design of the job and job-related stressors (Ashkanasy et al., 2002).

AET casts affect as a central experience in the workplace, with job satisfaction as a consequence of such experiences. Also, AET emphasizes events as proximal causes of affective reactions, with environmental factors (such as national culture) as distal influences.

This theory provides a relevant framework for understanding the relationship between the workplace context and employee attitudes and behaviors. We propose that workplace practices such as reward systems can act as stressors for employees if these practices are not congruent with the employee's cultural values. Based on AET, this stress can mediate the relationship between an employee's perceptions of reward systems and outcomes such as job satisfaction and commitment to the organization.

Person–Organization (P–O) Fit Framework

To fully explicate the relationship between employee cultural values in relation to perceptions of reward systems, we integrate AET with the P–O fit perspective. Like the AET, the P–O fit framework also takes an "interactional" perspective on the relationship between employee attitudes and behaviors and the work environment. Under the interactional framework, characteristics of the employee and the context jointly influence attitudes and behaviors (Chatman, 1989; Schneider, 1987). P–O fit has been defined as the "congruence between the norms and values of the organization and the values of persons" (Chatman, 1989, p. 339). The extent to which there is a reciprocal or interactional relationship, employees and their work contexts will be determined by the extent of fit between individuals and their environment (Chatman, 1989; Schneider, 1987). In the domestic U.S. setting, P–O fit has been found to significantly predict job satisfaction, organizational commitment, turnover, tenure, and intent to stay (see Kristof, 1996, and Meglino, Ravlin, & Adkins, 1992, for a detailed review). We extend the P–O fit perspective to understand how the fit between individual cultural orientation and organization's human resources practices (specifically reward systems) may influence employee attitudes such as satisfaction and commitment and behaviors such as turnover.

Based on P–O fit perspective we propose that the conjoint effects of an employee's cultural values and organization's reward systems may better predict employee outcomes than either main effect. In a service setting, Testa, Mueller, and Thomas (2003) found that fit between an employee's cultural orientation and organizational culture predicted satisfaction, self-efficacy, and willingness to perform. The P–O fit perspective was also supported in a study on work teams by Newman and Nollen (1996). Newman and Nollen found that work unit performance was higher when management practices corresponded with national cultural dimensions such as power distance, individualism–collectivism, and masculinity–femininity. In our subsequent discussion we define *cultural fit* as the congruence between employees' cultural values and specific characteristics of organizational reward systems.

Attitudinal and Behavioral Outcomes

AET proposes that workplace conditions can act as "hassles or uplifts" that lead to positive or negative emotions; these emotions can predict attitudes and behavioral responses among employees (Ashkanasy, 2002, p. 14). When affective events are positive, employees are likely to experience positive mood states that foster positive evaluations of the workplace. Negative affective events arising from job-related stressors are likely to generate negative moods such as anger and resentment.

We have also outlined empirical evidence relating P–O fit with outcomes such as satisfaction and commitment. More specifically, perceived P–O fit has been found to positively predict employee attitudes such as job satisfaction (Chatman, 1991) and instrumental and normative organizational commitment (O'Reilly, Chatman, & Caldwell, 1991). P–O fit is negatively related to employee stress (Chesney & Rosenman, 1980), turnover intentions, and turnover (Chatman, 1991; O'Reilly et al., 1991). We integrate these two perspectives to argue that a lack of cultural fit is a job-related stressor acting as an *affective event* that translates into proximal and distal affective and behavioral outcomes. These proximal outcomes include job satisfaction, commitment, and stress. The congruence between employees' culture orientation and rewards will also influence more distal outcomes of interest to organizations, such as turnover and intention to quit. Based on our review of the pertinent literature, we offer exploratory propositions to help guide empirical research on the effects of (mis)fit between cultural values and compensation and reward practices.

Drawing on the AET and P–O fit perspectives, when individualistic employees are in employment situations where all employees are rewarded equally regardless of their contributions (an affective event caused by lack of cultural fit), they may experience negative emotions such as anger and resentment (an affective state) that will lead to job dissatisfaction and turnover (Weiss & Cropanzano, 1996). Similar outcomes can be envisioned for collectivistic employees in employment situations where individual contributions are emphasized and reward systems reflect this emphasis. Therefore we propose:

Proposition 3a: The degree of cultural fit between the employees' individualism–collectivism and available monetary rewards and benefits will predict proximal outcomes such as employee stress, job satisfaction, and commitment, as well as more distal outcomes such as turnover.

Based on AET and P–O fit theories we would also predict that feminine employees in employment contexts where reward systems are not aligned with family needs and work–family balance would experience job dissatisfaction, lack of commitment, and stress. Ultimately, these attitudes may manifest in turnover. Masculine employees in organizations that do not provide rewards and recognition for achievement and performance may experience similar reactions. More specifically we propose:

Proposition 3b: The degree of cultural fit between the employees' masculinity–femininity and available monetary rewards and benefits will predict proximal outcomes such as employee stress, job satisfaction, commitment, as well as more distal outcomes such as turnover.

CONCLUSIONS AND FUTURE DIRECTIONS

Recent demographic shifts and immigration patterns in the United States have transformed the workforce. The multicultural composition of the U.S. workforce has significant implications for the design and implementation of compensation and reward systems. In this chapter we call for a reassessment of existing assumptions that govern the design of reward systems. Clearly, reward systems that are governed solely by the equity principle may no longer be sustainable in the current workplace. We suggest propositions that may serve as a guide to employers who want to incorporate the differing needs and preferences of their employees. However, as they introduce these options, they should consider the cultural values of the workforce may be pertinent.

From a research standpoint we call for more rigorous inquiry into the relation between employees' cultural orientation and preferences for specific monetary and nonmonetary rewards. These propositions should be subjected to empirical scrutiny and possible revision to facilitate the development of finer tuned hypotheses. Such empirical work should assess whether employees are aware of the specific design features of compensation practices that we only conjecture matter from the standpoint of P–O fit. Obviously, employers provide a range of options for their employees. To facilitate employers' selection of optimal choices, researchers should subject these propositions to empirical scrutiny and possible revision to facilitate the development of finer tuned hypotheses. Such empirical work should assess the extent to which the design characteristics of compensation and reward systems are salient to employees, and which features relate to specific cultural value statements listed in Table 8.1. At this point, we are able only to conjecture that specific design features of compensation practices matter from the standpoint of P–O fit.

We also call for more research relating the masculinity–femininity dimension to employee perceptions of rewards and benefits in the organization. The core values of this dimension relate specifically to employees' beliefs regarding quality of life, work–family balance, and job performance. Relating these values to employee preferences for rewards and benefits may provide additional insights into the design and effectiveness of reward systems.

REFERENCES

Adler, N. J., & Jelinek, M. (1986). Is "organizational culture" culture bound? *Human Resource Management, 25,* 73–90.

Ashkanasy, N. (2002). Studies of cognition and emotion in organizations: Attributions, affective events, emotional intelligence and perception of emotion. *Australian Journal of Management, 27,* 11–20.

Ashkanasy, N., Hartel, C., & Daus, C. (2002). Diversity and emotion: The new frontiers in organizational behavior research. *Journal of Management, 28,* 307–338.

Ayman, R., & Chemers, M. N. (1983). Relationships of supervisory ratings to work group effectiveness and subordinate satisfaction among Iranian managers. *Journal of Applied Psychology, 68,* 338–341.

Banker, R. D., Field, J. M., Schroeder, R. C., & Sinha, K. K. (1996). Impact of work teams on manufacturing performance: A longitudinal field study. *Academy of Management Journal, 39,* 867–890.

Becker, G. (1975). *Human capital.* New York: National Bureau of Economic Research.

Chatman, J. A. (1989). Improving interactional organizational research: A model of person-organization fit. *Academy of Management Review, 14,* 333–349.

Chatman, J. A. (1991). Matching people and organizations: Selection and socialization in a public accounting firm. *Administrative Science Quarterly, 36,* 459–484.

Chesney, M. A., & Rosenman, R. H. (1980). Type A behavior in the work setting. In C. L. Cooper & R. Payne (Eds.), *Current concerns in occupation stress* (pp. 187–212). New York: Wiley.

Cox, T. (1996). The complexity of diversity: Challenges and directions for future research. In S. E. Jackson & M. Ruderman (Eds.), *Diversity in work teams: Research paradigms for a changing workplace* (pp. 235–246). Washington DC: American Psychological Association.

Cox, T., & Tung, R. (1997). The multicultural organization revisited. In C. L. Cooper & S. E. Jackson (Eds.), *Creating tomorrow's organizations* (pp. 7–27). London, UK: Wiley.

Cox, T. H., Lobel, S. A., & McLeod, P. L. (1991). Effects of ethnic group cultural differences on cooperative versus competitive behavior on a group task. *Academy of Management Journal, 34*, 827–847.

Deutsch, M. (1975). Equity, equality, and need: What determines which value will be used as the basis for distributive justice? *Journal of Social Issues, 31*, 137–149.

Dulles, F. R., & Dubofsky, M. (1993). *Labor in America: A history.* Arlington Heights, IL: Harlan Davidson.

Earley, P. C. (1989). Social loafing and collectivism: A comparison of the United States and the People's Republic of China. *Administrative Science Quarterly, 34*, 565–581.

Earley, P. C. (1993). East meets west meets mideast: Further explorations of collectivistic and individualistic work groups. *Academy of Management Journal, 36*, 319–348.

Erez, M. (1994). Toward a model of cross-cultural industrial and organizational psychology. In H. C. Triandis, M. Dunnette, & L. Hough (Eds.), *Handbook of industrial and organizational psychology* (2nd ed., Vol. 4, pp. 557–607). Palo Alto, CA: Consulting Psychologists Press.

Erez, M., & Earley, P.C. (1993). *Culture, self-identity, and work.* New York: Oxford University Press.

Goodstein, L. D. (1981, Summer). American business values and cultural imperialism. *Organizational Dynamics*, 49–54.

Hackman, J. R., & Oldham, G. R. (1976). Motivation through the design of work: Test of a theory. *Organizational Behavior and Human Performance, 16*, 250–279.

Hanson, G., Scheve, K., Slaughter, M., & Spilimbergo, A. (2001). *Immigration and the U.S. economy: Labor-market impacts, illegal entry, and policy choice.* Unpublished report submitted to the International Monetary Fund.

Herskovits, M. J. (1955). *Cultural anthropology.* New York: Knopf.

Hofstede, G. (1980a). *Culture's consequences: International differences in work-related values.* Beverly Hills: Sage.

Hofstede, G. (1980b). Motivation, leadership, and organizations: Do American theories apply abroad? *Organizational Dynamics, 9*, 42–63.

Hofstede, G. (1983, Fall). The cultural relativity or organizational practices and theories. *Journal of International Business Studies, Fall*, 75–89.

Hofstede, G. (1991). *Cultures and organizations.* London: McGraw-Hill.

Hofstede, G. (1993). Cultural constraints in management theories. *Academy of Management Executive, 7*, 81–94.

Hulin, C. L. (1991). Adaptation, persistence, and commitment in organizations. In M. D. Dunnette & L. M. Hough (Eds.), *Handbook of industrial and organizational psychology* (2nd ed., Vol. 2, pp. 445–505). Palo Alto: Consulting Psychologists Press.

Kirkman, B. L., & Shapiro, D. L. (1997). The impact of cultural values on employee resistance to teams: Toward a model of globalized self-managing work team effectiveness. *Academy of Management Review, 22,* 730–757.

Kristof, A. L. (1996). Person-organization fit: An integrative review of its conceptualizations, measurement and implications. *Personnel Psychology, 49,* 1–49.

Little, J. S., & Triest, R. K. (2002). The impact of demographic change on U.S. labor markets. *New England Economic Review, First Quarter,* 47–68.

Locke, E. A. (1976). The nature and causes of job satisfaction. In M. D. Dunnette (Ed.), *The handbook of industrial and organizational psychology.* Chicago: Rand McNally.

Mann, L. (1980). Cross-cultural studies of small groups. In H. C. Triandis & R.W. Brislin (Eds.), *Handbook of cross-cultural psychology* (Vol. 5, pp. 77–109). Boston: Allyn & Bacon.

Markus, H. R., & Kitayama, S. (1991). Culture and self: Implications for cognition, emotion and motivation. *Psychological Review, 98,* 224–253.

Martocchio, J. J. (2004). *Strategic compensation: A human resource management approach* (3rd ed.). Upper Saddle River, NJ: Prentice-Hall.

Meglino, B. M., Ravlin, E. C., & Adkins, C. L. (1992). The measurement of work value congruence: A field study comparison. *Journal of Management, 18,* 33–44.

Meindl, J. R., Hunt, R., & Lee, W. (1989). Individualism-collectivism and work values: Data from the United States, China, Taiwan, Korea, and Hong Kong. In G. Ferris & K. Rowland (Eds.), *Research in personnel and human resource management* (pp. 59–77). Greenwich, CT: JAI Press.

Mikula, G. (1980). *Justice and social interaction.* New York: Springer.

Mowday, R. T., Porter, L. W., & Steers, R. M. (1982). *Employee-organization linkages: The psychology of commitment, absenteeism, and turnover.* New York: Academic Press.

Newman, K. L., & Nollen, S. D. (1996). Culture and congruence: The fit between management practices and national culture. *Journal of International Business Studies, 27,* 753–779.

O'Reilly, C. A., Chatman, J. A., & Caldwell, D. F. (1991). People and organizational culture: A profile comparison approach to assessing person-organization fit. *Academy of Management Journal, 34,* 487–516.

Orpen, C. (1982). The effect of social support on the reactions to role ambiguity and conflict: A study among white and black clerks in South Africa. *Journal of Cross-Cultural Psychology, 13,* 375–384.

Robert, C., Probst, T., Martocchio, J. J., Drasgow, F., & Lawler, J. J. (2000). Empowerment and continuous improvement in the United States, Mexico, Poland, and India. *Journal of Applied Psychology, 85,* 643–658.

Salisbury, D. L. (Ed.). (1998). *Do Employers/Employees Still Need Employee Benefits?* Washington, DC: Employee Benefit Research Institute.

Schneider, B. (1987). The people make the place. *Personnel Psychology, 40,* 437–453.

Schoonhoven, C. B. (1981). Problems with contingency theory: Testing assumptions hidden within the language of contingency theory. *Administrative Science Quarterly, 26,* 349–377.

Schuler, R. S., & Jackson, S. E. (1987). Linking human resource practices with competitive strategies. *Academy of Management Executive, 1,* 207–219.

Singelis, T. M., Triandis, H. C., Bhawuk, D. P. S., & Gelfand, M. (1995). Horizontal and vertical dimensions of individualism and collectivism: A theoretical and measurement refinement. *Cross-Cultural Research, 29,* 240–275.

Solnick, L. (1985). The effect of the blue collar unions on white collar wages and benefits. *Industrial and Labor Relations Review, 38,* 23–35.

Testa, M., Mueller, S., & Thomas, A. (2003). Cultural fit and job satisfaction in a global service environment. *Management International Review, 43,* 129–148.

Triandis, H. C. (1994). Cross-cultural industrial and organizational psychology. In H. C. Triandis, M. Dunnette, and L. Hough (Eds.), *Handbook of industrial and organizational psychology* (2nd ed., Vol. 4, pp. 103–172). Palo Alto, CA: Consulting Psychologists Press.

Triandis, H. C. (1995). *Individualism and collectivism.* Boulder: Westview Press.

Triandis, H. C. (1998). Vertical and horizontal individualism and collectivism: Theory and research implications for international comparative management. *Advances in International Comparative Management, 12,* 7–35.

Triandis, H. C., Bontempo, R., Villareal, M. J., Asai, M., & Lucca, N. (1988). Individualism and collectivism: Cross-cultural perspectives on self-ingroup relationships. *Journal of Personality and Social Psychology, 54,* 323–338.

Triandis, H. C., McCusker, C., & Hui, C. H. (1990). Multimethod probes of individualism and collectivism. *Journal of Personality and Social Psychology, 59,* 1006–1020.

U.S. Bureau of Labor Statistics. (1919). Welfare work for employees in industrial establishments in the United States. *Bulletin No. 250,* 119–123.

U.S. Department of Commerce. (2003). *Statistical abstracts of the United States* (123rd ed.).

Weathington, B. L., & Tetrick, L. E. (2000). Compensation or right: An analysis of employee "fringe" benefit perception. *Employee Responsibilities and Rights Journal, 12,* 141–162.

Weiss, H., & Cropanzano, R. (1996). Affective events theory: A theoretical discussion of the structural consequences of affective experiences at work. In B. M. Staw & L. L. Cummings (Eds.), *Research in organizational behavior* (Vol. 18, pp. 1–75). Greenwich, CT: JAI Press.

Zhou, J., & Martocchio, J. J. (2001). Chinese and American managers' compensation award decisions: A comparative policy-capturing study. *Personnel Psychology, 54,* 115–145.

9

Cultural Variations in Employee Assistance Programs in an Era of Globalization

RABI S. BHAGAT AND PAMELA K. STEVERSON
University of Memphis

JAMES C. SEGOVIS
Bryant University

Employee assistance programs (EAPs) are programmatic efforts undertaken by work organizations to help individuals, and their families, who are adversely affected by stressful events in their work and personal lives. The rationale for these programs is to assist individuals to deal with the dysfunctional consequences of organizational and personal life stressors so they can maintain their health and psychological well-being in addition to performing adequately in their work roles. In a Fisher Vista survey (2001), 96% of Fortune 500 companies indicated that they had an EAP in force. Work organizations generally vary in the nature of services that they provide to their employees, such variations being a function of the established practices and historical traditions found in the industry. For example, larger organizations have more resources to provide a diversity of services designed to assist employees in coping with chronic (i.e., persistent) and episodic (i.e., periodic) encounters with stressful experiences in the domain of work and personal life.

Organizations with limited resources are generally not able to provide well-designed EAPs for their employees despite the relevance of such programs in enhancing employee and organizational health. It is often the case that an organization's mission, resources, structure, and other bureaucratic mechanisms, coupled with the specific needs of the workforce, determine the amount of responsibility assumed by the EAP. The primary objectives of EAPs are as follows:

1. To promote and maintain the mental health and, to a lesser extent, the physical health of the workforce in the organization
2. To retain valued employees with skills and experience and lessen adverse consequences of turnover and job burnout
3. To promote the organizational health and well-being with a constant vigilance for improving organizational effectiveness.

The United Kingdom Employee Assistance Professionals Association (EAPA) defines an EAP as "a mechanism for making counseling and other forms of assistance available to a designated workforce on a systematic and uniform basis, and to recognize standards" (EAPA, 1994).

An EAP is a referral service that may be provided either by the work organization on their premises or by a contracting agency that supervisors or employees can use to seek professional treatment for various problems that are generally induced by stress, either in the domain of work or non-work. For example, when Campbell's Soup Company incorporated mental health treatment and counseling into its EAPs, medical costs associated with visits to psychiatrists decreased 28% in one year (Stetzer, 1992). EAPs vary widely but tend to share some basic elements. First, the programs are usually identified in the official human resources documents and brochures (such as the employee handbook available in personnel and human resources departments). Supervisors, division chiefs, and union representatives when relevant are trained to use the referral service for employees whom they identify as having mental health–related issues. For example, an employee going through the traumatic consequences of a painful divorce or loss of a loved one, generally noted as two of the stressful life events in the Holmes and Rahe Social Readjustment Ratings Scale, might be quite ill-prepared to face the demanding and constraining features of a job. A supervisor has the moral and ethical responsibility to counsel with such an employee and refer him or her to the EAP of the organization. Second, EAPs are evaluated in terms of their costs and benefits (as measured in terms of generally quick return to work, decreased absenteeism, improved work performance, and complete recovery from substance use). Although the effectiveness of EAPs is a concern in the field of occupational health psychology and human resource management (Cooper, Dewe, & O'Driscoll, 2003), this research on effectiveness occurred in EAPs within the United States, the United Kingdom, and other parts of Western Europe. It finds that there is limited information regarding the prevalence as well as effectiveness of such programs in other globalizing and emerging economies (e.g., China, India, Brazil, Ireland, Turkey, Egypt, etc.).

EAPs exist in various parts of the world, and our survey of the theoretical and applied literature in this area suggests that their evolution, maintenance, and even possibly their growth are likely to be affected by the level of affluence in a given country as a function of its globalization, culture-based variations in societal and organizational contexts, and predispositions on the part of employees to seek out and utilize such services. Subsidiaries of multinational and global corporations are also influenced by their company-wide human resource management practices. However, as competition in the global economy intensifies, there will be strong concerns in the human resource management departments of multinational and global corporations to design and implement EAPs in line with national, economic, political, legal, and cultural expectations.

Competition among multinational and global organizations is changing all the time and becoming more complex. Competition induces both continuous and abrupt changes in employment practices, resulting in significant stressful events in the workplace. Such changes are further accelerated by rapid changes in technology, modes of processing knowledge, and the pressures for innovation and increased demographic diversity. Furthermore, as knowledge-based competition intensifies around the world, workers, primarily knowledge workers, are often regarded as the most important organizational assets, which in turn results in increased top management concern for their continued well-being. However, there is a lack of systematic theoretical inquiry that might provide an adequate background to accomplish this objective. There are strong national and cultural variations in the design, implementation, and effectiveness of EAPs, and this is precisely our focus in this chapter.

Which countries and cultures are likely to be more favorably predisposed toward embracing EAPs of the kind that we know today? What are the various organizational and contextual factors that influence the effectiveness of EAPs in improving employee mental health and emotional well-being across national borders and cultures? In this chapter, we (a) discuss the evolution of EAPs from a historical perspective, with an objective of discerning their central concerns, (b) present an overview of the etiology of human stress and coping in work organizations whose economic activities span across national borders and dissimilar cultures, (c) present a conceptual model for understanding cross-cultural variations of human stress and cognition in organizations with the objective of understanding differential emphases of EAPs as a function of societal and organizational culture-based variations in an international perspective, and (d) advance a theoretical framework for examining the determinants of EAP effectiveness in a global perspective. This framework is developed especially for guiding future research endeavors that seek to incorporate cultural variations in EAPs in the current era of globalization. Implications for future research on the effects of cultural variations on the evolution, sustenance, and growth of EAPs are also explored.

EVOLUTION OF EMPLOYEE ASSISTANCE PROGRAMS: A HISTORICAL PERSPECTIVE

It is somewhat of a paradox that the earliest EAPs evolved in the Western world, where there is an inherent belief that individuals should be responsible for themselves, rather than in the Eastern world which, in its collectivist traditions, has long known the value of group support for its members. Whereas the emotional well-being of the employee and his or her family has been the primary focus of the EAP since its inception, the spirit of EAPs has always been consistent with the Judeo-Christian work ethic of the Anglo-Saxon context, that is, helping the employee gain a sense of mastery over his or her stress-inducing environment and, at the same time, ensuring that productivity is maintained on a ongoing basis. The primary impetus for EAPs has always been economic in nature. Although estimates of the costs of worker mental and emotional health problems vary widely, almost no one disputes that their impact is substantial.

Since the latter part of the 19th century, U.S. work organizations have offered employee assistance in many guises: social betterment, personnel counseling, occupational mental health, and alcoholism treatment (Sonnenstuhl & Trice, 1986). Management concerns for productivity and humanitarian values are combined in each of these approaches. The core management belief underpinning each is that helping employees with their problems increases productivity. However, by the mid-1930s, the social betterment movement had ended, as employees became disillusioned with corporate paternalism and companies lost the struggle against unionism (Sonnenstuhl & Trice, 1986).

The history of present-day EAPs is rooted in occupational health programs for alcoholism. In the 1940s, Alcoholics Anonymous (AA) emerged as an effective method of recovery from alcoholism by achieving total abstinence. Workers who had been terminated were rehired when they were able to maintain sobriety with the help of AA. Many organizations began to develop alcohol treatment programs because workers who went through these programs demonstrated astonishing work productivity improvements. The aim of these early programs was to identify alcoholic employees and get them help before termination resulted from poor job performance (absenteeism, tardiness, etc.). The threat of job loss became the final straw to be used in the alcoholic's denial, and it had excellent results. It was found that jobs meant more to workers, including alcoholics, than had previously been noted. This was indeed important knowledge, as historically the workplace was seen in a negative light with regard to ego-reinforcement (Masi, 1984).

During the 1940s, the majority of the innovative alcohol treatment programs did not progress from the design stage. Programs faced social stigma, industrial apathy, and denial of alcoholism as a major problem, as well as a lack of available resources (Masi, 1984). The idea was to train supervisors to recognize alcoholism-related symptoms among subordinates and encourage these individuals to seek help. The system generally allowed management to view alcoholism as an "affliction of the lower echelons" (Masi, 1984, p. 8). Workers were strongly discouraged from displaying any symptoms of alcoholism in their immediate work group in order to avoid detection and possible reprimands, including termination.

The front-line supervisors had limited capabilities in many other aspects. First-line supervisors lacked adequate training to deal with practicing alcoholics who had years of experience in manufacturing excuses for responsibility failures. Supervisors often unintentionally aided the practicing alcoholic by covering up his or her mistakes because they lacked an understanding of alcoholism as a progressive disease. Supervisors also leaned toward postponing referral until they could completely verify their suspicion, because there was such a strong social stigma attached to alcoholism. Most individuals referred for help, therefore, had already reached the end stages of the disease process, where the chance for recovery was remote. As a result, treatment opportunities were limited, as was the development of occupational alcoholism programs.

Companies with successful alcoholism recovery programs included Eastman Kodak and du Pont in the early 1940s, as well as later programs at North American Aviation, Consolidated Edison, New England Electric, and Caterpillar (Masi, 1984). These early EAPs focused primarily on alcoholism and alcohol-related problems, and their initial efforts remained mostly informal. The dedicated efforts of early EAP workers were instrumental in gaining management acceptance and approval. Without clear evidence from the early EAPs supporting the benefits to the organization in terms of worker performance, there would have been no justification for business involvement in their workers' personal problems.

Occupational alcoholism programs were implemented in many companies and unions during the 1950s and 1960s, as support for the concept widened. Governments and health care providers jumped on the bandwagon supporting the EAP basic delivery model. Organizations began utilizing external contractors for consultation, training, and service delivery during this period. In the United States, idea sharing among EAP professionals was fostered by the development of local and national professional associations such as the Labor-Management Administrators and Consultants on Alcoholism (Spicer, 1987), which was renamed the Employee Assistance Professionals Association, or EAPA, in 1989.

The focus of EAPs in the 1970s shifted from a sole focus on alcoholism to identifying impaired job performance. The development of the *broadbrush* (Spicer, 1987), or comprehensive approach, to human problems was spurred by the requests of employees for help with other problems in addition to substance abuse, as well as by the desire to make programs more palatable by taking away the stigmatizing impact of the term *alcoholism* (Masi, 1984). EAPs broadened the range of their services. As a necessity, EAPS could not ignore emotional problems affecting declines in performance if the EAP was a performance-based model. Supporters of the broadbrush model provided evidence that this approach encouraged workers to safely present problems other than alcohol and drug dependency, and also that the underlying chemical dependency could be found through the assessment process (Spicer, 1987). The Comprehensive Alcohol Abuse, and Alcoholism Prevention, Treatment and Rehabilitation Act of 1970 (also known as the Hughes Act) helped speed the advancement of EAPs in the United States. The Act identified alcoholism as a physical and psychological disease, which effectively decriminalized alcoholism. As a result, more systematic and thorough efforts to mobilize treatment resources for employed alcoholics emerged.

In the 1980s, there was increasing involvement of public treatment centers and private practitioners in EAP services, which contributed to the continued growth of EAPs. During that time, a void in treatment programs occurred as a result of government fiscal cutbacks. Eager entrants into the EAP field included alcohol and drug treatment centers, public and mental health agencies, and private consulting firms, partnering with industry for future survival. A focus on prevention emerged with new capabilities, highlighting stress management and health or wellness and addiction problems (smoking, overeating, etc.). Although innovative, programs that proposed controlling stress and encouraging healthier lifestyles among employees, which could reduce or prevent many of the problems dealt with in those occupational alcoholism programs and EAPs, were controversial.

In the 1990s, EAPs became a mainstay of many organizations, concomitant with workforce trends including downsizing, mergers and acquisitions, globalization, and changing workforce demographics (i.e., aging workers, increased ethnic diversity) (Phatak, Kashlak, & Bhagat, 2005). EAPs grew in number and functioned as a source of support for employees who balanced increasingly complex work and life demands (Kramer & Rickert, 2006). EAPs were forced to continue to evolve to accommodate unexpected socioeconomic trends impacting the workplace.

Organizations have been forced to deal with an ever-changing world, requiring them to make difficult and often painful decisions. The challenges faced by organizations regarding EAPs may be viewed as opportunities in some organizations, whereas others find the process of making the necessary alterations quite daunting. The EAPs of today are shaped, defined, and even coerced by external forces, which muddy traditional program values and sometimes inhibit proper functioning (Googins, 1990).

The evolution of EAPs has necessitated that people move in directions that conflict with the past and possibly with their culture. Historically, organizations have separated EAP efforts from disciplinary actions, clearly distinguishing between the two. Because of legal and security issues that have emerged in recent years, in some organizations these distinctions are no longer clear. For example, in some organizations EAP professionals are now asked to refer employees for drug testing and report results to the employer. Similarly, cost constraints may impose limitations on the EAP that are counter to the values of the organization and its employees. Conflicts such as these make establishing, selecting, and/or refining EAP models and functions difficult at best.

Higher health care costs are eroding the competitiveness of industries and negatively impacting the services of EAPs. For example, in the United States, health care costs consume an estimated 13 percent of the gross national product and have risen unabated since the early 1970s (Luthans & Davis, 1990). Escalating health care costs have been fueled by rising employee wages, changing demographics, the high cost of medical technology, increasing malpractice insurance rates, and a shift in consumer attitudes. Traditionally, unions and private employers have almost exclusively borne the burden of rising health care prices through higher insurance premiums or in the payment of direct claims. However, in recent years this has changed with the advent of managed care and relentless attempts to shift part, if not all, of the burden of health care costs to the employees.

Organizations have turned to managed care because they are confronted by two competing organizational goals. Organizations must reduce health care costs, while at the same time they must continue to provide prompt and effective treatment (particularly in the areas of mental health and substance abuse) to their workforce to maintain a competitive edge. Maintaining worker productivity is critical in achieving this goal and in fact, job performance must continue to be a key focus or EAPs will be in danger of elimination as budgets tighten. In organizations demanding highly skilled labor in areas where the labor pool is not easily replaced, there is an impetus for the development and maintenance of EAPs. However, EAPs must simultaneously balance cost-containment and quality concerns in addressing the needs of the workforce.

Today EAPs are typically found primarily in larger organizations, although it is not uncommon for smaller businesses to outsource EAP services. In the United States, in-house, on-site provision is still the predominant mode of program delivery, whereas in Britain and Europe, the later development of EAPs in a dissimilar and stricter economic climate has prompted external contractors to be the delivery method of choice (Cooper, et al., 2003).

EAPs are usually regarded as an essential component of the human resources function. Many standard human resources texts identify EAPs as part of the human resource (or personnel) function. In recent years, EAPs have expanded their services to address wellness and health promotion to supplement assistance for a broad range of mental and emotional problems, such as marital, parental, and familial difficulties; financial and legal issues; individual psychological issues; work stress; and substance abuse. Professionals offer a variety of services in disciplines such as education, psychology, social work, and substance abuse. Present-day EAPs may serve dependents and retirees as well current employees. The problems of these people may or may not impact employee work performance directly. Despite the recognition and a general acceptance of the benefits an EAP can provide, the function and prevalence of EAPs still vary from setting to setting. The role, if any, EAPs should play in the present and future remains a subject of debate within the management profession. Increased fragmentation and internal conflict threaten the future of the EAPs (Spicer, 1987). Although the effectiveness of EAPs has been analyzed (Arthur, 2000; Berridge & Cooper, 1994; Highley & Cooper, 1994), relatively little is known about the theoretical foundations of such intervention programs (Cooper et al., 2003). Furthermore, the role of international and cross-cultural variations on the etiology and significance of EAP programs has been overlooked.

Employee assistance programs exist in Canada, Ireland, the United Kingdom, Japan, China, and other countries. The International EAP Association, headquartered in Arlington, Virginia; Fashion Group International (FGI), headquartered in Toronto, Canada; and other private associations and consulting services provide EAPs. A network of services also exists for organizations and EAP professionals in different parts of the world. Our research clearly revealed that EAPs are more prevalent in western European countries, Canada, Australia, and the United States. Such programs are either nonexistent or exist in very few organizational contexts in east Asia, south Asia, Africa, southern Europe, and Latin America. When they do exist in these countries, they are usually found in the subsidiaries of multinational and global corporations. The reasons for the nonexistence of EAPs in these regions are economic; companies in developing countries cannot afford organized assistance to employees. Such companies may have good reasons to think about implementing EAPs as programmatic interventions for constructive and supportive management of employees, but they may not have the resources to do so.

Having discussed the central concerns of EAPs in a historical perspective, we are now in a position to examine the etiology of human stress, cognition, and coping in a cross-cultural perspective. Our objective is to understand the selective role that EAPs play in managing the dysfunctional consequences of stresses emanating from organizational as well as non-work-related demands, along with various coping strategies, social support mechanisms, and organizational, institutional, and personal preventative strategies.

HUMAN STRESS, COGNITION, AND COPING: A CROSS-CULTURAL PERSPECTIVE

It is well known that stressful experiences from the domains of both work and non-work have adverse effects on individuals (Bhagat, Allie,

& Ford, 1991; Bhagat, McQuaid, Lindholm, & Segovis, 1985; Quick, Bhagat, Dalton, & Quick, 1987; Quick, Cooper, Nelson, Quick, & Gavin, 2003). Psychological and physical strains are reported by individuals undergoing increased pressures from work, conflicting or unclear expectations about how to perform their work, and persistence of severe work–family conflicts. Research documenting the deleterious effects of organizational stress has been burgeoning since the classic studies of role ambiguity and conflict by Robert Kahn and his colleagues (Kahn, Wolfe, Quinn, Snoek, & Rosenthal, 1964) from the University of Michigan. Reviews of work stress literature may be found in Beehr (1995), Beehr and Bhagat (1985), Cooper (1998), Cooper, Dewe, and O'Driscoll (2001), Cooper and Payne (1998), Kahn and Byosiere (1992), and Quick et al. (2003), among others. In their recent handbook, Quick and Tetrick (2003) provide a detailed history of occupational health psychology in the United States. From a careful review of this handbook, it is clear that the prevention, detection, and treatment of work-related stresses are receiving increasing attention from human resources departments of organizations, as well as from health care agencies, payers of health care costs (i.e., insurance companies and governmental programs such as Medicare and Medicaid), and federal and state regulators (e.g., Occupational Health and Safety Administration in the United States). The primary emphasis of all of these preventative stress management programs is to enable the individual to cope with the deleterious effects of chronic and episodic types of stressful experiences and regain complete mastery of his or her environment, be it in the domain of work or non-work.

We seem to know a lot about the etiology of both work- and non-work-related stressors and their implications for health and well-being (see Quick et al., 2003, for a complete overview) and strategies for preventive management (Quick, Quick, Nelson, & Hurrell, 1997), but relatively little about how these strategies might be either appropriate or applicable in dissimilar national and cultural contexts. Individuals appraise stressful events in the domains of work and non-work as a function of their unique cognitive styles, belief systems, personal values as well by reflecting on their repertoire of past experiences (Folkman & Lazarus, 1988; Lazarus, 1991; Lazarus & Folkman, 1984). Cognitive styles, personal values, and belief systems of individuals are largely shaped by the dominant cultural orientations of one's national and cultural context (Triandis, 1989, 1994a, 1994b, 1995, 1998, 2002). Lazarus and his colleagues, whose works have been among the most influential in the area of human stress and coping, suggest that it is not necessarily most useful to identify conditions of work or non-work that affect most workers. The experience of stress is ultimately an individual phenomenon; that is, individuals subjectively construe the significance of stressful experiences in terms of their negative, positive, and neutral effects consisting of primary and secondary appraisals. *Primary appraisal* is concerned with those evaluative beliefs that are invoked to determine whether the individual has any immediate personal stake at the onset and during the initial phases of the stressful encounter. Thoughts such as Am I in danger? Am I going to be confronting an upset supervisor? Am I going to be laid off or terminated? are the kinds of thoughts that are invoked in the primary appraisal stage. *Secondary appraisal* concerns the assessment of available coping options and resources for dealing with the harm, threat, or challenge associated with the stressful event or experience. The effectiveness of coping lies in the inherent capacity or the cognitive style of the individual in integrating these two sets of psychological forces operating in an adaptational transaction. Personal beliefs, values, agendas, and goals, combined with a stressful event or experience and the environmental demands, jointly determine the outcome as to whether the individual will have mastery of the situation, or if the situation will be more dominant and its deleterious effects on the individual in terms of negative mental and physical consequences that might emerge.

Culturally sanctioned patterns of thinking, mores, and social norms, as well as organizational and social support mechanisms, also exert their influences in determining the outcome of transactional adaptation of the individual (or even a work or social group) experiencing the stressful event or experience (Bhagat, Krishnan, Harnisch, & Moustafa, 2004; Bhagat, 1994; Spector et al., 2001). In continuing their interest in exploring the moderating role of coping in a situation-specific and culturally determined phenomenon, Bhagat and his associates (1994, 2001, 2004) completed a series of investigations into the relative efficacies of problem-focused versus emotion-focused coping in dealing with organizational stress, first by utilizing U.S. workers and later non-U.S. workers sampled in eight countries which varied considerably in terms of their cultural dimensions as specified by Hofstede (1991, 2001). Following Lazarus and Folkman's (1984) conceptualization, *problem-focused coping* was defined as proactive attempts to alter or manage the situation (e.g., "Got the person responsible for creating the excess workload to change his or her mind" or "Made a plan of action and worked on it"). *Emotion-focused coping* was defined as attempts to reduce or manage distress associated with the experience of stress (e.g., "Looked for the 'silver lining in the cloud'" or "Tried to look on the brighter side of things" or "God willing, things are going to get better in the near future"). In studies conducted in the 1990s with a U.S.-based workforce located in the southwestern United States, Bhagat et al. (1991) found the superiority of problem-focused coping in coping with feelings of depersonalization, emotional exhaustion, and serious illness. Problem-focused coping was also a moderator of negative personal life stress and satisfaction with work.

In their investigation with professional workers from financial services and high-tech organizations of seven countries, Bhagat et al. (2004) expected problem-focused coping to emerge as a more effective moderator of work-related stress and psychological strain in individualistic contexts and emotion-focused coping to emerge as a more effective moderator of the relationship between organizational stress and strain in collectivistic contexts. The countries explored in this international study were Germany, New Zealand, Australia, and the United States (predominately individualistic in their cultural orientation, the United States being the most individualistic among them) and South Africa, Spain, and India (predominately collectivistic in their cultural orientation, India being the most collectivistic among them). Individualism and collectivism are shared patterns of beliefs, attitudes, and values organized as one theme. *Individualism* is defined as a social pattern that consists of loosely linked individuals who view themselves as independent of their immediate in-groups and collectives and who are primarily motivated by their own set of personal needs, agendas, rights, and contracts. *Collectivism*, on the other hand, is defined as closely linked individuals who view themselves as interdependent with each other and as belonging to one or more in-groups (e.g., family, work group, work organization, tribe, etc.) and who are largely motivated by social norms, duties, and obligations of these collectives. Collectivists' selves are spread and rooted in the conception of selves of other individuals in the immediate social context. When a member of a collectivistic context experiences pain or discomfort, other members consider it to be their duty and moral obligation to come the rescue of the affected party. This is not likely to be the case in individualistic contexts, where individuals are expected to take care of their own sense of well-being (including their subjectively experienced pain and discomfort). Whereas problem-focused coping (an organizationally and managerially determined prerogative) acted independently on organizational stress to reduce the level of psychological strain in six of the seven countries and decision latitude had independent effects in all seven of the countries, emotion-focused coping had virtually no direct or indirect effects on ameliorating the level of organizational strain that subjects experienced in all seven countries.

However, Bhagat et al. (2001), in their attempts to test the validity of these findings (the U.S.-based findings in 1995 were in consonance with Lazarus and Folkman's 1984 theory of coping concerning these adaptational mechanisms initiated at the individual level) across dissimilar national and cultural contexts, utilizing data from the seven countries from the Bhagat et al. (1994) study and additional data from Japan (collectivistic in orientation), found (a) organizational stress adversely affected psychological strain in all of the eight countries, (b) problem-focused coping did not moderate the relationship in any of the countries, (c) emotion-focused coping moderated the relationship between organizational stress and psychological strain in the context of South Africa, and (d) decision latitude (the amount of job-related autonomy that an individual has in executing his or her duties and responsibilities) had the strongest independent effect on lowering psychological strain in all seven countries regardless of the underlying cultural variations (Bhagat, 1994; Bhagat et al., 2001). The researchers of these studies attributed the tendency toward problem-focused coping as opposed to emotion-focused coping in all these countries to the nature of the workforce sampled. All of the workers were of the professional and white-collar variety, and it is quite likely that their educational background had socialized them to successfully deal with organizationally relevant stressful encounters by using a problem-solving orientation (Bhagat et al., 1994, p. 104). However, they noted that the measurement of both problem-focused and emotion-focused coping was not sufficiently culture specific (i.e., emic in character) and therefore might not have adequately captured the very essence of the iterative process of coping, which is deeply rooted in the cultural fabric of the society in which the individual functions. Studies by Spector and his colleagues (2002) involving cross-national data from 24 nations/territories also found marginal support for the role of individualism–collectivism in the prediction of well-being. They also noted methodological limitations of their measures and discussed the role of social desirability and response sets in masking the possible role of cultural variations in influencing the intricate relationships between stressful experiences at work and its various consequences as affected by various individual level moderators. The primary problems associated with studies done by these U.S.-based teams is their lack of culture-sensitive measures of coping. To deal with these issues, we believe it is important to grasp the essence of the stress and coping process by incorporating explicitly the role of cultural and national variations. Figure 9.1 depicts our approach.

CROSS-CULTURAL VARIATIONS OF THE STRESS PROCESS: A CONCEPTUAL MODEL

Figure 9.1 shows that both organizational and non-work (personal life–related) demands and stressors lead to the possibility of experiencing decision-making or problem-solving situations characterized by their uncertainty, importance, and duration (Beehr, 1998; Beehr & Bhagat, 1985). Stress is viewed as a multiplicative function of uncertainty, importance, and duration (i.e., $S = U_c \times I \times D$). This multiplicative function suggests that the individual does not experience stress in a situation where the individual (a) lacks a set of important outcomes to obtain, (b) lacks uncertainties associated with obtaining rewards or other valued outcomes, and (c) experiences these conditions for almost no length of time (duration is close to zero). This formulation as advanced by Beehr and Bhagat (1985) is presumed to be etic (i.e., generalizable across cultures) in character. The experience of stress can be modified by effective coping on the part of the individual and also by the availability of effective social support mechanisms (Beehr, 1995, 1998). Cultural variations rooted in societal and organizational contexts jointly influence, to a large, extent the nature of coping that one engages in and also the kind of social support systems that are likely to be available in the immediate and in

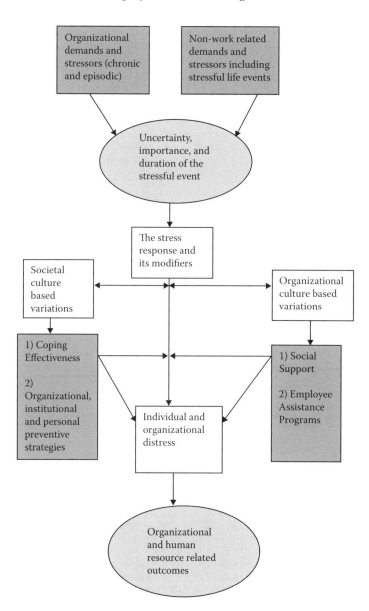

Figure 9.1 A conceptual model of cross-cultural variations of the stress process.

the long term. Organizational, institutional, and personal preventive strategies act as moderators of this relationship. Equally important (as Figure 9.1 shows) is the role of EAPs; in particular, well-designed EAPs can go a long way in ameliorating the effects of sustained and episodic stressful experiences on individual and organizational distress. Lessening of individual and organizational distress will also result in improved organizational and human resource–related outcomes.

Our approach also shows that EAPs—especially their intent, design, and effectiveness—are influenced by organization-based and culture-based variations. EAPs, just like social support mechanisms, exist in the context of work organizations. Having stated this, we must also note that socioculturally-based variations indirectly influence both the design and the effectiveness of EAPs, as well as their availability of high-quality, social support–related systems and mechanisms. Nations that are highly collectivistic are likely to provide appropriate mechanisms for evolving work-related social support in the context of one's immediate work environment but may not foster the kind of formal EAPs that are prevalent in the West. In fact, it is our thesis that vertical collectivistic countries (e.g., China, India, Egypt, Brazil, Argentina, Mexico, and Turkey) are likely to emphasize social support initiatives in the domains of both work and non-work, more so than horizontal individualistic countries such as Australia, Sweden, and Denmark. Culture is to society what memory is to an individual (Triandis, 1994a, 1994b, 1995, 2002). The four cultural grids that are relevant to examining the prevalence of EAPs around the globe are *vertical individualism, vertical collectivism, horizontal individualism,* and *horizontal collectivism* (see Table 9.1). Verticalness is concerned with propensity of the members of a culture to stand out (i.e., be different) from others in their

TABLE 9.1   Prevalence of Employee Assistance Programs in Four Different Grids of Societal Cultural Variations

Vertical	**In Vertical Individualistic Countries** (e.g. US, UK) EAPs are mostly institutional, company driven	**In Vertical Collectivistic Countries** (e.g. India, Japan) Less frequent in number and are generally a function of the state of globalization and economic well-being of the population in the country
Horizontal	**In Horizontal Individualistic Countries** (e.g. Australia, Sweden) Strongly embedded in social, legal, and political framework	**In Horizontal Collectivistic Countries** (e.g. Egypt, Israeli Kibbutzim) Existence of EAPs largely unknown; if known are highly dependent on the nature of social relations found in the country
	Individualism	**Collectivism**

significant circle of friends, associates, neighbors, and so forth. Verticals view people as differing in social status and think it is appropriate, even highly desirable, to stand out from the crowd. Horizontals, on the other hand, see themselves as people who have more or less the same status as others in their significant circle of friends, family, and so on. Horizontals do not like to stand out from others. This cultural pattern emerges when the individuals see their concept of self as an integral aspect of the in-group, family, and community. When one's self tends to merge with those of the members of one's own in-group, similar tastes and preferences, including how to cope with organizationally and personally induced stresses, emerge. The Israeli kibbutz is an example of a horizontal collectivistic cultural pattern.

The state of globalization of the country and the degree of economic affluence also influence the prevalence of EAPs in the countries in the vertical collectivistic grid. As a general rule (see Hofstede, 2001; Triandis, 1989), individualistic countries (whether they are horizontal or vertical in orientation) are more affluent than collectivistic countries (whether they are horizontal or vertical in orientation). We find that organizations in countries such as Japan, South Korea, India, and Brazil have EAPs only if they are actively participating in the global marketplace and experience the need of providing appropriate counseling mechanisms for employees who are functioning in overseas contexts. In contrast, in vertical individualistic countries, EAPs are primarily initiated by human resources management departments. There is a strong concern for maintaining the privacy of the individuals and their families (e.g., the recent Health Insurance Portability and Accountability Act [HIPAA] in the United States). Given the fact that relational concerns are kept to a minimum in the vertical individualistic cultural context (Sanchez-Burks, 2004), EAPs are supposed to act as strong buffers so that employees can maintain acceptable role performance and exhibit adequate levels of psychological functioning in the workplace. Another way to analyze the high prevalence of EAPs in those societal cultural contexts is to note that contractual arrangements in the workplace are strong. However, although there is a strong recognition that stressful encounters of a chronic and episodic nature adversely affect employees' ability to function effectively, there is also an equally strong ambient culture of leaving it up to the employees to solve their stress-related reactions and psychological distress with the help of EAPs provided by the institutional and human resource management context of the employing organization.

In horizontal collectivistic countries, EAPs are largely unknown. Of course, it should be emphasized that these countries are relatively poor (i.e., not affluent in resources) and are not participants in the global arena in any sense of the word and therefore are unlikely to possess the institutional and economic resources that are necessary for institutionalizing EAPs. Finally, in horizontal individualistic countries, there is a strong sense of social well-being inherent in the political, social, and legal framework of the country. In our survey of EAPs, it was clear that EAPs are institutionalized much more effectively from the public agencies in the cultural context of horizontal individualism. Sweden, Denmark, Norway, Finland, the Netherlands, and Australia are good examples of countries where the primary thrust for the evolution, sustenance, and growth of these EAPS come from governmental initiatives in the public sector and less so from the private sector. This is in contrast to what we found in the case of vertical individualism, where the thrust for institutionalizing these programs comes more from the private sector than from governmental initiatives. Even though various public agencies in the United States (e.g., the National Institute of Occupational Safety and Health [NIOSH], the National Institute of Mental Health [NIMH], and the Occupational Health and Safety Administration [OSHA]) may play some role in assisting company-sponsored EAPs to operate more effectively, the fact remains that the primary initiative has to originate from the human resources departments of these organizations with the explicit goal of maintaining adequate levels of psychological effectiveness in their own work environment.

As Figure 9.1 shows, organizational culture-based variations not only influence social support mechanisms and the existence of EAPs, but they also have direct effects on individual and organizational distress. In Table 9.2 we provide a cultural matrix of coping, social support mechanisms, and differential emphasis of EAPs in four types of organizational cultures. These cells are created by considering two dimensions of culture variations that are particularly useful for classifying organizational cultures for the purposes of generating insights into the differential emergence, sustenance, and growth of EAPs. These two dimensions are (a) *employee oriented* versus *job oriented* (Hofstede, 2001) and (b) *rule based* versus *relationship based* (Hooker, 2003). In employee-oriented organizational cultures, there is a concern for people as opposed to a concern for getting the job done immediately. Hofstede notes (2001) that in employee-oriented cultures, personal problems are given careful attention and the organization takes responsibility for employee welfare. In contrast, in job-oriented organizational cultures, individuals experience a strong pressure for getting the job done, and there is a strong perception that the organization is primarily interested in workers' productivity as opposed to their personal and family welfare. Extending the work of Hooker (2003) pertaining to relationship-based versus rule-based cultures, we advance the notion of relationship-based versus rule-based organizational cultures. Relationship-based organizational cultures are likely to focus on maintaining harmonious relationships even at the expense of immediate organizational productivity. Conflicts between individuals and among work groups are likely to be disdained. These organizational cultures are likely to be found in non-industrialized or in highly collectivistic parts of the world. In contrast, rule-based organizational cultures are interested in doing things by the book; there is strong emphasis on formal organizational procedures and contractual

TABLE 9.2   An Organizational Culture-Based Matrix of the Prevalence of Styles of Coping, Social Support Mechanisms, and Differential Emphasis of Employee Assistance Programs

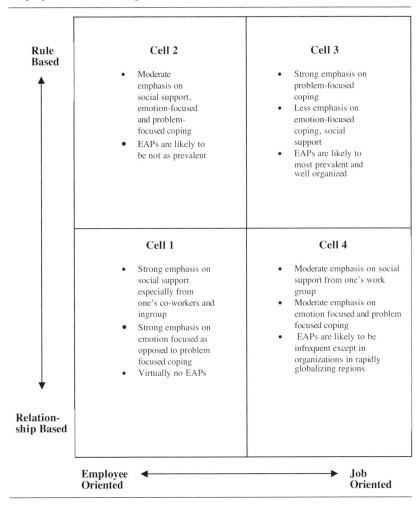

Rule Based	Cell 2	Cell 3
	• Moderate emphasis on social support, emotion-focused and problem-focused coping • EAPs are likely to be not as prevalent	• Strong emphasis on problem-focused coping • Less emphasis on emotion-focused coping, social support • EAPs are likely to most prevalent and well organized
	Cell 1	Cell 4
Relation-ship Based	• Strong emphasis on social support especially from one's co-workers and ingroup • Strong emphasis on emotion focused as opposed to problem focused coping • Virtually no EAPs	• Moderate emphasis on social support from one's work group • Moderate emphasis on emotion focused and problem focused coping • EAPs are likely to be infrequent except in organizations in rapidly globalizing regions
	Employee Oriented	Job Oriented

arrangements. One is unlikely to receive a special consideration of any kind (e.g., a longer maternity leave) than is usually sanctioned or provided in the human resource policy and procedures.

In Table 9.2, Cell 1 is populated by organizations that are largely employee-oriented and are also concerned with maintaining harmonious relationships in the workplace. Such organizations are found in countries, especially in rural areas, largely untouched by the process of globalization. Small family-owned organizations in horizontal or vertical collectivistic cultures (such as rural China, India, Brazil, Mexico, most rural parts of Latin America, the Middle East, and Africa, as well as the Israeli kibbutz) are likely to exhibit the tendencies of strong social support and strong emotion-focused, as opposed to problem-focused, coping. In Mexico, for example, work relationships, like other relationships in the non-work context, are strongly guided by the cultural tradition of *simpatia* (Diaz-Guerrero, 1967; Triandis, Marin, Lisansky, & Betancourt, 1984). This relational style is highly valued and in many ways resembles the search for social harmony and strong concern for others in the immediate network that is also characteristic of many east Asian cultures. EAPs are virtually unknown in these work cultures.

Organizations characterized by the cultural prototype as depicted in Cell 2 are likely to moderately emphasize social support mechanisms, problem-focused coping, and emotion-focused coping. Employee assistance programs in these contexts are likely to be somewhat infrequent. Organizations in urban areas of the newly globalizing world (such as South Korea, China, Taiwan, and India) are likely to exhibit these characteristics. Organizations in Cell 3 are found in highly industrialized and information-intensive societies. The United States, a majority of the countries in western Europe, Australia, and Canada are populated predominately by organizations whose cultural prototype fit this pattern, that is, job oriented and rule based. There are strong and subtle messages in the organizational context that one must deal with one's difficult encounters in life through problem-focused coping. Emotion-focused coping is to be avoided at all costs, especially in the workplace. Sanchez-Burks' (2002, 2004) findings strongly support the notion that organizations located in countries such as the United States have a strong preference for dealing with affective and relational concerns away from work. EAPs are likely to be highly institutionalized and offered frequently in such organizational cultures. Organizations in Cell 4 are job oriented and relationship based. There will be moderate emphasis on social support from one's in-group and also moderate emphases on problem-focused and emotion-focused styles of coping. These organizations are likely to emphasize the principle of *gunaxi*, that is, a sense of interconnectedness with and caring for one's in-group members (Hooker, 2003, p. 183; Leung & White, 2004). EAPs are likely to be infrequent except in rapidly globalizing regions. Examples of organizations in Cell 4 are likely to be found in South Korea, Singapore, Taiwan, Thailand, and globalized urban regions of China (e.g., Shanghai, Canton, Beijing, etc.) and India (e.g., Bangalore, Bombay, Chennai, etc.).

EFFECTIVENESS OF EAPS IN AN ERA OF GLOBALIZATION

Increasingly, it is being recognized that there are strong benefits of EAPs, not only in economic terms, but also in terms of employee productivity, health, and well-being. Multinational and global organizations stand to gain a great deal by assisting their employees of terms of psychological distress and emotional trauma. Although stress related to expatriate adjustments in overseas locations is an important concern, one should not forget the destabilizing effects of shifting employment patterns and ongoing relocations of manufacturing facilities to various overseas locations. Corporations that traditionally cared for their employee and family well-being, such as IBM, General Motors, Ford, and Toyota, are moving many of their less profitable functions to overseas locations and, in the process, creating unemployment for home country–based workers. Although it may cost less to employ a Mexican or Chinese worker to produce a television or a computer, the fact remains that assembly workers in the high-tech and other manufacturing facilities in the United States and other G-8 countries lose jobs when production is outsourced to overseas locations. White-collar workers, who used to be immune from shifting patterns of unemployment in the previous decades, are becoming increasingly vulnerable to such outsourcing practices (Heckscher, 1995). Outsourcing of various services is becoming the dominant norm in the global economy. The resulting stress on the employee and his or her family can be enormous and challenge traditional family structures (Overell, 2005). At first glance, it might appear that workers and their families in the globalizing parts of the world will consider the opportunities to work in the jobs provided by these global corporations rather happily. However, although this trend is true for some countries, this is not likely to always be the case. For example, employees in call center locations in India, Philippines, Singapore, and Ireland are required to work during U.S. working hours, which are between 7 p.m. and 6 a.m. at the local time. Half of Indian call center workers reported working overtime in a recent survey (Marquez, 2006) and call center attrition rates range from 30 to 40 percent (Overell, 2005). The strain of pretending to be an American on the phone has led to questions of identity and feelings of tension. Global corporation leaders are willing to utilize Western EAP providers but Indian organizations have been slow to partner with them (Overell, 2005). Skeers (2005) reported that Indian staff, primarily women, who work in call center operations experience significant health problems including chronic fatigue, anxiety, and depression because of work demands and the inability to successfully balance their work and social roles. India's cultural values are largely collectivistic, and women are expected to fulfill certain culturally sanctioned roles and duties in society. We find similar effects in other collectivistic countries (e.g., Thailand, Philippines, South Korea, and Hong Kong) as well, not only in the context of call center operations but also in the manufacturing units and subsidiaries of multinational and global corporations.

The importance of EAPs come into play precisely in ameliorating stressful effects associated with the process of globalization, not only in the context of developed G-8 countries but also in the rapidly globalizing and emerging economies of the world. In Figure 9.2, we present a framework for examining the effectiveness of EAPs in a global perspective. The figure shows that effectiveness of EAPs in a global perspective at any given location is a function of (a) the extent of globalization that exists in the given locale, (b) societal culture-based variations in terms of prevalence of EAPs (as shown in Table 9.1), (c) organizational culture-based variations in terms of prevalence of EAPs vis-à-vis emphasis on styles of coping and social support mechanisms (as shown in Table 9.2), and (d) last, but not the least, the role of demographic and cultural predisposition inherent in the population to seek out EAPs.

Our research reveals that EAPs are primarily rooted in, and evolve out of, the cultural context of Western and vertical individualistic societies. Although they do exist in one form or another in other parts of the world (non-Western and collectivistic societies), their evolution, maintenance, and effectiveness are strongly affected by the state of globalization existing in the locale, economic realities, and societal and organizational culture-based variations. There are also cultural variations in the propensity to seek mental health counseling and use EAPs (Kossek, Meece, Barratt, & Prince, 2005; Reynolds & Lehman, 2003; U.S. Department of Health & Human Services, 1999). Especially in the context of organizations in Cell 1 (see Table 9.2), in vertical collectivistic cultures, the demographic and cultural predisposition is to strongly seek out social support mechanisms and heavily rely on emotion-focused coping and other organized rites and rituals for managing stressful encounters.

International and cultural variations operate in ways not easily discerned from a casual glance at the literature. In fact, there have been no systematic investigations into the interplay of culture-specific factors and their role in fostering the evolution, maintenance, and growth of EAPs around the globe. EAPs are generally designed to address the complex issues associated with coping and adaptational processes that are uniquely interpreted in the cultural context of society. By their very definition, EAPs are designed to assist and enable the employee to function more effectively so that his or her psychological and physical health is not adversely affected, and to find ways to have him or her perform in a consistent manner and contribute steadily to organizational effectiveness (Cooper et al., 2003). The Employee Assistance Professionals Association (EAPA) lists 33 chapters; the majority of them, as one would expect, are in the United States, with many in the United Kingdom and countries with a strong Anglo-Saxon cultural heritage. Ireland, Canada, Australia, New Zealand, and even Hong Kong, are countries where EAPs are found. Among the non-Anglo-Saxon countries, Brazil, Japan, Greece, and India are good examples. However, the number of organizations providing EAPs is rather small in these countries. Our research also indicates that violence in the workplace and Critical Incident Stress Debriefing (CIDS) are some of the major services provided in the network of non-Anglo-Saxon EAPs (Employee Assistance Professionals Association, 2007).

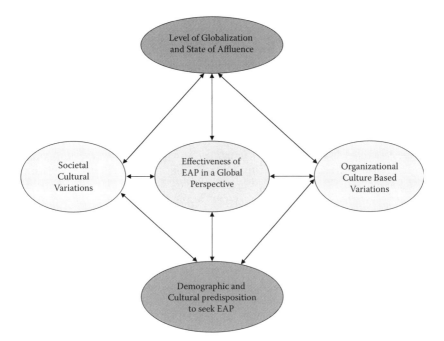

Figure 9.2 Effectiveness of employee assistance programs in an era of globalization.

Private consulting agencies such as Stuecker & Associates, head-quartered in Louisville, Kentucky, provide EAP services in public and private sector organizations in the United States, the United Kingdom, Mexico, and Puerto Rico. Their clients also include organizations in the transportation, manufacturing, and health-care industries as well as in the local, state, and federal branches of the government. Services typically consist of employee counseling, including family counseling, conflict resolution skills, substance abuse programs, coping with traumatic experiences and life transitions, financial counseling, work–life balancing, and other recent innovations such as online counseling. EAP International, owned by Horizon Behavioral Services of Louisville, Texas, specializes in global EAPs and provides customized services in conjunction with human resource management departments and offers risk management procedures for dealing with medical, safety, and legal issues. They are also known to provide childcare and eldercare counseling and referral services. Although their EAP services are largely concentrated in the United States, they do provide services in selected cities in Australia, Canada, New Zealand, Switzerland, the United Kingdom, Singapore, Mexico, Hong Kong, Russia, and Japan. ComPsy Corporation, located in Chicago, Illinois, provides services to 23 million individuals and over 6,000 organizations in 92 countries. They are known for providing comprehensive online and, often, customized services on a 24-hour/7-days-a-week basis. They recently began designing programs for assisting expatriates of global corporations to cope with stressful encounters with culture shock and related phenomenon associated with the experience of moving into unfamiliar locales.

Besides the U.S. providers, examples of internationally oriented EAPs include the K2 Corporation, Inc., headquartered in Tokyo, Japan; EAP Solutions, headquartered in Dublin, Ireland; and Dovedale Counselling Ltd., headquartered in London. Burgess (2001) noted that with the expanding global economy, EAPs are becoming increasingly involved in helping executives deal with the unfamiliar issues of managing and coping with demands in various subsidiaries of multinational and global corporations. It seems that the evolution of EAPs in non-U.S.-based corporations is perhaps due to the success of EAPs provided by U.S. multinationals for their expatriates and families in various parts of the world. In other words, there is a process of slow diffusion of these programs in parts of the world that are not necessarily Anglo-Saxon and individualistic in terms of their cultural orientation. However, the process of this diffusion is rather slow, as we have discovered in our survey of the international literature on EAPs. Buon (2006) reported the majority of supervisors in the non-English speaking countries have little awareness of EAPs. The EAP material available is typically from the North American countries, UK, and Australia and written in English describing contexts and problems common in these countries (Buon, 2006). In addition, it seems clear that affluent countries that also happen to be Anglo-Saxon and individualistic in character (Triandis, 1989, 1995) are able to afford EAPs on a scale that is still the stuff of dreams in many developing nations and emerging economies, such as Venezuela, Colombia, Mexico, China, India, Egypt, and Nigeria. Japan and South Korea are two developed and affluent but predominately collectivistic countries and also non-Anglo-Saxon in terms of their ethnic heritages. We did not find evidence of strong networks of EAP providers in these two nations. Reports of company-specific EAP activities in global corporations such as Toyota Corporation, Mitsubishi, Inc., Samsung, Inc., Lucky and Goldstar, Inc., of South Korea are not often mentioned in trade and related professional publications. It seems that the scientific discourse dealing with the benefits and related standardization procedures of EAPs are more prevalent in Western countries, in sharp contrast to non-Western countries, however developed or affluent they may be.

In fact, as competition in the global economy intensifies, EAPs will be designed increasingly in line with national, economic, political, legal, and cultural expectations. The framework provided in Figure 9.2 should aid in this process toward understanding the determinants of EAPs in a global perspective.

WHERE DO WE GO FROM HERE

In our future attempts to assess the effectiveness of EAPs, it will be necessary to understand the various national and culture-based determinants as depicted in Figure 9.2. Whereas EAPs are generally found to be effective in the cultural context of the United Kingdom and the United States (Cooper et al., 2003), their significance in dissimilar cultural contexts needs to be evaluated along with the existing roles of social support, prevailing patterns of coping strategies, and demographic and cultural predisposition to seek EAPs. For example, as the process of globalization adversely affects women in collectivistic countries (who are culturally predisposed to not seek mental health counseling and EAPs), human resource managers should seek ways to work with culturally sanctioned patterns of coping and related rites and rituals that are unique to the context in which the organization or the subsidiary is located. The purpose will be (a) to design and implement EAPs in line with culturally sanctioned patterns of coping, social support mechanisms, and other forms of organized rites and rituals; and (b) to augment the effectiveness of existing EAPs and align them not only with cultural variations, but with constant vigilance to the demographic and cultural predispositions to seek EAPs in the given locale. There will be many situations when such EAPs have to be considerably redesigned in order to incorporate selective influences from culture-specific variations in the society and in the organization. We should recognize that despite the effectiveness of EAPs and other preventative stress management programs (Cooper et al., 2003; Quick et al., 2003) in improving health and well-being at work in individualistic contexts, their straightforward application in the collectivistic contexts of work organizations might be problematic. Relationship-based and employee-oriented organizational cultures are likely to not endorse EAPs as strongly. Although job-oriented and relationship-based organizational cultures in the globalizing parts of the world are likely to endorse EAPs, they often lack the financial resources to implement and institutionalize EAPs. Given the current state of knowledge concerning how EAPs evolve and function in the global context, it is important that future research be directed toward understanding the relative efficacies of various styles of coping, social support systems, and EAPs in dissimilar cultural contexts. The conceptual model provided in Figure 9.1 and the framework for evaluating the effectiveness of EAPs in Figure 9.2 are offered as stimuli to begin serious investigation in this relatively unexplored area of research.

REFERENCES

Arthur, A. R. (2000). Employee assistance programmes: The emperor's new clothes of stress management? *British Journal of Guidance and Counseling,* *28,* 549–559.

Beehr, T. A. (1995). *Psychological stress in the workplace.* London: Routledge.
Beehr, T. A. (1998). An organizational psychology meta-model of occupational stress. In C. L. Cooper (Ed.), *Theories of organizational stress* (pp. 6–27). Oxford, UK: Oxford University Press.
Beehr, T. A., & Bhagat, R. S. (Eds.). (1985). *Human stress and cognition in organizations: An integrated perspective.* New York: John Wiley.
Berridge, J., & Cooper, C. L. (1994). The employee assistance programme: Its role in organizational coping and excellence. *Personnel Review, 23,* 4–20.
Bhagat, R. S., Allie, S. M., & Ford, D. L. (1991). Organizational stress, personal life stress and symptoms of life strains: An inquiry into the moderating role of styles of coping. *Journal of Social Behavior and Personality, 6,* 163–184.
Bhagat, R. S., Ford, D. L., O'Driscoll, M., Frey, L., Babakus, E., & Mahanyele, M. (2001). Do South African managers cope differently from American managers? A cross-cultural investigation. *International Journal of Intercultural Relations, 25,* 301–313.
Bhagat, R. S., O'Driscoll, M. P., Babakus, E., Frey, L. T., Chokkar, J. S., Ninokumar, H., Pate, L. E., Ryder, P. A., Gonzalez, F., Ford, Jr., D. L. T., & Mahanyele, M. P. (1994). Organizational stress and coping in seven national contexts: A cross-cultural investigation. In G. Keita & J. J. Hurrell (Eds.), *Job stress in a changing workforce.* (pp. 93–105) Washington, DC: American Psychological Association.
Bhagat, R. S., Krishnan, B. C., Harnisch, D. L., & Moustafa, K. S. (2004, April). Organizational stress and coping in twelve countries: Implications for a cultural theory of stress. Presented at the annual meeting of the *Society for Industrial and Organizational Psychology,* Chicago.
Bhagat, R. S., McQuaid, S. J., Lindholm, H., & Segovis, J. C. (1985). Total life stress: A multi-method validation of the construct and its effects on organizationally valued outcomes and withdrawal behaviors. *Journal of Applied Psychology, 70*(1), 202–214.
Buon, T. (2006). Non-English speaking countries: Adjusting for cultural differences. *Journal of Employee Assistance, 36*(3), 27–28.
Burgess, K. M. (2001, December). *The employee assistance program: An inappropriate model for supporting expatriates and families overseas.* Paper presented at the 8th annual Counseling in Asia conference, Taipei, Taiwan.
Cooper, C. L. (Ed.). (1998). *Theories of organizational stress.* New York: Oxford University Press.
Cooper, C. L. & Payne, R. (Eds.). (1988). *Causes, coping and consequences of stress at work.* Great Britain: Biddles Ltd. Guidlford and King's Lynn.
Cooper, C. L., Dewe, P. J., & O'Driscoll, M. P. (2001). *Organizational stress: A review and critique of theory, research, and applications.* Thousand Oaks, CA: Sage Publications.
Cooper, C. L., Dewe, P. J, & O'Driscoll, M. P. (2003). Employee assistance programs. In J. C. Quick & L. E. Tetrick (Eds). *Handbook of occupational health psychology.* Washington, DC: American Psychological Association.
Diaz-Guerrero, R. (1967). *Psychology of the Mexican: Culture and personality.* Austin, TX: University of Texas Press.
Employee Assistance Professionals Association (EAPA). (1994). *Standards of practice and professional guidelines for employee assistance programs.* London: EAPA.

Employee Assistance Professionals Association. (2007). Guide to employee assistance programs and services. Retrieved July 24, 2007 from http://www.eapassn.org/public/providers

Fisher Vista (2001). Fisher Vista's survey of Fortune 500 decision-makers reveals untapped market opportunities for work-life service providers. Available from Fisher Vista Website, http://www.fishervista.com/news_100123.htm.

Folkman, S., & Lazarus, R. S. (1988). The relationship between coping and emotion: Implications for theory and research. *Social Science and Medicine, 26,* 309–317.

Googins, B. K. (1990). Strengthening the mission: We need to strongly say who we are, what we stand for and what our values are. *Employee Assistance, 2*(12), 29–30.

Heckscher, C. (1995). *White-collar blues: Management loyalties in an age of corporate restructuring.* New York: Basic Books.

Highley, J. C., & Cooper, C. L. (1994). Evaluating EAPs. *Personnel Review, 23,* 46–59.

Hofstede, G. (1991). *Cultures and organizations: Software of the mind.* London, UK: McGraw-Hill.

Hofstede, G. (2001). *Culture's consequences: Comparing values, behaviors, institutions, and organizations across nations* (2nd ed.). Thousand Oaks, CA: Sage.

Hooker, J. (2003). *Working across cultures.* Stanford, CA: Stanford University Press.

Kahn, R. L., & Byosiere, P. (1992). Stress in organizations. In M. D. Dunnette & L. M. Hough (Eds.). *Handbook of industrial and organizational psychology* (pp. 571–650). Palo Alto, CA: Consulting Psychologists Press.

Kahn, R. L., Wolfe, D. M., Quinn, R., Snoek, J. D., & Rosenthal, R. A. (1964). *Organizational stress.* New York: Wiley.

Kossek, E. E., Meece, D., Barratt, M. E., & Prince, B. E. (2005). U.S. Latino migrant farm workers: Managing acculturative stress and conserving work-family resources. In S. A. Y. Poelmans (Ed.). *Work and family: An international research perspective.* Mahwah, NJ: Lawrence Erlbaum Associates.

Kramer, R. M. & Rickert, S. (2006). Health and productivity management: market opportunities for EAPs: By integrating with health and wellness and disease management programs, EAPs can offer employers a powerful workforce productivity tool. *Journal of Employee Assistance, 36*(1), 23–25.

Lazarus, R. S. (1991). *Emotion and adaptation.* New York: Oxford University Press.

Lazarus, R. S., & Folkman, S. (1984). *Stress, appraisal, and coping.* New York: Springer.

Leung, K., & White, S. (2004). Taking stock and charting a path for Asian management. In K. Leung & S. White (Eds.), *Handbook of Asian management* (pp. 3–18). Norwell, MA: Kluwer Academic.

Luthans, F., & Davis, E. (1990, February). The healthcare cost crisis: Causes and containment. *Personnel,* 24–30.

Marquez, J. (2006). Union cites high stress at call centers in India. *Workforce Management, 85*(21), 14.

Masi, D. A. (1984). *Designing employee assistance programs.* New York: American Management Association.

Overell, S. (2005, July 8). Stress hits India's outsourced and overworked work-force programmes: Disruption to wellbeing caused by long working hours could create a market for employee support. *Financial Times*, p. 12.

Phatak, A. V., Bhagat, R. S., & Kashlak, R. J. (2005). *International management: Managing in a diverse and dynamic global environment*. Burr-Ridge, IL: McGraw-Hill.

Quick, J. C., Bhagat, R. S., Dalton, J. E., & Quick, J. E. (1987). *Work stress: Health care systems in the workplace*. New York: Praeger.

Quick, J. C., Cooper, C. L., Nelson, D. L., Quick, J. D., & Gavin, J. H. (2003). Stress, health, and well-being at work. In J. Greenberg (Ed.), *Organizational behavior: The state of the science* (2nd ed., pp. 53–89). Mahwah, NJ: Erlbaum.

Quick, J. C., Quick, J. D., Nelson, D. L. & Hurrell, Jr., J. J. (1997). *Preventive stress management in organizations*. Washington, DC: American Psychological Association.

Quick, J. C., & Tetrick, L. E. (Eds.). (2003). *Handbook of occupational health psychology*. Washington, DC: American Psychological Association.

Reynolds, G. S., & Lehman, W. E. K. (2003). Levels of substance abuse and willingness to use the Employee Assistance Program. *Journal of Behavioral Health Services & Research*, *30*(2), 238–248.

Sanchez-Burks, J. (2002). Protestant relational ideology and (in)attention to relational cues in work settings. *Journal of Personality and Social Psychology*, *79*(2), 919–929.

Sanchez-Burks, J. (2004). Protestant relational ideology: The cognitive underpinnings and organizational implications of an American anomaly. *Research in Organizational Behavior*, *26*, 265–306.

Skeers, J. (2005). Study documents exploitation in Indian call centres. Retrieved July 24, 2007 from the World Socialist Web site of the International Committee of the Fourth International at: http://www.wsws.org/articles/2005/nov2005/indi-23n.shtml

Sonnenstuhl, W. J., & Harrison, H. M. (1986). *Strategies for employee assistance programs: The crucial balance*. Ithaca, NY: ILR Press.

Spector, P. E., Cooper, C. L., Sanchez, J. I., O'Driscoll, M., Sparks, K., Bernin, P., et al. (2001). Do national levels of individualism and internal locus of control relate to well-being: An ecological level international study, *Journal of Organizational Behavior*, *22*, 815–832.

Spector, P. E., Cooper, C. L., Sanchez, J. I., O'Driscoll, M. P., Sparks, K., & Bernin, P. (2002). A 24-nation/territory study of work locus of control in relation to well-being at work: How generalizable are western findings? *Academy of Management Journal*, *45*(2), 453–466.

Spicer, J. (1987). EAP program models and philosophies. In J. Spicer (Ed.), *The EAP solution: Current trends and solutions*. Center City, MN: Hazeldon Foundation.

Stetzer, E. (1992). Bringing insanity to mental health. *Business Health*, *10*, 72.

Triandis, H. C. (1989). Cross-cultural studies of individualism and collectivism. In J. Berman, Ed., *Nebraska Symposium*. Lincoln, NE: University of Nebraska Press, pp. 41–130.

Triandis, H. C. (1994a). Cross-cultural industrial and organizational psychology. In H. C. Triandis, M. D. Dunnette, & L. M. Hough (Eds.), *Handbook of industrial and organizational psychology* (2nd ed., Vol. 4, pp. 103–172).

Triandis, H. C. (1994b). *Culture and social behavior*. New York: McGraw-Hill.

Triandis, H. C. (1995). *Individualism and collectivism*. Boulder, CO: Westview Press.

Triandis, H. C. (1998). Vertical and horizontal individualism and collectivism: Theory and research implications for international comparative management. *Advances in international comparative management, 12,* 7–35.

Triandis, H. C. (2002). Generic individualism and collectivism. In M. J. Gannon & K. L. Newman (Eds.), *The Blackwell handbook of cross-cultural management* (pp. 16–45). Oxford, UK: Blackwell Business.

Triandis, H. C., Marin, G., Lisansky, J., & Betancourt, H. (1984). Simpatia as a cultural script of Hispanics. *Journal of Personality and Social Psychology, 47,* 1363–1375.

U.S. Department of Health and Human Services. (1999). *Mental Health: A Report of the Surgeon Genera*. Rockville, MD: U.S. Department of Health and Human Services, Substance Abuse and Mental Health Services Administration, Center for Mental Health Services, National Institutes of Health, National Institute of Mental Health, 1999.

NOTE:

Please direct all correspondences to:

Professor Rabi S. Bhagat
Professor of Organizational Behavior and International Management
University of Memphis
Memphis, TN 38152
Phone: (901) 678-3436
E-mail: rbhagat@memphis.edu

Work and Family Concerns and Practices:
A Cross-National and -Cultural Comparison of Ireland and the United States

JEANETTE CLEVELAND AND JODI L. HIMELRIGHT
Pennsylvania State University

ALMA MCCARTHY
National University of Ireland, Galway

Employees strain to balance personal and professional responsibilities. In the United States, there is still the belief that work should take precedence over family life, and that it is the woman's responsibility to take care of the children. On the other hand, the European Union, through legislation, has made it possible for parents to take time off from work to raise children with fewer negative career consequences compared with parents in the United States. Even with the enactment of the Family and Medical Leave Act of 1993 (FMLA), U.S. policies regarding family care continue to compare poorly with policies in other developed countries, including France, Sweden, Canada, and Finland, where family care is institutionalized. In the global labor market, work and family policies have emerged as key competitive factors for businesses. As a result, organizations that do not address these work–life issues are increasing the risk of negative consequences for their employees, which may eventually affect the organization (Neal & Hammer, 2006). The reconciliation of work and family demands is therefore an important human resource issue in organizations.

One frequently studied outcome of managing multiple work and family roles is work–family conflict, or the conflict that results from the difficulty in meeting demands in one domain due to demands in another (Greenhaus & Beutell, 1985). Work–family conflict has been related to greater work withdrawal, including higher absenteeism and turnover (Barling, MacEwen, Kelloway, & Higginbottom, 1994; Hepburn & Barling, 1996; Kossek, 1990; Kossek & Nichol, 1992; MacEwen & Barling, 1994) and more negative work attitudes (Aryee, 1992; Bedian, Burke, & Moffett, 1988; Boles, Johnston, & Hair, 1997; Burke, 1988; Kossek & Ozeki, 1998), as well as decreased family satisfaction (Higgins, Duxbury, & Irving, 1992) and decreased life satisfaction (Bedian et al., 1988; Pleck, Staines, & Lang, 1980). Additionally, negative mental and physical health outcomes have been related to high levels of work–family conflict (Barnett & Rivers, 1996; Boles et al., 1997; Frone, 2000; Frone et al., 1992; Frone et al., 1997; Thomas & Ganster, 1995). These findings suggest that the potential negative consequences of work and family conflict are significant at individual, organizational, and societal levels.

In the current chapter, we will discuss work–family or work–life policies and practices through a cultural lens. Figure 10.1 depicts a multilevel model of work and family policy and practice influences. This model will be used as a framework for discussing work and family issues from a cultural perspective, comparing Ireland and the United States. These two countries provide a particularly interesting comparative base because both countries are considered individualistic (Hofstede, 1980), both have high female workforce participation rates, both countries are achievement oriented, and both countries are classified as having liberal welfare regimes (Esping-Andersen, 1990). Yet, there are significant differences in work and family policy and practice in these countries, which we discuss in this chapter.

Comparing the United States and Ireland, we draw from multiple disciplines and literatures to understand the role that cultural context plays in shaping how societies, organizations, and individuals manage two of the major domains of life: work and family. We also discuss the interplay between policy and practice and highlight the idea that what appears to be good work-family policy does not always translate into effective work and family practice. We begin by describing what is meant by culture, and several approaches to characterizing cultures and societies are presented, including Esping-Andersen's (1990, 2002) typology of welfare state regimes and Hofstede's four dimensions of culture and values, with particular focus on two of these dimensions: individualism–collectivism and masculinity–femininity. Each of these

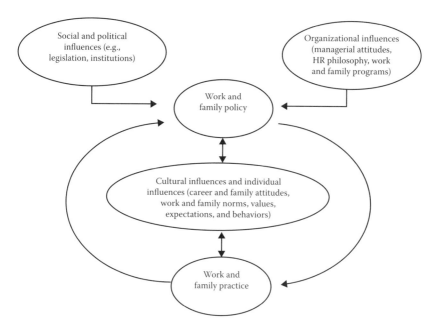

Figure 10.1 A multilevel model of work and family policy and practice influences.

cultural frameworks either discusses gender directly or articulates implications for work and family. Therefore, following the discussion of cultural frameworks and their implications for individual work and family preferences, we address the role of gender as it relates to work and family roles. The following section reviews the work and family policies and programs found in the United States and in Ireland, with links back to both Hofstede's (2001) and Esping-Andersen's (2002) conceptualizations of culture and to issues of gender. In the next section, we present the work and family case in Ireland and in the United States, focusing on government, legislative, and organizational policy and responses to work and family issues. Finally, the chapter concludes with a discussion of the implications of this cross-national comparison of Ireland and the United States for work and family research and practice.

WHAT IS CULTURE?

Culture is the human aspect of the environment. It has both objective elements, including the nature of the physical environment, its infrastructure, and tools, and subjective elements, including categories, association, beliefs, attitudes, norms, roles, and values. Todeva (1999) refers to four perspectives that view the cultural factor as important in international and comparative research. The first research perspective focuses on cultural values, attitudes, structures, and relationships, at the national and organizational levels, which act as means of comparing countries and companies operating in different national cultures. The social and political contexts of countries are also important, and Todeva (1999) argues that this research perspective has developed through social anthropology. The second perspective of research is interested in international dimensions of organizational behavior, such as cross-cultural leadership, employee attitudes, and international career management. The third perspective of international culture research focuses on general and strategic management and is interested in how multinational corporations (MNCs) shape strategy across different countries and cultures. The fourth perspective of research explores international dynamics in management practices, such as international human resource management. The primary area of interest for the discussion in this chapter is the first perspective of international and comparative culture research, because it explores cultural influences at a variety of levels including social and political context. This model of comparative analysis correlates well with Figure 10.1, which proposes a multilevel model of the influences on work and family policy and practice.

According to Hofstede (2001), the comparison of cultures assumes that each culture is not so unique that no possible parallels can be drawn (e.g., comparing apples with oranges). In research on culture, there have been two approaches: one stressing the unique aspects of culture (emic) and the other stressing the comparable aspects of cultures (etic). One approach is not necessarily better than the other; nor should one approach preclude the other. It is the task of the cross-cultural organizational psychologist to sort out the universal from the culture-specific (Tannenbaum, 1980). In this chapter, we discuss two countries that initially appear quite similar, especially in terms of individualism and masculinity. However, there are facets of each country that are unique and are critical in influencing and shaping how work and family interfaces are addressed. The following section explores the political and social influences that impact work and family attitudes, norms, and behaviors in Ireland and the United States.

POLITICAL AND SOCIAL INFLUENCES ON WORK AND FAMILY

An important contextual layer that influences social behavior within regions and countries is the interplay of markets, families, and government in determining social policy (Esping-Andersen, 2002). Den Dulk (2001) argues that the market, the family, and the state shape different backgrounds in which the combination of work and family life is addressed. This section reviews the social and welfare state context when discussing work–family issues, with particular reference to the Irish and U.S. contexts.

According to Esping-Andersen (1990), there are three types of welfare state regimes. The first is the social-democratic regime, which promotes equality among all citizens and where gender equality is strongly promoted and facilitated. The welfare system is driven by the state, and there are usually widespread and sophisticated public work–family arrangements. The system is supported by high individual taxation. However, Esping-Andersen (2002) argues that these taxes are no more costly than lower-tax regimes if a holistic view is taken, because individuals in less social-democratic regimes pay for social services such as child care, health care, and elder care out of their pockets. Sweden and Denmark are examples of social-democratic states.

The second classification of welfare state presented by Esping-Andersen (1990) is the conservative or the corporatist regime, of which Germany, France, and Italy are examples. Under this regime, social policy is less individualized, and men and women are not necessarily treated as equals. The traditional concept of family where the mother is responsible for child-care duties underpins this regime, and thus there are very few state-driven work–family initiatives and arrangements. Essentially, work–family arrangements are not seen to be a necessary social policy debate because mothers are not expected to participate in the labor force during the child-rearing years. Not surprisingly, in conservative welfare states, female labor force participation rates are low.

The liberal state is the third type of welfare state classified by Esping-Andersen (1990). Liberal welfare states operate under the assumption that the forces of the market regulate the economy and that state intervention should only occur as a last resort. Not unlike the conservative regime, the provision of work–family arrangements is not seen as a state-supported responsibility. Rather, it is believed that child care is an activity that will be provided by the market through the normal supply and demand dynamics. Further, public responsibility and intervention in these regimes is limited to extreme market failures and benefits are only targeted at the very needy. According to Esping-Andersen (1990), the United States is a good representation of this welfare state regime and the United Kingdom and Ireland most closely correspond with this regime in Europe. Table 10.1 summarizes some of the characteristics of the three different types of welfare state regimes.

Esping-Andersen's (1990) typology of welfare states reveals different attitudes toward the relative importance of the family and family life in society. The typology suggests that in conservative regimes like Italy and Spain, the family plays a key role in the social and political agenda. However, in liberal regimes, it is the market that dominates and provisions for family are seen to operate like any other commodity and can be facilitated by the market. It is expected that liberal regimes have little state provision for child care because the family plays a marginal role. While Ireland's classification as a liberal regime might signal very limited work and family reconciliation interventions at the state level,

TABLE 10.1   Characteristics of Three Types of Welfare State Regimes

	Social-democratic regime	Conservative regime	Liberal regime
Role of family	Marginal	Central	Marginal
Role of market	Marginal	Marginal	Central
Role of state	Central	Marginal	Marginal
Dominant locus of solidarity	State	Family	Market
Examples	Sweden	Italy	United States, Ireland, United Kingdom

Note: Adapted from Esping-Andersen, G. (1990) *The three worlds of welfare capitalism.* Oxford: Polity Press.

the influence of E.U. social policy has had a direct impact on Ireland's work–family environment.

CULTURAL DIMENSIONS AND INDIVIDUAL WORK AND FAMILY PREFERENCES

According to Hofstede (1991), there are four defining dimensions of culture, including individualism–collectivism, power distance, uncertainty avoidance, and masculinity–femininity. The most frequently researched construct has been individualism–collectivism. *Individualism* is the extent to which people emphasize personal or group goals. For example, if people live in nuclear families that allow them to do as they please, it is considered individualism; on the other hand, if people live together with extended families or tribes that control their behavior, it is indicative of *collectivism*. The essence of collectivism is giving preference to group goals over individual goals (Triandis, 1988, 1990). Examples of strongly collectivist countries include Venezuela, Colombia, and Pakistan, and individualistic cultures include the United States, the United Kingdom, and Ireland.

Schwartz (1990, 1992) outlines that collectivist values include respect for tradition, elders, and sexuality. Individualist values include pleasure, a variable life, and an exciting life. Individualists tend to focus on the development of a unique personality and identity and are inclined to put personal preferences, priorities, and needs before those of others. Individualists emphasize individual needs over group needs; they continue to be a member of the group as long as the group is instrumental in the attainment and satisfaction of individual goals (Ramamoorthy & Carroll, 1998). Chen, Chen, and Meindl (1998) suggest that individualists' expressive motives center around actualizing the true or potential self, and terms such as individuality, autonomy, agency, independence, self-direction, and self-reliance are commonly used to describe individualists' behavior.

Collectivists, in contrast, view the groups to which they belong as being most important, and membership in these groups contributes greatly to the determination of one's identity (Robert & Wasti, 2000; Triandis, 1995). Collectivists keep the group needs and goals foremost in their minds. Terms that are associated with collectivist behavior in the literature include self-discipline, self-restraint, loyalty, solidarity, and sociality (Chen et al., 1998).

In an extensive review of the literature, Triandis (1995) summarizes four defining attributes of the individualism–collectivism construct: (a) conceptions of self: individualists define the self as an autonomous entity independent of groups, whereas collectivists define the self in terms of its connectedness to others in various groups; (b) goal relationships: personal goals have priority over group goals in individualism, but they are subordinated to the group goals in collectivism. If conflict arises, individualists find it permissible to give priority to self-interest, whereas collectivists feel obliged to give priority to group interests; (c) relative importance of attitudes and norms: social behaviors of collectivists are more likely to be driven by social norms, duties, and obligations, whereas those of individualists are more likely to be driven by their own beliefs, values, and attitudes; and (d) emphasis on relationships: individualists are primarily oriented toward task achievement, sometimes at the expense of relationship building, whereas collectivists put more emphasis on harmonious relationships, sometimes at the expense of task accomplishment.

In the context of work and family, this cultural dimension provides a useful lens for interpreting certain preferences from one culture or country to the next. Spector et al. (2004) report that there is a stronger relationship between hours worked and work–family pressure in individualistic, as compared with collectivist, cultures. Employees working in individualistic cultures would appear to be more interested in the work domain of their lives, and those working in collectivistic cultures would be expected to have more tendencies toward family and building strong familial relationships and bonds. Because both Ireland and the United States are considered to be individualistic (Hofstede, 1980), it is expected that individual preferences would be similar in both countries. With the advent of the strong performing Irish economy, or Celtic Tiger, there is growing emphasis on career and career progression for men and, more particularly, for women in the past 10 years. Employees in the United States report high career salience suggesting that employees in both countries place a high level of importance on their work and career lives (Harris et al., 2004). This places even greater importance on the issue of achieving an effective balance or reconciliation between personal and professional life demands and responsibilities.

Power distance is the second cultural factor, according to Hofstede (1980), and refers to the extent that members of a culture accept inequality and whether they perceive much distance between those with significant power and those with little power. The third cultural factor, uncertainty avoidance, is reflected in an emphasis on ritual behavior, rules, and stable employment. Although these are important cultural considerations, we will not focus on linking them to work and family policies.

Masculinity, the fourth of Hofstede's cultural dimensions, is one of the least researched dimensions. Masculinity is found in societies that differentiate very strongly by gender, whereas femininity is characteristic of cultures where sex differentiation is minimal. Feminine cultures emphasize quality of life more than job advancement and give more of their gross national product to developing countries. The most masculine countries include Japan, Austria, and Venezuela, and the most feminine are Sweden, Norway, and the Netherlands (both the U.S. and Ireland are considered more masculine than feminine countries).

High masculinity countries are characterized by people who prefer having a higher salary over working shorter hours and who emphasize achievement; in low masculinity countries, people prefer shorter working hours to having a higher salary, and they work to live rather than live to work. The centrality of work in a person's life is greater in the masculine cultures than it is in the feminine cultures. Antecedents are unclear, but perhaps the length of time that gender differentiation was not especially instrumental to perform work or nonwork activities may be relevant. In Scandinavia and Netherlands, industrialization, emphasis on commerce, and emphasis on influence through peaceful (economic) rather than forceful means have prevailed for at least the past 200 years.

Leveling, or not trying to stand out, is a widely observed form of social behavior in low-masculinity countries, as is the emphasis on solidarity, equality, and sympathy for the weak. In high masculinity countries, there is a higher need for formal rules of behavior; an emphasis on competitiveness, equity, and sympathy for the strong; and greater rigidity of sex-role job differentiation. When combinations of the dimensions occur, there tend to be variations in social behavior as well. For example, achievement motivation is high, relative to relationship motivation in high masculine, low uncertainty-avoidance countries. Further, acceptability of machismo styles of management tends to be greater in high power distance and high masculine cultures.

In the work and family context, masculinity has important implications. Cultures that display high masculinity tend to place more importance on work and career than do cultures with low masculinity. This would indicate that employees in Ireland and the United States tend to place more importance on their professional lives than their family lives. This has significant implications for work and family policy and practice. If this is the case, it would follow that individuals in high masculinity cultures would require much more support for child and elder care, as they would tend to place more emphasis on spending their time in the work domain of their lives. Again, the motivation for achievement is greater than the motivation for building relationships, either inside or outside the family, in high masculinity cultures.

Gender within Cultural Contexts

Within the cultural and economic contexts, international gender research indicates that women face unique challenges in the international business and professional contexts (Harris, Moran, & Moran, 2004). First, many national cultures discriminate against females in the work environment—if women are allowed to work at all. Second, when women are admitted to the workplace, they are often constrained by obsolete organizational cultures and norms. Finally, when they begin to succeed under such circumstances, they are further limited by attitudes and policies within the global management subcultures (Harris et al., 2004).

A number of developments in society have resulted in issues regarding the reconciliation of work and family life being placed at the heart of the social, public, and political agenda. These changes include increased female workforce participation leading to an increase in dual-income families, rising child-care costs, and increasing demands for flexibility in terms of working time and place (Den Dulk, 2001). For example, today in the United States, women comprise about 60% of the workforce, compared to about 37% in 1970 (U.S. Bureau of Labor Statistics, 2001). Nearly 80% of women between the ages of 25 and 54 are in the labor force today (U.S. Bureau of Labor Statistics, 2000). This increase of women in the paid labor force has led to a number of changes in the family, including a redistribution of traditional gender role responsibilities, increases in the number of dual-earner couples, and an increase in the interdependency between work and family (e.g., Barnett, 1998).

As female labor participation has grown, so too has a concern for the groups traditionally cared for by women including elders and children. In addition to the aging population and the increased number of women in the workplace, the number of three-generation households is growing, with grandparents raising grandchildren in increasing numbers (U.S. Census Bureau, 2001). Among the 45- to 55-year-olds examined in a recent AARP (2001) study, nearly 17% reported living in multigenerational households (e.g., grandparents, parents, and grandchildren).

Although women increasingly are managing multiple roles, global barriers continue to hinder their advancement. For example, women are more likely to be pigeonholed into less challenging positions than men. Women often are found in support or staff positions than in line positions and are given less visible assignments that often have less responsibility (Harris et al., 2004). These practices may be linked to global expectations that a woman's role is as mother or primary caretaker in the family. It is a common stereotype that if a woman's focus is on childbearing and child rearing, she will take time off and thus cannot be considered an effective executive.

In addition, significant pay gaps continue to exist in the U.S. between women and men in the same positions. The median salary for male corporate types is $765,000, whereas for women it is $518,696. Informally exclusive corporate cultures reflect male-oriented cultures. Women within these settings are under pressure to adapt or transform their styles of working. Further, this dominant culture is associated with limited access to information among women, fewer contacts, and fewer high-level networking opportunities. Fewer women participate in executive development programs, employer-sponsored training programs or "fast track" programs. In addition, women are less likely to be asked to take on risky assignments such as expatriate positions. These patterns emerge within organizations across numerous countries and cultures including the U.S. and Ireland (Harris et al., 2004).

COUNTRY CASE 1: IRELAND

Ireland is part of the European Union and is, therefore, heavily influenced by social and political E.U. policy, which is placing increasing emphasis on reconciling the relationship between professional and family life. The 1998 Amsterdam Treaty detailed the promotion of employment as one of the key community objectives in its European Employment Strategy. The aim of this strategy is

> the achievement of a high level of employability for all groups, including those most distanced from the labor market; to develop skills of those already in work, especially in exposed or vulnerable sectors; to broaden the capacity for entrepreneurship and to ensure the equal participation of women and men in the labor market. (European Employment Strategy, p. 4)

It is commonly believed that a greater focus on work and family balance will significantly positively impact the latter of these objectives.

In 2001, the European Council guidelines for member states regarding employment policies emphasized the following key point concerning work and family life: "Policies on career breaks, parental leave and part-time work, as well as flexible working arrangements which serve the interest of both employers and employees, are of particular importance to women and men" (The European Foundation for the Improvement of Living and Working Conditions Foundation Paper No. 1, 2002: 6). The challenge Ireland (as well as other E.U. countries) faces is to ensure these aims are translated into effective action at the national and local levels.

The importance of balancing professional and family life is further highlighted as a fundamental right in other E.U. documents (European Union 2000/C 364/01) where it is specifically stated that the family will be protected legally, economically and socially, and in order to reconcile family and work life, all individuals have protection rights from dismissal due to maternity and have the right to paid maternity and paternity leave. In Ireland, some of these E.U. policy positions have been adopted and Irish policy makers have increasingly noted the importance of work–life balance. The reconciliation of work and family life was a central objective in the national wage agreement, the Programme for Prosperity and

Fairness (PPF), signed in March 2000. The PPF is a collective agreement between the social partners and deals with a variety of social and employment issues such as pay, working conditions, employee rights, and social inclusion. This agreement specifically provided for the promotion and development of family-friendly policies and established the National Framework Committee for Family Friendly Policies.

The Legal and Institutional Framework

Ireland, as a member of the European Union, is governed by E.U. legislation through regulations and directives. A directive is a form of order to member states to implement national legislation to achieve a specific result within a particular time frame. It is up to the national governments to decide on the form and method of the legislation. There have been a number of E.U. regulations and directives dealing specifically with the reconciliation of family and professional life and the protection of atypical employment, including parental leave, maternity leave, atypical employment (hours), minimal leave, dependent care leave, and part-time work.

A number of statutory entitlements regarding family leave exist in Ireland. These have either been introduced by the E.U. through regulations or directives or have been devised at a national level. The Parental Leave Directive (96/34/EC) grants men and women workers in all E.U. member states an individual right to parental leave on the grounds of the birth or adoption of a child to enable them to take care of that child, for at least 3 months, until a given age of up to 8 years. The act also stipulates time off from work on grounds of *force majeure* which entitles workers to time off from work, in accordance with national legislation, collective agreements and/or practice, for urgent family reasons in cases of sickness or accident making the immediate presence of the worker indispensable. The directive does not indicate a minimum requirement in terms of time.

In Ireland, the Parental Leave Act (1998) operates as the local legislation for this directive. The act provides that an employee who is the natural or adoptive parent of a child is entitled to parental leave without pay from his or her employment for a period of 14 working weeks to enable him or her to take care of each child up to the age of 5 years. Subject to the consent of the employer, this leave can be taken as a block or as specific days over a period of time or in terms of hours. An important provision of the act relates to *force majeure* leave, which can be taken with respect to any of the following persons: (a) a person of whom the employee is the parent or adoptive parent, (b) the spouse of the employee or a person with whom the employee is living as husband or wife, (c) a person to whom the employee is *in loco parentis*, (d) a brother or sister of the employee, and (e) a parent or grandparent of the employee. The entitlement under *force majeure* leave in Ireland is up to 3 days in any period of 12 consecutive months or 5 days in any period of 36 consecutive months and is paid leave.

The Council Directive 92/85/EEC provides for at least 14 weeks maternity leave for female employees in all E.U. member states and also stipulates time off work for antenatal care without loss of pay. In Ireland, the Maternity Protection (Amendment) Act 2003 provides for 18 weeks paid leave and an optional eight weeks unpaid leave can be taken. It is specifically stated in the explanatory memorandum for the act that the implementation of the act is aimed to fulfill a statutory component of the work–life balance programs to which the government is committed under the Sustaining Progress agreement. The act provides for time off work fully paid for the expectant mother to attend ante-natal classes and also entitles the expectant father to time off fully paid to attend the last two ante-natal classes. Similar legislation exists specifically relating to adoption providing for fourteen weeks paid leave for an adopting mother or sole adopting father. There is no legal entitlement to paternity leave in Ireland.

There is also national legislation providing for time off to care for dependents other than children in Ireland. The Carer's Leave Act (2001) allows employees to leave their employment temporarily to provide full-time care for a period of 65 weeks. Employers are not required to pay employees on care leave but are required to provide employees with the same job on their return. Employees can take up to 130 weeks for care of two dependent individuals.

Statutory provisions aimed at working time and the protection of atypical employees also assist in facilitating work and non-work life balance. In 1993, the European Union adopted the Working Time Directive (93/104/EC), which provides that member states shall take the measures necessary to ensure that the average working time for each 7-day period, including overtime, does not exceed 48 hours. In Ireland, the Organization of Working Time Act 1997 brings the directive into national legislation. The act also provides for minimum annual leave entitlements (4 working weeks in a leave year in which an employee works at least 1,365 hours (unless it is a leave year in which he or she changes employment). Furthermore, the act specifically states that "the times at which annual leave is granted to an employee shall be determined by his or her employer having regard to work requirements and subject to the employer taking into account the need for the employee to reconcile work and any family responsibilities."

The European Union adopted the Framework Agreement on Part-Time Work in 1997 (97/81/EC), which sets out the general principles and minimum entitlements relating to part-time work. Previously, employees engaged in part-time working had not enjoyed pro-rata benefits comparable to their full-time colleagues. In Ireland, the Protection of Employees (Part-Time Work) Act 2001 provides for the removal of discrimination against part-time workers where such exists. It aims to improve the quality of part-time work, to facilitate the development of part-time work on a voluntary basis, and to contribute to the flexible organization of working time in a manner that takes account of the needs of employers and workers. Recognition of the legitimacy of atypical, nonpermanent forms of employment in legislation has an inherent work–life balance objective.

It is clear that the statutory environment provides a particular set of entitlements aimed at improving the interface between an employee's work and personal life. Many of these initiatives have been driven by the E.U. employment and social affairs agenda. Such statutory provisions represent the minimum entitlements for employees but organizations have much discretion in terms of adopting both temporal and locational flexibility arrangements and these initiatives are reviewed below.

Organizational Responses to Work and Family Issues

In addition to the context of social, political, and legal influences, the choice that is made regarding work and family policy and practice at an organizational level is also a significant factor. Den Dulk's (2001) classification of work and life balance initiatives and arrangements is used to review the main work–family balance schemes in operation in Ireland where provision is at the discretion of management. Where possible, statistics are presented to demonstrate the availability of these arrangements and the level of utilization by employees. We draw on two recent surveys of work and family in Ireland. Drew, Humphreys, and Murphy (2003) conducted a study commissioned by the National Framework Committee for Family Friendly Policies in Ireland which examined the nature, availability, and up-take of family-friendly/work–life balance policies and practices in Ireland. The study includes perspectives from 912 employers and 1006 employees in both the private and public sectors across a range of industries, organization sizes, and regions. The second study referenced in this section was conducted by Fine-Davis, Fagnani, Giovannini, Hojgaard, and Clarke (2004) and is a cross-national comparison of work–life balance issues across Ireland, France, Italy, and Denmark exploring people's attitudes and experiences in coping with balancing work and family with particular reference to the different perspectives of men and women.

Work Flexibility

The organization of work itself in terms of time and place is one set of factors organizations use to reconcile conflicting demands between work and non-work commitments. One of the most common arrangements offered is **part-time** employment where employees work less than normal hours to suit their personal requirements. From an Irish perspective, part-time employment as a percentage of total employment rose from 6.7% in 1983 to 16.7% by 1999 (Coughlan, 2000). Part-time work is more prevalent among women than men. Women's increased labor market participation is cited as the explanation for much of the growth in part-time employment in Ireland (Coughlan, 2000).

Drew et al. (2003) report that 66% of organizations surveyed have part-time employment availability for staff and 76% of these organizations offer it to 15% of their staff. Fine-Davis et al. (2004) report that part-time work is available to 66% of male respondents and 83.7% of female respondents in Ireland. Of these taking advantage, the rate is 12% for males and 42% for females. Job sharing has also become a popular form of part-time working in recent years. Fynes et al. (1996) define job-sharing as "dividing one former full-time position into two or more positions while retaining all the rights and privileges attached to the full-time position" (p. 121). There are a number of forms that job-sharing can take. Split week and week on/week off are the most popular means of sharing jobs. Fine-Davis et al. (2004) report that, in Ireland, job-sharing is available to 60% of male respondents and 54% of female respondents. Of these, only 4% of males use this arrangement and 12% of females job-share.

Another popular form of temporal flexibility is **flexitime**. This scheme allows employees to vary their starting and finishing times and must be present during a compulsory core hours period. In the civil service, for example, a person may start work between 8:30 a.m. and 10 a.m. and finish between 4 p.m. and 6:30 p.m. A person may build up hours during a 4-week flexible period which can be taken as leave in a later period; this is termed *flexi-leave* (Humphreys et al., 2000).

Drew et al. (2003) report that flextime is available to some staff in 52% of organizations surveyed. However, they go on to report that in nearly half of these organizations which have flexitime in operation, it is only available to less than 5% of the staff. Fine-Davis et al. (2004) report that 21% of respondents in Ireland have a formal flexitime arrangement at work and 60% report that an informal agreement exists. Flexitime is available to 48% of the male respondents and 50% of the females. Of these, 36% of males take advantage of the scheme and the corresponding figure for females is 38%. The difference between levels of available flexitime arrangements reported in the two studies might be accounted for by the fact that Fine-Davis et al. (2004) also included informal arrangements.

Term-time is a new initiative and is a form of temporal flexibility which allows parents time off to care for school-age children over the summer holidays. Parents can usually take up to 13 weeks unpaid leave from June until the end of August to match their working arrangements to their children's summer holidays (Humphreys et al., 2000). Drew et al. (2003) report that 23% of organizations surveyed have term-time working available to some staff. However, in most companies, the term-time working arrangement is only available to a small number of staff. Term-time employment is most prominently available in the public sector.

Teleworking is an initiative aimed at making the work location more flexible. In a teleworking arrangement, the employee works from a home office for some or all of the week. He or she maintains a presence in the office electronically via computer, telephone, fax, and e-mail. Ireland has often been presented as a country with strong drivers towards high levels of e-working, including a young workforce, a large Information and Communications Technology (ICT) sector, a proactive government that promotes e-working, high business property prices and urban traffic congestion. However, results of surveys indicate that compared with the rest of Europe, the existence of e-work is modest in Ireland (Bates et al., 2002). According to Butler and Connolly (2002), teleworking/e-working is the least common nonstatutory, family-friendly policy.

Drew et al. (2003) report that 47% of respondent organizations have some form of working from home arrangement available to employees. However, the extent to which this arrangement is available to staff is limited with 90% of these organizations only offering teleworking to less than 5% of staff. Fine-Davis et al. (2004) report that teleworking is available to 34.7% of male respondents and 20% of females. Only 10% of males engage in some form of teleworking and the corresponding figure for females is 8.2%.

Child care and supportive arrangements.

There are a number of financial and nonfinancial supports organizations can use to assist with child care and managing work and family life. On-site child-care facilities are available in some organizations. Others provide advice on child care locally or may offer subsidies for child care in certain facilities. Nonfinancial supports include employee counseling and assistance programs, work–life/stress management training, and supply of information. The availability of family child care and support arrangements in the Irish organizations studied by Drew et al. (2003) was very minimal. Only 3% of organizations provide employees with information about local child care and only 2% of organizations have in-company day-care facilities. Only less than 1% subsidize day-care costs. It is interesting to note that while a significant majority of organizations report that work–family arrangements are important, the presence of child-care supportive arrangements is almost nonexistent.

Compliance and Utilization of Work and Family Policies in Ireland

At a policy level, it would appear that an active E.U. role has led to important change in Ireland. However, some reports are critical of the impact E.U. directives and entitlements are actually making to the experience of managing professional work and personal family. The European Commission itself published a review of parental leave (including maternity leave) arrangements in 2002 and reports that while countries have complied with the regulations set out in directives, many countries have taken a minimalist approach. Furthermore, the report claims that while a good number of mothers utilize parental leave, most fathers do not. Drew et al. (2003) provide statistics on the use of the various statutory provisions that exist in Ireland and the findings of the European

TABLE 10.2   Uptake Rates of Statutory Leave Entitlements

Leave Arrangement	Uptake	
	% Men	% Women
Force majeure leave	8	5
Maternity leave	—	10
Parental leave	1	3
Carer leave	0.5	0.5
Adoptive leave	0.3	0.3
Compassionate leave*	18	12

Note: From Drew, E., Humphreys, P., & Murphy, C. (2003). *Off the tread-mill: Achieving work/life balance.* Dublin: Stationary Office.
* Compassionate leave is not a statutory entitlement.

Commission are reflected in the low numbers actually availing of the entitlements (Table 10.2). Research is required to explore the reasons why utilization levels are quite low with many of these statutory provisions. It may be the case that employees feel that the career consequences for using these provisions are negative. Fine-Davis et al.'s (2004) study reveals that quite a large percentage of employees do not know if certain schemes are available to them or not in their workplace. Furthermore, many respondents indicated that they were unaware of the statutory provisions. There needs to be greater communication about initiatives, arrangements, and entitlements with all employees.

Deven and Moss (2002) argue that Ireland, the United Kingdom, and the United States have weak leave policies and advocate that this is due to their liberal welfare state regime whereby the role of the state in terms of welfare is limited. However, Ireland and the United Kingdom have many more statutory provisions compared with the United States, where there is no maternity or parental leave save the 12 week per annum unpaid family and medical leave entitlement. Policy makers play a critical role in shaping the policy context in which men and women make choices concerning balancing their work and family responsibilities. Policies that are well designed can make it easier for parents to participate in the workforce and can support them in their choices in how they want to do so.

Within the political framework discussed above, the Joint Employment Report (2002) sets out the principal measures each member state has undertaken to comply with E.U. Employment Guidelines. In a recent publication evaluating the impact of the European Employment Strategy in Ireland, it is reported that "rates of flexibilization of work continue to be lower in Ireland than elsewhere in the European Union." These findings indicate that Ireland needs to invest more resources in family-friendly working arrangements and establish clearer mechanisms to implement policy.

In the Department of Enterprise, Trade and Employment's recent strategy statement for Ireland, "the adoption of family friendly practices such as teleworking, work sharing, annualized hours etc, to attract and retain employees, including females and older people" is specifically highlighted as a key labor policy priority (Department of Enterprise, Trade and Employment, 2003, p. 42). However, the report fails to address how this priority will be achieved or indeed how its progress will be measured, and there are no specific guidelines given regarding how it will be implemented in real terms. This highlights the issue of homage being paid to the concept of improving the experience of working parents with their family lives but little being done in terms of making this a reality.

At an organizational level, the most popular form of work–family arrangement is flexitime. This is also the most widely adopted arrangement by employees. This offers a convenient option for employers and employees because terms of work, salary, and benefits essentially remain the same as traditional arrangements. This might account for the increased utilization of this form of flexibility over others such as part-time work and job-sharing where salary and terms of employment are significantly altered.

There is some evidence of the increasing adoption of family-friendly working arrangements in Ireland over the past few years, which is accompanied by statutory entitlements regarding family leave. However, there is limited evidence of the attitudes of Irish employees regarding these developments and their perception of the effectiveness of these initiatives. It is a matter of concern that there is little to no evidence of evaluation of discretionary family-friendly programs in organizations. Drew et al. (2003) report that nearly a quarter of employers surveyed do not evaluate family-friendly working arrangements at all, and those employers who do engage in some form of evaluation use indicators such as changes in employee turnover, changes in absenteeism, and anecdotal information to assess family-friendly working arrangements. However, some of these indicators, unless directly assessed in the context of family friendliness, might not capture the precise issues relating to family-friendly employment. Much more needs to be done in terms of assessing the impact of these programs on important work-related variables such as commitment, job satisfaction, life satisfaction, stress, and work–family balance, and productivity.

COUNTRY CASE 2: THE UNITED STATES

Employer/Organizational and Governmental Responses in the United States

Employee benefits, as provided in the United States, have two primary purposes. The first is to provide income security by insuring against loss of income should the wage earner die, become disabled, or voluntarily retire. The second is to raise the standard of living through the provision of certain vital services, such as medical care (Employee Benefit Research Institute [EBRI], 1990; Kossek & Ozeki, 1999; Piacentini & Cerino, 1990).

However, compared to Ireland, the U.S. employee benefit system is a partnership between employers, individuals, and the government (Kossek & Ozeki, 1999; Piacentini & Cerino, 1990). Although some employment-based benefits are mandated by the government, most are organizationally based and offered only at the discretion of the organization. The corporate availability or offering of work–family friendly practices has waxed and waned with labor supply (e.g., when the labor supply of men is strong, the demand for female workers decreases (Neal & Hammer, 2006)).

Early employee benefits programs have existed since colonial time and addressed employees' retirement and health-care needs. Benefits that are specifically family-oriented date back to the industrial revolution, when women (and children) began to work outside the home in the first factories and mills (Kamerman, 1983; Morgan & Tucker, 1991). Once government social programs were more widely available through New Deal legislation (Kamerman, 1983), the need for organization-based programs decreased. Federal government involvement resulted in expansions in health insurance and retirement benefits (Wiatrowski, 1990). Some of these increases were mandated; others were implemented voluntarily by employers as a result of tax incentives (Piacentini & Cerino, 1990).

World War II changed the employee benefits scene once again (Wiatrowski, 1990). Men left to serve in the military, the need for production increased, and supply of labor in relation to demand increased thereby raising the value of women as workers. Employer interest in family concerns increased (Morgan & Tucker, 1991, p. 22) and government funding became available for communities to provide child-care services. Further, in response to problems with absenteeism resulting from child-care problems, some organizations created their own child-care centers (Morgan & Tucker, 1991). However, following the end of the war, with men returning to the workforce and the lower demand for female workers, federal support for child care was eliminated and child-care centers associated with war-industry companies closed (Morgan & Tucker, 1991). Employee benefits plans, however, increased again in the 1960s when the federal government supplemented child-care programs, especially for the children of low-income parents (Morgan & Tucker, 1991).

Organizational concern for employment-based work–family programs typically was financially driven and occurred during periods of our history when women were needed in the workplace to fill jobs left by men serving in the military (e.g., during the two World Wars). Employers viewed such family supports (i.e., child-care programs) as a strategy to attract and retain needed workers (Neal & Hammer, 2006). For most of the 19th and 20th centuries in the United States, however, managing the intersection of work and family was seen as the sole responsibility of the workers themselves.

During the 1970s and 1980s, as increasing numbers of women began to enter and remain in the workforce, the prevailing belief that family life and family responsibilities could and should be left at home was challenged by the realities facing workers. Although working adults struggled to manage their work and family obligations, employer efforts to assist working parents were slow to respond and increased gradually (Morgan & Tucker, 1991). Finally, in 1993, the federal Family and Medical Leave Act (FMLA) was passed by Congress. Several states also passed family leave legislation with additional benefits, generally applying to larger employers (e.g., those organizations with 25 or more employees, rather than 50; Martocchio, 2003). None of this leave was mandated to be paid leave, however, until 2002, when the state of California enacted the first Paid Family Leave Law in the United States (Dube & Kaplan, 2002). In sum, currently the United States has no national level **paid** leave policy for maternity or dependent care.

Types of Workplace-Based Supports for Employees With Family Responsibilities in the United States

In the United States, employers have implemented a range of workplace-based supports that can be of assistance to employees with family responsibilities. Although some supports are intended for the entire workforce or other groups, some are targeted specifically to employees with families. Employers' primary motivation in implementing these supports has been to lessen employees' work–family conflict and thereby improve worker productivity.

Unlike Ireland, most of the work–family programs in the United States, with the exception of FMLA, are offered volitionally by organizations rather than mandated by government directives. Neal, Chapman, Ingersoll-Dayton, and Emlen (1993) make a distinction between three general types of family-friendly workplace supports provided by organizations. These categories include: (a) policies concerning work schedule, place, and leave, (b) benefits, and (c) services. In general, these three categories of employer support options involve different levels of employer involvement and investment. Policies usually represent the least amount of employer involvement, ultimately, in the lives of employees, while services require the most employer involvement.

Policies provide guidelines, either formal or informal, for dealing with certain situations, such as the ways in which employees' work and leave schedules are handled (Ontario Women's Directorate, 1990). They can be supportive of employees with caregiving responsibilities, although they usually are not designed exclusively for these employees. Generally, policies involve no direct compensation or cash benefit. *Benefits* are forms of compensation, direct or indirect, that provide protection against loss of earnings, payment of medical expenses associated with illness, injury, or other health-care needs, or paid time off for vacations or personal needs. Benefits may also include full or partial payment for other services, such as legal, educational, or dependent-care services (Kamerman & Kingston, 1982). *Services* are programs that are provided directly by or through the employer to address specific employee needs. Services are a tangible form of help but are not direct compensation. These services can be organized into broad categories that, again, vary in the level of employer involvement and investment (Neal et al., 2001).

Policies.

In the United States, similar to Ireland, flexibility in the structure of work is viewed as one of the most important types of support that employers can provide for employees who have dependent-care responsibilities. Time to deal with family issues is seen by employees as a crucial need (Byars & Rue, 2004). Policies that increase work flexibility include those that increase flexibility in the work schedule and place of work, provide options for paid or unpaid leave, and provide mechanisms for the implementation, creation and review of workplace-based supports (Neal & Hammer, 2006).

Flexibility in work schedule.   There has been a growing trend in the implementation of alternative work schedules in U.S. organizations since the 1970s (Grover & Crooker, 1995; Olmsted & Smith, 1989). The percentage of workers on flexible work schedules rose from 12.3 in 1985 to 15.1 in 1991 (U.S. Bureau of Labor Statistics, 1994). We will describe four alternative work schedules (for a comprehensive review, see Pierce, Newstrom, Dunham, & Barber, 1989). Unfortunately, in contrast to Ireland, part-time workers in the U.S. do not receive the same pay level, health, or retirement benefit protections as do full-time employees in otherwise identical jobs.

One example of an alternative work schedule involves reducing the number of hours worked. Specifically, employers may allow employees to work part-time, defined by the U.S. Department of Labor as less than 35 hours of work per week (Rosin & Korabik, 2002). The number of part-time workers increased from almost 17 million in 1980 to almost 21 million in 1993 (U.S. Bureau of Labor Statistics, 1994). Some employers have established alternative career paths for professionals who work part-time (Morgan & Tucker, 1991).

Job sharing is a second option and a variation of part-time employment in which a single full-time job is shared by two (or more) individuals (Byars & Rue, 2004; Pierce, Newstrom, Dunham, & Barber, 1989). Two individuals with complementary skills share one job, but the tasks performed and levels of responsibility may differ (job splitting) or two individuals take equal responsibility for all job tasks (job pairing).

A third option is flexible work hours, or flextime. Although employees are given some discretion in arranging their daily schedules (e.g., the start–stop times for work), constraints are imposed by employers through the use of bandwidths (i.e., the organization's daily span of operating hours) and core times (i.e., management-imposed times when employees are required to be on the job; Baltes, Briggs, Huff, Wright, & Neumann, 1999; Kossek & Ozeki, 1999; Olmsted & Smith, 1989; Thomas & Ganster, 1995).

Finally, in compressed work weeks, the number of days per week in which full-time work is performed is reduced (e.g, from 5 days to 4), without a corresponding reduction in the number of weekly hours. Variations of this scheme exist (e.g., 10 hours a day for 4 days a week; 12 hours a day for 3 days a week).

Flexibility in the location work is performed. Another work flexibility policy involves the place or locale of work. Specifically, the employers have flexplace or telecommuting policies that allow employees to work from home or at some other site besides the main office or job site (Christensen & Staines, 1990; Hill, Miller, Weiner, & Colihan, 1998).

Leave Options.

However, in practice most U.S. employers offer their full-time employees some form of paid sick or vacation leave. Personal sick leave is often used (legitimately or not) for the care of sick children or elders, which then leaves employees with less time to take care of themselves (Health Action Forum of Greater Boston, 1989). Further, this leave option is often not available for part-time employees. Yet, some employers have implemented family leave options for the birth or adoption of a child or for the care of an ill or disabled family member (Christensen & Staines, 1990; Martocchio, 2003). For employers with 50 or more employees, offering such leave is mandated by the federal FMLA of 1993. The FMLA allows an employee to take up to 12 weeks of leave, with a guarantee of being able to return to his or her same or similar job at the same pay and benefits. This leave, however, is unpaid. Also, only employers with 50 or more employees must comply. Thus, it is not universally available to employees; for example those who work for small employers, those who feel they cannot afford to take time off without compensation, or those who fear that the progress of their careers will be jeopardized, are not able to use this leave (Allen, 2001; Thompson, Beauvais, & Lyness, 1999). Moreover, there is evidence that firms do not always comply with the FMLA (Scharlach, Sansom, & Stanger, 1995).

As of July 1, 2004, one state, California, has mandated that family leave be paid. Employees who work for employers having 50 or more employees may receive up to 6 weeks of paid leave per year to care for a new child or an ill family member, which is financed through the State Disability Insurance (SDI) system. The benefit covers all workers who have an SDI deduction taken from their paychecks, and employers are required to hold the job for an employee who goes on paid family leave (Neal & Hammer, 2006).

Benefits.

Benefits have more government involvement. Employers are required by federal law to provide certain employee benefits including Social Security retirement (a lifetime annuity), Social Security disability (for individuals who are disabled and unable to work), Medicare Part A (hospitalization for elderly persons), workers' compensation (for workers who become disabled on the job), and unemployment insurance (for workers who are temporarily unemployed; Byars & Rue, 2004). However, the majority of U.S. employers' benefits packages are offered only at the discretion of the organization and may be withdrawn or discontinued with little notice to employees. Discretionary benefits include health insurance; life insurance; participation in a pension plan and/or profit sharing; paid time off for holidays, vacations, and sick leave; and short-term disability. Additional benefits, such as dental care, vision care, dependent care, long-term disability, and liability insurance, are also sometimes offered (Byars & Rue, 2004). Further, nearly all of these benefits are available only to full-time employed workers.

Benefits may be offered through a *standard* (or *traditional*), a *flexible* (or *cafeteria*), or a *life-cycle* (or *life-span*) plan. Flexible benefits and life-cycle plans are more family-responsive than standard ones, in that they recognize that individual employees' benefits needs differ depending on the employee's age, salary, and family status. For example, flexible spending accounts are accounts in which employees can allocate either their own pretax dollars, credits, or flexible-benefits dollars given to them by their employer to pay for certain expenses (e.g., medical, dental, legal, dependent care) not covered under the standard package.

Long-term care refers to the health care, personal care, and social services needed by persons of any age who have physical or mental limitations and who have lost or never acquired some degree of functional capacity (Byars & Rue, 2004). The only federal program that finances long-term care extending beyond a few months is Medicaid, which is available only to low-income individuals. Therefore, some employers have begun offering group long-term care insurance for employees, their spouses, and sometimes their parents and parents-in-law, and/or retirees and their spouses (Martocchio, 2003; Neal et al., 1993; Scharlach et al., 1991; U.S. Department of Labor, n.d.).

Services.

The first step that companies often take to address employees' family-care needs includes providing education and instructional materials (Kossek & Ozeki, 1999). Organizations may establish a library with print, audio, and videotaped materials on the premises in order to distribute newsletters and guidebooks, and provide educational seminars. In addition, organizationally–sponsored caregiving fairs may be conducted where local providers of service set up tables or booths and distribute information (Neal et al., 1993; Scharlach et al., 1991). Finally, organizations may make computers available so employees can access information (Kuzmits, 1998).

Further, information (or resource) and referral/case management is another type of service that employers may offer their caregiving employees. For employees with children, this generally involves having a list of child-care providers or facilities, along with questions employees should ask to determine the quality of care provided or to identify where a variety of services are available. Finally, employers may opt to provide working caregivers with individual counseling or support group assistance. This service is intended for employees who need help coping with their family responsibilities (Lambert, 2000; Rosin & Korabik, 2002). Professional counseling is generally offered to employees through Employee Assistance Programs (EAPs) either within or external to the organization, or through health and wellness programs (U.S. Department of Labor, n.d.). Support groups have also been established directly by employers or through EAPs. Here, employees with similar kinds of work–family issues get together and talk, generally with facilitation provided by a professional counselor (Ingersoll-Dayton, Chapman, & Neal, 1990).

A few U.S. companies help employees to deal with their dependent care needs by providing services for care recipients, such as on-site or near-site day-care facilities, or by offering subsidies, vouchers, or discounts for such services provided in the community. Corporate child-care centers are much more common than are adult day-care centers (Friedman & Johnson, 1999; Scharlach et al., 1991; Wagner & Hunt, 1994). According to Neal & Hammer (2006), other direct services may include take-home dinners from the company's cafeteria; employee convenience centers that will do grocery shopping, rent videos, and drop off/pick up dry cleaning for employees while they work or do dry cleaning, laundry, and shoe repair on site; and provision of door-to-door transportation in employee-driven vans (Morgan & Tucker, 1991). The benefit consists of the time and travel costs saved; employees pay for the actual services.

Prevalence and Utilization of Family-Supportive Programs in the United States

Although a wide range of policies, benefits, and services to assist employees with family responsibilities has been provided by U.S. employers, it is important to consider how widely such initiatives have in fact been utilized. In 1990, Kingston concluded that American businesses had made only modest progress in instituting family-friendly practices. Further, Davis and Krouze (1994) state, "The United States consistently falls behind other industrialized countries in its treatment of family-related issues" (p. 20).

Currently, family-responsive supports are much more likely to be offered by large organizations with at least 500 employees; the many workers employed by smaller organizations do not have access to this assistance (Allen, 2001; Grandey, 2001; Hughes & Galinsky, 1988; Kamerman, 1983). Moreover, the types of supports offered by small and large employers differ. For example, Hayghe (1988, cited in Raabe, 1990) noted that larger employers offer more direct family support services, while smaller ones are more likely to offer flexible leaves and alternate work patterns. Such forms of support are more feasible for small employers to provide than day-care centers, for example, which require a certain number of users to be economically viable. The Society for Human Resources Management (SHRM) (2003) survey found, for instance, that employees of small companies (less than 100 employees) were much more likely to be allowed to bring their children to work in an emergency (39%) than were employees of large companies (more than 500 employees; 21%). In contrast, large employers were much more likely than small employers to offer child-care referral (27% versus 12%), as well as on-site child care (10% vs. 1%). Finally, frequently not all policies, benefits, and services offered by an employer are available to all of its employees (Grandey, 2001). For example, research has consistently shown that even within a given company, employees in certain positions experience greater work schedule flexibility than those in other positions. Further, employees sometimes feel penalized, such as through loss of seniority or resentment from coworkers, when they use work schedule flexibility and leave policies (Grandey, 2001).

Utilization of Workplace Supports.

Even after family care benefits and services have been made available, they often are not used as extensively as expected or are sometimes used by those not expected to use them (Fierman, 1994; Wagner & Hunt, 1994). Regulatory restrictions limit the usefulness of many governmental initiatives. For example, with respect to dependent care, only expenses incurred directly as a result of the employee's working can be reimbursed. Further, care must be provided by someone other than an employee's dependent (e.g., child or nonemployed spouse), and receipts or invoices indicating the care provider's name, place of business, and Social Security or tax identification number must be submitted. Any funds that have been set aside for use but that remain in the account at the end of the year are forfeited. Estimating the amount of money that should be placed in such an account is difficult, especially for employees caring for dependent elders, whose needs for assistance fluctuate (Byars & Rue, 2004).

Finally, some services may not adequately meet the needs of employed caregivers. For example, traditional employee assistance program (EAP) services typically are not very beneficial to caregivers of the elderly because the counselors are unfamiliar with elder care–related problems and resources for older people (Gorey, Brice, & Rice, 1990). With 2 full days of training, however, Gorey and colleagues estimate that EAP staffs' expertise could be greatly improved.

Barriers to the Widespread Implementation of Family-Care Supports

Kingston (1990) argued that the incentives for American employers to respond to work– family conflict may not be as strong as they first appeared. For example, labor shortages may have been overstated; job growth has occurred among jobs that are low-paying, require little experience, and have few benefits; and the economic benefits of family-friendly policies and practices has yet to be demonstrated. Others agree (Aldous, 1990) that few businesses see it as in their self-interest to institute family benefits. One reason for this may be that there is little evidence that such programs pay off in organizational level profitability. Further, there is little integrated evidence linking how benefits ease the lives of employees with families

As benefits become more widely available (SHRM, 2003), the research on their effectiveness is increasing with more studies documenting positive outcomes associated with the use of supports. Flexible work schedules, for instance, have been linked to increased performance (Kossek & Ozeki, 1999), increased job satisfaction (Scandura & Lankau, 1997), and reduced work–family conflict (e.g., Christensen & Staines, 1990). Hill, Miller, Weiner, and Colihan (1998) found positive effects of telecommuting on flexibility and productivity. Grover and Crooker (1995) found that use of dependent care benefits reduces intentions to quit and improves organizational commitment. Rothausen, Gonzales, Clarke, and O'Dell (1998) found a relationship between the use of on-site child care and satisfaction with organizational support. These and other studies have strengthened the business case in favor of providing supports. As Fernandez (1990) pointed out, "Companies look only at the cost and not at the return on the dollars spent" (p. 188), and these returns typically are very favorable for companies. Companies fare better if they focus their supports according to actual need (Neal et al., 1993). The MetLife (1999) study assessed the economic costs of lost productivity to employers and estimated these costs to range between $11.4 and $29 billion.

Davis and Krouze (1994) pointed, as well, to the lack of evidence of long-term positive results from offering elder care benefits, in particular. Also, there remains a lack of awareness and inadequate information about employees' caregiving-related needs and the costs associated with providing many types of supports (Galinsky et al., 1991; Liebig, 1993). Both the quantity and the quality of research examining the effectiveness of family-responsive supports have been lacking (Neal, Chapman, Ingersoll-Dayton, & Emlen, 1992; Raabe, 1990).

A second barrier to the implementation of family care supports is employer concern about equity and fears of backlash. Family-friendly backlash occurs when policies, benefits, or services are available to employees with dependent care responsibilities, but are not balanced with other types of policies, benefits, and services made available to employees without dependent care responsibilities. Employers fear that some groups of employees (e.g., those with family responsibilities) will be seen as favored, or receiving extra benefits, when supports such as elder or child care benefits are offered (Grandey, 2001; Rothausen, Gonzalez, Clarke, & O'Dell, 1998). Likewise, if employees believe that they have differential access to such family-friendly policies, they may feel unfairly treated, resulting in negative backlash feelings against those who have access. This situation ultimately may result in feelings of inequity and resentment experienced by the group of employees without dependents (Grandey, 2001).

When employees perceive that they will be treated or thought of in a negative way for making use of family-friendly supports, they may tend to not make use of such supports. Thus, this backlash can result in diminished use of existing benefits. Ultimately, how people respond to organizational family-friendly supports depends on their philosophical perspective. Specifically, if people believe that everyone should be treated the same, instead of the belief that people who need benefits should be given benefits, then perceptions of inequity and backlash are likely to occur. For example, childless workers may not feel particularly comfortable with the idea that their own benefit allocation is used to "subsidize" that of workers with children (Kossek & Nichol, 1992; Rothausen, Gonzalez, Clarke, & O'Dell, 1998). On the other hand, if people believe that benefits should be distributed based on need, then backlash is less likely to occur.

Organizations are making attempts to diminish the negative effects of backlash by reframing family-friendly initiatives as "work–life" initiatives with the hope that the term would be more inclusive. Furthermore, offering cafeteria-style benefit plans that allow employees to choose benefits they need helps reduce the negative effects of backlash. Finally, introducing benefits that are attractive to employees without dependent care responsibilities to offset more family-oriented benefits, such as health club memberships and concierge services, help to reduce the negative effects of backlash.

A third barrier to the implementation of family-friendly supports is the lack of universal agreement that (a) family responsibilities negatively impact productivity at work, and/or (b) it is even appropriate for employers to attempt to address employees' family needs. Some employers maintain that the traditional division between an employee's work life and his/her family life is a real and important one to maintain.

Fourth, corporate management is not always unified in its dedication or willingness to support employees with family responsibilities. For example, although the top management may be committed to the establishment of work–life programs (an element argued to be crucial for successful implementation; Axel, 1985; Galinsky & Stein, 1990), middle managers often become barriers to supports such as flexible work hours and time off (Grandey, 2001). Primary reasons may be that often no incentives for adhering to family-sensitive policies are offered, and in fact, managers may be penalized if the standards for evaluating their performance do not take into account short-term productivity shortfalls that can result when employees are allowed to take time off when necessary to perform their family care duties (New York Business Group on Health, 1986). Finally, other barriers include a lack of community resources to address employees' dependent care needs (Liebig, 1993).

DISCUSSION AND IMPLICATIONS FOR CROSS-CULTURAL WORK AND FAMILY RESEARCH AND PRACTICE

The case of Ireland and the United States is an interesting pair of countries for cross-national comparison of work and family policy and practice, both at a political/social level and at an organizational level in terms of discretionary initiative and programs employers can offer employees. Both countries are considered to have liberal welfare regimes and display similar cultural preferences in terms of individualism and masculinity. It is apparent from the discussion above that Ireland has a much wider range of legislative and statutory entitlements available to employees compared with the United States. There are potentially two reasons for this. First, the trade union movement has historically played an important role in influencing working conditions in Ireland more so than in the United States. Trade unions and employee representatives are an integral part of the "social partnership" model which exists in Ireland for determining pay and working conditions. Social partnership is a form of centralized collective bargaining where government, employer representatives, employee representatives, and other interested parties collectively agree to pay and working conditions. These social partnerships have given particular significance to work and family/work and life issues over the past 6 years. The role of employee representatives in the United States is not as influential as in Ireland and this is possibly one explanation of the difference that exists at a social policy between the two countries. Second, the influence of the European Union has been substantial in shaping work and family policy in Ireland, particularly through E.U. directives that must be transposed into national legislation. There are many statutory provisions in terms of leave entitlements which have emanated from E.U. social policy which are statutory entitlements in Ireland (e.g. parental leave, maternity leave, and the working time directive). In the United States, there are few federal provisions for work and family leave or entitlements, save the FMLA.

It would appear that reconciling work and family responsibilities in Ireland would be somewhat easier than in the United States given the significantly better statutory entitlements in Ireland. Yet, we see that the utilization of these entitlements is not that extensive in Ireland. This raises an important issue worthy of further research scrutiny. The existence of policy, either in terms of statutory entitlements or discretionary organizational programs, does not necessarily indicate greater levels of utilization by employees. Thompson, Beauvais, and Lyness (1999) report that work–family culture is an important factor that affects utilization of work–family benefits in the United States. It is interesting to note that in Ireland, work–family culture (including managerial support, career consequences, and organizational time expectation dimensions) is perhaps a factor that is moderating the relationship between various work and family policy initiatives/programs and actual utilization. Further research is needed to explore other factors that might influence the relationship between availability/prevalence and utilization across different cultures, because the Irish case shows clearly that availability, through statutory entitlements, may not be enough on its own to positively influence work and family reconciliation.

Much of the research cited here relates to studies conducted in large companies, most of which are multinational. Much of the economic activity of both the United States and Ireland is generated by the small enterprise sector, known as small and medium enterprises (SMEs) in Ireland. Research is needed to explore how work and family initiatives and issues are managed in smaller organizations.

REFERENCES

AARP (2001). *In the middle: A report on multicultural boomers coping with family and aging issues.* Washington, DC: Author.

Aldous, J. (1990). Specification and speculation concerning the politics of workplace family policies. *Journal of Family Issues, 11,* 355–367.

Allen, T. D. (2001). Family-supportive work environments: The role of organizational perspectives. *Journal of Vocational Behavior, 58,* 414–435.

Aryee, S. (1992). Antecedents and outcomes of work-family conflict among married professional women: Evidence from Singapore. *Human Relations, 45,* 816–837.

Ashkanasy, N. & Jackson, C. (2001). Organizational Culture and Climate. In N. Anderson, D. Ones, H. Sinangil & C. Viswesvaran (Eds.), *Handbook of industrial, work and organizational psychology.* Thousand Oaks, CA: Sage.

Axel, H. (1985). *Corporations and families: Changing practices and perspectives* (Report No. 868). New York: The Conference Board.

Baltes, B. B., Briggs, T. E., Huff, J. W., Wright, J. A., & Neuman, G. A. (1999). Flexible and compressed workweek schedules: A meta-analysis of their effects on work-related criteria. *Journal of Applied Psychology, 84,* 496–513.

Barling, J., MacEwen, K. E., Kelloway, E. K., & Higginbottom, S. F. (1994). Predictors and outcomes of elder-care-based interrole conflict. *Psychology and Aging, 9,* 391-397.

Barnett, R. (1998). Toward a review and reconceptualization of the work/family literature. *Genetic, Social, and General Psychology Monographs, 124*(2), 125–183.

Barnett, R. C., & Rivers, C. (1996). *She works/he works: How two-income families are happier, healthier, and better-off.* New York: Harper Collins.

Bates, P., Bertin, I. and Huws, U. (2002) *E-Work in Ireland,* Report No. 394. Dublin: The Institute for Employment Studies.

Bedian, A. G., Burke, B. G., & Moffett, R. G. (1988). Outcomes of work-family conflict among married male and female professionals. *Journal of Management, 14,* 475–491.

Boles, J. S., Johnston, M. W., & Hair, J. F. (1997). Role stress, work-family conflict and emotional exhaustion: Inter-relationships and effects on some work-related consequences. *Journal of Personal Selling & Sales Management, 1,* 17–28.

Burden, D. S., & Googins, B. (1987). *Balancing job and homelife study: Managing work and family stressing corporations.* Boston, MA: Boston University School of Social Work.

Burke, R. J. (1988). Some antecedents and consequences of work-family conflict. *Journal of Social Behavior and Personality, 3,* 287–302.

Byars, L. L. & Rue, L. W. (2004). *Human resource management.* New York, NY: McGraw-Hill/Irwin.

Chen, C.C., Chen, X.P. and Meindl, J.R. (1998) How can cooperation be fostered? The cultural effects of individualism-collectivism. *Academy of Management Review, 23,* 285-305.

Christensen, K. E., & Staines, G. L. (1990). Flextime: A viable solution to work/family conflict? *Journal of Family Issues, 11,* 455–476.

Coughlan, A. (2000). *Family-friendly/work-life balance policies.* Dublin: IBEC Publishing.

CSO (2006) Central Statistical Office, Ireland on-line database www.cso.ie

Davis, E., & Krouze, M. K. (1994). A maturing benefit: Eldercare after a decade. *Employee Benefits Journal, 19*(3), 16–20.

Den Dulk, L. (2001) *Work-family arrangements in organizations: A cross-national study in the Netherlands, Italy, the United Kingdom, and Sweden.* Amsterdam: Rozenberg Publishers.

Department of Enterprise, Trade and Employment (2003) *Strategy Statement 2003-2005.* Dublin: Stationary Office

Deven, F. and Moss, P. (2002) Leave arrangements for parents overview and future outlook. *Community, Work and Family, 5 (3),* 237-255.

Drew, E., Humphreys. P. and Murphy, C. (2003) *Off the treadmill: Achieving work/life balance.* Dublin: Stationary Office.

Dube, A. & Kaplan, E. (2002). *Paid family leave in California: An analysis of costs and benefits* (Working Paper No. 2). Berkeley, CA: University of California at Berkeley, Labor Project for Working Families.

Employee Benefit Research Institute (EBRI). (1990). *Fundamentals of employee benefit programs* (4th ed.). Washington, DC: Author.

Esping-Andersen, G. (1990) *The three worlds of welfare capitalism.* Oxford: Polity Press.

Esping-Andersen, G. (2002) Towards the Good Society Once Again? In G. Esping-Andersen, D. Gallie and J. Myles (Eds.) *Why we need a new welfare state* (pp. 1-26). Oxford: Oxford University Press.

European Commission (2002) *Report on the implementation of Council Directive 96/34/EC of 3rd June on the framework agreement on parental leave concluded by UNICE, CEEP, and the ETUC.* Brussels: European Commission.

Fernandez, J. P. (1990). *The politics and reality of family care in corporate America.* Lexington, MA: D.C. Heath and Company.

Fierman, J. (1994, March 21). Are companies less family-friendly? *Fortune,* 129(6) 64–67.

Fine-Davis, M., Fangani, J., Giovannini, D., Højgaard, L., and Clarke, H. (2004) *Fathers and mothers:Dilemmas of the work-life balance.* Netherlands: Kluwer Academic Publishers.

Frone, M. R, Russell, M., Cooper, M. L. (1997). Relation of work-family conflict to health outcomes: A four-year longitudinal study of employed parents. *Journal of Occupational & Organizational Psychology, 70,* 325–335.

Frone, M. R. (2000). Work-family conflict and employee psychiatric disorders: The national comorbidity survey. *Journal of Applied Psychology. 85,* 888–895.

Frone, M. R., Russell, M., & Cooper, M. L. (1992). Antecedents and outcomes of work-family conflict: Testing a model of the work-family interface. *Journal of Applied Psychology, 77,* 65–78.

Fynes, B., Morrisey, T., Roche, W.K., Whelan, B.J., Whelan and Williams, J. (1996). *Flexible working lives—the changing nature of working time arrangements in Ireland.* Dublin: Oak Tree Press.

Galinsky, E., & Stein, P. J. (1990). The impact of human resource policies on employees: Balancing work/family life. *Journal of Family Issues, 11,* 368–383.

Galinsky, E., Friedman, D. E., Hernandez, C. A., with Axel, H. (1991). *Corporate reference guide to work-family programs.* New York: Families and Work Institute.

Gorey, K. M., Brice, G. C., & Rice, R. W. (1990). An elder care training needs assessment among employee assistance program staff. *Employee Assistance Quarterly, 5(3),* 71–93.

Grandey, A. A. (2001). Family friendly policies: Organizational justice perceptions of need-based allocations. In R. Cropanzano (Ed.), *Justice in the workplace: From theory to practice* (pp. 145–173). Mahwah, NJ: Lawrence Erlbaum Associates.

Greenhaus, J. H., & Beutell, N. J. (1985). Sources of conflict between work and family roles. *Academy of Management Review, 10,* 76–88.

Grover, S. L., & Crooker, K. J. (1995). Who appreciates family-responsive human resource policies: The impact of family-friendly policies on the organizational attachment of parents and non-parents. *Personnel Psychology, 48,* 271–288.

Harris, P. R. Moran, R. T., & Moran, S. V. (2004). *Managing cultural differences: Global leadership strategies for the 21st century.* Elsevier Butterworth-Heinemann: Oxford.

Hayghe, H. V. (1988, September). Employers and child care: What roles do they play? *Monthly Labor Review, 111,* 38–44.

Health Action Forum of Greater Boston. (1989). *Eldercare: The state of the art.* Boston: Author.

Hepburn, C. G., & Barling, J. (1996). Eldercare responsibilities, interrole conflict, and employee absence: A daily study. *Journal of Occupational Health Psychology, 1,* 311–318.

Hewitt Associates, LLC (2004). *SpecSummary: United States Salaried Work/Life Benefits, 2003-2004.* Retrieved July 21, 2006 from, http://www.catalystwomen.org/files/quicktakes/Quick%20Takes%20-%20Work-Life.pdf

Higgins, C.A., Duxbury, L. and Irving, L. (1992). Work-family conflict in the dual-career family. *Organizational Behavior and Human Decision Processes, 51,* 51-75.

Hill, E. J., Miller, B. C., Weiner, S. P., & Colihan, J. (1998). Influences of the virtual office on aspects of work and work/life balance. *Personnel Psychology, 51,* 667–683.

Hofstede, G. (1980) *Culture's consequences: International differences in work-related values.* Beverly Hills, CA: Sage.

Hofstede, G. (1991) *Cultures and organizations: Software of the mind.* London: McGraw-Hill.

Hofstede, G. (2001). *Culture's consequences: Comparing values, behaviors, institutions and organizations across nations.* Thousand Oaks, CA: Sage.

Hughes, D., & Galinsky, E. (1988). Balancing work and family lives: Research and corporate applications. In A. E. Gottfried & A. W. Gottfried (Eds.), *Maternal employment and children's development: Longitudinal research* (pp. 233–268). New York: Plenum.

Humphreys, P. C., Fleming, S. and O'Donnell, O. (2000). *Flexible Working in the Public Service,* CPMR Research Report 3. Dublin: IPA.

Ingersoll-Dayton, B., Chapman, N. J., Neal, M. B. (1990). A program for caregivers in the workplace. *The Gerontologist, 30 (1),* 126-130.

Joint Employment Report (2002), Brussels, Commission of the European Communities.

Kamerman, S. B. (1983). *Meeting family needs: The corporate response* (Work in America Institute Studies in Productivity, Vol. 33). New York: Pergamon.

Kamerman, S. B., & Kingston, P. W. (1982). Employer responses to the family responsibilities of employees. In S. B. Kamerman & C. D. Hayes (Eds.), *Families that work: Children in a changing world* (pp. 144–208). Washington, DC: National Academic.

Kingston, P. W. (1990). Illusions and ignorance about the family-responsive workplace. *Journal of Family Issues, 11,* 438–454.

Kossek, E. E. (1990). Diversity in child care assistance needs: Employee problems, preferences, and work-related outcomes. *Personnel Psychology, 43,* 769–791.

Kossek, E. E., & Nichol, V. (1992). The effects of on-site child care on employee attitudes and performance. *Personnel Psychology, 45,* 485–509.

Kossek, E. E., & Ozeki, C. (1998). Work-family conflict, policies, and the job-life satisfaction relationship: A review and directions for organizational behavior-human resources research. *Journal of Applied Psychology, 83,* 139–149.

Kossek, E. E., & Ozeki, C. (1999). Bridging the work-family policy and productivity gap: A literature review. *Community, Work and Family, 2,* 7–32.

Kuzmits, F. E. (1998). Communicating benefits: A double-click away. *Compensation & Benefits Review 14(9),* 60–64.

Lambert, S. J. (2000). Added benefits: The link between work-life benefits and organizational citizenship behavior. *Academy of Management Journal, 43*, 801–815.

Liebig, P. S. (1993). Factors affecting the development of employer-sponsored eldercare programs: Implications for employed caregivers. *Journal of Women & Aging, 5(1)*, 59–78.

Lovell, V. (2004). *No time to be sick: Why everyone suffers when workers don't have paid sick leave.* Washington, DC: Institute for Women's Policy Research.

MacEwen, K. E., & Barling, J. (1994). Daily consequences of work interference with family and family interference with work. *Work and Stress, 8*, 244–254.

Martocchio, J. J. (2003). *Employee benefits: A primer for human resource professionals.* New York, NY: McGraw-Hill/Irwin.

Metropolitan Life Insurance Company (1997, June). *The MetLife study of employer costs for working caregivers.* Westport, CT: Author.

Morgan, H. & Tucker, K. (1991). *Companies that care: The most family-friendly companies in America—What they offer and how they got that way.* New York: Simon & Schuster/Fireside.

Neal, M. B., & Hammer, L. B. (2006). *Working couples caring for children and aging parents: Effects on work and well-being.* Mahwah, NJ: Lawrence Erlbaum and Associates.

Neal, M. B., & Hammer, L. B., with Brockwood, K. J., Caubet, S., Colton, C., Hammond, T., Huang, E., Isgrigg, J., & Rickard, A. (2001). *Supporting employees with child and elder care needs: A work-family sourcebook for employers.* Portland, OR: Portland State University. [www.sandwich.pdx.edu]

Neal, M. B., Chapman, N. J., Ingersoll-Dayton, B., & Emlen, A. C. (1993). *Balancing work and caregiving for children, adults, and elders.* Newbury Park, CA: Sage.

Neal, M. B., Chapman, N. J., Ingersoll-Dayton, B, & Emlen, A. (1992, November). *Assessing the Impacts of Work-Elder Care Conflict and Corporate Initiatives.* Paper presented at the 45th Scientific Meeting of the Gerontological Society of America, Washington, D.C.

New York Business Group on Health. (1986). *Employer support for employee caregivers.* New York: Author.

Ontario Women's Directorate. (1990). *Work and family: The crucial balance.* Toronto: Author. (Available from Consultative Services Branch, Suite 200, 480 University Avenue, Toronto, Ontario, M5G1V2, (416) 597-4570.)

Piacentini, J. S. & Cerino, T. J. (1990). *EBRI databook on employee benefits.* Washington, DC: Employee Benefit Research Institute.

Pierce, J. L., Newstrom, J. W., Dunham, R. B., & Barber, A. E. (1989). *Alternative work schedules.* Boston: Allyn & Bacon.

Pleck, J. H., Staines, G. L., Lang, L. (1980). Conflicts between work and family life. *Monthly Labor Review, 103*, 29-32.

Programme for Prosperity and Fairness (2000) Dublin: Stationery Office.

Olmstead, B., & Smith, S. (1989). *Creating a flexible workplace: How to select and manage alternative work options.* New York: American Management Association.

Raabe, P. H. (1990). The organizational effects of workplace family policies: Past weaknesses and recent progress toward improved research. *Journal of Family Issues, 11*, 477–491.

Ramamoorthy, N. and Carroll, S. (1998) Individualism/collectivism orientations and reactions toward alternative human resource management practices. *Human Relations, 51,* 571-588.

Robert, C., & Wasti, S. A. (2000) *Individualism/collectivism and the exploration of person-organization fit.* Paper presented at the annual meeting of the Society for Industrial and Organizational Psychology. New Orleans, LA, April.

Rosin, H. M., & Korabik, K. (2002). Do family-friendly policies fulfill their promise?: An investigation of their impact on work-family conflict and work and personal outcomes. In D. L. Nelson & R. J. Burke (Eds.), *Gender, work stress, and health* (pp. 211–226). Washington, DC: American Psychological Association.

Rothausen, T. J., Gonzalez, J. A., Clarke, N. E., & O'Dell, L. L. (1998). Family-friendly backlash—Fact or fiction? The case of organizations' on-site child care centers. *Personnel Psychology, 51,* 685–706.

Scandura, T. A., & Lankau, M. J. (1997). Relationships of gender, family responsibility and flexible work hours to organizational commitment and job satisfaction. *Journal of Organizational Behavior, 18,* 377–391.

Scharlach, A. E., Lowe, B. F., & Schneider, E. L. (1991). *Elder care and the work force: Blueprint for action.* Lexington, MA: Lexington.

Scharlach, A. E., Sansom, S. L., & Stanger, J. (1995). The Family and Medical Leave Act of 1993: How fully is business complying? *California Management Review, 37*(2), 66–79.

Schwartz, S. H. (1992). The universal content and structure of values: Theoretical advances and empirical tests in 20 countries. *Advances in Experimental Social Psychology, 25,* 1-62.

Schwartz, S. H. (1990). Individualism-Collectivism: Critique and proposed refinements. *Journal of Cross-Cultural Psychology, 21,* 2.

Society for Human Resources Management (SHRM) (2003). *2003 Benefits Survey.* Alexandria, VA: Society for Human Resource Management, SHRM Research Department.

Spector, P. E., Cooper, C. L., Poelmans, S., Allen, T. D., O'Driscoll, M., Sanchez, J. I., Siu, O., et al. (2004) A cross-national comparative study of work-family stressors, working hours, and well-being: China and Latin America versus the Anglo World. *Personnel Psychology, 57,* 119-142.

Sustaining Progress: Social Partnership Agreement 2003–2005. Dublin: Stationery Office.

Thomas, L. T., & Ganster, D. C. (1995). Impact of family-supportive work variables on work-family conflict and strain: A control perspective. *Journal of Applied Psychology, 80,* 6–15.

Thompson, C. A., Beauvais, L. L. & Lyness, K. S. (1999). When work-family benefits are not enough: The influence of work-family culture on benefit utilization, organizational attachment, and work-family conflict. *Journal of Vocational Behavior, 54,* 392–415.

Todeva, E. (1999) Models for comparative analysis of culture: The case of Poland. *The International Journal of Human Resource Management, 10,* 606-623.

Triandis, H. C., Leung, K., Villareal, M. B. and Clark, F. L. (1985) Allocentric versus ideocentric tendencies: Convergent and discriminant validation, *Journal of Research in Personality, 19,* 395-415.

Triandis, H. C. (1995). Individualism and collectivism. Boulder, CO: Westview Press.

Trompenaars, F. (1994). *Riding the waves of culture.* London: Nicholas Brealey.

U.S. Bureau of Labor Statistics (2000). USDL 00-127. Retrieved on May 21, 2004 from, http://stats.bls.gov/news.release/famee.nr0.htm

U.S. Bureau of Labor Statistics (2001). *Employment characteristics of families.* Retrieved on June 18, 2004 from, www.bls.gov/news.release/famee.t02. htm

U.S. Bureau of Labor Statistics. (2001). *Work experience of the population in 2000.* Retrieved September 11, 2003, from, http://www.bls.gov/news. release/work.t01.htm

U.S. Bureau of Labor Statistics (2005). *Workers on flexible and shift schedules in May 2004.* Retrieved on July 21, 2006, from, http://www.bls.gov/news. release/pdf/flex.pdf

U.S. Bureau of Labor Statistics (2005). *Women in the labor force: A databook.* Retrieved on July 21, 2006, from, http://www.bls.gov/cps/wlf-data-book2005.htm

U.S. Bureau of Labor Statistics (2006). *Employee benefits survey.* Retrieved on July 21, 2006, from, http://data.bls.gov/cgi-bin/surveymost

U.S. Census Bureau (October 2001). *The 65 Year and Over Population: 2000— Census 2000 Brief.* Retrieved on September, 30, 2004 from, www.census. gov/prod/2001pubs/c2kbr01-10.pdf

U.S. Census Bureau (September, 2001). *Age: 2000—Census 2000 Brief.* Retrieved on October 25, 2004 from, www.census.gov/prod/2001pubs/ c2kbr01-12.pdf

U.S. Department of Labor, Office of the Secretary, Women's Bureau. (Undated). *Work and family resource kit.* Washington, DC: Author. (Available from Clearinghouse on Implementation of Child Care and Elder Care Services, 1-800-827-5335.)

Wagner, D. L., & Hunt. G. G. (1994). The use of workplace eldercare programs by employed caregivers. *Research on Aging, 16,* 69–84.

Wiatrowski, W. J. (1990, March). Family-related benefits in the workplace. *Monthly Labor Review, 113*(3), 28–33.

11

A Sensemaking Approach to Understanding Multicultural Teams:
An Initial Framework

C. SHAWN BURKE, HEATHER A. PRIEST,
CHRISTIN L. UPSHAW, AND EDUARDO SALAS
University of Central Florida

LINDA PIERCE
Army Research Laboratory

> "In any organizational experience a person's most pressing cognitive task is to make sense of the situation, to account for it, to understand it in meaningful terms."
>
> (Gioia, 1989, p. 221)

Although it has been argued that making sense of situations is a dominant cognitive activity for organizational members, in no place is it more relevant than in examining and promoting effective team interaction and adaptation within multicultural teams. Multicultural teams (MCTs) require individuals from different nations and cultures to cooperate and work together as a team, often with varying concepts of how teams should operate and how tasks are completed in order to solve complex problems (Ilgen, LePine, & Hollenbeck, 1997). While diverse perspectives have been argued to provide the potential for better identification of problems and the creation of better solutions (Ilgen et al., 1997), they also add ambiguity and complexity to an already dynamic work environment. Therefore, instead of enhancing team effectiveness, diversity within teams often serves to hinder the communication, coordination, and adaptive performance that results in effective team performance outcomes.

Part of the process loss that often occurs in MCTs is a result of team members' failure to make accurate sense of member interactions within this environment due to a reliance on stereotypes and hidden assumptions about values, beliefs, and actions. These assumptions are often faulty when it comes to multicultural teams, as they are driven by each member's own cognitive frame (i.e., mental model). These cognitive frames guide interactions with fellow team members. Differences among cultures in views on time (Maznevski & Chudoba, 2000) and rules pertaining to status (Merriam et al., 2001) are frequently reported as areas that cause friction among multicultural teams. For example, consider the expatriate who must work within a team where members' orientation to time varies along the continuum of concrete to fluid. Unless these differences are understood, members may be seen as lazy, nontask orientated (i.e., those whose view of time is continuous) or rude (i.e., those who have a discrete view of time). Conversely, when multicultural team members effectively make sense of the situation, diversity can be an added benefit.

Given the complexity present within multicultural teams and the prevalence of globalization (e.g., more than 60,000 multicultural companies; Copeland, 2006) it has become imperative to better understand multicultural team effectiveness. However, within the field of psychology, an understanding of how to create effective multicultural teams is still in its infancy. Most of the work that has been conducted has taken a rather narrow view, which relies heavily on the promotion of cultural awareness (often at a microlevel) and the original cultural dimensions (or various expansions of them) proposed by Hofstede (1980). Moreover, this approach has been psychology-centric in that in attempting to better understand multicultural team effectiveness, team researchers have tended to not stray far into other literatures.

Although this approach has been useful in providing a baseline, the current paper argues that to more fully understand multicultural teams, we need to move beyond the psychology-centric view that has tended to dominate their study. In addition, it will be argued that examining multicultural teams through the lens of sensemaking is a useful way to begin to better understand what happens within effective multicultural teams. Therefore, the purpose of this chapter is threefold. First to broaden our view of culture by examining the contributions that the literature on sensemaking can provide to the understanding of multicultural teams. Multicultural teams will be briefly described in order to set the context. Second, to develop a framework that offers a heuristic by which multicultural teams can be examined. The framework takes a multidisciplinary perspective by incorporating concepts from a wide range of disciplines, including cultural anthropology, organizational psychology, and cognitive psychology. Specifically, the proposed framework builds from four theoretical drivers: sensemaking, culture/global context, social identity, and teams. Finally, the potential practical implications of the framework and areas in need of future research will be discussed.

MULTICULTURAL TEAMS

MCTs are defined as teams (see Salas, Stagl, Burke, & Goodwin, in press) whose members have diverse values that are based in their national culture. The effectiveness of MCTs lies in their ability to manage the need for consensus versus the need for diversity (Argote & McGrath, 1993). This "dilemma" suggests that although the team may benefit from diverse members with a wide range of talents, skills, personal experiences, and perspectives, it also needs a common perspective and the ability to carry out a coordinated plan of action (Argote & McGrath, 1993). Team members drawn from various nationalities tend to differ in ways that have substantial implications for team functioning, and some mixtures of cultures may create higher levels of heterogeneity than others (Hambrick, Davison, Snell, & Snow, 1998; Ilgen et al., 1997).

Heterogeneous teams have the *potential* to achieve a constructive synergy beyond that achievable in a homogeneous team (Adler, 1986). For example, complementary heterogeneity can bring different cognitions and values to the task, thereby broadening the problem-solving capacity (Hambrick et al., 1998). However, heterogeneous teams also have the potential to be ineffective and may experience interpersonal aversion, distrust, and dysfunction (Hambrick et al., 1998). Currently, the general contention is that homogeneity promotes integration, trust, and ease of communication and that these outweigh any disadvantages of narrowness or redundancy within the team. Others contend that the benefits and costs of team heterogeneity depend on the nature of the team's task (Filley, House, & Kerr, 1976; Jackson, 1992) and the specific dimensions on which heterogeneity is being considered (Jackson, 1992; Pelled, 1996; Triandis, Hall, & Ewen, 1965). In some ways, the argument over which type of team is better is a moot point from a practical standpoint; many MCTs do not have a choice. Within organizational teams, diversity is often a feature that cannot be escaped but is simply a function of the operating environment. The question, instead becomes "What does within-team diversity in MCTs mean for team interaction (i.e., teamwork)?" It is this very question that served as the impetus for the development of the conceptual framework presented in Figure 11.1.

A CONCEPTUAL FRAMEWORK OF MULTICULTURAL TEAMS

In an effort to push the understanding of MCTs forward, several steps were taken to choose the constructs included in the conceptual framework displayed in Figure 11.1. First, multicultural teams and the challenges facing such teams were illustrated. As a predominant number of the challenges faced by multicultural teams revolve around issues of adaptive team coordination and the individual level teamwork processes that comprise it, adaptive coordination serves as the performance outcome within the proposed framework. Adaptive team coordination was defined, specifying the core constructs characterizing teamwork: leadership, back-up behavior, mutual performance monitoring, and communication. Next, given that metaphors of teamwork have been found to differ across cultures (Gibson & Zellmer-Bruhn, 2001), the processes by which meaning is assigned to specific teamwork processes within multicultural teams were delineated. The first step in this process was to examine how members make sense of their environment (in this case, their internal team environment). In order to accomplish this, a multidisciplinary perspective was taken as literature on cognition, systems engineering, organization theory, and information science to examine. Finally, to contextually bound our framework, the literature bases in cultural anthropology, cross-cultural psychology, and organizational psychology were examined to identify the contextual variables that serve to drive the sensemaking process within multicultural teams. From this literature base, three primary sets of constructs (i.e., contextual drivers) were identified: global context, national culture, and social identity. These, in turn, serve as proximal inputs to the sensemaking process within our framework.

It is important to note that at this early stage of development Figure 11.1 presents a conceptual framework by which multicultural teams can be understood; this, as can be seen, *is not* a predictive model. Whereby a conceptual framework identifies the constructs of interest within a particular domain, a model goes beyond identification to proposing specific relationships between constructs. Such an effort goes beyond the scope of the current forum. In this chapter, we provide a framework, as opposed to a predictive model, due to space limitations and where we are in our thinking. As we engage in more conceptual and empirical work, the framework will be expanded into a predictive model. Therefore, at this time specific propositions are not included in the body of the main text, but within the section on future research several research questions are posed which flow from the content contained within the framework.

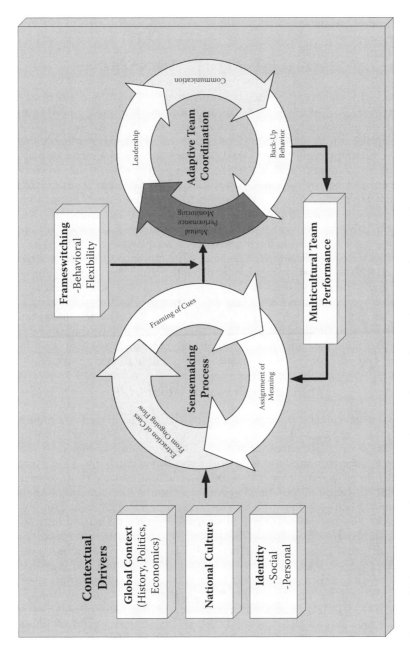

Figure 11.1 A sensemaking approach to understanding multinational teamwork.

The next section will begin to describe each of the variables within the framework starting with the proposed performance outcome, adaptive team coordination.

ADAPTIVE TEAM COORDINATION

Figure 11.1 identifies individual team member (i.e., mutual performance monitoring, back-up behavior, communication, leadership) and team level (i.e., adaptive team coordination) processes that provide the basis for adaptive action within multicultural teams. High performing teams require planning, well-defined goals and direction, and a blend of team members who not only bring the needed skills, but who are able to work in a cooperative environment. Specifically, direction that is articulated through the process of leadership serves to provide the conceptual foundation for the planning process, and behaviors such as communication, back-up behavior, mutual performance monitoring, and leadership are the processes that provide the foundation for adaptive team coordination. Adaptive team coordination is a team-level phenomenon that involves the team adaptively organizing and sequencing team member actions (Burke, Stagl, Salas, Pierce, & Kendall, 2006). Although it has been argued that adaptive team coordination is a key mechanism in allowing teams to capitalize on potential synergy, it is very often the place where things fail within multicultural teams. In the subsections that follow, the nature of these team member processes, how they facilitate adaptive team coordination, and potential cultural roadblocks or facilitation are addressed.

Mutual Performance Monitoring

Mutual performance monitoring can be defined as a team member's ability to "keep track of [a] fellow team member's work while carrying out their own. . . . to ensure that everything is running as expected and . . . to ensure that they are following procedures correctly" (McIntyre & Salas, 1995, p. 23). Primarily a cognitive action, mutual performance monitoring requires that team members observe the actions of their teammates regularly to watch for mistakes, slips, lapses, errors, and performance discrepancies. The goal of mutual performance monitoring is to catch these errors and correct them in a timely manner in order to minimize their negative effects. Mutual performance monitoring enables adaptive team performance within multicultural teams in that it is the mechanism by which members recognize when others need help (Marks & Panzer, 2004). In addition, it promotes adaptive coordination by facilitating team members' awareness of the timing and pacing of collective actions (Kozlowski, 1998) and facilitates greater situation awareness (Salas, Prince, Baker, & Shrestha, 1995). Finally, mutual performance monitoring encourages adaptive action through facilitation of error correction (Dickinson & McIntyre, 1997). Specifically, mutual performance monitoring is often the first step in highlighting an over-loaded team member or error in direction of a member.

Although mutual performance monitoring has been highlighted as a key feature of adaptive team coordination (Burke, Stagl, Salas, et al., 2006; Entin & Serfaty, 1999), this work has been conducted primarily within the United States using a U.S.-centric view of teamwork. Think-ing back to the earlier discussion, one might expect some difficulty in using this process effectively within multicultural teams. For example, the manifestation of cultural norms with regard to how monitoring occurs, the manner in which signs of distress occur, or from whom mon-itoring is accepted is likely to vary. This, in turn, drives a need to be able to recognize and interpret these novel cue patterns (see Figure 11.1).

Back-up Behavior

Closely related to performance monitoring is back-up behavior, defined as "the discretionary provision of resources and task-related effort to another member of one's team that is intended to help that team mem-ber obtain the goals as defined by his or her role when it is apparent that the team member is failing to reach those goals" (Porter et al., 2003, p. 391–392). It is the information gathered through mutual performance monitoring and expressed through feedback or other forms of back-up behavior (e.g., physical action, offloading of tasks) that boosts the team from the sum of individual performance to the synergy of teamwork and so promotes team adaptation. However, back-up behavior does not universally lead to team adaptation.

Within teams, back-up behavior may be offered in response to spe-cific requests for help or it may be based on the recognition that there is a workload distribution problem in the team. Porter et al. (2003) found that its role in promoting team performance may vary depending on the actual team need for the offered back-up behavior. If back-up behavior is provided when it is not needed, it can decrease performance by leading to redundancy of effort. For example, if team members misinterpret the cues offered within heterogeneous teams, they may provide back-up when it is not needed, neglect the cue that signals help is needed, or provide back-up in a manner that is culturally inappropriate. Given this example, it becomes easy to see how heterogeneous teams may have more difficulty in back-up behavior due to misinterpretations and miscommunications. In addition, given some cultural orientations, the explicit manner in which Americans conduct back-up behavior might be seen as threatening, rude, or embarrassing (e.g., within collectivistic cultural orientations).

Communication

Communication is defined as "the process by which information is clearly and accurately exchanged between two or more team members in the prescribed manner with proper terminology; the ability to clarify or acknowledge the receipt of information" (Cannon-Bowers, Tannen-baum, Salas, & Volpe, 1995, p. 345). Communication is essential to teams in that it helps team members develop and update the shared knowledge structures that serve to guide adaptive action, and it provides the foundation for effective monitoring behavior. For example, if a team member monitors fellow members' actions, yet never communicates feedback in the form of back-up behavior, the monitoring is not functional for the team.

Communication is a team process that is consistently highlighted as an issue within multicultural teams. Some of the difficulty lies in the fact that team members who are from different cultures, therefore from different nations or regions, often have differences in language, dialect, slang, or communication norms. For example, a team member from one culture may perceive verbal corrections as rude, and another may be considered harsh for the way he verbalizes feedback. Other difficulties with communication have been reported, such as that much information or the intended meaning is often lost within multicultural teams. Therefore, heterogeneous teams who may already have process barriers could face additional loss due to communication problems.

Team Leadership

There are benefits of leadership in teams and this has been well-documented in the literature (see Burke, Stagl, Klein, et al., 2006). These benefits include the ability of the leader to serve as a coordinator of operations, a liaison to external teams or management, and as a guide for setting the team's vision (Zaccaro & Marks, 1999). Beyond that, leaders also contribute to adaptation in that they can play a key role in facilitating a team's propensity to adapt by choosing how and when to intervene to promote review and revision of procedures and methods (e.g., Gersick & Hackman, 1990; Hackman & Wageman, 2005). Leaders contribute to adaptive coordination processes by facilitating flexible plan execution and team problem-solving through cognitive processes, coordination processes, and the team's collective affective status (Salas, Burke, & Stagl, 2004). In this vein, the leadership processes enacted by the team leader can play a key role in promoting the conditions required for adaptive action. Particularly in heterogeneous teams, strong leadership can help teams adapt to difficulties in execution and process loss. However, complicating the picture within multicultural teams is that research has shown that while there is some agreement in desired leadership characteristics and styles, there are also many differences across cultures concerning what is deemed "effective" leadership.

Teamwork in MCTs

Although the discussions above begin to highlight the complexity when it comes to teamwork within multicultural teams, individuals from various cultures have been found to ascribe different meaning to what defines teamwork behaviors and place different levels of importance on teamwork (Cox, Lobel, & McLeod, 1991; Gibson & Zellmer-Bruhn, 2001). Cultures differ in their preferences for teamwork and structured interactions (Hambrick & Brandon, 1988; Hofstede, 1980). Some members may expect clearly differentiated roles, whereas others may be less concerned with defining roles (Cohen & Bailey, 1997). Likewise, clear outcomes may be important to some members, and others see multiple implicit outcomes possible (McGrath, 1984). For instance, it was demonstrated by Gibson and Zellmer-Bruhn (2001) that people around the globe hold different definitions of teamwork, as illustrated by the metaphors they use when they talk about their teams. Specifically, individualistic cultures commonly use sports team metaphors to describe their notions of teamwork; whereas other cultures use family, military, or community as metaphors for teamwork. These metaphors carry with them indications of the expectations for how teams will be managed and how team processes will unfold (Gibson & Zellmer-Bruhn, 2001). Research is needed to further probe into the metaphors used, as a deeper understanding can assist team members in making sense of cultural preferences based on member communication.

It has also been suggested that culture affects preferences for certain task solutions, group processes, and cognition (Postman, Bruner, & McGinnies, 1948). By evaluating these differences, insight may be gained as to the preferred practices that have been noted across cultural contexts. In addition, culturally contingent definitions of teamwork will help members understand the expected behaviors within teams and the culture those teams reside in (Gibson & Zellmer-Bruhn, 2001).

So how do members of multicultural teams make sense of team interaction? What distinguishes the good teams, the ones that get it from those that don't? To begin to answer this question, we argue that team researchers and practitioners must broaden their views on culture to incorporate literature from cultural anthropology, cognitive psychology, as well as organizational psychology. Specifically, the search for an approach to understanding multicultural teams begins, in our view, with an examination of the sensemaking literature within cognitive and organizational psychology. For this reason, sensemaking forms the basis of our conceptual framework (see Figure 11.1).

SENSEMAKING

Sensemaking Defined: Sensemaking has been defined in various ways. Starbuck and Milliken (1988) argue that sensemaking "involves placing stimuli into some kind of framework" (p. 51). Similarly, Ring and Rands (1989) argue that it is "a process in which individuals develop cognitive maps of their environment" (p. 342). Others take it one step further by arguing that it is "the reciprocal interaction of information seeking, meaning ascription, and action" (Thomas, Clark, & Gioia, 1993, p. 240). Finally, Weick (1995) offers perhaps the most comprehensive definition in that, "sensemaking is about such things as placement of items into frameworks, comprehending, redressing surprise, constructing meaning, interacting in the pursuit of mutual understanding, and patterning" (p. 6). Despite the researcher, almost all definitions involve the idea that it is a process by which individuals place stimuli into a framework that allows them to understand and make sense of what is happening. In addition, researchers, such as Weick, argue that sensemaking is more than just interpretation as it also involves how the cues to be interpreted got there in the first place (e.g., how they were singled out from ongoing experience).

To better delineate this process, sensemaking has been characterized by seven properties: It is (a) grounded in identity construction, (b) retrospective, (c) enactive of sensible environments, (d) social, (e) ongoing, (f) focused on and by extracted cues, and (g) driven by plausibility (Weick, 1995). As a cognitive process, it is grounded in identity construction whereby it's influenced by the cognitive frames that individuals hold, including one's self-concept and personal identity. This aspect of sensemaking begins to suggest some of the antecedents that one may examine in understanding multicultural teams (e.g., social identity literature, cultural anthropology literature; see Figure 11.1). The highly cognitive nature of this process also means that it is retrospective or grounded in past experience. Sense cannot be made before an event happens, it is always retrospective (e.g., it's triggered by some event; in the case of multicultural teams, this is often a breakdown in adaptive team coordination). It is a continuous cognitive process that takes place mostly on a tacit level, until team members are confronted by an unexpected event or result (Gioia, 1989). It is a social process that involves noticing and extracting specific cues from the environment as well as the contextual interpretation of those cues (Leedom, 2001). Finally, the purpose of all this activity lies within the enactment of a *sensible, plausible* environment. While the literature on sensemaking would suggest that the product of sensemaking doesn't have to reflect reality (it must only be plausible), it is a recursive, cyclical process whereby meaning is continually calibrated.

Sensemaking has been argued to involve such cognitive processes as: extraction of cues from the ongoing flow of experience, and the placement of these cues into cognitive frameworks that provide context for the cues, aiding in their interpretation (Hill & Levanagan, 1995; Thomas et al., 1993; Weick, 1995). These three cognitive processes comprise the higher order process of sensemaking as depicted in Figure 11.1. Specifically, the process of environmental scanning leads to the extraction of the cues that trigger sensemaking. In turn, an initial level of cue interpretation is fostered by the placement of cues into frameworks, and a deeper level of interpretation is formed when cues are embellished through the use of contextual explanations (Weick, 1995).

Embellishment of contextual explanations for why the extracted cues are important in the context (frame) leads to individuals understanding the reasoning behind the sense that is being offered. Even though the above definitions of sensemaking and its seven properties help to distinguish sensemaking from similar processes (e.g., interpretation) and illustrate the highly cognitive nature of this process, on a practical level there is still much that needs to be explained. Within the next few paragraphs the three component processes involved in sensemaking will be described in more detail.

Extraction of Cues from Ongoing Experience

The impetus for this initial phase is a break or change in the flow of experience (i.e., ecological change; Weick, 1979). However, due to issues pertaining to working memory, team members do not attend to all the information contained within the break but actively construct the information that they do attend to (Choo, 2006). In other words, members selectively extract a subset of cues from all those available. Cue recognition determines which cues get extracted and has been identified as the mechanism by which experts make decisions (Carlson, 1997; Salas, Cannon-Bowers, Fiore, & Stout, 2001). Essentially, when an expert is "presented with a cue pattern, a series of recognition processes proceed, which results in the activation of a vast store of information used in decision making" (Salas et al., 2001, p. 176). However, it is important to note that that expert's improved performance (e.g., decision making) is not due to their ability to search the environment but to knowing what cues should be searched (Charness, 1989).

This improved performance, due to an increased ability to recognize what cues to search in order to extract the most appropriate information, is also applicable to social interactions often containing more abstract cues, such as those within multicultural teams. For example, social intelligence is based on searching the most appropriate social cues to make a decision about feelings, behaviors, and attitudes in a particular setting and to determine the most appropriate response (Ford & Tisak, 1983; Marlowe, 1986; Zaccaro, Gilbert, Thor, & Mymford, 1991). Ultimately, within social intelligence, and we would argue within social interactions that take place within MCTs, "it is important that [individuals] identify and specify what specific critical cues are in the situation in hand" (Salas et al., 2001, p. 177). Within the context of multicultural teams, the cues that should form an initial basis would be those that deal with the intersection of the set of variables on the left-hand side of Figure 11.1 (global context, national culture, social identity) and adaptive coordination. In some cases, team members may not have the expertise that enables effective cue recognition, therefore, they may actively intervene within the environment to create new features in an effort at hypothesis testing (Choo, 2006).

Framing of Cues

Once cues have been extracted, the next step is to place them within a cognitive framework (e.g., schema, mental model) that will assist in cue interpretation. By comparing cues to mental models of similar situations, cue interpretations are then selected that best fit with past understandings. In this case, similar situations may involve prior team interactions or interactions with culturally diverse populations. This framing is similar to processes that occur within recognition primed decision making as discussed within the cognitive engineering literature. Recognition primed decision making is a strategy used by experts in which typical themes are recognized and familiarity with similar situations is used as a basis to form quick situation assessments (Klein, 1998). If the cues are not easily diagnosable, mental simulation may be used to envision how best to proceed in the current situation. A similar argument can be made for the second phase of the sensemaking process.

Meaning Assignment

Guided by the placement of cues into frameworks, meaning is assigned. As members may not always have the expertise within their current cognitive frames to make sense on their own, they may turn to other sources. Guidance as to what these sources might be can be gleaned from the literature on newcomer socialization. Specifically, Louis (1980) argued that newcomers within an organization may rely on several sources to "make sense" of their environment: (a) similar past experiences, (b) general personnel characteristics, (c) cultural assumptions, and (d) information and interpretations from others in the situation. Depending on the novelty of the situation, these sources may be inadequate and thus cause the member to form inaccurate or incomplete cognitions that will, in turn, serve to guide their actions. As with newcomers, members of MCTs are often at a disadvantage with some of the aforementioned sources of information. For example, depending on members' cultural experience and cultural distance, team members may not have an adequate history in the setting to fully appreciate why and how events discrepant from their current cognitions occur. This, in turn, may cause them to rely heavily on past experiences or internal attributes, often causing faulty mental models.

Summary   At its most basic, understanding multicultural teams can be seen as a problem of sensemaking for team members, practitioners, and researchers. Within this frame, the actions that individuals are attempting to make sense of are the interactions within the team (see Figure 11.1). Multicultural team members need not only to make sense of their external setting, they also must make sense out of the interaction requirements necessary within the situation at hand, as well as of the various contingencies that may affect how they respond (e.g., member KSAOs) individually, as well as collectively. The data sources argued for by Louis (1980), combined with what is known about team-work within multicultural settings, begin to offer a starting point for understanding what cues are likely to be extracted from ongoing experience within MCTs and the variables that impact how they might be interpreted. If one accepts this view as a starting point, the following question arises: Within multicultural teams, what are the cues that are likely to get singled out from the ongoing flow of experience? In other words, what are the drivers of the sensemaking process within multicultural teams? For answers to these questions we next turn to the literatures of cultural anthropology, organizational, and cognitive psychology to examine a series of contextual drivers that provide input to the sensemaking process within multicultural teams.

CONTEXTUAL DRIVERS

In an effort to begin to identify the proximal factors that impact the sensemaking process within MCTs, we first turn to the literature on cultural anthropology as well as to linguists who study cultural diversity within organizations. These two literature bases serve to inform our framework and suggest the first two of three identified proximal inputs to sensemaking: national culture, global context (see Figure 11.1). Within the next section, the argument is made that it is not enough to understand cultural dimensions; but in order to truly understand sensemaking within MCTs, one must also consider the global context that surrounds the cultures that comprise one's team. Finally, the last proximal factor that will be discussed in relation to the proposed framework (see Figure 11.1) originates within organizational psychology. Specifically, social identity and the role that it plays in understanding the sensemaking process will be described. As is described below, it is expected that these three aspects will impact each stage of the sensemaking process within MCTs.

What Can Be Learned from Cultural Anthropology and Linguists?

Within the cultural anthropology literature, culture is often defined as being "synonymous with 'a nation' or 'a people'—that is, as an intergenerational community, more or less institutionally complete, occupying a given territory, or homeland, sharing a distinct language and history" and "a set of institutions, covering both public and private life, with a common language, which has historically developed over time on a given territory, which provides people with a wide range of choices about how to lead their lives" (Kymlicka, 1995, pp. 17–18).

Psychologists tend to focus on the human mind in relation to the individual and the group; in contrast, cultural anthropology widens the focus and goes beyond the human in the equation. For example, cultural anthropologists believe that "culture is inscribed in the public world of artifacts, texts, and practices, and also in the minds of the individuals who produce these artifacts and texts and enact these practices" (Quinn & Strauss, 2006, p. 267). Moreover, cultural anthropologists acknowledge that they should consider not only the global context, but also "the meanings and actions of particular persons" (Quinn & Strauss, 2006, p. 269).

The multidisciplinary and multidimensional study of culture that is adopted by anthropologists can be useful to psychologists in better understanding the richness of culture and the depth of its influence on the sensemaking process, which drives the enactment of team behavior in multicultural teams. Ultimately, anthropologists agree that culture must be classified as both intrapersonal and extrapersonal (D'Andrade, 1995; Hannerz, 1992; Shore, 1991; Strauss & Quinn, 1997). These two classifications will be briefly reviewed, and their relation to the sensemaking process within multicultural teams will be described.

National Culture (Intrapersonal).

A number of cultural factors have been discussed in the literature. Traditionally, psychological researchers have defined culture based on the descriptions of Hofstede (1980), Trompenaars (1993), and the like, who classify national culture based on norms and means along general cultural dimensions (e.g., time orientation, collectivism–individualism). Within the work of psychologists studying culture and teams, the primary conceptual basis has been the work of Geert Hofstede (i.e., power distance, individualism/collectivism, uncertainty avoidance, masculinity/femininity, time orientation). Although Hofstede's work is indeed important, it has been criticized along a number of dimensions (see later discussion), and it is time for psychologists to move beyond Hofstede to consider other dimensions of national culture. In an effort to look outside our traditional box, several cultural dimensions proposed by linguists who study culture and organizational behavior are offered. Specifically, we sought to examine the dimensions that would tie directly back to the sensemaking process described earlier in the paper. As such, we focus on dimensions that pertain to: (a) the process by which information is gathered; (b) methods of communication; and, due to the coordination requirements that multicultural team members are attempting to make sense of, we focus on (c) time orientation.

Cultural differences in information gathering (data vs. dialogue).
Within multicultural teams, as with all teams, information gathering is essential to maintain adaptive team coordination and effective

performance outcomes. For example, leaders gather information during boundary spanning activities, and information gathering is an essential activity within the sensemaking process. Cue extraction and the activities involved when members are attempting to reconcile new information with existing cognitive frames may all be considered to involve information gathering. In addition, within teams, interaction involves the process of gathering information from the environment, which includes other team members. However, within multicultural teams, confusion may arise due to differences in cultural preferences with regard to information gathering. In this vein, Lewis (1999) identified dialogue-oriented and data-oriented cultures. Members of data-oriented cultures act based on information that has been gathered by doing a great deal of research. Specifically, data-oriented cultures (e.g., Swedes, Germans, and Americans) rely on solid databases gathered from reliable sources. Members of data-oriented cultures tend to embrace the current, technology-driven resources that are widely available.

Dialogue-oriented cultures (e.g., Latinos, Arabs, and Indians) on the other hand, see interactions "in context" and rely on their own personal information network (Lewis, 1999). Instead of seeking out hard data sources, members of dialogue-oriented cultures will already know about the facts surrounding an interaction because they would have already consulted their immediate social network and learned the gossip or connections surrounding a possible interaction. This, in turn, helps them decide how to act. Therefore, data-oriented cultures are fact-driven, but dialogue-oriented cultures are relationship-driven. These differences will impact where cues are most likely to be extracted from during an ecological change. In addition, understanding how team members gather information will assist fellow team members in taking the perspective of other members.

Cultural differences in time (linear-active, multi-active).   Another cultural difference lies in views of time sequences. A culture's view of time is important in terms of planning, setting goals, and the sequencing of team behavior. Linear-active cultures (e.g., Swedes, Swiss, Dutch, Germans) "do one thing at a time, concentrate hard on that thing and do it within a scheduled timescale" (Lewis, 1999, p. 37). This is not just a preference for how it is done, but linear-active cultures believe this is the most efficient and effective way to do things. Conversely, multi-active cultures (e.g., Portuguese, Turkey, and Vietnam) are very flexible in their interactions and views of time. Multi-active cultures typically multitask and often do many things at once in an unplanned sequence. Members of this culture are not particularly interested in schedules or punctuality. These preferences are often implicit, yet they guide member action and will impact how goals are set, as well as how members expect coordination to occur (e.g., multitasking vs. sequential tasking).

Cultural differences in communication (reactive).   A final difference relates to how cultures communicate. Within multicultural teams this is obviously important, as communication is one of the essential constructs identified as comprising adaptive team coordination (see Figure 11.1). Differences will not only impact how members communicate, but the manner in which feedback is offered, how instructions are clarified, and how the outcomes from sensemaking are shared across team members. Although reactive cultures are multi-active and excitable, they are unique in that they are reactive in their interactions (Lewis, 1999). Reactive cultures (e.g., Japan, Taiwan, Finland) are good listeners, and do not let their minds wander when someone is talking to them. Reactive cultures tend to be introverts and communicate through body language more than by overt communication. Although reactive cultures do not specifically differ on time sequencing from linear-active and multi-active cultures, reactive cultures have tendencies that clash with both. For example, members of linear-active cultures will likely become frustrated with reactive members because they do not fit into their linear system (e.g., question/reply; cause/effect). Furthermore, multi-active cultural members get frustrated because they view reactive members as giving little or no feedback.

Although the broad cultural dimensions described above begin to offer some suggestion as to what cues may be seen as discrepant from members mental models and, as such, are singled out from ongoing experience. But they do not provide enough detailed information to offer assistance in determining how these extracted cues are assigned meaning. In line with the above argument, a debate has begun about the efficiency and accuracy of classifying individuals based on their national culture along these dimensions (e.g., Bearden, Money, & Nevins, 2006; Chiang, 2005; Jacob, 2005). In anthropology, a similar debate has been taking place. For example, proponents of "liberal multiculturalism" (e.g., Kymlicka, 1995; Taylor, 1992) have emphasized the stable nature of cultural dimensions and the diversity of these cultural tendencies between nations, but cultural anthropologists have borrowed from studies of other natures (e.g., feminist studies, media studies) to argue that "there is no end or exception to this criss-crossing and overlapping" and pointing out that cultures "overlap geographically and come in a variety of types" (Tully, 1995, p. 10). Culture is also described as "so varied, contested and constantly shifting" (Tully, 1995, p. 11) and referred to as "heterogeneous, dynamic, porous and hybrid" (Dhamoon, 2006, p. 360).

The recognition of variability within nations and individuals is an extremely useful contribution to the psychological study of culture. The seminal work in our field relies too heavily on self-report and generalizations. Although this methodology contributes to our knowledge base, valuable information is lost. For example, Hofstede's original study established the cultural dimensions used by most studies today and is now criticized, based on both methodological and interpretation issues.

Criticisms have pointed out that Hofstede's work only reports averages and does not describe individual situations so is therefore only valid for groups rather than individuals; harsher critiques cite Hofstede as a source of stereotyping that continues today (A. Marcus & Gould, 2000).

Despite where one falls in the debate, it seems obvious that Hofstede's dimensions are outdated and offer only a partial picture of culture. Anthropological methodologies specifically focused on global contexts offer a step forward in addressing this issue. Dimensions surrounding national culture offer a starting point to understanding sensemaking within MCTs, but to fully understand this process, the global context must also be taken into account. It is this global context that provides the knowledge needed to make sense within dynamic adaptive environments. The next section provides a brief discussion of the context provided by examining global variables (i.e., history, politics, and economy) and acknowledges the exclusion of other key variables (e.g., religion and language). Although future research needs to examine each of these global variables at a deeper level, an initial step forward is offered here.

Cultural Context: Historical, Political, and Economical Influences (Extrapersonal).

Historical influences.   To understand culture, anthropologists believe one must understand the historical underpinnings of a region. When examining interactions between team members, it is difficult to understand the meaning and rationale underlying team member actions if there is not an understanding of what that person has seen, done, or experienced (e.g., Roseberry, 1989; Silk, 1987). Historical events tell us about the transformation of long-term social structures and their meaning. For example, anthropologists argue that the conflicts and wars of our fathers infuse the development of values and norms used to make decisions today (Roseberry, 1989). Building on this example, World War II has influenced the culture of the United States by, among other things, increasing our ethnocentrism. A researcher could learn a great deal about American culture by the examination of the Great Depression, WWII, the Vietnam Conflict, and the Gulf Wars. All of these events helped shape the American national culture.

Political influences.   Intricately linked to historical events, political changes also influence the development of culture. Cultural anthropologists refer to culture and power or cultural politics to refer to a wide range of relationships not limited to governmental politics (Hess, 1995). Anthropologists actually borrow their idea of politics/power from sociology by using a classic definition from Max Weber's *Economy and Society:* "the ability of people or groups to get what they want, even when other people or groups want something else" (Hess, 1995, p. 12). To illiterate the influence of power/politics on culture, we point to interviews conducted with American soldiers who have been deployed to Iraq. Based on interviews with soldiers, the authors of this paper have a great deal of anecdotal evidence to support the impact that political events have on determining the manifestation and evolvement of cultural values. For example, soldiers argued for a need to understand the political and historical perspectives of Iraqi and Afghani citizens. The knowledge of power sources and how they came to arrive at that power is one aspect that fosters a greater understanding of the other culture. Specifically, within those cultures, there is a stringent political structure on who can interact with who and, similar to the anthropological definition of power, who to go to in order to get what you want. Understanding the power and politics of that country fosters an understanding not only of why they do what they do but how to operate within that culture. This, in turn, allows team members not only to make more accurate predictions concerning team member behavior, but when the unexpected happens, this contextual information is a window by which to frame and understand member interaction.

Economic influence.   Lastly, economics influences individual values and norms and drives team member interaction. The growth of the market, the inequalities between classes based on wealth, and the economic exchanges that take place within a community, whether global or local, influence how individuals interact and value each other (G. E. Marcus & Fischer, 1999). Cultural anthropologists describe economics, in as far as its influence on culture as "production, exchange, and consumption" (Wilk, 1996, p. 29). In addition to framing the definition of relationships (e.g., the "haves" vs. the "have nots"), the economic structure of a culture is also credited with driving human behavior based on needs (Malinowski, 1994). This too can be useful in understanding behaviors and interactions resulting from cultural tendencies. For example, observing the interactions at an economic hub can give cultural behaviors meaning and explain why individuals interact with each other in a particular way and help define cultural drivers such as class structure.

Summary   Understanding national culture at the dimension level forms an initial baseline for operation; however, nations are evolving, not static. Therefore, it becomes important to not only take into account national culture at the dimension level but also the context surrounding those dimensions (e.g., history, political, economic influences), as it is these sources that serve to update individual beliefs, values, and expected actions. However, we argue that in order to understand the variation that exists in individuals within a culture, the framework presented in Figure 11.1 must push further. Specifically, we argue that understanding what social identity a person is occupying during the sensemaking process and the cues that may trigger one identity over another will assist in truly understanding the frame of reference that each individual team member is operating within and, in turn, what is likely to draw their attention.

What Can Be Learned from Social and Organizational Psychology?

Social Identity.

Social identity theory aims to identify when and why individuals associate with social groups as well as why individuals behave as a part of social groups. According to this theory, individuals have both a personal and a social identity. An individual's personal identity is derived from individual personality traits and interpersonal relationships. One's social identity is derived from belonging to a certain group. In other words, the first level of an individual's identity is personal identity, which is different from that of other in-group members and the second level is the individual's social identity, which is shared with in-group members but not with out-group members (Haslam, Powell, & Turner, 2000).

When presented with ambiguous situations, such as those found when first operating within a multicultural team, members initially use categorization to reduce ambiguity. Categorization involves putting ourselves and other people into categories (i.e., American, Canadian, Arab, British). By categorizing others and ourselves, we are able to gain insight into our identity, similarities, and differences with others in the same group and in different groups. Identification entails an individual associating with groups they believe they belong to. This identification is one's social identity and often becomes apparent in "us" versus "them" dialogues. Individuals can identify with many groups and can think of themselves as group members or individuals interchangeably. Moreover, individuals can vary their group membership situationally, meaning that depending on the context of the situation, an individual can identify more or less with a certain group (e.g., identifying less as a Democrat when we disagree with a view taken).

The above argues that individuals have both a personal identity and a social identity, what is more difficult to understand is why and when an individual takes on one persona over the other. As depicted in Figure 11.1, recognition of the identity a person is occupying as well as the cues that trigger one identity over another are important; this is particularly true when taking a sensemaking perspective to understanding multicultural teams. Social identity will impact the particular cues that are likely to be extracted as well as the meaning that is assigned to those cues. Essentially, social identity serves as one aspect of the cognitive framework against which information is compared during sensemaking within multicultural teams. Ellemers, Spears, and Doosje (2002) developed a taxonomy of situations in which they define the conditions that cause an individual to portray one identity over the other. Within this taxonomy (Table 11.1) the horizontal axis reflects the type of threat (i.e.,

TABLE 11.1   Self-Identity and Social Identity Theory
(Ellemers, Spears, and Doosje, 2002)

	Group Commitment	
Threat Type	Low	High
No Threat		
Concern:	Accuracy/efficiency	Social meaning
Motive:	Noninvolvement	Identity expression
Individual-Directed Threat	Low	High
Concern:	Categorization	Exclusion
Motive:	Self-affirmation	Acceptance
Group-Directed Threat	Low	High
Concern:	Value	Distinctiveness, value
Motive:	Individual mobility	Group affirmation

Reprinted, with permission, from the *Annual Review of Psychology* Volume 53 ©2002 by Annual Reviews www.annualreviews.org.

none, individual-directed, group-directed), and the vertical axis reflects the level of group commitment (i.e., low, high). Next, the taxonomy will be briefly reviewed in order to identify how the type of threat and level of commitment interact to determine whether team members are likely to adopt a social or personal identity. The descriptions provided below are organized around the type of threat perceived.

No threat.   In situations where there is no threat to the individual's personal or social identity, individuals are primarily concerned with sensemaking and efficiency. When the individual's commitment to the group is low, the most common response is noninvolvement (Ellemers et al., 2002). Because neither the social nor the personal identity is threatened, the individual is more concerned with gathering information and making sense of the situation. In the taxonomy developed by Ellemers et al. (2002), researchers disagree as to whether this is a personal identity or social identity response.

When individuals have high commitment to the group, their primary concern is to express and confirm the group identity. Ellemers et al. (2002) note that the individual's response depends on whether his or her group identity is clear or is not yet developed. When the individual's group identity is definite, he or she conforms with the in-group and support group norms. When group identity is unclear, the individual attempts to "create a distinctive identity by distinguishing and differentiating the group from outgroups in the comparative context" (p. 169). In either case, individuals express their social identity when they have high group commitment and there is no threat to the personal or group identity. Ellemers et al. note that because there is no threat to the individual's identity, their response lacks the urgency it would have if there were a threat.

Individual-directed threat.   Threats to self-identity can occur when individuals are categorized into a group to which they have low commitment. In this situation the individual will resist categorization for a number of reasons, such as (a) to establish individuality, (b) because such categorization is irrelevant, (c) because other groups in which the individual belongs are more important, or (d) to prevent the loss of control when categorization is imposed by others (Ellemers et al., 2002). Spears and colleagues (1999) have found that when individuals believe they are being inappropriately categorized, they try to individuate the group and emphasize intragroup differences. Further, Ellemers, Kortekaas, and Ouwerkerk (1999) found that individuals who are categorized by others, as opposed to earning group membership, are less willing to be considered by that categorization. This effect can be seen when people use stereotypes to categorize individuals (e.g., women in mathematics). In summation, when individuals with low group motivation are categorized with that group, they express their personal identity as distinct from the group's characteristics.

The opposite phenomenon can occur when individuals have high group commitment and are not accepted by or categorized within the group. This can occur for a number of reasons, such as an individual developing a high commitment to the group to compensate for personal inadequacies. When highly committed group members are threatened by possible future rejection, these individuals communicate similarities of themselves with the in-group and conform with and support group norms (Jetten, Spears, & Manstead, 2001). Individuals who are threatened by exclusion from the group and have high group commitment will express their social identity by emphasizing their inclusion in and similarity with the group.

Group-directed threat.   When an individual's group's values are threatened, the individual's personal identity is also threatened. Even when individuals are low in group commitment, to preserve their personal identity, they attempt to minimize their association with the negative group identity and align with a group more favorable to their personal identity. Some researchers argue that when group values are threatened, there is no threat to the personal self for individuals with low group commitment, however this is untrue. For example, in situations where a group is stigmatized for any reason, "unless [group members] can hide their group membership, members of stigmatized groups are likely to be chronically treated in terms of their devalued group membership, regardless of their group commitment" (Ellemers et al., 2002, p. 174). These individuals, as members of a negatively viewed group, will attempt to distance themselves from the group by emphasizing their individual uniqueness and expressing social similarities with a more favorable group (Mussweiler, Gabriel, & Bodenhausen, 2000).

When individuals are high in group commitment, two important types of group threat can affect their actions: threat of group values and threat to the distinctiveness of the group. When there is a threat to the group values, individuals with high group commitment respond with group affirmation by emphasizing the homogeneity of the group, differentiating the group from others, and participating in self-stereotyping (Doosje, Ellemers, & Spears, 1995; Spears et al., 1999). Members of powerful groups, specifically, respond with anger, contempt, and may intend to move against the out-group. When the distinctiveness of the group is threatened, group members will express their commitment to the group by participating in self-stereotyping and distinguishing their group from other groups. Jetten and colleagues (1999) remark that the highest committed members of a group, when group distinctiveness was threatened, may attempt to differentiate the in-group from other groups so intensely that overt discrimination may be observed. Further, Keltner and Haidt (1999) explain displays of hatred and disgust for out-group members may result from this situation. Threats to an individual's group identity, whether it be the group value or its distinctiveness, will lead to individuals expressing their social identity, maintaining their group membership, self-stereotyping, and distinguishing the in-group from other groups.

Frameswitching.

The conceptual framework that has been described up to this point has specified the nature of sensemaking within multicultural teams through examining the primary target of sensemaking that occurs within the team (i.e., adaptive coordination requirements), as well as the manner in which the sensemaking process might be enacted. Finally, the conceptual framework highlights a series of potential intra- and extrapersonal constructs which may be especially relevant as drivers of the sensemaking process within multicultural teams. Additionally, it has been argued that the sensemaking process, as well as those processes comprising adaptive team coordination, is reciprocal and cyclical in nature. This implies, and the sensemaking literature would also argue, that sensemaking, in and of itself, does not need to be accurate in its reality—only plausible. In the context of promoting multicultural team effectiveness, it may be unlikely, especially for novice team members, that the resulting meaning will be exactly on target in all areas, but we would like to push it as close as we can in that direction. Therefore, the conceptual framework presented in Figure 11.1 also calls out frameswitching as a key construct that should be examined in seeking to understand effective multicultural teams. Frameswitching allows "individuals to interpret their surroundings and determine appropriate actions as they move between contexts that are primarily associated with one culture or another" (Briley, Morris, & Simonson, 2005, p. 351). The ability to switch frames is similar to the concept of perspective taking or seeing the world through the cultural lens of others (see H. A. Klein, 2004). Perspective taking involves "understanding how and why another person thinks and feels about the situation and why they are behaving as they are" (Sessa, 1996, p. 105), or more simply, putting oneself in another's shoes (Galinsky, Ku, & Wang, 2005). In order for individuals to take the perspective of others and adapt their behavior according to the situation, individuals must be high in self-monitoring (Densten & Gray, 2003). High self-monitoring individuals adapt to new situations better and more quickly than those low in self-monitoring (Zaccaro, Foti, & Kennedy, 1991).

Galinsky and Moskowitz (2000) suggest that perspective taking contributes to effectiveness within multicultural teams because it reduces stereotypic responses and increases the overlap "between representations of the self and representation of the outgroup" (p. 708). Research has identified many benefits of perspective taking, including reduction of stereotyping and prejudice, encouraging helping behavior, and promoting social coordination (Galinsky, Ku, & Wang, 2005; Galinsky & Moskowitz, 2000). Additionally, perspective taking facilitates better communication. Research indicates that individuals who engage in perspective-taking frame their conversations to be easily understood by others and disclose more information resulting in greater comprehension of their message by others and overall greater success in communications (Sessa, 1996). Given the above, we argue that to the extent that team members have this ability, it will allow them to get closer to reality in terms of the sensemaking process, as they can interpret the cues not only from their own ethnocentric view but should also be able to incorporate other cultural frames.

Our framework also identifies behavioral flexibility as a skill that should facilitate perspective taking within multicultural teams. When working with multicultural teams, faulty sensemaking and conflicts often occur because of differences in cultural norms, procedures, methods, and ideas. By implementing a strategy to understand others' beliefs and norms, these types of conflicts can be avoided. Team members who score high on measures of behavioral flexibility will have an easier time taking the perspective of others. Zaccaro et al. (1991) explain that behavioral flexibility is actually a two-step process; first individuals must recognize what is expected of them in a situation, which is called social perceptiveness, and then they must respond accordingly, which is the actual behavioral flexibility. Skills needed by individuals to practice behavioral flexibility include negotiation, coaching, persuasion, and conflict management (Zaccaro, 1999).

Other researchers have argued that intercultural competence reflects a form of behavioral flexibility. Davis and Cho (2005) define intercultural competence as an individual's ability to "change one's knowledge, attitudes, and behaviors so as to be open and flexible to other cultures" (p. 4). Rather than the result of something, intercultural competence is an ongoing, transformational process (Taylor, 2004, as cited in Davis &

Cho, 2005). With practice, individuals become skilled at flexible behavior, which leads to the ability to adapt to and become competent in other cultures. Those who have intercultural competence avoid stereotypical judgments about new people and cultures and are able to shed or modify their own cultural norms to accommodate the norms of others (Davis & Cho, 2005). Davis and Cho (2005) explain that for individuals to have intercultural competence, they must also possess other skills and abilities, such as openness, empathy, person-centered communication, and perspective-taking. Behavioral flexibility and intercultural competence is an ongoing process which, if practiced by members of multicultural teams, can facilitate the sensemaking process and prevent the conflicts and pitfalls normally associated with heterogeneous teams.

PRACTICAL IMPLICATIONS

The nature of team interaction within multicultural teams is a complex phenomenon which is not yet well understood. The conceptual framework set forth in Figure 11.1 takes a multidisciplinary perspective in an attempt to examine multicultural teams from a broader perspective than is typically seen within the team's literature. Although the conceptual framework only begins to scratch the surface, a few practical implications can be drawn from the framework and the theoretical underpinnings that have driven its development. A few of these implications will be discussed next. The implications that will be briefly discussed are organized around four themes: methodologies used during investigation, training, design of real-time job aides, and system design. Space and focus preclude us from delving in depth into every aspect of organizational functioning, but a sampling is presented below.

METHODOLOGICAL IMPLICATIONS

Within the discussion of the framework, the importance of examining multicultural teams from a broad, multidisciplinary perspective was noted. The constructs included in Figure 11.1, begin to highlight a multidisciplinary perspective and point to the importance of examining both intrapersonal and extrapersonal factors in the quest to understand the factors impinging on multicultural team effectiveness. The typical way to learn about multicultural teams within the psychology literature has been through surveys, but methods from cultural anthropology add additional insight. The main method of cultural study within anthropology revolves around embedding the phenomena of interest within the context of a world system through ethnographic methodology (G. E. Marcus, 1995). The acceptance within anthropology that "public culture" is internalized and becomes "meaningful and motivating to people" (Quinn & Strauss, 2006, p. 268) allows psychologists and behavioral scientists to more easily incorporate this methodology into our human focused world. By including the methodology of ethnographic studies into organizational and behavioral studies of culture, we can incorporate the anthropological definition of culture and provide structure for individual actions and begin to understand the motivation for the differences in observable behaviors between cultures. This can enable us to better understand how effectively heterogeneous teams may or may not be able to work together, and if not, why not (Dodd, 1991; Helmreich, 2000).

Therefore, research using ethnographic studies, we argue, can help HR and organizational practitioners get at the global context portion of our framework. The embedded global context is a key mechanism in determining what influences an individual team member's social identity and their interaction with team members of different cultures. In addition, an examination of the constructs included in Figure 11.1 are highly cognitive-driven and may be operating at a tacit level; by combining traditional methodologies with ethnographic methods, these constructs can be further unpacked.

Training Implications

To further illustrate the utility of the framework, we point to the application of the framework to develop training for multicultural teams with the ultimate objective of promoting multicultural team effectiveness through adaptive team coordination. The framework begins to highlight the types of processes that practitioners and human resource personnel need to be developing within organizational work teams that are culturally diverse. In addition, the framework begins to identify the manner in which team leaders may be able to engineer the situation such that cues trigger the one type of identity (i.e., social, personal) dependent on team needs.

By virtue of the constructs included, the framework can also begin to highlight some implications in terms of the manner in which team members are developed. For example, scenario-based training (SBT) and storytelling are both methods that, though not traditionally used to train multicultural teams, could offer a benefit to practitioners. Scenario-based training uses scenarios as content and allows training to take place within relevant context. The method consists of "trigger" events and metrics tied to learning objects which are embedded within scenarios to illicit the targeted behaviors. The use of SBT would benefit the training of MCTs in a number of ways. For example, SBT is immersive and engaging, in that scenarios within SBT allow trainees to interact with "realistic situations that will facilitate learning" (Oser, Cannon-Bowers, Salas, & Dwyer, 1999, p. 454). Moreover, as Figure 11.1 points to a need for training to go beyond knowledge (i.e., needed in terms of the contextual drivers), it also points to the importance of guided practice so that skills such as sensemaking can be developed in an efficient manner. Moreover, the notation of behavioral flexibility suggests that training needs to create team member mental models, which have the breadth to allow pattern matching along a variety of axes in order to promote behavioral flexibility. SBT relies on the foundation of guided practice that is grounded in context, in which the presentation of a variety of scenarios can be accomplished in a relatively short time frame. This exposure, in turn, serves to increase the breadth of trainees' mental models by creating varied learning opportunities. Scenarios embedded within SBT allow learners to see how different performance strategies can be applied across a number of situations and how those strategies work out (Oser, Cannon-Bowers, Salas, & Dwyer, 1999). This, in turn, promotes behavioral flexibility through the acquisition of intercultural competence based on practice, which leads to the ability to adapt to and become competent in other cultures. Ultimately, SBT enables learners to create a "microworld" that increases the psychological fidelity, experimental realism, and learner experimentation (Bowers & Jentsch, 2001; Senge, 1990). Therefore, SBT provides "rich experiences" during training, which accelerate learning and the acquisition of expertise relevant to multicultural environments.

In addition to SBT, storytelling is a method by which the knowledge and value components contained within the framework can be promoted. Bruner (1990) argues that creating stories is one manner in which individuals make sense of a complex situation. Storytelling has been described as a social experience, a means to connect to others and develop professional identities (Shank, 2006). Moreover, it has been argued that storytelling has a number of purposes, among them, to: communicate who you are, instill organizational values, build collaboration, transmit knowledge and understanding, neutralize rumor, create vision (Denning, 2005). As a matter of fact, storytelling is a key way that many cultures transmit cultural values. Although useful as a stand-alone method through which more tacit type of information and values may be transmitted, it could also be embedded within the SBT framework as a component piece for how scenarios are crafted.

Job Aid Implications

Another practical application of this framework is in the guidance of system design in the form of job aids. Job aids are tools that organizations develop to help or assist users in how they perform their tasks (Swezey, 1987) and may facilitate transfer. Job aids help decrease the amount of training time workers need and minimize the cognitive load, ultimately improving performance. Job aids can be informational, procedural, or decision making and coaching (Rossett & Gautier-Downes, 1991). The type of job aid that should be developed depends on the needs of the worker performing the task. For example, informational job aids are used during a task and provide access to large amounts of information (e.g., online databases). Procedural aids, on the other hand, provide step-by-step instructions on how to complete a task (e.g., directions for installing software), and decision making and coaching provide heuristics for guiding users though tasks.

The conceptual framework presented in Figure 11.1 serves to begin to identify the factors important in seeking to understand multicultural teams, specifically the need to promote adaptive team coordination. In doing so, some portions could be extracted and the information provided to team members in the form of a job aid. For example, knowing that a team needs to understand the context of other team members, job aids can be designed to provide historical and political background offering global context from another perspective. Additionally, job aids may be designed to assist members in determining the cues that will elicit others' attention, or cue them to enact a social or personal identity; all of which impact how meaning is assigned and, in turn, what is expected.

System Design Implications

A final example from the current framework relates to interface design. Specifically, one issue that comes out of this framework is the lack of a common picture among those coming from different backgrounds, who are thus influenced by different global contexts. Individuals on a team need to identify with the others on their team, despite these differences. Displays for systems can be designed to provide MCTs with a common ground view of the world. Some cultures depend more on data; others depend more on dialogue because of their emphasis on history or cultural tendency toward hard facts. As discussed earlier, this can be examined within terms of dialogue- versus data-driven cultural team members (Lewis, 1999). System design based on the information provided in the proposed framework will be informed by the drivers of these tendencies allowing for more culturally focused and, ideally, efficient utility of the system. For example, interfaces could be designed to target either data or dialogue, depending on both the global context and the cues needed for the team to form a group identity. Thus, interface can be designed to provide data to data-oriented cultures and a more historical, storytelling-themed interface for dialogue-oriented team members. In this way, the entire team can obtain the cues they need in the way that makes sense for them culturally. For example, knowing that design implications, though still in need of exploration, should be driven by the needs of the teams outlined in this framework.

The framework and corresponding discussion also highlights the fact that within multicultural teams, much information remains hidden or tacit. System designers should strive to not only develop displays that will facilitate the creation and maintenance of common ground. But, as this is a lofty goal, another approach is to design such systems so that they facilitate the uncovering of tacit assumptions. This could be through the use of probes related to exposing team member backgrounds or by designing systems that present information in multiple modalities so that cultural preferences are likely to be met and cues extracted in a more timely manner.

THE ROAD AHEAD: FUTURE RESEARCH

Given the globalization movement and technological advances, it would appear that multicultural teams are here to stay. One of the finest features of multicultural teams is their *potential* to outperform homogeneous teams due to their diverse perspectives, experiences, and backgrounds. Yet, within many teams, this potential is not realized. Current methods for understanding multicultural teams have tended to rely almost solely on the use of Hofstede's cultural dimensions or compared teams that were not necessarily multicultural, as they were internally homogeneous. To illustrate the latter point, research has often compared an American team's performance of a particular task to that of an Asian team on the same task. As a field, we have not yet even begun to scratch the surface in understanding what truly comprises effectiveness within multicultural teams. What distinguishes effective multicultural teams from those that are less effective? How different are the challenges they face from those faced by traditional teams? Because of the present dearth of research that truly examines multicultural teams, there are rich opportunities for further fine-tuning and extending our understanding of multicultural teams.

Figure 11.1 was designed as an initial framework and not a prescriptive model; however, there are still many research questions which can be derived even at the framework level. Below we present five such questions, which are organized to tap each aspect of the conceptual framework.

Research Direction 1: Future research needs to examine the nature of adaptive team coordination within MCTs.

A few researchers (e.g., Sieck, Smith, & McHugh, 2005; Sutton et al., 2006) have begun to examine how the different teamwork dimensions so commonly identified within the United States are operationalized across different cultures, but much remains to be done. Not only are there questions pertaining to differences across culture in their manifestation, but also about how these differences interact when you have a multicultural team? The work that has been conducted by Gibson and Zellmer-Bruhn (2001), H. A. Klein (2004), Chao and Moon (2005), as well as Harrison and Klein (in press) might provide a starting point to further examine these questions.

Research Direction 2: Future research should delineate how each stage of the sensemaking process occurs across cultures?

Additionally, several research questions are driven by the sensemaking approach to understanding adaptive team coordination within multicultural teams, which was taken in the current paper. The description offered of the sensemaking process within the current framework is only a first step, and the information found in the sensemaking literature on the actual stages within the overarching process was rather abstract. Therefore, the current paper attempted to pull guidance from other literature domains in an effort to make the description of the process a bit more concrete. Future research should not only continue to delve deeper into these processes but also examine the manner in which each stage (e.g., cue extraction, cue framing, meaning assignment) is actually operationalized across cultures. The current framework only begins to touch the surface by suggesting several contextual drivers that may impact the cues that are extracted. Research needs to further drill down into the exact manner in which this happens. It seems that there are more questions than answers at this point in the study of multicultural teams, but that means that it is an area rich for examination and, therefore, a very exciting time. We look forward to continued thought and dialogue on this topic and hope that the conceptual framework offered herein provides an impetus for future work.

Research Direction 3: Future research should examine the KSAs which contribute to frameswitching and how this process moderates the relationship between sensemaking and adaptive team coordination.
The ability to switch frames or engage in perspective taking, in which members are able to view the world from the lens of the cultures with whom they are interacting, has been argued to be key in determining the accuracy of the sensemaking process. The larger literature on sensemaking would argue that the outcomes of sensemaking do not need to be accurate—only plausible. However, when members are interdependent and coordination is required, the outcome of this process needs to be fairly accurate. The resulting cognitive states, which are a proximal outcome to the sensemaking process, are what guide the behaviors within the adaptive coordination cycle. The framework presented in Figure 11.1 would suggest that the degree to which members can volley back and forth between different cultural lenses or viewpoints will assist in the sensemaking process. However, research is not only needed to verify this proposition but also to investigate the antecedents to frameswitching, as well as the KSAs which comprise the construct. Additionally, research should examine if the ability to switch frames is differentially important across the various phases of the sensemaking process.

Research Direction 4: Future research needs to examine the sensemaking process within multicultural teams at a much finer level of detail.
Within this chapter we have argued that by taking a sensemaking approach to understanding multicultural teams, the field can begin to move beyond traditional cross-cultural research, where the focus is primarily on a small set of dimensions on which nations are said to vary. However, although sensemaking is the first step, a necessary but not sufficient condition, toward team effectiveness within multicultural teams, the sensemaking literature base fails to offer much in the way of

prescriptive guidance. There is no question that as humans we engage in sensemaking on a daily basis, nor that it consists of processes such as cue extraction, cue framing, and meaning assignment; however, when one really begins to probe in terms of how each one of these phases occurs, the detailed information is not there. Future research needs to begin to investigate descriptive models of the process within multicultural teams that contain enough detail such that practitioner guidelines can be developed.

Research Direction 5: Future research should examine the drivers of sensemaking within multicultural teams.

The last future research direction that will be discussed pertains to research that begins to identify the drivers or antecedents to the sensemaking process. For example, sensemaking involves the extraction of cues from the environment, but exactly how are these cues extracted from the ongoing flow of experience? What are the factors which cause cues to stand out? Within this chapter we have suggested at a high level what some of these factors may be, but future research needs to examine these. Is there a common set of drivers that exists across multicultural teams regardless of culture?

The framework presented in Figure 11.1 also identifies social and personal identity as contextual drivers of sensemaking within multicultural teams. Within multicultural settings, exactly what are the situational contexts that cause one to assume one identify over the many they possess? Again, although we can begin to extract some propositions from within the broader literature on identity theory, we really know very little in terms of how the situational context impacts the manner in which individual team members act within multicultural contexts (see Matsumoto, in press).

CONCLUDING REMARKS

The framework advanced herein is one attempt to push the field forward. It is of theoretical importance in that it extends previous theoretical endeavors in at least three ways. First, the framework represents a multidisciplinary view of multicultural teams through the incorporation of literature from cultural anthropology, cognitive engineering, communication, organizational, cognitive, cross-cultural and social psychology. Second, rather than taking the traditional cultural awareness view of multicultural teams, the framework moves beyond to begin to suggest the manner in which members make sense of the adaptive coordination requirements in multicultural teams. Specifically, the framework begins to highlight not only the processes involved in the sensemaking but, more importantly, contextual drivers that serve to determine what cues are extracted from the ongoing work flow, as well as how their meaning is interpreted. This framework is perhaps the first to take such an approach to understanding multicultural teams. Most of the work done on multicultural teams has focused almost exclusively on the need to understand how countries differ along Hofstede's dimensions and how this may impact team member interactions. Finally, though the framework needs to be expanded further and developed into a conceptual model, it serves to highlight the cyclical and recursive nature of not only adaptive team coordination (see Burke et al., 2006, for further information), but the sensemaking process in and of itself. Moreover, it acknowledges the fact that culture is not static, but fluid and dynamic both within and across cultures. This, in turn, drives the need to understand more than just culture per se, but the economic, political, historical, and religious aspects that underlie culture and cause it to shift in time. At an individual level, social identity theory is also an important addition, given that researchers such as Triandis, as well as cultural anthropologists, argue for variation within individuals.

We hope that the framework proposed within the current chapter serves to promote discussion, debate, and food for thought. It was purposely created as a framework which could be expanded into a conceptual (and predictive) model with formal propositions as more work is conducted and thought put forth. We hope the thoughts, framework, and practical implications discussed herein are the first steps in understanding the complexity in multicultural teamwork.

Author Note: This work was supported by funding from the Army Research Laboratory's Advanced Decision Architecture Collaborative Technology Alliance (Cooperative Agreement DAA D19-01-2-0009). All opinions expressed in this chapter are those of the authors and do not necessarily reflect the official opinion or position of the University of Central Florida, the U.S. Army Research Laboratory or the Department of Defense.

REFERENCES

Adler, N. (1986). *International dimensions of organizational behavior.* Boston: Kent.

Argote, L., & McGrath, J. E. (1993). Group processes in organisations: Continuity and change. *International Review of Industrial and Organisational Psychology, 8,* 333–389.

Bearden, W. O., Money, R. B., & Nevins, J. L. (2006, February). Multidimensional versus unidimensional measures in assessing national culture values: The Hofstede VSM 94 example. *Journal of Business Research, 59*(2), 195–203.

Bowers, C. & Jentsch, F. (2001). Use of commercial, off-the-shelf, simulations in team research. In E. Salas (Ed.), *Advances in Human Performance and Cognitive Engineering Research, Vol. 1* (pp. 291–315). Amsterdam, NL: Elsevier Science.

Briley, D. A., Morris, M. W., & Simonson, I. (2005). Cultural chameleons: Biculturals, conformity motives, and decision making. *Journal of Consumer Psychology, 15*(4), 351–362.

Bruner, J. S. (1990). *Acts of meaning.* Cambridge, MA: Harvard University Press.

Burke, C. S., Stagl, K. C., Salas, E., Pierce, L., & Kendall, D. (2006). Understanding team adaptation: A conceptual analysis and model. *Journal of Applied Psychology, 91*(6), 1189–1207.

Cannon-Bowers, J. A., Tannenbaum, S. I., Salas, E., & Volpe, C. E. (1995). Defining competencies and establishing team training requirements. In R. Guzzo & Salas (Eds.), *Team effectiveness and decision making in organizations* (pp. 333–380). San Francisco: Jossey-Bass.

Carlson, R. A. (1997). *Experienced cognition.* Mahwah, NJ: Erlbaum.

Chao, G. T., & Moon, H. (2005). The cultural mosaic: A metatheory for understanding the complexity of culture. *Journal of Applied Psychology, 90*(6), 1128–1140.

Charness, N. (1989). Expertise in chess and bridge. In D. Klahr & K. Kotovsky (Eds.), *Complex information processing: The impact of Herbert A. Simon.* Hillsdale, NJ: Erlbaum.

Chiang, F. (2005, September). A critical examination of Hofstede's thesis and its application to international reward management. *International Journal of Human Resource Management, 16*(9), 1545–1563.

Choo, C. W. (2006). *The knowing organization: How organizations use information to construct meaning, create knowledge, and make decisions.* New York: Oxford University Press.

Cohen, S. G., & Bailey, D. E. (1997). What makes teams work: Group effectiveness research from the shop floor to the executive suite. *Journal of Management, 23,* 239–290.

Copeland, M. V. (2006). The mighty micro-multinational. *Business 2.0 Magazine, 7*(6). Retrieved on October 2, 2006, from http://money.cnn.com/magazines/business2/

Cox, T. H., Lobel, S. A., & McLeod, P. L. (1991). Effects of ethnic group cultural differences on cooperative and competitive behavior on a group task. *Academy of Management Journal, 34*(4), 827–847.

D'Andrade, R. (1995). *The development of cognitive anthropology.* Cambridge, UK: Cambridge University Press.

Davis, N., & Cho, M. O. (2005). Intercultural competence for future leaders of educational technology and its evaluation. *Interactive Educational Multimedia, 10,* 1–22.

Denning, S. (2005). *A leaders' guide to storytelling.* San Francisco, CA: Jossey-Bass.

Densten, I. L., & Gray, J. H. (2003). *Leadership applications: Organizational effectiveness* (CFLI Contract Research Rep. No. CR02-0620). Kingston, ON: Canadian Forces Leadership Institute.

Dhamoon, R. (2006). Shifting from "culture" to "the cultural": Critical theorizing of identity/difference politics. *Constellations, 13*(3), 354–373.

Dickinson, T. L., & McIntyre, R. M. (1997). A conceptual framework for team measurement. In M. T. Brannick, E. Salas, & C. Prince (Eds.), *Team performance and measurement: Theory, methods, and applications* (pp. 19–43). Mahwah, NJ: Erlbaum.

Dodd, C. (1991). *Dynamics of intercultural communication* (3rd ed.). Dubuque, IA: William C. Brown.

Doosje, B., Ellemers, N., & Spears, R. (1995). Perceived intragroup variability as a function of group status and identification. *Journal of Experimental Social Psychology, 31,* 410–436.

Ellemers, N., Kortekaas, P., & Ouwerkerk, J. W. (1999). Self-categorization, commitment to the group and social self-esteem as related but distinct aspects of social identity. *European Journal of Social Psychology, 28*, 371–398.

Ellemers, N., Spears, R., & Doosje, B. (2002). Self and social identity theory. *Annual Review of Psychology, 53*, 161–186.

Entin, E. E., & Serfaty, D. (1999). Adaptive team coordination. *Human Factors, 41*, 312–325.

Filley, A. C., House, R. J., & Kerr, S. (1976). *Managerial process and organizational behavior.* Glenview, IL: Scott, Foresman.

Ford, M. E., & Tisak, M. S. (1983). A further search for social intelligence. *Journal of Educational Research, 75*, 196–206.

Galinsky, A. D., Ku, G., & Wang, C. S. (2005). Perspective-taking and self-other overlap: Fostering social bonds and facilitating social coordination. *Group Processes and Intergroup Relations, 8*(2), 109–124.

Galinsky, A. D., & Moskowitz, G. B. (2000). Perspective-taking: Decreasing stereotype expression, stereotype accessibility, and in-group favoritism. *Journal of Personality and Social Psychology, 78*(4), 708–724.

Gersick, C. J. G., & Hackman, J. R. (1990). Habitual routines in task performing groups. *Organizational Behavior and Human Decision Processes, 47*, 65–97.

Gibson, C. B., & Zellmer-Bruhn, M. E. (2001). Metaphors and meaning: An intercultural analysis of the concept of teamwork. *Administrative Science Quarterly, 46*, 274–303.

Gioia, D. A. (1989). Self-serving bias as a self-sensemaking strategy: Explicit versus tacit impression management. In R. Giacalone & P. Rosenfeld (Eds.), *Impression management in the organization* (pp. 219–234). Hillsdale, NJ: Erlbaum.

Hackman, J. R., & Wageman, R. (2005). A theory of team coaching. *The Academy of Management Review, 30*(2), 269–287.

Hambrick, D. C., & Brandon, G. (1988). Executive values. In D. C. Hambrick (Ed.). *The executive effect: Concepts and methodologies for studying top managers.* Greenwich, CT: JAI Press.

Hambrick, D. C., Davison, S. C., Snell, S. A., & Snow, C. C. (1998). When groups consist of multiple nationalities: Towards a new understanding of the implications. *Organization Studies, 19*, 181–205.

Hannerz, U. (1992). *Cultural complexity: Studies in the social organization of meaning.* New York: Columbia University Press.

Harrison, D. A., & Klein, K. J. (in press). What's the difference? Diversity constructs as separation, variety, or disparity in organizations. *Academy of Management Review.*

Haslam, S. A., Powell, C., & Turner, J. C. (2000). Social identity, self-categorization, and work motivation: Rethinking the contribution of the group to positive and sustainable organizational outcomes. *Applied Psychology: An International Review, 49*(3), 319–339.

Helmreich, R. L. (2000). On error management. Lessons from aviation. *British Medical Journal, 320*, 781–785.

Hess, D. J. (1995). *Science & technology in a multicultural world.* New York, NY: Columbia University Press.

Hill, R. C., & Levenhagen, M. (1995). Metaphors and mental models: Sensemaking and sensegiving in innovative and entrepreneurial activities. *Journal of Management, 21*(6), 1057–1074.

Hofstede, G. (1980). *Culture's consequences: International differences in work-related values.* Beverly Hills, CA: Sage.

Ilgen, D. R., LePine, J. A., & Hollenbeck, J. R. (1997). Effective decision making in multinational teams. In P. C. Earley & M. Erez (Eds.), *New perspectives on international industrial/ organizational psychology* (pp. 377–409). San Francisco: New Lexington Press/Jossey-Bass.

Jackson, S. E. (1992). Team composition in organizational settings: Issues in managing a diverse workforce. In S. Worchel, W. Wood, & J. Simpson (Eds.), *Group process and productivity* (pp. 138–173). Thousand Oaks, CA: Sage.

Jacob, N. (2005). Cross-cultural investigations: Emerging concepts. *Journal of Organizational Change Management, 18(5),* 514–528.

Jetten, J., Spears, R., & Manstead, A.S.R. (1999). Group distinctiveness and intergroup discrimination. In N. Ellemers, R. Spears & B. Doosje (Eds.), *Social identity: Context, commitment, content* (pp. 107–126). Oxford: Blackwell.

Jetten, J., Spears, R., & Manstead, A.S.D. (2001). Similarity as a source of discrimination: The role of group identification. *European Journal of Social Psychology, 31(6),* 621–640.

Keltner, D., & Haidt, J. (1999). Social functions of emotions at four levels of analysis. *Cognition & Emotion, 13,* 505–521.

Klein, G. (1998). *Sources of power: How people make decisions.* Cambridge, MA: MIT Press.

Klein, H. A. (2004). Cognition in natural settings: The cultural lens model. In M. Kaplan (Ed.), *Advances in human performance and cognitive engineering research: Vol. 4. Cultural ergonomics* (pp. 249–280). Amsterdam: Elsevier.

Kozlowski, S. W. J. (1998). Training and developing adaptive teams: Theory, principles, and research. In J. A. Cannon-Bowers & E. Salas (Eds.), *Making decisions under stress: Implications for individual and team training* (pp. 115–153). Washington, DC: American Psychological Association.

Kymlicka, W. (1995). *Multicultural citizenship: A liberal theory of minority rights.* Oxford, UK: Oxford University Press.

Leedom, D. K. (2001). *Final Report: Sensemaking Symposium.* (Technical Report prepared under contract for Office of Assistant Secretary of Defense for Command, Control, Communications & Intelligence). Vienna, VA: Evidence Based Research. Inc.

Lewis, R. D. (1999). *When cultures collide: Managing successfully across cultures.* London: Nicholas Brealey.

Louis, M. R. (1980). Surprise and sense making: What newcomers experience in entering unfamiliar organizational settings. *Administrative Science Quarterly, 25,* 226–250.

Malinowski, B. (1994). The problem of meaning in primitive language. In J. Maybin (Ed.), *Language and literacy in social practice: A reader* (pp. 1–10). Philadelphia: Open University Press.

Marcus, A. & Gould, E. W. (2000). Crosscurrents: Cultural dimensions and global web user-interface design. *Interactions, 7(4),* 32–46.

Marcus, G. E. (1995, October). Ethnography in/of the world system: The emergence of multi-sited ethnography. *Annual Review of Anthropology, 24,* 95–117.

Marcus, G. E., & Fischer, M. J. (1999). *Anthropology as cultural critique: An experimental moment in the human sciences* (2nd ed.). Chicago: University of Chicago Press.

Marks, M. A., & Panzer, F. J. (2004). The influence of team monitoring on team processes and performance. *Human Performance, 17*, 25–42.

Marlowe, H. A. (1986). Social intelligence: Evidence for multidimensionality and construct independence. *Journal of Educational Psychology, 78*(1), 52–58.

Matsumoto, D. (2001). Culture and Emotion. In D. Matsumoto (Ed.), *The Handbook of Culture and Psychology*. New York: Oxford University Press.

Maznevski, M. L., & Chudoba, K. M. (2000). Bridging space over time: Global virtual team dynamics and effectiveness. *Organization Science, 11*(5), 473–489.

McGrath, J. E. (1984). *Groups: Interaction and performance*. Englewood Cliffs, NJ: Prentice-Hall.

McIntyre, R. M., & Salas, E. (1995). Measuring and managing for team performance: Emerging principles from complex environments. In R. Guzzo & E. Salas (Eds.), *Team effectiveness and decision making in organizations* (pp. 149–203). San Francisco: Jossey-Bass.

Merriam, S. B., Johnson-Bailey, J., Lee, M. Y., Kee, Y., Ntseane, G., & Muhamad, M. (2001). Power and positionality: Negotiating insider/outsider status within and across cultures. *International Journal of Lifelong Education, 20*(5), 405–416.

Mussweiler, R. T., Gabriel, S., & Bodenhausen, G. V. (2000). Shifting social identities as a strategy for deflecting threatening social comparisons. *Journal of Personality Social Psychology, 79*, 398–409.

Mutman, M. (2006, June). Writing culture: Postmodernism and ethnography. *Anthropological Theory, 6*(2), 153–178.

Ortner, S. B. (2005, March). Subjectivity and cultural critique. *Anthropological Theory, 5*(1), 31–52.

Oser, R. L., Cannon-Bowers, J. A., Salas, E., & Dwyer, D. J. (1999). Enhancing human performance in technology-rich environments: Guidelines for scenario-based training. In E. Salas (Ed.), *Human/technology interaction in complex systems* (Vol. 9, 175–202). Greenwich, CT: JAI Press.

Pelled, L. H. (1996). Demographic diversity, conflict, and workgroup outcomes: An intervening process theory. *Organization Science, 7*, 615–631.

Porter, C. O., Hollenbeck, J. R., Ilgen, D. R., Ellis, A. P. J., West, B. J., & Moon, H. (2003). Backing up behaviors in teams: The role of personality and legitimacy of need. *Journal of Applied Psychology, 3*, 391–403.

Postman, L., Bruner, J. S., & McGinnies, E. (1948). Personal values as selective factors in perception. *Journal of Abnormal and Social Psychology, 43*, 142–154.

Quinn, N., & Strauss, C. (2006). Introduction to special issue on the missing psychology in cultural anthropology's key words. *Anthropological Theory, 6*(3), 267–279.

Ring, P. S., & Rands, G. P. (1989): Sensemaking, understanding, and committing: Emergent interpersonal transaction processes in the evolution of 3M's microgravity research program. In A. H. Van den Ven, H. L. Angle, & M. S. Poole (Eds.), *Research on the management of innovation. The Minnesota studies* (pp. 337–366). New York: Ballinger.

Roseberry, W. (1989). *Anthropologies and histories: Essays in culture, history, and political economy*. New Brunswick, NJ: Rutgers University Press.

Rosset, A. & Gautier-Downes, J. (1991). *A handbook of job aids.* San Francisco: Jossey-Bass Pfieffer.

Salas, E., Burke, C. S., & Stagl, K. C. (2004). Developing teams and team leaders: Srategies and principles. In D. Day, S. J. Zaccaro, & S. M. Halpin (Eds.), *Leader development for transforming organizations* (pp. 325–355). Mahwah, NJ: Erlbaum.

Salas, E., Cannon-Bowers, J. A., Fiore, S. M., & Stout, R. J. (2001). Cue-recognition training to enhance team situation awareness. In M. McNeese, E. Salas, & M. Endsley (Eds.), *New trends in cooperative activities: Understanding system dynamics in complex environments* (pp. 169–190). Santa Monica, CA: Human Factors and Ergonomics Society.

Salas, E., Prince, C., Baker, D. P., & Shrestha, L. (1995). Situation awareness in team performance: Implications for measurement and training. *Human Factors, 37,* 123–136.

Salas, E., Stagl, K. C., Burke, C. S., & Goodwin, G. F. (2007). Fostering team effectiveness in organizations: Toward an integrative theoretical framework of team performance. In W. Spaulding & J. Flowers, (Eds.), *Modeling complex systems: Motivation, cognition and social processes* (pp. 185–243). Lincoln, NE: University of Nebraska Press.

Senge, P. M. 1990. *The Fifth Discipline.* New York: Doubleday/Currency.

Sessa, V. I. (1996). Using perspective taking to manage conflict and affect in teams. *Journal of Applied Behavioral Science, 32*(1), 101–115.

Shank, M. (2006, August). Teacher storytelling: A means for creating and learning within a collaborative space. *Teaching and Teacher Education, 22(6),* 711–721.

Shore, B. (1991). Twice-born, once conceived: Meaning construction and cultural cognition. *American Anthropologist, 93*(1), 9–27.

Sieck, W., Smith, J. L., & McHugh, A. P. (2005). Team competencies in multinational collaboration. Year 5 Final Report (#05TA2-SP1-RT1). Prepared through participation in the Advanced Decision Architectures Collaborative Technology Alliance sponsored by the US Army Research Laboratory under Cooperative Agreement DAA D19-01-2-0009.

Silk, J. B. (1987). Social behavior in evolutionary perspective. In B. B. Smuts, D. L. Cheney, R. M. Seyfarth, R. W. Wrangham, & T. T. Struhsaker (Eds.), *Primate societies* (pp. 318–329). Chicago: University of Chicago Press.

Spears, R., Doosje, B., & Ellemers, N. (1999). Commitment and the context of social perception. In N. Ellemers, R. Spears, & B. Doosje (Eds.), *Social identity: Context, commitment, content* (pp. 59–83). Oxford, UK: Blackwell.

Starbuck, W. H., & Milliken, F. J. (1988). Executive perceptual filters: What they notice and how they make sense. In D. Hambrick (Ed.), *The executive effect: Concepts and methods for studying top managers* (pp. 35–65). Greenwich, CT: JAI Press.

Strauss, C., & Quinn, N. (1997). *A cognitive theory of cultural meaning.* Cambridge, UK: Cambridge University Press.

Sutton, J. L., Pierce, L. G., Burke, C. S., & Salas, E. (2006). Cultural adaptability. In C. S. Burke, L. Pierce, & E. Salas (Eds.), *Advances in human performance and cognitive engineering research* (pp. 143–173). Oxford, UK: Elsevier Science.

Swezey, R. W. (1987). Design of job aids and procedure writing. In G. Salvendy (Ed.), *Handbook of human factors* (pp. 1039–1057). New York: Wiley.

Taylor, C. (1992). The politics of recognition. In A. Gutmann (Ed.), *Multiculturalism and the politics of recognition* (pp. 25–73). Princeton, NJ: Princeton University Press.

Thomas, J. B., Clark, S. M., & Gioia, D. A. (1993). Strategic sensemaking and organizational performance: Linkages among scanning, interpretation, action, and outcomes. *Academy of Management Journal, 36*(2), 239–270.

Triandis, H. C., Hall, E. R., & Ewen, R. B. (1965). Some cognitive factors affecting group creativity. *Human Relations, 18*(1), 33–35.

Trompenaars, F. (1993). *Riding the waves of culture: Understanding cultural diversity in business.* London: Nicholas Brealey Publishing.

Tully, J. (1995). *Strange multiplicity: Constitutionalism in an age of diversity.* Cambridge, UK: Cambridge University Press.

Weick, K. E. (1979). *The social psychology of organizing.* Reading, MA: Addison-Wesley.

Weick, K. E. (1995). *Sensemaking in organizations.* Thousand Oaks, CA: Sage.

Wilk, R. R. (1996). *Economies and cultures: Foundations of economic anthropology.* Boulder, CO: Westview Press.

Zaccaro, S. J. (1999). Social complexity and the competencies required for effective military leadership. In J. G. Hunt, G. E. Dodge, & L. Wong (Eds.), *Out-of-the-box leadership: Transforming the twenty-first-century army and other top-performing organizations* (pp. 131–151). Stamford, CT: JAI Press.

Zaccaro, S. J., Foti, R. J., & Kenny, D. A. (1991). Self-monitoring and trait-based variance in leadership: An investigation of leader flexibility across multiple group situations. *Journal of Applied Psychology, 76*(2), 308–315.

Zaccaro, S. J., Gilbert, J., Thor, K. K., & Mumford, M. D. (1991). Leadership and social intelligence: linking social perceptiveness and behavioral flexibility to leader effectiveness. *Leadership Quarterly, 2,* 317–331.

Zaccaro, S. J., & Marks, M. A. (1999). The roles of leaders in high-performance teams. In E. Sundstrom & Associates (Eds.), *Supporting work team effectiveness: Best management practices for fostering high performance* (pp. 95–125). San Francisco: Jossey-Bass.

12

Culture and Human Resource Management:
Prospects for the Future

EUGENE F. STONE-ROMERO
AND DIANNA L. STONE
University of Texas at San Antonio

As the chapters in this book clearly suggest, the cultural diversity of organizations has increased markedly in the past three decades. As a result, organizations are facing a growing need to deal with the consequences of this increased cultural diversity for various human resource management (HRM)-related processes and practices. Among the processes and practices considered by chapter authors are recruitment, selection, training, motivation, and compensation and benefits administration. Triandis and Wasti (Chapter 1) describe numerous dimensions along which cultures differ and briefly consider the impact of cultural differences on HRM-related processes and practices.

A MODEL OF THE EFFECTS OF CULTURE ON HRM PROCESSES AND PRACTICES

Figure 12.1 shows the effects of culture on such processes and practices on three general phases: pre-hire, selection, and post-hire. Two categories or types of culture have a bearing on HRM processes and practices.

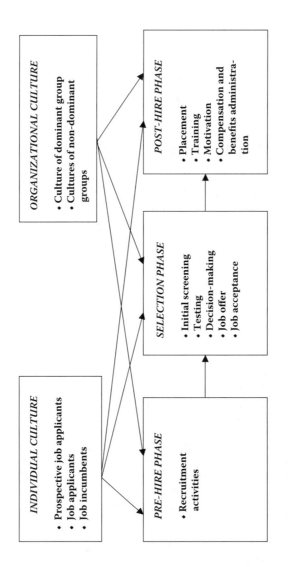

Figure 12.1   Impact of Individual Culture and Organizational Culture on Human Resource Management Processes and Practices.

The first is the culture of individuals, including prospective job applicants, job applicants, and job incumbents. The second is organizational culture, which is a function of the cultures of the dominant and nondominant groups in an organization (Stone-Romero & Stone, 2007). We believe that the cultures of individuals may influence HRM processes and practices at all of the just-noted phases. At the pre-hire phase, the cultures of prospective job applicants (e.g., culture-based values) influence the degree to which they will be attracted to an organization and motivated to become organizational members. This is illustrated by Stone, Isenhour, and Lukaszewski's chapter on recruitment (Chapter 2). At the selection phase, the cultures of job applicants affect their responses to tests designed to assess their predicted job success, and thereby the odds of their being offered a job. Stone-Romero and Thornson (Chapter 4) address this issue with respect to the use of personality measures in selection. Finally, at the post-hire phase, the cultures of job incumbents influence their reactions to job conditions. Joshi and Martocchio (Chapter 8) show this effect in the context of individuals' reactions to compensation systems and the administration of benefits.

We posit that HRM processes and practices also are a function of organizational culture. It is determined largely by the culture (e.g., values, ideologies) of the dominant group (e.g., able-bodied, white, male, Anglo-Saxon, Protestants) in an organization (Stone-Romero & Stone, in press). However, members of nondominant groups (e.g., females, racial minorities, people with disabilities) may also have an effect on an organization's culture. Thus, for example, as a result of a number of forces (e.g., social, legal), relative to the mid-20th century, organizations now have cultures that are far more family friendly and accepting of racial diversity. Cleveland, McCarthy, and Himelright (Chapter 10) consider the former issue. In addition, as noted by Ferris and Treadway (Chapter 6), organizational culture influences the design of performance appraisal systems and the way that appraisal information is used to influence the behavior of ratees. Moreover, as detailed by Bhagat, Steverson, and Segovis (Chapter 9), organizational culture influences the design of employee assistance programs.

IMPLICATIONS FOR RESEARCH

Relative to research on other phenomena of interest to scholars in such fields as industrial and organizational psychology, HRM, and organizational behavior, research on the influence of culture on HRM processes and practices is very limited. In addition, any given study on this topic typically considers only a limited number (e.g., two or three) of cultures. In view of the paucity of studies, we are unable to detail how specific dimensions of culture (e.g., individualism, uncertainty avoidance, masculinity) influence various HRM processes and practices across a wide range of cultures or subcultures. Thus, research is needed that addresses this general issue. However, conducting these studies will prove problematic because of the need to develop and validate needed measures. In addition, it will be very difficult to control possible confounds in cross-cultural studies. Moreover, unless studies use large samples that are representative of the targets of generalization, their external validity will be open to question. Nevertheless, we believe that a great increase in research effort is needed to develop a better understanding of the influence of culture on HRM processes and practices.

IMPLICATIONS FOR PRACTICE

Cultural differences have important implications for the design of HRM policies, processes, and practices. Most of the HRM practices in U.S. organizations were designed to attract, motivate, and retain individuals who are members of the dominant culture (e.g., Anglo-Saxons, males, able-bodied individuals). Given the changing composition of the workforce, we believe, as do others (Cox, 1993), that current HRM processes and practices should be modified to meet the needs and values of people from diverse cultures and subcultures.

For example, in order for organizations to attract and retain members of diverse cultures, they may first have to recognize that job applicants and incumbents vary in terms of their cultural values. As a result, organizations might alter their recruitment and reward systems to meet the needs of individuals from varying cultural backgrounds. At present, many U.S. organizations use individualistically oriented incentive systems (e.g., merit pay). Such systems may not be as motivating to workers who stress collective values as they are to those who endorse individualistic values. Thus, instead of using standardized reward systems that appeal to only members of the dominant culture, organizations might adopt cafeteria-based reward systems that allow individuals to select the types of job outcomes or rewards that best meet their needs. Stated somewhat differently, to the extent possible, compensation and benefit systems should be aligned with the cultural values of the new diverse workforce.

In addition, although current selection systems in U.S. organizations are designed to assess the knowledge, skill, and ability levels of job applicants, they often measure individual characteristics that are valued by dominant organizational cultures (e.g., assertiveness, competitive achievement, individualism). As a result, selection systems are often biased in favor of people who endorse traditional value systems (Stone-Romero, 2005). Thus, organizations that want to increase employee diversity may have to modify their selection systems to ensure that predictors assess the knowledge, skill, and ability levels of applicants rather than their cultural characteristics. Similarly, selection techniques (e.g., cognitive ability tests, interviews) may have to be altered to ensure they have criterion-related validity for job applicants from different cultural backgrounds.

Furthermore, in view of the changing nature of the workforce, training systems should be congruent with the needs and cultural values of individuals from diverse cultures. For instance, additional training may be needed to ensure that employees and supervisors understand both cultural differences among workers and the fact that individuals often enter the world of work with different, culture-based work scripts and role conceptions (Stone-Romero, Stone, & Salas, 2003). Similarly, performance management systems may need to be modified to ensure they are effective with individuals from diverse cultural backgrounds. For instance, in many U.S. organizations, individuals are expected to work independently and be self-reliant. As a result, individuals who have different work scripts (e.g., they prefer working with others or asking for help or assistance when appropriate) may be rated more negatively than those who have work scripts that are consistent with the dominant culture (e.g., working alone, being self-sufficient). Thus, performance appraisal systems may be biased in favor of members of the dominant group. To avoid this problem, organizations may want to modify their performance criteria and appraisal systems to ensure that individuals have the freedom to use their own methods of performing the job as long as job-related goals are met.

Finally, until recently, many U.S. organizations emphasized the separation of work and family and were not very "family friendly." For instance, they did not offer workers family-oriented work benefits. However, as the composition of the workforce has changed, an increasing number of firms are offering alternative family-oriented benefits (e.g., day care, family leave, domestic partner benefits) that meet the needs of workers who value such outcomes. Overall, we believe that organizations should adopt cafeteria-based compensation and benefit packages that will enable them to attract and retain productive workers who come from various cultural backgrounds.

CONCLUSION

Clearly, a great deal of research is needed on the impact of cultural diversity on HRM processes and practices and the effects of such processes and practices on job applicants and job incumbents. The same research should contribute to not only an improved understanding of cultural diversity issues in organizations but also the betterment of practice. We hope that the chapters in this book motivate and facilitate both the needed research and the changes in practice.

REFERENCES

Cox, T. H. (1993). *Cultural diversity in organizations: Theory, research, and practice*. San Francisco: Berrett-Koehler.

Stone-Romero, E. F. (2005). Personality-based stigmas and unfair discrimination in work organizations. In R. L. Dipboye, & A. Colella (Eds.), *Discrimination at work: The psychological and organizational bases* (pp. 255–280). Mahwah, NJ: Lawrence Erlbaum.

Stone-Romero, E. F., & Stone, D. L. (2007). Cognitive, affective, and cultural influences on stigmatization and its impact on human resource management processes and practices. *Research in Personnel and Human Resource Management, 26,* 117–167.

Stone-Romero, E. F., Stone, D. L., & Salas, E. (2003). The influence of culture on role conceptions and role behavior in organizations. *Applied Psychology: An International Review, 52,* 328–362.

AUTHOR INDEX

A

AARP, 243, 262
Abrahamsen, M., 58, 75, 83
Ackerman, G., 48
Adams, G., 9, 20
Aditya, R. N., 12, 22
Adkins, C. L., 200, 204
Adler, N. J., X, 13, 115, 118, 119,
    120, 130, 182, 202, 271, 299
Aguinis, H., 91, 94, 106
Ahlstrom, D., 64, 73, 75, 77
Ajzen, I., 20, 28, 32, 47, 48, 49, 89,
    105, 108
Akbar, N., 101, 105
Albright, M. D., 166, 178
Aldag, R. J., 29, 50
Alderfer, C. P., 158, 177
Alderton, D. L., 147, 154
Ali, A. J., 57, 67, 77, 149, 150
Allen, J., 140, 155
Allen, T. D., 255, 258, 262, 267
Allie, S. M., 214, 230
Allik, J., 81
Allison, S. T., 146, 150
Aldous, J., 259, 262
American Society For Training and
    Development (ASTD), 120, 130
Americans with Disabilities Act of
    1990, 103, 105
Anderson, N., 58, 59, 60, 72, 82, 84,
    262
Anderson, S. K., 72, 82
Aneshensel, C. S., 113
Angle, H. L., 303
Antonioni, D., 140, 150
Appley, M. H., 158, 177
Argote, L., 119, 130, 271, 299
Arminas, D., 58, 77

Army Medicine, 97, 105
Arnold, H. J., 29, 30, 48
Arthur, A. R., 214, 229
Arthur, W., 104, 105, 126, 130
Arvey, R. D., 148, 149, 150
Aryee, S., 236, 262
Asai, M., 14, 24, 186, 205
Ash, R., 26, 48
Ash, S. R., 120, 131
Ashford, S. J., 166, 177, 178
Ashkanasy, N., 199, 200, 202, 262
Ashmore, R. D., 107
Ashton, M. C., 94, 105
Atkins, P. W., 140, 150
Aycan, Z., 68, 69, 77
Ayman, R., 187, 202
Axel, H., 261, 262, 264

B

Babakus, E., 217, 230
Bae, J., 11, 22
Bagley, C., 23
Bailey, C., 101, 106
Bailey, D. E., 277, 300
Bakan, D., 102, 106
Baker, D. P., 274, 304
Baker, W. E., 10, 22
Baltes, B. B., 255, 263
Bandura, A., 20, 47
Banker, R. D., 192, 202
Barber, A. E., 29, 47, 254, 266
Barling, J., 236, 263, 265, 266
Barnett, R., 236, 243, 263
Barnett, R. C., 263
Barnum, D. T., 152
Baron, H., 57, 66, 67, 68, 81, 82
Barratt, M. E., 226, 231

313

Barrett, G. V., 57, 78
Barrick, M. R., 86, 88, 94, 106
Bartol, K. M., 145, 153
Baskett, G., 99, 106
Bass, B. M., 57, 78
Bates, P., 249, 263
Bearden, W. O., 284, 299
Beattie, A. E., 55, 79
Beauvais, L. L., 255, 262, 267
Becker, G., 189, 202
Bedian, A. G., 236, 263
Beehr, T. A., 140, 150, 215, 218, 230
Bem, S. L., 102, 106
Benjamin, L., 132
Ben-Nahum, Z., 139, 152
Bennett, J. M., 126, 130
Bennet, W., 124, 130
Berger, C. R., 164, 177
Berkerman, Z., 132
Berkowitz, L., 154
Bernin, P., 232
Berridge, J., 214, 230
Bertin, I., 263
Best, D. L., 102, 113
Betancourt, H., 5, 24, 38, 45, 224, 233
Beckmann, J., 47
Beutell, N. J., 236, 264
Beyer, J. M., 27, 39, 42, 44, 50, 93, 113
Bhagat, R. S., 8, xiv, 122, 130, 144, 148, 150, 207, 212, 214, 215, 216, 217, 218, 230, 232, 233, 309
Bhawuk, D. P. S., 16, 21, 46, 50, 63, 64, 83, 120, 124, 125, 130, 147, 151, 185, 205
Bishaw, A., 97, 106
Bishop, R. C., 63, 80
Björkmann, I., 73, 75, 78
Blaauw, E., 144, 155
Black, J. S., 145, 152
Blancero, D. A., 36, 47
Blancero, D. M., 36, 47
Blass, R., 152
Bledsoe, K., L., 101, 108
Block, J., 94, 106
Blozis, S. A., 46, 51
Bly, P. R., 168, 179
Bochner, S., 10, 24
Boelter, C. M., 101, 113
Bodenhausen, G. V., 289, 303

Bohn, M. J., 88, 113
Bokemeier, J. L., 29, 49
Boles, J. S., 236, 263
Bond, M. H., 72, 78, 79, 110, 129, 130, 132, 148, 154, 159, 171, 178, 179
Bond, R., 5, 21
Bontempo, R., 14, 24, 186, 205
Booth-Kewley, S., 147, 154
Borman, W. C., 109, 137, 138, 149, 150, 151, 153, 177
Bowen, D. E., 78
Bowers, C., 294, 299
Bowen, M. G., 137, 151, 152
Boykin, A. W., 101, 106, 113
Bracken, D. W., 177
Brandon, G., 277, 301
Brannick, M. T., 300
Breaugh, J. A., 25, 27, 43, 44, 48
Bretz, R. D., 26, 28, 30, 34, 38, 44, 48, 49
Brewer, M. B., 6, 21, 24
Brewster, C., 145, 154
Brice, G. C., 259, 264
Brief, A. P., 96, 106
Briggs, T. E., 255, 263
Briley, D. A., 290, 299
Brislin, R. W., 16, 24, 120, 124, 125, 130, 133, 204
Brockner, J., 46, 48
Brockwood, K., J., 266
Bruner, J. S., 277, 294, 300, 303
Brush, D. H., 137, 150
Bruton, G. D., 75, 77
Brutus, S., 167, 177
Buck, M. L., 158, 178
Buckley, M. R., 148, 151
Buon, T., 228, 230
Burden, D. S., 263
Burgess, K. M., 228, 230
Burke, B. G., 236, 263
Burke, C. S., 11, xiv, 133, 274, 275, 276, 299, 300, 303, 304
Burke, M. J., 96, 106
Burke, R. J., 236, 263
Burlew, K., 105
Burns, J. J., 125, 131
Bussema, E., 124, 131
Burrough, B., 117, 130
Butler, M. C., 74, 83, 249
Byars, L. L., 254, 256, 258, 263
Byrne, D., 97, 98, 106

C

Cable, D. M., 30, 34, 44, 48, 49, 92, 106
Caldwell, D. F., 200, 204
Camara, W. J., 104, 106
Campbell, J. P., 137, 151, 158, 160, 177
Campion, J. E., 29, 51
Canavan, P. J., 136, 152
Cannon-Bowers, J. A., 115, 122, 123, 124, 125, 126, 131, 133, 276, 279, 293, 294, 300, 302, 303, 304
Cappelli, P., 70, 84
Cardy, R. L., 141, 151
Carlson, R. A., 279, 300
Carnevale, P., 24
Carroll, S., 240, 267
Cartwright, D., 152
Cartwright, S., 152
Carver, C. S., 87, 106
Cascio, W. F., 90, 91, 94, 96, 106, 158, 177
Cattell, R. B., 88, 106
Caubet, S., 266
Caudron, S., 120, 121, 122, 131
Cawley, B. D., 166, 178
CSO (Central Statistical Office), 263
Cerino, T. J., 252, 266
Chan, D. K-S., 46, 50
Chan, E. S., 73, 75, 77
Chao, G. T., 60, 78, 296, 300
Chapman, N. J., 253, 257, 260, 265, 266
Charness, N., 279, 300
Chatman, J. A., 34, 48, 95, 106, 199, 200, 202, 204
Chemers, M. N., 187, 202
Chen, C., 167, 177
Chen, C. C., 240, 241, 263
Chen, M., 64, 78
Chen, Y.-R., 6, 21
Chen, X. P., 240, 263
Chen, Z. X., 48
Cheng, J., 24
Cheng, B. S., 139, 151
Cheney, D. L., 304
Chesney, M. A., 200, 202
Chew, I., 76, 79
Chi, T. H., 131
Chiang, F., 284, 300
Child, J., 144, 151

Cho, M. O., 291, 292, 300
Choi, I., 61, 78, 81
Choi, S.-C., 24, 109, 111
Choo, C. W., 279, 300
Chou, V., 108
Chow, C. W., 118, 131
Christensen, K. E., 255, 259, 263
Chudoba, K. M., 270, 303
Chung, B. J., 58, 67, 73, 84
Chung, Y. H., 146, 151
Church, A. T., 59, 79
Clark, B. D., 179
Clark, F. L., 267
Clark, L. A., 104, 113
Clark, S. M., 278, 304
Clark, T., 58, 78
Clarke, H., 247, 264
Clarke, N. E., 259, 260, 267
Clegg, C. W., 179
Cleveland, J. N., x, xiv, xvii, 137, 153, 235, 309
Cliffordson, C., 95, 107
Cofer, C. N., 158, 177
Cohen, A., 118, 132
Cohen, D., 4, 7, 21, 24
Cohen, J., 171, 176, 177
Cohen, S. G., 277, 300
Cohn, S., 96, 107
Colarelli, S. M., 70, 76, 78
Cole, M., 1, 21
Colella, A., 50, 78, 112, 312
Colihan, J., 255, 259, 265
Collins, C., 96, 97, 113
Colquitt, J. A., 10, 22, 112
Colton, C., 266
Contrada, R. J., 97, 107
Conway, J. M., 109, 138, 151
Cooke, N. J., 128, 131
Coon, H. M., 100, 101, 107, 111
Cooper, C. L., 130, 202, 203, 208, 213, 214, 215, 226, 229, 230, 231, 232, 267
Cooper, M. L, 264
Copper, C., 126, 131
Copeland, M. V., 270, 300
Costa, P. T., 59, 80, 94, 104, 107, 110
Coughlan, A., 247, 263
Coups, E., 107
Cox, T. H., xii, xv, 26, 33, 48, 146, 151, 181, 187, 203, 277, 300, 310, 311
Crooker, K. J., 254, 259, 264

Cropanzano, R., 81, 183, 184, 199, 201, 205, 264
Crosby, F. J., 12, 23, 85, 112
Crosby, M., 12, 23
Cummings. L. L., 133, 154, 166, 177, 205
Cunningham, M., 59, 79
Curtis-Holmes, J., 55, 78

D

Dafflon, A.-C., 102, 110
Daily, B., 118, 120, 131
Dalal, R., 61, 78
Dalessio, A., 98, 107
Daly, C. L., 29, 47
Dalton, J. E., 215, 232
D'Andrade, R., 282, 300
Daus, C., 199, 202
Davis, E., 213, 231, 257, 259, 263
Davis, N., 291, 292, 300
Davison, S. C., 271, 301
Day, A. L. D., 60, 82
Day, D., 303
De Cieri, H., 26, 50
Dawis, R. V., 88, 110
De Cuir, A. D., 168, 179
de Forest, M. E., 72, 78
Den Dulk, L., 238, 243, 247, 263
De Stefano, J. J., 46, 49
de Vargas, M. C., 12, 23
Deller, J., 69, 77
Denes-Raj, V., 55, 78
Denning, S., 126, 131, 294, 300
Densten, I. L., 291, 300
Department of Enterprise, Trade and Employment, 251, 263
Desaulniers, J., 13, 22
Deschamps, J. C., 100, 108
Deshpande, S. P., 120, 131
Deutsch, M., 193, 203
Deven, F., 250, 263
Dewe, P. J., 215, 230, 208, 213, 214
Dhamoon, R., 284, 300
Diaz-Guerrero, R., 49, 224, 230
Dickinson, T. L., 274, 300
Diefendorff, J., 158, 178
Diener, C., 8, 21
Diener, E., 8, 21
Diener, M., 8, 21
Digman, J. M., 88, 94, 107
Dillihunt, M. L., 101, 113

Dipboye, R. L., ix, xiii, 50, 56, 62, 78, 97, 103, 107, 112, 312
Dilova, M. L., 12, 21
Distefano, J. J., 118, 131
Dobbins, G. H., 99, 110, 139, 141, 151
Dodd, C., 293, 300
Dodge, G. E., 305
Dohrenwend, B. P., 96, 97, 107, 110
Dohrenwend, B. S., 96, 107
Doosje, B., 287, 288, 290, 300, 301, 302, 304
Dorfman, P. W., 18, 22, 46, 48, 276, 302
Dos Santos-Pearson, V. M., 14, 21
Douglas, C., 152
Douglas, M., 159, 177
Dowling, P. J., 26, 50
Drasgow, F., 12, 23, 183, 204
Dreher, G. F., 26, 48
Drew, E., 247, 248, 249, 250, 251, 263
Driskell, J. E., 126, 127, 131
Drost, E. A., 76, 84
Dube, A., 253, 263
Dubofsky, M., 195, 203
Du Brin, A. J., 96, 107
Dugan, S., 14, 23
Duggan, C., 107
Dulles, F. R., 195, 203
Dumais, S. T., 131
Dunham, R. B., 254, 266
Dunnette, M. D., xii, xvi, 26, 48, 50, 78, 80, 94, 108, 109, 150, 151, 152, 158, 177, 178, 179, 203, 204, 205, 231, 232
Durso, F. T., 131
Duxbury, L., 236, 265
Dwyer, D. J., 124, 125, 131, 133, 293, 294
Dwyer, P., 115, 131, 303

E

Earley, P. C., xii, xv, xvi, 8, 11, 14, 15, 21, 22, 26, 44, 46, 48, 83, 99, 107, 132, 158, 167, 177, 178, 182, 187, 203, 302
Eaton, N. K., 94, 109
Eaves, L. J., 109
Eber, H. W., 88, 106
Ebling, R., 67, 83

Edwards, J. E., 147, 154
Edwards, V., 73, 83
Egeth, J. P., 107
Ehrenstein, A., 133
Eisenberg, J., 22
Eisenhardt, K. M., 136, 151
Ekeberg, S. E., 168, 179
Eleftheriou, A., 58, 78
Ellemers, N., 287, 288, 289, 290,
    300, 301, 302, 304
Ellen, P. S., 32, 49
Ellingson, J. E., 102, 111
Ellis, A. P. J., 303
Elsik, W., 149, 152
Emlen, A. C., 253, 260, 266
Employee Assistance Professionals
    Association (EAPA), 208, 211,
    226, 231
Employee Benefit Research Institute
    (EBRI), 252, 263
Endsley, M., 304
Engardio, P., 115, 131
Entin, E. E., 275, 301
Entrekin, L., 146, 151
Epstein, S., 55, 78
Erez, M., xii, xv, xvi, 11, 12, 18, 21,
    22, 26, 44, 46, 48, 83, 99, 107,
    132, 158, 178, 182, 186, 203, 302
Erofeev, D., 140, 150
Esping-Andersen, G., 236, 237, 238,
    239, 240, 264
European Commission, 249, 264
Evans, J., 55, 78
Ewen, R. B., 271, 305
Eyring, A. R., 29, 51
Eysenck, H. J., 89, 94, 100, 107, 109
Eysenck, M. W., 89, 107
Eysenck, S. B., 100, 109

F

Fadil, P., 72, 78
Fairlie, P., 22
Fangani, J., 264
Farh, J.-L., 14, 21, 99, 110, 139, 151
Farley, J. U., 75, 78
Farmer, R. N., 150
Farmer, S. M., 143, 151
Farr, M. J., 127, 131
Fay, D., 95, 107
Fedor, D. B., 50, 112, 142, 143, 151
Feldman, D. C., 29, 30, 48

Ferguson, M. W., 36, 49
Fernandez, J. P., 141, 147, 151, 259,
    164
Ferner, A., 59, 78
Ferris, G. R., ix, xiv, 50, 78, 112, 135,
    136, 141, 142, 143, 144, 146, 147,
    148, 149, 150, 151, 152, 155, 204,
    309
Fiedler, F. E., 16, 21
Field, J. M., 192, 202
Fierman, J., 258, 264
Filley, A. C., 271, 301
Fine-Davis, M., 247, 248, 249, 250,
    264
Fischer, M. J., 286, 302
Fishbein, M., 28, 48, 89, 108
Fisher, G. B., 75, 78
Fisher Vista, 207, 231
Fiske, A. P., 159, 178
Fiske, S., 55, 79
Fiore, S. M., 279, 304
Fitzgibbons, D. E., 142, 152
Fleishman, E. A., xvii
Fleming, S., 265
Fletcher, J. D., 133
Florkowski, G. W., 148, 154
Flowers, J., 304
Foley, S., 73, 77
Folkman, S., 215, 231
Fong, C. P. S., 61, 79
Ford, D. L., 215, 230
Ford, J. K., 122, 131, 145, 153
Ford, M. E., 279, 301
Fortmann, K., 59, 79
Fortune, xi, xvi
Foti, R. J., 291, 305
Fowler, S. M., 124, 131
Fowles, J. E., 133
Fowlkes, J., 124, 131
Fox, S., 139, 152
Fraboni, M., 109
Francesco, A. M., 48
Frayne, C. A., 74, 79
Freeman, M. A., 102, 108
French, J. R. P., 5, 142, 152
Frese, M., 95, 107
Frey, L. T. 217, 230
Fried, J., 42, 49
Friedman, D. E., 257, 264
Frink, D. D., 136, 142, 146, 147, 148,
    149, 151, 152
Frone, M. R., 236, 264

Furnham, A., 10, 24, 103, 109
Fynes, B., 248, 264

G

Gabriel, S., 289, 303
Gabrielidis, C., 14, 21
Gaines, S. O. J., 101, 108
Galang, C., 78
Galang, M. C., 146, 149, 151, 152
Galinsky, A. D., 291, 301
Galinsky, E., 258, 259, 261, 264, 265
Gallagher, E., 178
Ganster, D. C., 236, 255, 267
Garcia, L. F., 77
Gary, M. L., 107
Gavin, J. H., 215, 232
Gay, G., 101, 108
Gelfand, M. J., 24, 48, 109, 185, 205
George, J. M., 96, 106, 108
Gerganov, E. N., 12, 21
Geringer, J. M., 74, 79
Ghiselli, E. E., 94, 108
Giacalone, R., 301
Giannantonio, C. M., 29, 47
Gibson, C. B., 14, 21, 121, 132, 167,
    177, 272, 277, 296, 301
Gilbert, J., 279, 305
Giles, H, 177
Gilligan, C., 102, 108
Gilliland, S. N., 60, 63, 69, 70, 83
Gilmore, D. C., 147, 151
Gioia, D. A., 141, 153, 269, 278, 301,
    304
Giordano, J., 34, 49
Giovannini, D., 247, 264
Goethals, G. R., 49
Goffin, R. D., 109
Goffman, E., 92, 108
Goldstein, I. L., 122, 128, 131
Goldston, J., 132
Gomez, C., 44, 48
Gomez-Mejia, L., 75, 79
Gonzalez, F., 230
Gonzalez, J. A., 260, 267
Goodman, J. S., 143, 151
Goodstein, L. D., 182, 203
Goodwin, G. F., 271, 304
Googins, B., 263
Googins, B. K, 212, 231
Gorey, K. M., 259, 264

Gottfried, A. E., 265
Gottfried, A. W., 265
Gottier, R. F., 86, 94, 105, 108
Gould, E. W., 285, 302
Graf, I. K., 142, 155
Grandey, A. A., 258, 260, 261, 264
Gray, J. H., 291, 300
Graziano, W. G., 104, 105
Green, E. G. T., 100, 108
Greenberg, J., 48, 112, 232
Greenhaus, J. H., 236, 264
Greenwald, A. G., 167, 178
Greer, C., 74, 79
Gregerson, H. B., 145, 152
Griffitt, W., 99, 108
Grimm, S. D., 59, 79
Grover, S. L., 254, 259, 264
Grugulis, I., 53, 80
Gu, H., 61, 62, 84
Guganowski, D., 140, 150
Guion, R. M., 86, 91, 94, 105, 108
Gully, S. M., 60, 69, 81
Guopei, G., 72, 79
Gupta, V., 18, 22, 31, 46, 48, 276,
    302
Gutmann, A., 304
Guzzo, R., 300, 303

H

Hackman, J. R., 188, 203, 176, 301
Hagendoorn, L., 15, 16, 23
Hagman, J. D., 126, 133
Haidt, J., 290, 302
Hair, J. F., 236, 263
Hall, A. T., 152
Hall, E. R., 305
Hall, E. T., 140, 152
Halpin, S. M., 303
Hambrick, D. C., 271, 277, 301, 304
Hammer, L. B., 236, 252, 254, 256,
    257, 266
Hampden-Turner, C., 62, 84, 90, 99,
    113
Hammond, K., 55, 79
Hammond, T., 266
Hanges, P. J., 18, 22, 46, 48, 276, 302
Hannerz, U., 282, 301
Hansen, C. P., 140, 150
Hanson, G., 181, 182, 203
Harrell-Cook, G., 148, 151
Harnisch, D., 216, 230

Harrison, D. A., 296, 301
Harrison, G. L., 118, 131
Harrison, H. M., 232
Harris, M., 98, 108
Harris, M. M., 139, 152
Harris, P. R., 241, 243, 264
Hartel, C., 199, 202
Härtel, C. E. J., 75, 78
Hartman, M., 26, 30, 50
Haslam, S. A., 287, 301
Hatvany, N., 57, 69, 79
Hayashi, C., 17, 21
Hayes, C. D., 265
Hayghe, H. V., 258, 264
Health Action Forum of Greater
    Boston, 255, 265
Heath A. C., 109, 264
Heckscher, C., 225, 231
Heine, S. J., 13, 21, 100, 108
Heinisch, D. A., 63, 80
Helmes, E., 94, 105
Helmreich, R. L., 117, 120, 128, 131,
    132, 293, 301
Hepburn, C. G., 236, 265
Herbig, P., 72, 79
Herdt, G., 23
Herlocker, C. E., 146, 150
Hernandez, C. A., 264
Herriot, P., 60, 79, 82, 84
Herskovits, M. J., 184, 203
Hess, K. P., 133
Hess, D. J., 285, 301
Hewitt Associates, 265
Higgins, C. A., 144, 152, 236, 265
Higginbottom, S. F., 236, 263
Highley, J. C., 214, 231
Hill, E. J., 255, 259, 265
Hill, R. C., 278, 301
Hilliard, A., 101, 108
Hiltrop, J. M., 60, 83
Himelright, J. L., x, xiv, 235, 309
Hirokawa, R. Y., 148, 152
Hite, J. M., 145, 152
Hochwarter, W. A., 148, 151, 152
Hodgetts, R. M., 121, 132
Hofstede, G., 65, 66, 69, 72, 79, 86,
    90, 93, 99, 100, 108, 117, 132,
    144, 152, 159, 162, 167, 171, 172,
    178, 182, 184, 185, 187, 191, 193,
    203, 216, 221, 222, 231, 236, 238,
    240, 241, 265, 270, 277, 282, 285,
    301

Hoenig, S., 75, 78
Hoffman, L. R., 118, 132
Hogan, R. T., 86, 87, 94, 108
Hojgaard, L., 247, 264
Hollenbeck, J. R., 132, 137, 152, 270,
    302, 303
Holling, H., 179
Holman, D., 179
Hooker, J., 222, 224, 231
Hopkins, S. A., 69, 81
Hopkins, W. E., 69, 81
Hopper, H., 136, 152
Horenczyk, G., 118, 119, 132
Horwitz, Fr. M., 76, 79
Hoshino-Browne, E., 4, 21
Hough, L. M., xii, xvi, 26, 48, 50,
    86, 94, 101, 103, 108, 109, 150,
    151, 152, 158, 178, 179, 203, 205,
    231, 232
House, R. J., 12, 18, 22, 46, 48, 271,
    276, 301, 302
Howard, A., 179
Howe, H. E., 23
Huang, H. J., 75, 79
Huang-Fu. E., 81
Huang, E., 266
Huff, J. W., 255, 263
Huffcut, A. I., 95, 109
Hughes, D., 258, 265
Hui, C. H., 16, 24, 36, 46, 48, 50,
    100, 109, 186, 205
Humphreys, P., 247, 248, 250,
    263
Humphreys, P. C., 265
Hunt, G. G., 257, 258, 268
Hunt, J. G., 305
Hunt, R., 185, 204
Hunter, J. E., 55, 59, 82
Huo, Y. P., 70, 73, 75, 77, 79,
    178
Huntington, S. P., 27, 48
Hurley-Hanson, A. E., 72, 78
Hurlock, R. E., 127, 132
Hurrell, J. J., 215, 230, 232
Huselid, M. A., 26, 48, 158, 178
Huws, U., 263
Hwang, K. K., 100, 109
Hyatt, D., 112

I

Iceland, J., 97, 106

Ilgen, D. R., 109, 118, 119, 132, 137, 152, 158, 177, 178, 270, 271, 302, 303
Ineson, E. M., 83
Imada, A., 98, 107
Inger, M. E., 59, 82
Ingersoll-Dayton, B., 253, 257, 260, 265, 266
Inglehart, R., 10, 22
Inouye, J., 94, 107
Insko, C. A., 64, 82
Irving, L., 236, 265
Isenhour, L., ix, xiii, 33, 50, 309
Isgrigg, J., 266
Ivanitskaya, L., 140, 150
Iwao, S., 46, 50
Iwawaki, S., 100, 109

J

Jackofsky, E., 65, 82
Jackson, C., 262
Jackson, C. L., 10, 17, 22
Jackson, D. N., 86, 88, 94, 105, 109, 113
Jackson, S., 22
Jackson, S. E., 65, 82, 118, 132, 158, 178, 184, 203, 204, 271, 302
Jackson, T., 99, 108
Jacob, N., 284, 302
Jacobs, L., 72, 79
Janis, I. L., 118, 132
Javidan, M., 18, 22, 48, 276, 302
Jelinek, M., 182, 202
Jentsch, F., 294, 299
Jetten, J., 289, 290, 302
Ji, L., 121, 132
Jin, K., 64, 81
Johnson, R. D., 26, 30, 50
Johnson, S. K., ix, xiii, 53
Johnson-Bailey, J., 303
Johnston, M. W., 236, 263
Joint Employment Report, 250, 265
Jones, E. E., 143, 153
Jones, G. R., 96, 108
Jones, J. L., 59, 81
Jones, S. D., 168, 179
Joshi, A., x, xiv, 181, 309
Judge, T., 28, 30, 34, 38, 44, 48, 49, 92, 106, 141, 142, 144, 149, 152
Jurgensen, C. E., 29, 49

K

Kacmar, C. J., 152
Kahn, R. L., 89, 109, 215, 231
Kagitçibasi, C., 24, 111
Kamerman, S. B., 252, 254, 258, 265
Kamoche, K., 57, 76, 79
Kamp, J. D., 94, 109
Kanungo, R. N., 69, 77
Kaplan, E., 253, 263
Kaplan, M., 132, 133, 302
Karakowsky, L., 145, 153
Kashima, Y., 102, 109
Kashlak, R. J., 212, 232
Katz, D., 89, 109
Katz, I., 118, 132
Kazdin, A. E., 24
Keita, G., 230
Kehoe, J. F., 81
Kelley, K., 112
Kelley, L., 144, 153
Kelloway, E. K., 236, 263
Kelly, C., 14, 22, 143, 153
Kelly, J. C., 14, 22
Keltner, D., 290, 302
Kemmelmeier, M., 100, 101, 107, 111
Kendall, D., 274, 300
Kendler, K. S., 104, 109
Kenny, D. A., 77, 305
Keon, T. L., 30, 38, 51
Kerbo, H. R., 96, 109
Kerr, S., 271, 301
Kessler, R. C., 97, 109, 110
Kieser, A., 144, 151
Kim, U., 24, 109, 111
Kim-Prieto, C., 61, 78
King, T. R., 142, 147, 151, 152
Kingston, P. W., 254, 257, 259, 265
Kiniciki, A., 117, 132
Kipnis, D., 142, 143, 144, 147, 153
Kirchmeyer, C., 118, 132
Kirkman, B. L., 17, 22, 121, 132, 182, 204
Kitayama, S., 2, 5, 8, 13, 14, 21, 22, 30, 35, 49, 61, 80, 81, 100, 108, 111, 162, 178, 186, 204
Klahr, D., 300
Klein, G., 280, 302
Klein, H. A., 116, 132, 291, 296, 302
Klein, K. J., 296, 301
Klimoski, R. J., 109, 155, 139, 177
Kluckhohn, C., 1, 22

Kluckhohn, F. L., 2, 9, 22, 45, 49
Knudstrup, M., 72, 78
Kohn, M. K., 3, 5, 22, 96, 110
Kohn, N., 140, 155
Kohlberg, L., 6, 22
Kolodinsky, R. W., 152
Konrad, A. M., 85, 110
Korabik, K., 254, 257, 267
Kortekaas, P., 289, 301
Kozlowski, S. W. J., 274, 302
Kossek, E. E., 38, 49. 231, 236, 252, 255, 256, 259, 260, 265
Kotovsky, K., 300
Kraiger, K., 145, 153
Kramer, R. M., 154, 212, 231
Kras, E. S., 65, 72, 80, 148, 153
Kreitner, R., 117, 132
Kristof-Brown, A. L., 34, 49, 95, 98, 110, 200, 204
Krouze, M. K., 257, 259, 263
Ku, G., 291, 301
Kudoh, T., 111
Kuhl, J., 47
Kumar, K., 120, 134
Kurman, J., 59, 80
Kurshid, A., 69, 77
Kuzmits, F. E., 257, 265
Kwang-Kuo, H., 72, 78
Kymlicka, W., 281, 284, 302

L

Lacy, W. B., 29, 49
Lambert, S. J., 257, 266
Lammers, F., 179
Landis, D., 130
Lang, L., 236, 266
Lankau, M. J., 259, 267
Latham, G. A., 73, 80
Laurent, A., 145, 153
Lause, K., 119, 133
Law, K. S., 75, 80, 84
Lawler, J. J., 11, 12, 22, 23, 183, 204
Lay, C., 15, 22
Lazarus, R. S., 215, 216, 217, 231
Lee, A., 107
Lee, M. D., 158, 178
Lee, M. Y., 303
Lee, W., 185, 204
Leedom, D. K., 278, 302
Lehman, D. R., 13, 21, 100, 108
Lehman, W. E. K., 226, 232

Leighton, D., 100, 110
Lennon, M. C., 96, 110
Lepak, D. P., 158, 178
Le Pine, J. A., 132, 270, 302
Lerner, J. S., 137, 153
Leslie, C., 59, 79
Leslie, J. B., 167, 177
Leung, A. K.-Y., 4, 21
Leung, K., 6, 8, 13, 14, 22, 23, 129, 130, 132, 224, 231, 267
Leong F., 73, 80
Levav, I., 107
Levenhagen, M., 301
Levenson, R. W., 67, 83
Levin, I., 96, 110
Levine, S., 107
Levy, P. E., 158, 166, 167, 178
Lévy-Leboyer, 57, 58, 59, 80
Lewin, K., 153
Lewis, J., 80, 108
Lewis, R. D., 283, 284, 295, 302
Li, F., 80
Li, H. Z., 118, 132
Li, J., 145, 153
Liden, R. C., 142, 155
Liebig, P. S., 259, 261, 266
Lin, S. L., 14, 24
Lin, S.-C., 14, 21
Lin, T., 99, 110
Lin, Y., H-W., 64, 82
Lindholm, H., 215, 230
Lindsay, D. S., 131
Link, B. G., 96, 97, 107, 110
Lisansky, J., 5, 24, 36, 38, 50, 224, 233
Littrell, L. N., 121, 132, 133
Little, J. S., 182, 204
Liu, I., 100, 110
Lobel, S. A., 38, 49, 187, 203, 277, 300
Locke, E. A., 184, 204
Lockett, M., 75, 80
Lockyer, C., 70, 80, 82
Lofquist, L. H., 88, 110
London, M., 140, 153
Longenecker, C. O., 141, 153
Loo, R., 100, 110
Lopez, S. R., 26, 45, 47
Lorenzi-Cioldi, F., 102, 110
Louis, M. R., 280, 281, 302
Love, K. G., 80
Lovell, V., 266

Lowe, B. F., 267
Lowe, K. B., 121, 132, 178
Lu, Y., 73, 75, 78
Lucca, N., 14, 24, 186, 205
Lukaszewski, K. M., xiii, 25, 33, 50
Luo, Y., 75, 81
Luthans, F., 121, 132, 213, 231
Lyness, K. S., 255, 262, 267
Lyons, R., ix, xiii, 115

M

Maass, A., 13, 22
MacDermid, S. M., 158, 178
MacEwen, K. E., 236, 263, 266
MacGuire, M. A., 136, 154
Madden, T. J., 32, 49
Mahanyele, M., 217, 230
Maier, N. R. F., 118, 132
Makin, P. J., 57, 58, 59, 75, 82
Malinowski, B., 23, 286, 302
Mann, L., 187, 204
Manstead, A. S. R., 289, 302
Marchington, M., 53, 80
Marcus, A., 285, 302
Marcus, B., 60, 80
Marcus, G. E., 286, 292, 302
Marelich, W. D., 101, 108
Marin, B. V., 34, 38, 39, 40, 42, 45, 49
Marin, G., 5, 24, 34, 35, 36, 38, 39, 40, 42, 45, 49, 50, 224, 233
Marks, M. A., 274, 276, 302, 305
Markus, H. R., 2, 5, 13, 14, 21, 22, 30, 35, 49, 80, 100, 108, 111, 162, 178, 186, 204
Marlowe, H. A., 279, 303
Marshall, R., 102, 111
Marshall, V., 155
Marquez, J., 225, 231
Martella, D., 13, 22
Martin, D. C., 145, 153
Martin, J. N., 122, 133
Martocchio, J. J., x, xiv, 12, 23, 152, 183, 188, 193, 198, 204, 205, 253, 255, 256, 266, 309
Maruyama, M., 76, 80
Masi, D. A., 210, 211, 212, 231
Maslyn, J. M., 143, 151
Masuda, T., 61, 80
Matsumoto, D., 102, 111
Matsumoto, H., 5

Maybin, J., 302
Maznewski, M. L., 118, 131, 270, 303
McAdams, D. P., 94, 110
McCarthy, A., x, xiv, 235, 309
McLeod, P. L., 187, 203, 277, 300
McCloy, R. A., 94, 109
McCormick, M. J., 168, 179
McCrae, R. R., 59, 80, 81, 94, 104, 107, 110
McCulloch, S., 58, 80
McCusker, C., 186, 205
McDonald-Mann, D., 167, 177
McFarland, L., 57, 82
McFarlin, D. B., 63, 69, 70, 81
McGinnies, E., 277, 303
McGoldrick, M., 34, 35, 38, 49
McGowen, E. G., 150
McGrath, J. E., 119, 130, 271, 277, 299, 303
McKenzie, R. C., 55, 82
McHugh, A. P., 296, 304
McKinnon, J. L., 118, 131
McLeod, P. L., 187, 203, 277, 300
McIntyre, R. M., 274, 300, 303
McMahan, G. C., 158, 180
McManus, M. A., 36, 49
McNeese, M., 304
McQuaid, S. J., 144, 150, 215, 230
Meece, D., 226, 231
Meglino, B. M., 200, 204
Meindl, J. R., 185, 204, 240, 263
Mendonca, M., 69, 70, 77
Merenda, P. F., 104, 106
Merriam, S. B., 270, 303
Merritt, A. C., 120, 128, 131
Metropolitan Life Insurance Company, 266
Meyer, J. W., 121, 133
Michaelsen, L. K., 120, 134
Middleton, K. L., 59, 81
Middleton, V. A., 72, 82
Mikula, G., 193, 204
Miles, R. H., 143, 154
Miller, B. C., 255, 259, 265
Milliken, F., 277, 304
Milliman, J. F., 79, 158, 167, 176, 178
Minne, C., 107
Mintzberg, H., 141, 143, 153
Mischel, W., 90, 111
Mishra, R. C., 102, 111
Misumi, J., 17, 22

Mitchell, T. R., 16, 21, 136, 152
Miyamoto, Y., 61, 81
Mobley, W. H., 80
Moemeka, A. A., 101, 111
Moffett, R. G., 236, 263
Money, R. B., 284, 299
Montague, W. E., 127, 132
Montei, M. S., 63, 80
Moon, H, 296, 300, 303
Moran, R. T., 243, 264
Moran, S. V., 243, 264
Morgan, H., 252, 253, 254, 257, 266
Morris, M. W., 13, 22, 290, 299
Morrisey, T., 264
Moscoso, S., 82, 91, 111
Mosley, M., 105
Moskowitz, D. S., 13, 22
Moskowitz, G. B., 291, 301
Moss, P., 250, 263
Motowidlo, S. J., 137, 138, 149, 150,
    153, 155
Mount, M. K., 86, 88, 94, 106
Moustafa, K. S., 216, 230
Mowday, R. T., 184, 204
Mueller, S., 200, 205
Muhamad, M., 303
Muldron, T. W., 55, 82
Mumford, M. D., 305
Muniz, E. J., 32, 37, 49
Murphy, C., 247, 250, 263
Murphy, K., 106, 109, 137, 153, 155
Murray, R., 107
Mussweiler, T., 289, 303
Mutman, M., 303

N

Nachbar, J., 119, 133
Napier, N. K., 73, 75, 79, 80
Nason, S., 178
Naveh, G., 107
Naylor, J. C., 158, 160, 164, 178
Neal, M. B., 236, 252, 253, 254, 256,
    257, 259, 260, 265, 266
Neale, M. A., 154
Neale, M. C., 109
Neider, L., 152
Neisser, U., 106
Nelson, D. L., 215, 232, 267
Nelson, A., 59, 81
Nemec, P., 124, 131
Nemeth, C. J., 141, 154

Nesse, R. M., 104, 112
Neuberg, S., 55, 79
Neuman, G. A., 263
Nevins, J. L., 284, 299
Newcomb, T. M., 98, 111
Newell, S., 58, 59, 70, 75, 83
Newman, K. L., 182, 187, 188, 200,
    204, 233
Newstrom, J. W., 254, 266
New York Business Group on Health,
    261, 266
Nguyen, H.-H., 60, 78
Nichol, V., 236, 260, 265
Nickerson, R. S., 131
Nie, W., 69, 81
Ninokumar, H., 230
Nisbett, R. E., 6, 8, 22, 61, 80, 81,
    121, 132
Nkomo, S. M., 146, 151
Noe, R. A., 121, 133
Nollen, S. D., 182, 187, 188, 200,
    204
Norasakkunkit, V., 22
Norenzayan, A., 61, 81
Norris-Watts, C., 158, 178
Northcraft, G. B., 166, 178
Norton, S. M., 139, 154
Ntseane, G., 303
Nyfield, G., 66, 67, 68, 81

O

Ohbuchi, K-I., 14, 23
O'Dell, L. L., 259
O'Donnell, O., 265
O'Driscoll, M. P., 208, 213, 214, 215,
    216, 217, 230, 232, 267
O'Grady, M. A., 72, 81
Okun, B. F., 42, 49
Okun, M. L., 42, 49
Oldham, G. R., 188, 203
Olmstead, B., 266
Ones, D., 262
Ontario Women's Directorate, 253,
    266
Organ, D. W., 138, 154
O'Reilly, C. A., 200, 204
Orpen, C., 187, 204
Ortner, S. B., 303
Oser, R. L., 124, 125, 131, 133, 293,
    294, 303
Oswald, F. L., 86, 101, 109

Ottati, V., 36, 50
Ouchi, W. G., 136, 154
Ouwerkerk, J. W., 289, 301
Overell, S., 225, 232
Oyserman, D., 100, 101, 111
Ozawa, K., 12, 23
Ozeki, C., 236, 252, 255, 256, 259, 265

P

Pacini, R., 55, 78
Páez, D., 100, 108
Page, M. M., 23
Page, R., 57, 82
Paige, R. M., 122, 123, 133
Paik, Y., 72, 81
Palich, L., 75, 79
Panzer, F. J., 274, 302
Park, H., 61, 78, 140, 150
Park, S., 61, 84
Paspalanova, E. P., 12, 21
Paquin, A. R., 168, 179
Pate, L. E., 230
Paunonen, S. V., 94, 105, 109, 111
Payne, R., 202, 215, 230
Payne, S. C., 160, 179
Pearce, J. K., 49
Pearson, V. M. S., 14, 23
Pelled, L. H., 72, 271, 303
Peng, K., 61, 81, 121, 132
Peng, M. W., 75, 81
Peppas, S. C., 63, 64, 73, 81
Peppas, S. R., 63, 64, 73, 81
Perloff, R., 35, 49
Perreault, W. D., 143, 154
Pervin, L. A., 94, 111
Peterson, M. F., 14, 17, 23
Petkova, K. G., 12, 21
Petrick, J. A., 64, 66, 83
Pfeffer, J., 53, 81, 141, 154
Phalet, K., 15, 16, 23
Phelan, J. C., 113
Phatak, A. V., 212, 232
Phillips, J. M., 29, 47, 60, 69, 81
Phooi-Ching, L., 84
Phua, T. T. F., 63, 83
Piacentini, J. S., 252, 266
Pierce, J. K., 34
Pierce, J. L., 254, 266
Pierce, L., x, xiv, 274, 300
Pierce, L. G., 304

Pillai, R., 78
Pillinger, T., 140, 155
Pincus, A. L., 87, 113
Pleck, J. H., 236, 266
Ployhart, R. E., 86, 101, 109
Poelman, S. A. Y., 230, 231, 267
Poole, M. S., 303
Poortinga, Y. H., 59, 81
Porter, C. O., 275, 303
Porter, L. W., 178, 179, 184, 204
Postman, L., 277, 303
Powell, C., 287, 301
Prasad, P., 85, 110
Price, R. H., 97, 110
Prien, K. O., 122, 130
Priest, H. A., x, xiv, 269
Prince, B. E., 226, 231
Prince, C., 274, 300, 304
Pringle, K. K., 85, 110
Pritchard, R. D., ix, xiv, 158, 160, 161, 168, 169, 170, 177, 178, 179, 180
Probst, T. M., 12, 24, 183, 204
Programme for Prosperity and Fairness, 244, 266
Pruitt, J. S., 125, 131
Pucik, V., 57, 69, 79
Punnett, B., 154

Q

Quinn, N., 282, 292, 303, 304
Quinn, R. P., 89, 109, 215, 231
Quiñones, M. A., 133
Quick, J. D., 215, 229, 230, 232
Quick, J. E., 215, 232
Quintanilla, J., 59, 78

R

Raabe, P. H., 258, 260, 266
Ramakrishnan, M., 158, 178
Ramamoorthy, N., 240, 267
Ramstad, P. M., 160, 161, 168, 169, 170, 179
Rand, T., 99, 111
Rands, G. P., 277, 303
Raven, B. H., 142, 152
Ravlin, E. C., 200, 204
Redfield, I., 1, 23
Reed, S., 115, 131

Renz, G. L., 150
Repetti, R. L., 96, 113
Reynolds, G. S., 226, 232
Rice, R. W., 259, 264
Ricci, T., 22
Rickard, A., 266
Rickert, S., 212, 231
Riedel, S., 133
Ring, P. S., 277, 303
Rivera, A. A., 72, 82
Rivers, C., 236, 263
Robert, C., 11, 12, 15, 23, 24, 183,
    184, 204, 241, 267
Robertson, I. T., 57, 58, 59, 75, 78,
    81, 82, 130
Robinson, B. S., 96, 106
Roche, W. K., 264
Roe, A., 88, 111
Rogelberg, S. G., 110
Rokeach, M., 144, 154
Ronen, S., 171, 172, 179
Roseberry, W., 285, 303
Rosen, S. D., 152
Rosenfeld, H. M., 9, 23
Rosenfeld, P., 147, 154, 301
Rosenman, R. H., 200, 202
Rosenthal, R. A., 89, 109, 215,
    231
Rossier, J., 77
Rosin, H. M., 254, 257, 267
Roth, P. L., 95, 109, 168, 179
Rothstein, J. S., 74, 82
Rothstein, M., 86, 88, 94, 113
Rothstein, M. G., 94, 105
Rothausen, T. J., 259, 260, 267
Rousseau, D. M., 53, 63, 70, 82
Rowe, P., 60, 82
Rowe, P. M., 95, 99, 112
Rowland, K. M., 50, 112, 142, 150,
    152, 155, 204
Rowson, A. M., 140, 146, 154
Ruderman, M., 203
Rudman, L. A., 147, 154
Rue, L. W., 254, 256, 258, 263
Rusbult, C. E., 64, 82
Russ, G. S., 149, 152
Russell, M., 264
Ryan, A. M., 57, 58, 59, 65, 66, 67,
    68, 73, 75, 82, 98, 111
Ryder, P. A., 230
Rynes, S. L., 25, 27, 28, 29, 32, 33,
    37, 43, 44, 50

S

Sacco, J. M., 98, 111
Sackett, P. R, 102, 111
Salas, E., ix, x, xiii, xiv, 37, 50, 93,
    112, 115, 116, 118, 122, 123, 124,
    125, 126, 131, 132, 133, 148, 150,
    269, 271, 274, 276, 279, 293, 294,
    299, 300, 302, 303, 304, 311, 312
Salgado, J. F., 58, 59, 82
Salisbury, D. L., 195, 204
Sampson, E. E., 100, 111
Sanchez, J. I., 232, 267
Sanchez-Burks, J., 221, 224, 232
Sandal, G. M., 59, 82
Sansom, S. L., 255, 267
Sarkar-Barney, S., 128, 129, 133
Sato, T., 22
Sauquet, A., 57, 82
Scandura, T. A., 259, 267
Schaubroeck, J., 139, 152
Scharlach, A. E., 255, 256, 257, 267
Scheier, M. F., 87, 106
Schein, E., 95, 111
Schendal, J. D., 126, 133
Schermerhorn, J. R., 148, 154
Scheu, C. R., 98, 111
Scheve, K., 181, 203
Schiller, S., 115, 131
Schlevogt, K., 75, 82
Schmidt, F. L., 55, 59, 82
Schmidt, S. M., 142, 153
Schmidt, S. W., 142, 143, 144, 147,
    153
Schmitt, N., 98, 111, 150
Schneider, B., 93, 111, 199. 204
Schneider, E. L., 267
Schneider, R. J., 94, 109
Schneider, S. C., 145, 154
Scholarios, D., 70, 80, 82
Schooler, C., 96, 110
Schoonhoven, C. B., 184, 204
Schriesheim, C. A., 152
Schroeder, R. C., 192, 202
Schuler, R. S., 26, 50, 65, 74, 82,
    148, 154, 158, 178, 184, 204
Schulten, T., 117, 133
Schvaneveldt, R. W., 131
Schwab, D. P., 29, 50
Schwartz, S., 107, 159, 179
Schwartz, S. H., 144, 154, 240, 267
Scott, W. R., 121, 133

Sears, G. J., 95, 99, 112
Scotch, N. A., 107
Sedikides, C., 24
Seeman, T., 96, 113
Segall, M. H., 159, 179
Segalla, M., 57, 82, 83
Segovis, J. C., x, xiv, 215, 230, 309
Segrest-Purkiss, S. L., 72, 78
Sen, S., 31, 104, 112
Senge, P. M., 294, 304
Serfaty, D., 275, 301
Sessa, V. I., 291, 304
Sewell, A., 107
Seyfarth, R. M., 304
Shackleton, V., 58, 59, 70, 75, 83
Sham, P., 107
Shank, M., 167, 294, 304
Shapiro, D. L., 17, 22, 182, 204
Shen, J., 73, 83
Shenkar, O., 154, 171, 172, 179
Shepard, J. M., 29, 49
Shiomi, K., 100, 110
Shore, B., 282, 304
Shrestha, L., 274, 304
Shrout, P. E., 107
Shweder, R. A., 1, 23
Sieck, W., 296, 304
Siegel-Jacobs, K., 136, 154
Silk, J. B., 285, 304
Silverman, S. B., 158, 178
Simpson, J., 132, 302
Simonson, I., 290, 299
Sims, A. D., 153, 177
Sims, H. P., 141, 153
Sinangil, H., 262
Singelis, T. M., 3, 15, 24, 101, 112, 185, 205
Sinha, J. B. P., 17, 23, 46, 50, 57, 60, 68, 83
Sinha, K. K., 192, 202
Siu, O., 267
Skeers, J., 225, 232
Skodol, A. E., 96, 110
Slaughter, M., 181, 203
Slocum, J. W., 65
Smith, J. L., 296, 304
Smith, M., 58, 59, 75, 81, 83
Smith, P. B., 5, 14, 17, 21, 23, 59, 83, 171, 179
Smith, S., 254, 255, 266
Smith, W. D, 105
Smither, J. W., 140, 153

Smuts, B. B., 304
Snell, S. A., 158, 178, 271, 301
Snoek, J. D., 89, 109, 215, 231
Snow, C. C., 271, 301
Society for Human Resources Management (SHRM), 258, 267
Solnick, L., 195, 205
Sommer, S. M., 158, 164, 166, 167, 179
Sonnenstuhl, W. J., 210, 232
Sorrentino, R. M., 24
Soto, J., 67, 83
Sparks, K., 232
Sparrow, P., 60, 83, 179
Spaulding, W., 304
Spears, R., 287, 289, 290, 300, 302, 304
Spector, P. E., 216, 218, 232, 241, 267
Spence, L. J., 64, 66, 83
Spence, J. T., 30, 35, 50, 106
Spicer, J., 211, 212, 214, 232
Spilimbergo, A., 181, 203
Sriram, N., 59, 80
Stagl, K. C., 271, 274, 275, 276, 300, 303, 304
Stahl, G., 70, 81
Staines, G. L., 236, 255, 259, 263, 266
Stanger, J., 255, 267
Starbuck, W. H., 277, 304
Starke, M., 25, 27, 43, 44, 48
Staw, B. M., 108, 133, 141, 154, 205
St. Clair, R. N., 177
Steers, R. M., 184, 204
Steers, W. N., 101, 108
Stein, P. J., 261, 264
Steiner, D. D., 60, 63, 69, 70, 83
Steiner, I. D., 118, 133
Steiner, R. L., 120, 131
Stephan, C. W., 12, 23
Stephan, W. G., 12, 14, 21, 23
Stephens, G., 74, 79
Stepina, L., 72, 78
Stetzer, E., 208, 232
Steverson, P. K., x, xiv, 207, 309
Stigler, J. W., 23
Stockdale, M. S., 85, 112
Stohl, C., 65, 83
Stokes, J. P., 96, 110
Stoltenberg, S. F., 104, 112

Stone, E. F., 86, 103, 112
Stone, D. L., vii, ix, x, xiii, xv, xvii, xviii, 26, 30, 33, 36, 37, 38, 39, 40, 41, 43, 44, 50, 86, 87, 92, 93, 95, 98, 102, 103, 112, 113, 116, 133, 158, 162, 167, 168, 179, 309, 311, 312
Stone, G. J., 59, 83
Stone, N. J., 95, 109
Stone-Romero, E. F., ix, xiii, xv, xvii, xviii, 26, 30, 33, 34, 37, 39, 44, 50, 86, 88, 92, 93, 94, 95, 96, 98, 102, 103, 105, 112, 113, 116, 133, 158, 162, 167, 168, 179, 309, 310, 311, 312
Stout, R. J., 279, 304
Strauss, C., 282, 292, 303, 304
Strauss J., 49
Strodtbeck, F. L., 2, 9, 22, 42, 45, 49
Strong, E. K., 88, 112
Struhsaker, T. T., 304
Stuebing, K. K., 168, 179
Su, S. K., 13, 22
Suh, E. J., 13, 22
Suliman, A. M. T., 138, 154
Sully de Luque, M. F., 158, 164, 166, 167, 179
Sundstrom, E., 305
Super, D. E., 88, 113
Sussman, N. M., 9, 23
Sustaining Progress: Social Partnership Agreement 2003-2005, 246, 267
Sutton, J. L., 296, 304
Suutari, V., 145, 154
Swaffin-Smith, C., 147, 153
Sweeney, P. D., 63, 69, 70, 81
Swezey, R. W., 294, 304

T

Takahashi, Y., 14, 23
Takeuchi, S., 111
Tannenbaum, S. I., 276 300
Tatsuoka, M. M., 106
Taylor, C., 284, 291, 304
Taylor, S. E., 96, 97, 102, 113, 167, 179
Teagarden, M. B., 72, 74, 76, 81, 83, 84
Tellegen, A., 94, 113

Testa, M., 200, 205
Tetlock, P. E., 137, 153
Tetrick, L. E., 195, 205, 215, 230, 232
Tett, R., 86, 88, 94, 113
Theiderman, S., 148, 155
Thomas, A., 200, 205
Thomas, D. C., 118, 119, 120, 133
Thomas, J. B., 278, 304
Thomas, K. M., 44, 50
Thomas, L. T., 236, 255, 267
Thompson, C. A., 255, 262, 267
Thompson, E. R., 63, 83
Thor, K. K., 279, 305
Thornson, C. A., ix, xiii, 85, 309
Thornton, G. C., 139, 155
Timmreck, C. W., 177
Ting-Toomey, S., 14, 24
Tinsley, C., 53, 63, 70, 82
Tisak, M. S., 279, 301
Tixier, M., 57, 58, 66, 75, 83
Tobias, S., 133
Todeva, E., 237, 267
Tom, V. R., 30, 44, 50
Trafinow, D., 4, 7, 24
Travaglione, A., 155
Treadway, D. C., ix, xiv, 135, 142, 149, 152, 309
Triandis, H C., ix, xii, xiii, xvi, xviii, 1, 2, 3, 4, 5, 6 7, 8, 9, 10, 11, 13, 14, 16, 19, 20, 21, 23, 24, 26, 30, 35, 36, 38, 46, 48, 49, 50, 63, 64, 80, 83, 86, 99, 100, 101, 109, 111, 113, 118, 121, 133, 144, 145, 155, 158, 178, 179, 184, 185, 186, 203, 204, 205, 215, 220, 221, 224, 228, 232, 233, 240, 241, 267, 271, 299, 305, 307
Trice, H. M., 27, 39, 42, 44, 50, 93, 113
Trice, H. T., 210, 232
Triest, R. K., 182, 204
Trompenaars, F., 62, 63, 71, 84, 90, 99, 113, 159, 179, 268, 282, 305
Trubinsky, P., 14, 24
Tucker, K., 252, 253, 254, 257, 266
Tully, J., 284, 305
Tung, R. L., 57, 84, 181, 203
Turati, C., 57, 83
Turban, D. B., 29, 30, 38, 51
Turner, J. C., 287, 301
Tyler, K. M., 101, 113

U

United Nations Conference on Trade and Development, 26, 51
Upshaw, C. L., x, xiv, 269
U. S. Bureau of the Census, xi, xvi
U. S. Bureau of Labor Statistics, 194, 205, 243, 254 268
U. S. Census Bureau, 26, 27, 51, 106, 243, 268
U. S. Department of Commerce, 106, 195, 205
U. S. Department of Health and Human Services, 226, 233
U. S. Department of Justice, 113
U. S. Department of Labor, 113, 254, 256, 257, 268
U. S. Equal Employment Opportunity Commission, 113

V

Van Hemert, D. A., 59, 81
Van de Vijver, F. J. R., 59, 81
Van den Ven, A. H., 303
Van Knippenberg, B., 144, 155
Van Knippenberg, D., 155
Van Scotter, J. R., 137, 138, 153, 155
Vassiliou, V. A., 11, 24
Verardi, S., 77
Verma, G. K., 23
Vermunt, R., 144, 155
Villareal, L., 14, 21
Villareal, M. B., 267
Villareal, M. J., 24, 186, 205
Visweswaran, C., 120, 131, 262
Volpe, C. E., 276, 300
Von Glinow, M. A., 58, 67, 70, 72, 73, 76, 77, 79, 83, 84, 178
Vroom, V. H., 25, 27, 28, 44, 51, 89, 113, 158, 160, 180

W

Wageman, R., 276, 301
Wagner, D. L., 257, 258, 268
Wall, T. D., 179
Walley, L., 59, 81
Wallsten, T. S., 61, 62, 84
Wan, K. C., 129, 130
Wang, C. S., 291, 301
Wang, Z. M., 67, 84

Ward, C., 10, 16, 24
Wasti, S. A., ix, xiii, xviii, 11, 16, 20, 23, 24, 86, 113, 241, 267, 307
Watkins, W., 108
Watson, D., 104, 113
Watson, T. W., 150
Watson, W. E., 118, 119, 120, 134
Wayne, S. J., 142 144, 146, 155
Weathington, B. L. 195, 205
Webster, J., 96, 106
Weick, K. E., 278, 279, 305
Weiner, B., 168, 180
Weiner, I. B., 177
Weiner, S. P., 255, 259, 265
Weiss, H., 183, 184, 199, 201, 205
Wesson, M. J., 10, 22
West, B. J., 303
Wexley, K. N., 99, 111, 139, 155
Whatley, A., 120, 131
Wheeler, K. G., 69, 84, 129, 134
Whelan, B. J., 264
White, S., 224, 231
Whitney, W., 105
Wiatrowski, W. J., 252, 268
Widaman, K. F., 46, 51
Wiggins, J. S., 87, 113
Wilk, R. R., 286, 305
Wilk, S. L., 70, 84, 102, 111
Wilkinson, I., 142, 147, 153
Williams, D. R., 96, 97, 113
Williams, J., 264
Williams, J. E., 102, 113
Williams, J. R., 166, 178
Williams, M. C., 60, 82
Williams-Morris, R., 97, 113
Willis, R. P., 126, 131
Wilson, K. A., ix, xiii, 115, 133
Wink, P., 102, 113
Wise, P. G., 44, 50
Woehr, D. J., 104, 105
Wolfe, D. M., 89. 109, 215, 231
Wong, C-S., 73, 75, 80, 84
Wong, I. F. H., 84
Wong, L., 305
Wong, N. Y. C., 81
Wood, R. E., 140, 150, 155
Wood, W., 132, 302
Worchel, S., 132, 302
Worthley, R., 144, 153
Wortman, C. B., 97, 110
Wrangham, R. W., 304

Wright, J. A., 255, 263
Wright, N. S., 12, 22
Wright, P. M., 158, 180
Wu, A., 118, 131
Wyer, R. S., 61, 79

Y

Yamada, A. M., 15, 24
Yamaguchi, S., 11, 24, 109
Yan, Y., 73, 84
Yang, J. Z., 75, 78
Yates, J. F., 136, 154
Ybarra, O., 14, 21
Yi, J.-S., 61, 84
Yinon, Y., 139, 152
Yoon, G., 24, 111
Young, M. N., 73, 77

Youngcourt, S. S., ix, xiv
Yu, J., 139, 155
Yu, K., 69, 77
Yu, Y., 96, 97, 113
Yuki, M., 109

Z

Zaccaro, S. J., 276, 279, 291, 303,
    305
Zanna, M., 21, 24, 154, 179
Zapata-Phelan, C. P., 10, 22
Zeitling, L. R., 15, 24
Zellmer-Bruhn, M. E., 272, 277, 296,
    301
Zhang, Y., 80
Zhou, J., 147, 151, 193, 198, 205
Zuckerman, M., 94, 113

SUBJECT INDEX

A

accountability systems
  accountability to whom, 138–139
  defined, 136–137
  outcome accountability, 137
  performance appraisal and, 136
  process accountability, 137
  specificity of, 137
affective events theory, xiv, 183–184
  attitudes and, 200
  description of, 199
attitudes, xiii, xiv, xvii, 1, 45
  behaviors and, 183, 186, 199, 279
  beliefs and, 29
  cultural competence and, 291
  cultures and, 237–238
  cultural values and, 4, 7, 10, 182, 186–187, 217
  employee, 238
  gender and, 243
  job and work-related, 28–29, 31–32, 34,43–44, 236
  job application intentions and, 28, 32
  managerial, 237
  organization-related, 29
  performance-related, 170
  subjective culture and, 144
  time-related, 68
  training to influence, 121–123, 127
  validity as predictors, 59
  value congruence and, 184
  virtual social identity and, 92
  winning-related, 69
  work versus family-related, 237–239, 247, 251

B

benefits, employee, 183, 193–198
  administration of, 307–309
  cultural values in relation to, 43, 129, 193, 198, 201–202
  defined, 193–198
  discretionary, 194, 196–198
    accommodation and enhancement programs, 194, 198
    defined benefit plans, 197
    employee assistance programs, 208, 214
    health insurance, 252
    health protection programs, 197
    leave, sick and vacation, 255–256
    life insurance, 196
    long-term care, 256
    paid time-off, 198
    retirement plans, 196–197, 252
    services, employee, 256–257
    entitlement to, 195
    supports, workplace, 258–259
    barriers to, 259–261
  employee retention and, 16
  family-related, 194, 252–253, 255, 258–260, 262, 311
  functions or purposes of, 252
  legally mandated, 194, 195–196
    Social Security, 256
  unionization and, 195
  welfare practices and, 194
  work arrangements and, 246, 251, 256

C

communication
    cultural differences in, 284
    defined, 275
    in multicultural teams, 271–275,
        284, 292
    methods, 282
    norms about, 276
    problems, 276
    team effectiveness and, 270, 275
compensation and reward systems.
        See also, Benefits, employee.
    impact of culture on, 183–184,
        188–199, 201
    multicultural contexts of,
        181–183
    types of rewards and
        compensation, 188–191
        monetary rewards, 183,
            188–191
        seniority-based pay, 188–191,
            193, 195
        base pay, 188–190
        merit-based pay, 189–190, 192,
            310
        incentive-based pay, 183,
            188–189, 192
        competency-based pay,
            188–190, 192
control, perceived, 32–33, 35, 43
    collectivism and, 37
    defined, 20
    familism and, 38
    power distance and, 40–42
    Theory of Reasoned Action and,
        28
cultural values or dimensions , 3–10
    achievement, 7, 9, 27, 310
        compensation practices and, 188
        employee selection practices
            and, 62, 68–69
        individualism–collectivism and,
            7, 30, 35, 37, 241
        familism and, 38
        feedback giving and, 167
        idiocentricity and, 100
        job choice and, 30, 36
        masculinity–femininity and,
            185, 188, 193, 201, 242
        motivation and, 242
        national differences in, 71

    socialization and, 99
    workforce participation rates
        and, 236
achievement–ascription, 62, 68
allocentrism–idiocentrism, 10–11,
    186
    group work preferences and, 17
    well-being and, 15
collectivism, xiii, 2. *See also*,
        individualism–collectivism.
    beliefs about desirability of job
        attributes and, 35–36
    beliefs about desirability of
        recruitment sources and, 36
    conflict resolution and, 14
    defined, 3, 63, 159, 185, 217,
        240–241
    determinants of, 90, 100
    discrimination and, 11–12
    domains in which found, 4
    employee recruiting and, 35–38
    employment practices and,
        186–187
    ethnic differences in, 34–35
    feedback and, 167
    group, 6
    group or team effectiveness and,
        17, 117, 186, 200
    horizontal, 10, 185, 200
    institutional, 19
    job application process and,
        43
    job choice preferences and,
        30
    leader style and, 18
    measures, construct validity of,
        46
    motivation and, 162–164
    national differences in, 15–16,
        62–63, 100, 177, 187
    organizational, 17
    perceived control in job
        application process and,
        37–38
    psychological (allocentrism), 10,
        17, 100, 186
    relational, 6
    reward preferences or practices
        and, 129, 183, 190, 193
    self-ratings of performance and,
        139
    sex-based differences in, 102

training and, 121, 129
vertical, 10, 185, 200
well-being and, 218
work versus family issues and,
    237, 240
communication styles, 284–285
direct versus indirect, 140
individualism–collectivism and,
    64, 100
job performance and, 128
power distance and, 117
collectivism, 3–6. *See also*,
    individualism–collectivism.
group, 6
relational, 6
emotional expression, 9
familism, 38
individualism, 6–8, 159. *See
    also*, collectivism and
    individualism–collectivism.
individualism–collectivism, 35
    employee assistance programs
        and, 220–224
    employee behavior and, 186–187
    employee benefits and, 190, 198
    employee selection practices
        and, 62–64
    employment practices and,
        186–187
    incentive pay and, 193
    monetary rewards and, 190, 193,
        201
    motivation and, 162, 164–165
    reward and compensation
        practices and, 185, 190
    socialization basis of, 100–101,
        159
    stress and, 217
    work versus family preferences
        and, 240–241
information gathering, 282–283
    sensemaking and, 283
    team coordination and, 252
internal–external locus of control,
    defined, 69
    employee selection practices
        and, 69
masculinity–femininity, 159,
    184–186, 240
    compensation and monetary
        rewards and, 183, 185, 188,
        190–191, 193, 200–202

cross-cultural training and, 121
defined, 65, 185, 242
employee benefits and, 191
employee benefit and/or reward
    preferences and, 190, 193,
    198–199, 201, 242
employee motivation and,
    163–166
employee selection practices
    and, 65–66
employment practices and, 62,
    187–188, 309
gender stereotypes and, 65
interpersonal behavior and,
    242
national differences in, 65–66,
    71, 90, 99, 171–172, 184,
    238, 282
other values and, 163–165
reward practices and, 191
socialization practices and, 99
work versus family issues and,
    237, 242, 261
monochronic–polychronic, 9
    monochronic, 9
    polychronic, 9
    social, 9
neutral–affective, 67
power distance, 39–40, 99, 159,
    240
    defined, 39, 64, 159, 165, 241
    employee selection practices
        and, 64–65, 68
    employee motivation and,
        164–165
    ethnic differences in, 39, 45
    job choice preferences and, 30,
        40, 43
    labor unions and, 65
    measurement of, 46
    motivation and, 164–165, 184
    national differences in, 62, 64,
        71, 187
    other values and, 10, 17, 163,
        185, 242
    perceived control and, 41–42
    performance feedback and,
        200
    person-organization fit and,
        41–42
    reactions to employee selection
        procedures and, 69

recruitment source preferences
    and, 40–41
subjective norms and, 41
team performance and, 117
training and, 121, 128–129
well-being and, 19
work versus family preferences
    and, 241–242
sequential–synchronic
    defined, 68
    employee selection practices
        and, 62, 68–69
    national differences in, 62, 71,
        283
simple–complex, 3
specific–diffuse
    defined, 67
    employee selection practices
        and, 62, 67–68
    employee reactions and, 70
    feedback and, 70
    national differences in, 62, 67,
        71
tight–loose, 3, 11, 19
    defined, 67
    employee selection practices
        and, 62, 67
    national differences in, 62, 67,
        71
time orientation, 42, 283–284
    defined, 42
    employee motivation and,
        164–165
    ethnic differences in, 42, 45
    job application process and,
        42–43
    measures of, 43, 282
    national culture and, 282
    outcome preferences and, 43
uncertainty avoidance,
    defined, 65, 159, 242
    employee selection practices
        and, 165
    employee motivation and,
        162–164, 166, 242
    employee selection practices
        and, 62, 65, 70
    feedback and, 166
    national differences in, 19, 62,
        65, 71, 99
    reactions to selection practices
        and, 70

training and, 121
work versus family preferences
    and, 240, 242
universalism–particularism
    cultural differences in, 90
    defined
    employee selection practices
        and, 66–67
vertical–horizontal, 9
culture
    beliefs and, 2
    defined, 1–2, 99, 144–145, 159,
        184–185, 237–238
    dimensions of, 3–10
    ethnicity and, 45
    factors influencing, 2
        history, 285
        political systems, 285–286
        economic factors, 286
    impact on
        conflict resolution, 13–15
        emotional expression, 12
        employee assistance programs,
            207–229
        employee compensation and
            reward systems, 181–202
        employee recruitment, 25–47
        employee retention and
            attachment to organizations,
            15–17, 26
        employee selection, 11–12,
            53–77. *See also*, selection,
            employee.
        employees, 19–20
        groups and work teams, 17. *See
            also*, teams.
        individuals and their behavior,
            19–20
        job application intentions and
            behavior, 25–47
        job design, 12
        leadership and leader behavior,
            17–19, 187
        motivation, 157–177, 182
        organizations and organizational
            culture, 11–20, 27, 44–45
        performance evaluation/
            appraisal, 12–13,135–150
        sensemaking in multicultural
            teams, 269–299
        supervisor–subordinate
            relationships, 12–13

training, 15–16, 115–130. *See also* training.
work versus family issues, 235–262
material, 1–2
nationality and, 45
national differences in, 10, 18–19
nature of, 1
levels of analysis of, 10–11
lifestyles and, 2
organizational, 11
personality fit with, 10
socialization practices and, 31
stereotypes and, 2
subjective, 1–2
values and, 2, 45
cultural assimilator, 16, 121
Cross-Cultural Feedback Model, described, 167–168

E

employee assistance programs, xiv, 207–229
culture, influences on, 209–210, 220–224
defined, 207–208
types of, 210–214
alcohol treatment, 210–211
broadband programs, 211–212
managed care, 213
effectiveness of and globalization, 224–229
evolution of, 210–214
globalization and, 224–228
in various nations, 214, 226
organizational culture and, 223–224
purposes of, 208
work versus family issues and, 257–258
employee selection. *See* selection, employee.
expatriates,
employee assistance programs and, 228
performance appraisal and, 145
training and, 15, 121–122
Expectancy theory, 27
employee recruitment and, 28
personality variables and, 89

motivation models and, 160, 182
valences of outcomes and, 89

F

feedback
behavior, 158
culture and, 162, 157–158, 162, 164–168, 284
giving of, 157–159, 166–167, 276
interventions concerning, 168
model of, cross-cultural, 167–168
motivation and, 158, 160, 166–168
performance and, 166
performance appraisal and, 136, 139, 166, 275–276
reactions to, xiv, 70, 167–168
seeking of, xiv, 166–167
sources of, 140, 146
training and, 123–127

G

Globe study, 19
gender. *See also*, work-family issues and culture.
culture and, 243–244
employee selection and, 11, 66
job attribute preferences and, 29
masculinity–femininity and, 65, 185, 242
training and, 120
work-family issues and, 237, 239–244
groups
conflict resolution and, 13–14
culture and, 2, 4–5, 7, 10, 17, 36, 39, 45, 63–64, 100–101, 217, 241, 285
defined, 192,
ethnicity and, 45
external threats to, 289–290
impact of culture on, 17, 34, 44
in-groups and out-groups, 1, 4–5, 13, 36, 92–93, 98, 100, 187, 190, 290
job design and, 12
leader behavior and, 18
minority, xi, 26, 34, 44, 87, 96, 103, 147, 309

stigmatization of, xiii, 103, 298
human resource practices
    and, 26, 87, 96, 98, 100,
    102–103
multicultural, 47
organizational culture and, 222,
    308–309
performance appraisal and, 141,
    146–147
social identity and, 92, 93, 287
support, 257
values and, xi–xii, 187
work versus family issues and,
    243–244, 260

H

human resource management
    processes and practices,
    53–54
compensation and reward
    practices, 181–202
employee assistance programs,
    207–229
employee empowerment, 12
employee recruitment, 25–47
employee selection practices,
    53–77
    unfair discrimination and,
        85–105
performance appraisal, 135–150
performance feedback and
    motivation, 157–177
training, 115–130
universalistic, 11
work versus family issues,
    235–262

I

influence behavior,
    culture and, 146–148
    defined, 142
    performance appraisal and, 144,
        146–147
    strategies of, 143

J

job application intentions and
    behaviors, 25–47
    attitudes and, 28–29

culture and, 34–35, 37–39, 41–43
model of, 29
perceived control and, 32–33
research needs concerning, 44–45
subjective norms and, 31–32
job performance
    construct of, 137
    culture and standards of, 69
    dimensions of, 137–138
    employee assistance programs and,
        213
    measurement of, 137, 140
        culture and, 149
        biases in, 150
    negative influences on, 210–211
    prediction of, 91, 94
    rewarding of, 189, 192, 195

L

leadership. *See also* culture, impact
    on.
    culture and, xiii, 2, 17–19, 46, 185,
        190, 238, 276
    effectiveness of, 18
    employee selection and, 18, 74,
        101
    influence behavior and, 142
    nature of, 18
    styles of, 18–19, 276
    teams and, 272–274, 276
legislation
    Americans With Disabilities Act of
        1990, 103
    Career's Leave Act of 2001, 246
    Civil Rights Act of 1991, 104
    Council Directive 92/95/EEC,
        246
    European Employment Strategy,
        244
    European Union Legislation, 245
    Family Medical Leave Act of 1993,
        195–196, 235
    Health Insurance Portability and
        Accountability Act of 1996,
        221
    National Labor Relations Act of
        1935, 195
    Organization and Working Time
        Act of 1997, 246
    Paid Family Leave Law of 2002,
        253

Parental Leave Act of 1998, 245
Protection of Employees (Part-
    Time) Act of 2001, 246
Social Security Act of 1935,
    194–195

M

minorities,
    performance appraisal issues,
        146–148
    stigmatization of, xiii, 92–93
    recruiter preferences of, 37
    communication styles of, 118
    performance ratings of, 146
    impression management behaviors
        of, 147
    influence behaviors of, 147
    political skills of, 147
    effects of on organizational
        culture, 309
models
    A Conceptual Model of Cross-
        Cultural Variations of the
        Stress Process, 219
    A Multilevel Model of Work and
        Family Policy and Practice
        Influences, 237
    A Sensemaking Approach
        to Understanding
        Multinational Teamwork,
        273
    Effectiveness of Employee
        Assistance Programs In An
        Era of Globalization, 227
            Impact of
        Individual Culture and
        Organizational Culture
        on Human Resource
        Management Processes and
        Practices, 308
    Life Cycle of Scenario-Based
        Training, 125
            Model of Effects
        of Culture on Human
        Resource Management
        Processes and Practices,
        307–309
            Model of the
        Influence of Cultural
        Values on Job Application
        Intentions and Behaviors, 29

Model of the Influence of National
    Cultural Values and Reward
    Systems on Proximal and
    Distal Outcomes, 183
Motivation Model, 161
morality
    culture and, 6, 72, 145
    virtual social identity and, 92
motivation
    culture and, 5, 8, 157–177, 160–
        166, 176, 182–183, 242, 293
    defined, 158
    employee behavior and, 158
    employee recruitment and, 27
    feedback and, xiv, 157–177
    group, 289
    interventions to change, 168
    job application intentions and
        behaviors, 27, 31–32,
        35, 93
    models of, 158, 160–161, 170, 182
    reward and compensation practices
        and, 191
    theories of, 158–161
multiculturalism
    construct, complexity of, 284
    importance of understanding, 116
    in organizations, 116–120
    motivation models and, 182
    process gains and losses
        attributable to, 118–120. *See
        also* teams.

N

norms
    behavior and, 19–20, 100, 241
    collectivism and, 36
    communication-related, 276
    conformity with, 100
    coping with stress and, 216
    culture, subjective and, xiii, 1–4,
        6–7, 20, 32, 35–41, 43, 145,
        184–186, 217, 237, 241,
        282, 285
    defined, 186
    dominant, xii
    employee attitudes and, 186
    familism and, 39
    groups or teams and, 17, 286,
        288–289, 291–292
    in organizations, xi

job application intentions and
  behaviors and, 28–29,
  30–32, 34–35, 43, 45
justice-related, 60, 63
minority versus majority group
  differences in, xi
person-organization fit and, 199
power distance and, 41
organizational culture and, xii, 11,
  243
            performance
    appraisal and, 141, 275
subgroup norms in employee
  selection, 104
training and, 123
work versus family issues and, 237

O

organizations
  accountability in, xiv
  attitudes toward, 29–30, 33–34,
    36–38, 42, 44, 47, 135
  behavior in, 26, 45–46, 146, 148
  compensation and reward practices
    in, 181–202, 310–311
  cultural heterogeneity or
    homogeneity of, xii, xv,
  cultures of, 44, 47
  cultures of and norms, 11, 243
  cultural influences on or in, xii,
    xiii, 11, 27, 64–65, 67–68,
    117, 129, 187, 221, 236, 244
  design of, xii
  diversity of or in, xi, xii, 27, 33–34,
    44, 77, 121, 123, 135, 147,
    158, 307, 310–311
  dominant groups in, 92
  effectivness of, xv
  emotions in, 149
  employee assistance programs in,
    207–229
  employee performance in, 135, 149
            human resource
    management practices in, xii,
    xvii, 26–28, 32, 37, 43–44,
    46–47, 53–54, 77, 88, 96,
    136, 207–208, 307, 310
  influence behavior in, 142–143,
    145, 148
  motivation and feedback in,
    157–177

multiculturalism in, xiii, xv, 27,
  43, 116, 122, 182–183,
norms in, xi
performance appraisal in, 135–150,
  311
political aspects of, 141–142
role-taking in, 89
stigmatization in, 92,
stress and coping in, 207–229
training in, 115–130
work versus family issues in,
  235–262, 311

P

performance appraisal
  appraisal sources,
    self, 139
    peer, 139–140
    360 degree, 140–141
  as an influence process, 141–144
  criterion development in, 137
  cross-cultural studies of, 170–176
  liking of rates and, 143–144
  nature of systems for, 136,
    168–169
person–group fit,
  defined, 95
  personality and, 95
person–job fit,
  defined, 95
  personality and, 95
person–organization fit,
  defined, 95
  personality and, 95
  reward systems and, 199–200
personality
  age differences in, 102
  assessment of, 91–92
    interview methods of, 91–92
    standardized measurement of,
      92
  development of, 89–90
    impact of culture on, 85–86
    impact of socialization on,
      99–101
  employee selection using, 85–105
  ethnic differences in, 101–102
  human resource management
    practices, and, 90–91
  nature of, 87–88
  perspectives on, 88–89

sex differences in, 102
socioeconomic status differences in, 102
state versus trait views of, 96–97
political systems,
employee selection and, 71–73
practice, implications for
employee recruitment, 46–47
employee selection, 74–77
human resource management processes and practices, 310–311
multicultural teams, 292–296
work-family issues, 261–262

R

recruiting, employee, 25. *See also* job application intentions and behavior.
impact of values on, 35–43
collectivism and, 35–38
familism and, 38–42
time orientation and, 42–43
recruitment source desirability, 36, 40–41
model of, 28–34
process of, 27–28
research, implications for,
employee assistance programs, 229
employee recruitment, 44–46
human resource management processes and practices, 309–310
multicultural teams, 296–298
performance appraisal, 148–150
reward and compensation practices, 201–202
work-family issues, 261–262

S

scripts, work-related, and culture, 116
selection, employee, 53–77
applicant reactions to procedures, 60
cultural differences in, 69–70
best practices, 53–54
biases in, 97–99
personality biases, 99–103

relational demography biases, 98
similarity attraction biases, 97–99
culture and,
selection practice differences, 54, 56–59, 62–69
comparison of Mexico and U.S., 71–74
description of, 54
ideal employee stereotype biases, 98
legality of systems for, 60, 103–104
predictor variables,
interviews, unstructured and culture, 58
personality
rationale for use of, 86–87
criterion-related validity of, 94
references and culture, 58
application blanks and culture, 58
structured, quantitative and culture, 58–59
purposes of, 91
rational/analytic approach and culture, 55, 61–62
social/intuitive approach and culture, 55, 61–62
systems
criteria for evaluating, 59–60
use of subgroup norms in, 104–105
self-construal, 4
cultural differences in, 7
social identities
minorities, of, 146–147
reactions to threat and, 287–290
teams and, 287–290
virtual, determinants of, 92–93
socialization, culture-based, 99
stigmatization, personality-based, 92, 95
stress
collectivism and, 217
coping process, 215–216
primary appraisal, 215
secondary appraisal, 216
coping styles,
culture and, 222–224
problem focused, 216
emotion focused, 216
cross-cultural model of, 218–220

culture and, 215–218
  individualism and, 217
  work-related, 214–215

T

teams
  conceptual framework for
    multicultural teams,
    elements of,
  adaptive team coordination,
    274–277
    back-up behavior, 275
    communication, 275–276
    mutual performance
      monitoring, 274–275
    team leadership, 276
    teamwork, 276–277
  contextual drivers, discipline-
    based lessons, 281–282
  sensemaking,
    defined, 277–278
    extraction of cues from
      experience, 279–280
    framing of cues, 280
    meaning assignment, 280
    process, 278
  effectiveness of, 17
  frameswitching and, 280–292
  multicultural
    conceptual framework of,
      272–274
    defined, 271
    potential of, 271
    prevalence of, 270
    process losses and, 270
  theory, implications for employee
    recruitment-related, 44
Theory of Planned Behavior, 28
  belief-attitude relations, 29–30
  perceived control-behavioral
    intentions relations, 32–33
  subjective norms-behavioral
    intentions relations, 31–32
  values-beliefs relations, 30–31
  values-perceived control relations,
    33–34
  values-subjective norms relations,
    32

training
  concerned with multicultural
    differences, 123–126,
    128–129
  cross-cultural, 121–122
  diversity, 121–122
  multicultural interactions and,
    122–123
  research agenda for multicultural,
    127–130
  strategies for, 124–126
  transfer of, 129–130

U

Uniform Guidelines on Employee
  Selection Procedures, 103

V

values, cultural. *See* cultural values or
  dimensions.

W

welfare state regimes
  roles of family, state, and market
    in, 239–240
  types of, 239
work versus family issues, 235–262
  child care programs, 249
  cross-cultural differences,
    236–237
    Ireland, 244–251
    United States, 251–261
  model of factors affecting work
    versus family practices,
    236–237
  political and social influences on,
    238–240
  work-family conflict, defined,
    236
  work flexibility arrangements,
    247–249
    compressed work week, 255
    flexitime, 248, 254–255
    job sharing, 254
    part-time work, 247, 254
    teleworking, 248–249, 255